AI And Legal Reasoning Essentials

Advanced Series On
Artificial Intelligence (AI)
And Law

Dr. Lance B. Eliot, MBA, PhD

ISBN: 978-1-73-460165-7

DEDICATION

To my incredible daughter, Lauren, and my incredible son, Michael.

Forest fortuna adiuvat (from the Latin; good fortune favors the brave).

CONTENTS

Note: Visuals are collected together in Appendix B, rather than being interjected into the chapter contents, for ease of reading, enhanced flow, and to see the visuals altogether.

ACKNOWLEDGMENTS

I have been the beneficiary of advice and counsel by many friends, colleagues, family, investors, and many others. I want to thank everyone that has aided me throughout my career. I write from the heart and the head, having experienced first-hand what it means to have others around you that support you during the good times and the tough times.

To renowned scholar and colleague, Dr. Warren Bennis, I offer my deepest thanks and appreciation, especially for his calm and insightful wisdom and support.

To billionaire and university trustee, Mark Stevens and his generous efforts toward funding and supporting the Stevens Center for Innovation.

To Peter Drucker, William Wang, Aaron Levie, Peter Kim, Jon Kraft, Cindy Crawford, Jenny Ming, Steve Milligan, Chis Underwood, Frank Gehry, Buzz Aldrin, Steve Forbes, Bill Thompson, Dave Dillon, Alan Fuerstman, Larry Ellison, Jim Sinegal, John Sperling, Mark Stevenson, Anand Nallathambi, Thomas Barrack, Jr., and many other innovators and leaders that I have met and gained mightily from doing so.

Thanks to Ed Trainor, Kevin Anderson, James Hickey, Wendell Jones, Ken Harris, DuWayne Peterson, Mike Brown, Jim Thornton, Abhi Beniwal, Al Biland, John Nomura, Eliot Weinman, John Desmond, and many others for their unwavering support during my career.

And most of all thanks as always to Lauren and Michael, for their ongoing support and for having seen me writing and heard much of this material during the many months involved in writing it. To their patience and willingness to listen.

CHAPTER 1
AI AND LAW

Artificial Intelligence (AI) and the field of Law are synergistic partners.

Those interested in the intertwining of AI and Law can generally be categorized into two major approaches:

- **AI as applied to Law**
- **Law as applied to AI**

Let us consider each of those two approaches.

AI As Applied To Law

AI as applied to law consists of trying to make use of AI technologies and AI techniques involving the embodiment of law, potentially being able to perform legal tasks associated with the practice of law via AI systems.

Those scholars, experts, and practitioners that have this focus are using AI to aid or integrate artificial intelligence into how humans practice law, either augmenting lawyers and other legal professionals or possibly replacing them in the performance of various legal tasks.

Crafting such AI is especially hard to accomplish, problematic in many ways, and this book describes and analyses the myriad of attempts to achieve this difficult goal or aspiration.

The rise of LegalTech and LawTech, which is modern digital technology used to support and enable lawyers, law offices, and the like throughout the practice of law are gradually and inexorably being bolstered by the addition of AI capabilities.

There are many indications already of this trend rapidly expanding in the existing and growing LegalTech and LawTech marketplace. Notably, the potent AI and LegalTech/LawTech combination has been drawing the rapt attention of Venture Capitalists (VCs).

According to figures by the National Venture Capital Association (NVCA), the last several years have witnessed VC's making key investments of over one billion dollars towards law-related tech startups, many of which have some form of an AI capability involved (see Appendix B, Bibliography, reference [R.18]).

Most of the AI developed so far for LegalTech and LawTech is only able to assist lawyers and legal professions in rather modest and simplistic ways. For example, AI might speed-up the search for documents during e-discovery or might enhance the preparation of a contract by identifying pertinent contractual language from a corpus of prior contracts.

Where the field of applying AI to law is seeking to head involves having AI that can perform legal minded tasks that human lawyers and other legal professionals perform. In essence, create AI systems that can undertake legal reasoning.

This book is about using AI for Legal Reasoning (AILR).

In a sense, legal reasoning goes to the core of performing legal tasks and is considered the ultimate pinnacle as it were for the efforts to try and apply AI to law.

It is undoubtedly one of the most exciting areas of the AI-applied-to-law arena and one that holds both tremendous promise and perhaps some angst and possible somber qualms.

As you will learn in this book, there have been many attempts at getting AI to perform "legal reasoning" and have often done so with only mixed or limited success.

This is definitely still an open field with many unanswered questions and has a long way to go.

I'll be taking you through the storied backdrop of what legal reasoning seems to consist of, as per those that have tried ardently to figure this out, and then showcase the ways in which AI has been utilized to try and carry out or embody so-called legal reasoning.

This book intentionally dovetails together the broader conceptual aspects, ranging into the somewhat abstract philosophical elements, and yet also brings these academic matters back down to earth and covers the everyday practical elements too.

Law As Applied To AI

The other major approach that combines AI and Law focuses on Law as applied AI.

This is an equally crucial perspective on the AI and Law topic.

The focus is primarily on the governance of AI and how our laws might need to be revised, updated, or revamped in light of AI systems.

You likely already know that AI is experiencing quite a resurgence and has become a key focus of the tech field, along with gaining attention throughout society. AI is being rapidly infused into a wide variety of industries and domain specialties, including AI in the financial sector, AI in the medical domain, and so on.

This rapid pace of AI adoption has opened the eyes of society about the benefits of AI but also has gradually brought to the forefront many of the costs or negative aspects that AI can bring forth.

Some assert that our existing laws are insufficient to cope with the advances that AI is producing.

The topic of law as applied to AI is not covered extensively here (it is the emphasis of my next book), and, as such, within this book there are only occasional discussions about the matter, provided primarily to showcase the intertwinement with AI and legal reasoning.

Overall, the synergy between AI and Law is a duality, consisting of ways that AI can be applied to law, and ways in which law can be applied to AI.

If you are an AI specialist, you should certainly be interested in the AI-and-law topic, either due to the possibilities of advancing AI by discovering how to leverage AI into the legal domain, or due to the potential of how existing and future laws are going to impact the exploration and fielding of AI systems.

If you are a lawyer or legal specialist, you ought to be interested in the AI-and-law topic too, for the same reasons as the AI specialist, though perhaps with some added stake in the game.

What is the added stake?

If AI can ultimately become advanced enough to practice law, there is concern by some that it could potentially replace the need for human lawyers and other human legal-related law practitioners.

Some liken this to the famous and telling remark about commitment as exhibited via a chicken and a pig. A chicken and a pig are walking along and discussing what they might do together, and the chicken offers that perhaps they ought to open a restaurant that serves ham-n-eggs. Upon a moment of reflection, the pig speaks up and says that if they did so, the chicken would only be involved (making the eggs), while the pig would end-up being fully committed (being the bacon).

In that sense, AI specialists in this topic are involved, while legal specialists and lawyers are committed.

Meanwhile, for those of you squarely in the field of law, lest you think that AI specialists are to be spared the same fate of being overtaken by AI, you will be perhaps surprised to know that there are efforts underway to craft AI that makes AI, such as in the field of Machine Learning (ML), a specialty known as AutoML, which could potentially put human developers of AI out of a job.

What is good for the goose is good for the gander. Or, it might be that what is bad for the goose is equally bad for the gander.

On The Role Of Thinking And Legal Reasoning

One of the ongoing debates about the fundamental nature of legal reasoning revolves around a seemingly straightforward question and for which the answer has profound consequences.

Here is the perplexing question:

➔ **Does the act of legal reasoning by humans require all of the facets of human thinking, or does it only require some subset?**

If legal reasoning requires all facets of human thinking, presumably this suggests that to get a machine or computer to do likewise will require that we figure out all of those facets.

That's a rather tall order.

On the other hand, if you were to believe that legal reasoning is a subset of human thinking, perhaps there are areas of human thinking that we can avoid having to replicate in AI.

As such, the problem then of getting a machine or computer to undertake legal reasoning might be lessened.

That's not to imply that the carve-out makes the matter particularly easy.

It is still an extremely hard problem to solve.

Yet, if we can reduce the problem size, in whatever manner feasible, it nonetheless might aid in getting toward a solution, sooner than otherwise.

Your initial reaction to the posed question might be that yes, of course, legal reasoning is only a subset of human thinking.

Legal reasoning is only about laws, you might assert.

In that manner, maybe there is only needed a fraction of what human thinking consists of. That is a relief for those that want to make a computer or machine that can do the same efforts.

Do not though let the "obvious" blind you to the deeper nature of the provocative question.

Undoubtedly, legal reasoning does certainly require knowledge about law. No dispute there.

Though, as an aside, some might try to argue that you could have no knowledge per se about law and seemingly yet still invoke legal reasoning, but let us put that to the periphery for now (we will come back to it later on).

Just because there is a particular domain of knowledge needed, you can't then make the leap to the notion that the reasoning process is equally of a narrowed nature. It could very well be that the same range of thinking processes involved in doing legal reasoning is the same as the thinking processes used in other domains, such as say medicine.

Legal reasoning might require all of the otherwise gamut of reasoning processes, and merely be residing on top of a bed or layer of law and legal knowledge.

Similarly, it could be that medical doctors use otherwise all of the conceivable human reasoning processes and do so on top of a bed or layer of medical knowledge.

In short, be leery of believing that just because the domain itself is "narrow" that it ergo implies that the reasoning processes are also narrowed accordingly. The word "narrow" should be used cautiously, thus the basis for putting it in quotes herein, since many so-called narrow domains are bound to have tentacles that reach outward in a complex web fashion into many other areas of knowledge and reasoning.

This question about the range of human thinking that is required for the legal reasoning domain is one of many hurdles facing the advent of AI and legal reasoning systems.

The barrier to entry toward being able to codify and implement legal reasoning in AI might be higher if all of human thinking is involved. Some then point out that we will need to solve all of human reasoning as a prerequisite to achieving true AI legal reasoning, which makes for a daunting effort ahead.

Others insist that we might be able to achieve legal reasoning via AI and do so without having to cross the bridge of all of human thinking. Thus, they argue, push ahead on AI and legal reasoning, out of which too might come valuable insights for the rest or remainder of human thinking.

The debate is vocal, acrimonious, and ongoing.

About This Book

Now that you've gotten an initial taste regarding the topic of AI and Law, let's take a moment to consider what this book is all about.

This book provides an overview and guided tour of the field of AI and legal reasoning.

For ease of discussion, at times the combination of AI and legal reasoning is referred to herein as AILR, an acronym that is straightforward and used from time-to-time by those in this field of endeavor (though some eschew the acronym, so use it cautiously around specialists in this field).

The bulk of AILR efforts have been undertaken by researchers and university labs, thus the preponderance of this overview has to do with those academic efforts, though do not be misled into thinking that the work discussed is therefore solely abstract or conceptual.

By and large, most of the AILR efforts have been accompanied by attempts to design and construct some form of automata that will showcase the implementation of AI legal reasoning. In that sense, examining those "academic" efforts are worthwhile for both those that are interested in theories underlying AILR and those that are focused on the practical application of AI legal reasoning.

In some cases, AILR researchers have kindly opted to post their source code in publicly available online websites, which I mention as such during the discussions about the various AILR systems and the Appendix B contains links to the online sources (such code is usually housed in GitHub, a popular online repository for source code worldwide).

The source code is typically available for free and often considered "open source" (generally meaning that you can use the source code and adapt it for other uses, though make sure to observe any posted restrictions or potential licensing requirements).

Why provide a book that covers the breadth of the AI legal reasoning field?

The basis for doing so involves the hope that this book might encourage additional researchers and practitioners to join the fray and participate in making further progress in AILR.

Overall, it's both good news and somewhat bad news as a narrative about the current status of AI legal reasoning.

The good news is that there have been many prior and ongoing efforts to figure out AI legal reasoning, dating back to the earlier days of AI, and this book covers a substantial number of the key milestones and advances that have been made in AILR.

Alas, the bad news is that the progress has been rather stilted and slow, and if you are anticipating that you'll suddenly discover that there is a fully ready-to-go AI legal reasoning system that you hadn't already heard about, the plain answer is that no such system as yet exists.

This brings us back to the good news, namely that there are plenty of opportunities to contribute to the field of AILR.

And, for those of you with an entrepreneurial spirit, there is much promise for AILR startups and a great deal of investor money flowing into those budding efforts.

From an academic perspective, you can come from a variety of perspectives and disciplines in aiding the tackling of AILR, including perhaps being a computer scientist, or an AI researcher, or a legal scholar, a sociologist, a cognitive scientist, a philosopher, a lawyer, or be in other related fields and nonetheless become a contributor to AI legal reasoning advances.

Breakthroughs in AI legal reasoning can come from any of a number of varying kinds of expertise.

The potential impacts of AILR are also likely to be noteworthy for those that wish to make a mark on the world.

AI legal reasoning systems could change the practice of law, and in the chapters, we'll discuss ways that this might indeed occur.

Some assert that AILR might change the very nature of law itself.

There's another angle too, which entails the potential of advancing AI by whatever might be gleaned from trying to apply AI to the field of law.

In that manner, there is an equal opportunity that AI might not only change the law, but that simultaneously the attempts to combine the law and AI could offer new insights into how to design and build AI systems of any kind.

Throughout this book, the material is presented in a relatively non-technical manner, allowing readers to not be burdened by having to have an extensive prior background in tech and nor AI.

That being said, you are strongly encouraged to pursue the references cited and dig more deeply into the topic of AILR, and perhaps if you are a developer, consider accessing some of the source code of the cited AILR's to see what makes those systems tick and how they might be advanced.

For those in the legal field, this book aims to increase your awareness about the nature of AI legal reasoning, including why it has so far been stymied and generally unable to provide the type of AI capacity that you might assume should by now have been crafted.

There are lots of difficulties and roadblocks involved, and I've tried to identify quite a number of them to surface where the tensions exist.

Some readers might find this overview or guided tour to be somewhat wanting in terms of satiating their craving to get into greater details, and if so, as I say, please realize that there's only so much that can be packed into one book, thus, the taste provided herein will give you a semblance of what to pursue next.

In that sense, this book is the "forest for the trees" type of macro-view.

AILR specialists reading this book will hopefully see that I've tried to cover the key elements, and if your favorite piece of research or other aspect has not seemingly been included, please accept my sincerest regrets and drop me a line to let me know (there is a chance that I might be able to include the desired aspect in my next book).

In terms of how this guided tour is going to proceed, here's the overarching approach to the sequencing of the material, which I'll describe generally and in order of the chapters as presented.

The Chapters Of This Book

In the second chapter, coming up next, the crux of why AILR is so hard will be confronted head-on, pointing out that law is semantically indeterminate and therefore an immense challenge to embody in AI automation.

After covering this cornerstone as an impinger on what needs to be overcome, I tackle the disfavor of referring to AILR as "robo-lawyers" and explain why it is decidedly <u>not</u> a useful form of reference.

Then, the next several chapters examine what it means to refer to legal reasoning, along with exploring attempts that have been undertaken to form an ontological mapping of law. This dovetails into the aspect that even if we can computationally capture and use law, it could very well be intractable and therefore not computable in any reasonable sense of timing.

Prior to getting into the facets of some of the historically famous AILR's, the next several chapters explore what it means to practice law and what it means to be a lawyer, which, when cast in the light of the supposition that we will inevitably achieve true AILR, offers fascinating and unanswered questions about how AI will be positioned to undertake those human-performed legal tasks.

In the ninth chapter and through the nineteenth chapter, various AI legal reasoning systems are examined and discussed.

Included are notable systems such as TAXMAN, HYPO, CATO, SHYSTER, ROSS, AGATHA, IBP, NAI, VJAP, SCOTUS ML, and others.

Anyone versed in the field of AI legal reasoning needs to be aware of those systems.

The coverage herein seeks to showcase the contributions these notable AILR's have made to the field, and also highlight where gaps and opportunities continue to exist.

From the perspective of building AI legal reasoning systems, the chapters include a brief sampling of tools and utilities that are typically employed, along with AI programming languages, including ASPIC+, ASP, Prolog, LISP, and others.

In the latter part of the book, there is added attention to the nature of selected AI technologies, including Machine Learning (ML), Natural Language Processing (NLP), Knowledge-Based Systems (KBS), and the like.

One aspect that is a recurring point in the chapters is the importance of explainability in the field of law and the practice of law. This is such a vital element that a chapter is devoted to the topic (Chapter 23).

Toward the end of the book, I revisit various legal and societal implications that AI legal reasoning proffers.

The last chapter provides a perspective on how AI legal reasoning research has been undertaken and offers additional insights for those that are contemplating entering into the field and conducting new research.

For anyone opting to use this book in a class or course that pertains to these topics, note that Appendix A contains suggestions about how to use the book in a classroom setting.

Furthermore, Appendix B contains a set of slides that depict many of the salient points made throughout the book.

In some of my prior books, I've interspersed the slides into the chapter contents, but feedback by readers has generally been that readers prefer to not have the textual flow become disrupted by the slides, and instead prefer to have the supplemental material assembled altogether into an appendix.

To make sure that you are aware of those added materials, you'll notice that the ending of each chapter provides a quick reminder about the visual depictions that are available in Appendix B.

And so, with this overall orientation to the nature and structure of the book in mind, let's move to the next chapter and get further underway on examining the nature and quest of AI legal reasoning.

Note: *For supplemental materials depicting the aspects discussed in this chapter, refer to Appendix B, which contains various augmented diagrams, charts, and additional related facets of relevance.*

CHAPTER 2

LAW IS SEMANTICALLY INDETERMINATE

What is law?

This is not an esoteric question.

If we are seeking to somehow create an AI system that can undertake legal reasoning, it makes sense that we'd need to first ascertain what law is.

In other words, you can't hit a target when the target itself is not defined.

We'll need to pin down what it means to refer to law, in order to sensibly seek to have AI do something that we're going to refer to as legal reasoning.

To figure out what is meant by law, consider a historical reference.

Go back in time to about 1750 BC.

In Mesopotamia, there was a Babylonian code of law, known famously today as the Hammurabi Code [C.7], named after the sixth king of Babylonia.

He generally forced all of Mesopotamia to abide by his Code of Hammurabi. Legal historians tend to suggest that the Hammurabi Code was distinctive due to its extending beyond the prior Sumerian laws (e.g., Code of Ur-Nammu), and included an added boost toward physical penalties that were to be atoned upon those that violated his laws.

Notably too, it is said that his laws were an early initiator of the presumption-of-innocence precept, a significant transformative shift in the rule of law.

Of what we know about the Hammurabi Code, there were purported 282 laws [C.7].

After the discovery of the ancient artifact of Hammurabi Code in 1901, the language was translated and each of the laws has been extensively scrutinized and studied.

Let's take a look at law numbered 196.

Hammurabi Code law #196 [C.7] states this:

> **"If a man destroy the eye of another man, they shall destroy his eye."**

At first glance, this seems rather straightforward. It is the classic eye-for-an-eye axiom and nearly anyone that reads this law is certainly going to understand what it means.

Presumably, it is unambiguous.

Helpful too is that it is easy to remember, and easy to share with others.

Despite the innocuous appearance of law #196, there is more to this law than meets the eye. There is actually a lot of ambiguity in the stated rule.

Ponder the rule, and I'm sure you'll quickly come up with various loopholes, along with unspecified situations that could arise.

For example, consider these open-ended facets:

- Does the word "man" include that women are bound to this law too?
- Are children encompassed by this law (i.e., does "man" imply adults only)?
- What is the meaning of the first "destroy" -- suppose the person can still see, having only incurred damaged vision and was not entirely blinded?
- What does the second "destroy" mean as per the extent of damage or destruction that can be wrought in revenge or retribution?
- Who is the "they" that can destroy the eye of the other (is it the person whose eye was destroyed, or can someone else do so on their behalf)?
- Suppose that the first "eye" had already destroyed beforehand, as such, could someone nonetheless still be in trouble for destroying it (again)?
- Is time involved in the matter, for example, does the second destroy have any kind of time limit, perhaps needing to be done right away, or could the response by done years hence?
- Does "eye" mean that this refers only to eyes, or is it generalized to mean that leg-for-a-leg is also applicable, and hand-for-a-hand, foot-for-a-foot, etc.?
- And so on

I trust that this showcases that any law that seems to be apparent and obvious is not necessarily as crisp as one might assume.

The reason that I bring up this point is that some falsely assume that law would certainly be one of the easier areas or domains that could be automated by AI.

Why do they believe this?

Because laws are usually written down.

This makes it seem more amenable to automation, versus if we were trying to automate something that was only orally stated and not placed into writing.

Also, laws are usually indexed.

Laws are typically organized and structured in various ways.

In fact, anyone that studies law, such as budding lawyers, often find themselves overwhelmed with voluminous and extensive legal cases, along with a multitude of legal principles.

Those that aren't especially familiar with law are apt to assume that law is therefore well-defined, complete, exhaustive, and otherwise ripe for being automated, due to the notion that law is typically written down, voluminous, and has been pored over and devised by mankind by great effort and attention.

In truth of the matter, law is not complete, it is not exhaustive, and it is not as well-defined as might be assumed.

Law tends to be incomplete, insufficient as to its written form, and ill-defined to the extent that it is widely open to interpretation and the realization or production of multiple answers, along with being arguable and malleable as to its meaning over time (thus, a temporal factor is involved too).

Think for a moment about the core nature of laws.

Laws consist of words, formed into sentences, formed into paragraphs, and so on.

Those words all have meanings.

Those sentences have meanings.

Those paragraphs have meanings.

In that sense, the law itself is not somehow self-contained.

It requires that the reader of the law bring to the table a great deal of "understanding" about how to make those words, sentences, paragraphs, and narratives into something that has meaning, beyond the words on the pages alone.

In essence, there is semantic meaning that is not embodied directly in the words and that must be applied to make sense of the words.

This leaves law open to interpretation.

When an aspect of substance is left to interpretation, you have opened a Pandora's box that tends to defy conventional automation, and that challenges even AI.

As they say, beauty (or meaning) is in the eye of the beholder and each person that studies or uses law might reach their own conclusions about what the law constitutes and intends.

The malleability of the law arises due to its interpretability.

And, of course, laws change over time, as do the interpretations of the laws.

So, you've got a variance in how to interpret the laws, despite them being written down, and those laws also are bound to change over time.

You need to apply temporal reasoning to law, which amounts to having to interpret a law in a prior time context and a present time context.

Imagine though if law could be purely converted into a formalized set of logical statements that were unambiguous.

As seen via the Hammurabi Code, the law #196 might appear to be a logical statement of unambiguous nature, but clearly, it is woefully lacking by itself and would require many additional logical statements to bolster it.

Furthermore, one confounding irritant to anyone trying to make sense of law is that there is really no single "right" answer per se when trying to resolve a legal question.

The old lore is that if you get two lawyers into a room and ask them a legal question of an adversarial nature, you'll not get a single "right" answer and instead might get any number of legal answers, perhaps infinitely so (though whether an infinite argument can occur is an existential question to ponder).

In short, laws are said to be **semantically indeterminate**.

Laws are difficult to get a handle on. Trying to boil laws down into tangible logic is tricky and problematic.

One concern too is that the transformation of the porous wording into a formalized logic might lose something along the way. In that sense, the logic version would potentially no longer properly represent what was intended in the more ambiguous version.

Other distortions could happen too, such as the logic-based version opens up new avenues that weren't previously envisioned within the abstruse version.

Overall, many experts question whether law is truly amenable to being digitally formalized at all.

Do not misinterpret that contention. You can easily put law into a digital format.

This is done all the time, especially in our modern era, having progressed beyond paper-based laws (better than stone tablets) and gradually shifted laws to be embodied in electronic means.

But, having text that happens to be electronically stored and retrievable does not necessarily mean the same thing as having law that is digitally formalized.

There isn't any embedded sense of "understanding" that accompanies the conventional digitally formatted text.

The absence of having meaning and understanding bound within the textually digitalized law makes it deficient for legal reasoning purposes. If you will, it is like an apple pie that has everything but the apples in it. The crust is tasty, helps a lot, but without the apple, there's not much else you can do with the pie.

Many have sought for a long time to apply scientific principles and the rigors of science to law. Those doing so are hoping to find a kind of theory of relativity or other science-based principles that could apply to law.

If so, consider how much easier it would be to automate law if it was based on scientifically rigorous aspects. You could presumably have formalized legal proofs that abide by mathematical precision and rigor. You would merely crunch through the law and generate a pristine result, of which the proof for the result would be clearly delineated and absent of any debate or disagreement.

Law is not that codifiable, and there is no apparent reason to think that it will ever be, despite such depictions commonly used in science fiction tales.

Those that are trying to achieve legal reasoning in a machine are often times upbeat about turning the corner on this matter, including some that are convinced it is an inevitable certainty that law will be digitally formalized.

Others say that the pursuit is futile.

In the next chapters, we'll explore the pursuits toward codifying and formalizing law.

Conclusion

In 1732, John Gay famously wrote in "The Dog and the Fox" [C.8} about lawyers and indicated this:

> "I know you Lawyers can, with ease,
> Twist words and meanings as you please;
> That language, by your skill made pliant,
> Will bend to favour ev'ry client;
> That 'tis the fee directs the sense
> To make out either side's pretense.
> When you peruse the clearest case,
> You see it with a double face;
> For skepticism's your profession;
> You hold there's doubt in all expression.
> Hence is the bar with fees supply'd,
> Hence eloquence takes either side…"

Will John Gay ultimately be proven wrong?

Could it be that someday the law will not be twistable and pliant?

Time will tell.

In the next chapter, we'll start probing into the particulars of how law might be digitally formalized.

Note: *For supplemental materials depicting the aspects discussed in this chapter, refer to Appendix B, which contains various augmented diagrams, charts, and additional related facets of relevance*

CHAPTER 3
MISUSE OF ROBO-LAWYER MONIKER

Headlines often clamor that we are on the verge of having so-called **robo-lawyers** [C.11], which is a shortened moniker referring to robotic or robot lawyers.

It's a catchy way to describe AI that might eventually do what human lawyers do.

The phrase is revered by some since it encapsulates a vivid image.

In the classic, a "picture is worth a thousand words" notion, the robot part of the phrase conjures up a walking-talking robot that might be attired as an attorney might (what kind of attire is that in today's world), and do whatever lawyers do (we'll take a closer look at legal tasks shortly).

Perhaps we'll go into courtrooms one day and see a robot judge (robo-judges) and robot lawyers, all awaiting those irascible humans to come into the legal crucible to seek justice for human indiscretions against fellow humans.

Of course, most people aren't necessarily thinking of robot lawyers per se when they hear or see the robo-lawyer expression being used.

Instead, it is an easy means to imply that automation, especially AI (since we associate robots with being driven by AI), somehow is involved.

The advent of online chatbots has especially ramped up the use of robo-lawyer references.

Via an online chatbot, you might be doing a task such as trying to find a specific legal document, and all of a sudden a chatbot enters into your online effort and flags some legal cases or contracts that are possibly relevant to your work.

This chatbot is decidedly not truly an all-encompassing robo-lawyer, not at least in the sense of being able to undertake legal reasoning to the degree a human could, and so it is perhaps unfair or inappropriate to suggest it is a robo-lawyer.

In fact, some are outraged and enraged at the willy-nilly way in which robo-lawyer and robot lawyers are bandied around.

Some vendors that have a LegalTech or LawTech software package are apt to include the robo-lawyer reference into their marketing materials.

This presumably adds a glow of AI to their wares, regardless of whether there is any AI involved or not.

It is difficult to police the use of robo-lawyer as a phrase since it has no definitive meaning and has been used by so many in such various ways.

As such, purists would assert that we ought to ban the use of the robo-lawyer or robot lawyer monikers altogether.

There isn't any AI system today that warrants being called a robo-lawyer, assuming that you ascribe to the meaning that a robo-lawyer would need to be the equivalent of a human lawyer in all respects of legal practice.

Stop the use of it, curtail the click-bait, and hopefully bury it, until or if we someday really do achieve an AI capable of legal reasoning and can do the same as human lawyers.

This brings up another contemplative point.

Will we be able to achieve a robo-lawyer?

Ever?

Some prognosticators say we won't, some say we will. It depends upon whom you ask, and when you ask them.

For those of you that have studied law, you might know the name of William Orville Douglas.

He was an Associate Justice on the Supreme Court, serving as such from 1939 to 1975, an astounding 36 years and 211 days. A graduate of the 1925 law class of the Columbia Law School, he was obviously involved in quite a number of historic cases that occurred during his tenure on the Supreme Court.

William Douglas stated in 1948 this oft-quoted comment about the law [R.16]:

> **"The law is not a series of calculating machines where definitions and answers come tumbling out when the right levers are pushed."**

Why bring up this quote?

Some interpret that declaration by him as having signed the death warrant on the chances of achieving a true robo-lawyer or AI system that could be the equivalent of a human layer.

Assuming that a robo-lawyer or AI system is essentially a calculating machine, his remarks appear to place a dim view on having such machines be able to properly contend with the complexities and indeterminate nature of law.

Once again, we have another example of how words can be open to interpretation.

Some say that what he was trying to indicate is that the law is not cut-and-dry.

In that manner of speaking, it suggests that whatever automation is crafted has to be a lot better than simply calculating machines and expecting push-button results.

That's something I've already tried herein to emphasize too.

There are additional twists and turns about the remark.

Keep in mind that he made his comment in 1948.

This was during a time period in which computers barely existed, and when they did exist, such as the ENIAC (put into use in 1945), it was a monstrous sized system that though amazing for its time, can today be dwarfed easily by the computational power of even an everyday smartphone.

So, it could be that Douglas was merely noting that if there is a calculating machine that might someday take part in law, it has to be much better than the calculating machines of his day. Or, he might have not been able to envision what the calculating machines of the future could do, thus, based on a narrower perspective, you could say he was quite right that an ENIAC had no chance of becoming a robo-lawyer.

In any case, as I've already covered, we do all need to acknowledge that law is messy and fuzzy, and anyone thinking that law is crisp and precise is not going to make much advance on getting AI to do legal reasoning.

Beyond Calculations

Let's pursue the notion that law is more than mere calculations.

We can dig more deeply into the ingredients of the law and consider this comment by Thomas Hobbes, which he mentioned in his famous book *Leviathan* of 1651 [R.28]:

"The law is the public conscience."

This poignant line adds more fuel to the fire.

The fueled fire is that putting our arms around law is not so easily done, since it is a socio-legal artifact that is a complex miscellany, and if we can't get our arms around law, trying to craft an AI system to do so is going to be problematic.

When you look at the words on the page of any law book, you are witnessing something much more than words that perhaps one person crafted or wrote down.

Instead, you are looking at a compression.

Compressed within those words is a cacophony of input and viewpoints by a wide swath of society. Those words embody regulators, the judiciary, our culture, economics, history, ethics, and overall serve as a gigantic melting pot.

All squeezed down into a finite set of words.

Those words are not in a vacuum, they are in a whole stew of context, of which, by-and-large, the context is not present, and the bearer of the interpretation and use of those laws must have the context at their own fingertips.

Conclusion

Henceforth herein, I'm going to refrain from referring to robo-lawyer or robot lawyer, since I too find the phrasing to be misleading and confounding.

Meanwhile, the added lesson from this chapter is that anyone approaching the topic of AI and legal reasoning has their work cut out for them. It is an extremely tough problem, partially due to the aspect that the very artifact we want to use AI for is itself ill-defined and missing an essence that is needed to make it all into a workable and functional whole.

This problematic situation is especially exacerbated when trying to get AI into being an *autonomous* legal reasoning system.

You might have noticed that I used the word "autonomous" in that sentence.

As will be covered later on, it is one kind of struggle to have an AI legal reasoning system that can work when aided or propped up by a human lawyer (that kind of AI would be labeled as semi-autonomous, at best), and it is quite something much more pronounced of a fracas if the AI is to work without a human lawyer as its crutch (that would be the vaunted autonomous AI version).

Note: *For supplemental materials depicting the aspects discussed in this chapter, refer to Appendix B, which contains various augmented diagrams, charts, and additional related facets of relevance.*

CHAPTER 4
DEFINING
LEGAL REASONING

Let's start down the path of figuring out what legal reasoning consists of and how humans do it.

Once we get there, we can then delve into how AI might be able to do legal reasoning too.

Attempting To Define "Law"

First and perhaps foremost, it would seem relatively apparent to make the assertion that legal reasoning is something that depends upon law.

And, avoiding any debate over that apparent notion, what does it mean when someone refers to law?

A quick aside on a wording convention, if I may. When I refer to law, notice that I'm not saying, "the law" and instead I am just saying "law." I realize that it might be easier to read some of these passages if I indicated "the law" (compare the wording of "someone refers to law" to instead "someone refers to the law"), but if I did so, such wording at times could be conflated with an implication of a particular law or set of laws.

Likewise, some people like to refer to AI <u>and</u> law, while others prefer to say AI and <u>the</u> law (underlined for emphasis herein). Both means seem interchangeable, generally, yet for my taste, I usually prefer to omit the "the" of "the law" and merely say "law" (a simpler convention).

Back to considering what the word "law" even means. Popular definitions of "law" are often quite similar, and this example provides an indicative representation:

> **"A rule of conduct developed by a government or society over a certain territory, and that follows certain practices and customs, as controlled and enforced by the controlling authority"** [C.15].

Take a moment to reflect on that definition.

It seems like a reasonably accommodating definition. Let's assume it is good enough for our purposes herein. Nonetheless, I do want to point out that many disagree about what "law" is (there are entire many treatises written about the definition of law and numerous in-depth debates about the topic).

Among the ongoing debates about the nature of law and how it arises, there are differing philosophies about what law is or ought to be defined as, along with differing opinions about how law comes to be formulated and adopted.

Some of these philosophies about "law" has gradually coalesced into various relatively distinct schools or factions, each professing its own set of key underlying assumptions and arguments about what law is and how it arises.

The schools or factions have gradually been given names or otherwise labeled, which is a source of pride in some instances and an irritant in other cases. Few like the idea of being known by a simple naming convention and believe it undermines the scope and gravity of their respective beliefs and arguments.

In any case, here are some of the most frequently mentioned schools or philosophies about the nature of law:

- **Naturalist School** (court of justice decides all laws, not the legislature)
- **Positivistic School** (rules as politically used over political subjects)
- **Normative Science School** (not what must occur, prescribed rules to abide by)
- **Historical-Law School** (common consciousness of the people, our customs)
- **Sociological School** (law is social, exerts control, coercive, societally driven)
- **Realist School** (per Oliver Wendell Holmes [R.29]: "Law is a statement of the circumstances in which public force will be brought to bear upon through the courts")
- **Other**

These are serious matters, and some would assert strike at the heart of the entire field of law.

Without further angst over which school or faction is somehow best or right, let's proceed into the foray of identifying the facets of legal reasoning.

As such, momentarily accede that "law" is a rule of conduct, developed by the government or society, over a certain territory, and that follows certain practices and customs, as controlled and enforced by the controlling authority.

Parse out of that definition the part that says, "rule of conduct" and the part that says, "certain practices and customs."

If we want to pin down law, making it usable for legal reasoning, we need somehow to know what that "rule of conduct" consists of, along with how the "practices and customs" come to bear.

This brings us to the beguiling aspect that we perhaps need two major aspects to be resolved, namely reasoning and we need representation:

➔ **Legal Reasoning = Reasoning & Representation**

Another short side note related to wording, which is that the word "representation" is not meant in the way that you might think it is. The usual use of the word "representation" in the context of law would be that of a lawyer for example "representing" their client. That's not how the word "representation" is normally used in the AI field.

Representation in an AI context refers to how an object or entity will be codified into a computationally usable form.

Generally, conceptualize that "reasoning" is a process, while "representation" is some kind of object or things upon which a process can operate.

One form of representation might be a written set of laws.

In conventional writing and the written record, representation is essentially inactive, static shall we say, unmoving, and a collection of characters printed on a page.

The "reasoning" somehow uses those words and miraculously undertakes a process that makes them come into active use.

In short, we have now two aspects at hand:

- **Reasoning about the law**

- **Representation of the law**

If that seems rather obvious, there is a perhaps hidden point to this seemingly convoluted indication.

When someone says that they are undertaking "legal reasoning," the general belief is that there are really two aspects involved, reasoning *and* representation.

Thus, even though the word "reasoning" is found within the phrase "legal reasoning," there are in practical terms presumably two problems to be solved or conquered.

One problem is how does the process of doing legal reasoning exactly work, and the other problem is how the representation that underlies the act of that process is to be symbolized.

Stay with me and you'll soon see how crucial this simple revelation is.

Knowledge Representation

We are first going to tackle the representation side of the legal reasoning coin.

Within the legal domain, what kinds of representation might there be?

As anyone that has studied law can tell you, it includes at least, but is not limited to, these kinds of representation facets:

- Facts
- Procedures
- Rules
- Arguments
- Hypotheses
- Cases
- Analogies
- Standards
- Other

Those representation facets are the multitude of means by which the law is depicted, and for which are used to various degrees while reasoning about the law.

Knowledge representation is a significant topic and an unresolved issue when considering how we'll get an AI system to be able to do any kind of action, regardless of the domain of attention. Somehow, we'll need to provide a viable means of representing the law, such that the AI system might then process the law, exercising whatever the reasoning part of legal reasoning consists of.

As will be discussed in these chapters, there are numerous ways that you could consider representing the law, and it could very well be that the wrongly chosen kind of representation could undermine the efficacy of the legal reasoning effort.

You could, for example, have the law arranged or represented in a manner that say is a square shape (metaphorically), yet maybe the processing or reasoning side needs a round shape, and as such, things are afield of each other.

Numerous attempts have been made at devising ways to represent the law in terms of being amenable therefore to automation and particularly to using AI. Nobody has struck gold, as it were, in that there is still plenty of debate about what kinds of representation is going to win the day here.

To some degree, the attempts at representation have been varied and allowed for inspection and assessment, providing a means to assess the tradeoffs among different approaches to representation.

In that sense, what is less transparent perhaps is the "reasoning" side of the coin.

The debates on the reasoning facets are as fierce if not more so than those about representation and can readily get mired into grueling discussions about what happens inside our minds.

How so?

Well, if you ask a lawyer to explain their legal reasoning, here's what they might do.

First, they are likely to point at a legal case and highlight the facts of the case (the case itself being the "representation" of the legal matter, while the interpretation of it is the processing side of the coin).

They might then search for and find various legal rules or principles that pertain to the case.

Next, the lawyer could go into a mental legal analysis mode, concentrating on mulling over the case.

Out of that, perhaps the lawyer will offer several arguments about the nature of the case and try to tie together analogous cases, various rules, facts, and so on, aiming to make some assertion.

While watching the lawyer, as though they were in an experiment, you would likely easily see what written materials they referred to.

As such, for those wondering about the "representation" side of legal reasoning, it seems somewhat straightforward that the objects or entities needed while the lawyer undertook their legal reasoning would be those written records that they handled.

Is it as readily apparent as to what the lawyer did during that mental mulling portion?

You are only able to guess at what the "reasoning" consisted of (we'll be revisiting this point shortly).

Just as there are copious attempts at the "representation" of law, there are indubitably numerous attempts at portraying the "reasoning" aspects of law too.

One viewpoint is to refer to the reasoning as a kind of sense-making.

Here's a typical model of a sense-making process in law [C.5]:

Foraging

- Data leads to Search & Filter
- Search & Filter leads to Read & Extract
- Read & Extract leads to Schematize
- Schematize leads to Schema
- Schema leads to Build Case

Sensemaking

- Build Case leads to Hypotheses
- Hypotheses leads to Tell Story
- Tell Story leads to Presentation
- Presentation leads to Reevaluate & Search for Support
- Reevaluate & Search leads to Schema
- Schema leads to Search for Information
- Search for Information leads to Data

This might feel like a reasonable way to depict doing the reasoning part of legal reasoning.

Unfortunately, converting that kind of high-level depiction into something that's going to be undertaken by an AI system is just not specific enough and leaves a lot of unstated and ill-specified elements that still would need to be worked out.

Conclusion

This chapter has set the stage to consider two major problems to be tackled, the "reasoning" problem, and the "representation" problem that is associated with legal reasoning.

It might seem peculiar that in our attempts to solve the problem of figuring out AI legal reasoning that we've now spawned two problems, but it is considered by most to be a prudent divide-and-conquer means to proceed (though controversy abounds, as will be explained shortly).

Note: *For supplemental materials depicting the aspects discussed in this chapter, refer to Appendix B, which contains various augmented diagrams, charts, and additional related facets of relevance.*

CHAPTER 5
ONTOLOGY AND LAW

There are various elaborated models that try to bring together the "representation" and the "reasoning" into one big picture perspective.

Consider one such model that makes use of a pyramid shape (proposed by Ashley et al [R.6]).

At the base of the pyramid, there are legal cases, and out of those cases, a set of case facts are to be derived.

Next, using the case facts, derive a series of factors that pertain to the case facts, and have those case facts serve as the next layer in the pyramid (just above the base).

Then, use the identified factors to craft various legal claim elements, which becomes the layer atop of the factors layer.

At the apex, there would be legal policies and principles.

Thus, the pyramid is a representation of legal knowledge and would be used by a reasoning or inference mechanism to then compare the legal cases, make use of the factors, draw inferences, and make legal arguments.

This would then be a computational model of the law that would consist of:

- **Case Texts**
- **Case Facts**
- **Factors**
- **Legal Claim Elements**
- **Legal Policies/Principles**
- **Algorithms to:**
    - **Compare Cases**
    - **Draw Inferences**
    - **Make Arguments**

Again, though this is certainly helpful, and we need high-level depictions like this, the devil is ultimately in the details.

Suppose I gave you an architectural rendering to make a 50-story tall skyscraper. If the architectural rendering is primarily at a high-level, it's inarguably important and vital to the effort, but using that to go ahead and build a towering building is just not enough.

Where some turn to is the search for an ontology of law.

Essentially, if there was already an existent ontological layout of law, and that those that study law already had put together an architectural rendering along with needed blueprints, AI developers could start with that as a launchpad.

Turns out that the field of law is still in the midst of ongoing debates about the ontological aspects of law.

Researchers Valent and Breuker aptly state the situation [R.49]:

> "Ontological assumptions are the very heart of the enterprise of representing knowledge. In AI & Law, these assumptions reflect an underlying view of what law is made of, what legal knowledge is, which knowledge categories play a role in Law and how they interrelate. By and large, however, ontological issues have been rather neglected in AI & Law. The most common ontological view on Law is very simple and divides legal knowledge into two orthogonal types: rules and cases."

And, they provide what they consider a "functional ontology of law," which contains facets such as:

- **Real-world situation**
- **Terminological Knowledge (Legal Abstract Model)**
- **Causal Knowledge**
- **Legal Situation**
- **Normative Knowledge**
- **Responsibility Knowledge**
- **Reactive Knowledge**

Digging deeper, their functional ontology of the law contains these knowledge elements, suggesting that the representation of law needs to contain these kinds of objects:

- **Normative Knowledge**
  - Commanding Norms
  - Empowering Norms
  - Derogative Norms

- **Responsibility (Causal Knowledge)**
    - Legal Responsibility
    - Causal Responsibility
- **World Knowledge**
    - Definitional Knowledge
    - Situational Knowledge
- **Reactive Knowledge**
- **Positional Knowledge**
- **Creative Knowledge**

Conclusion

There isn't a standardized and sufficiently detailed ontology of law that can be used as a specification for an AI developer to follow.

As you'll soon see in the AI case studies about legal reasoning, the AI legal reasoning efforts to-date have forced each such instance to ferret out their own ontological mechanizations.

It has been a somewhat start-from-scratch or reinvent the wheel ordeal, each time, partially due to the aspect that the "wheel" hasn't even been invented as yet, and only crude mechanisms that kind of try to act like wheels have been previously put together.

In addition, no one can say with any substantive certainty what the "reasoning" part of legal reasoning consists of. All in all, it seems a bit daunting, and maybe downbeat, but I forewarned that this is a field with a lot of opportunity and upside potential.

Note: *For supplemental materials depicting the aspects discussed in this chapter, refer to Appendix B, which contains various augmented diagrams, charts, and additional related facets of relevance.*

CHAPTER 6
INTRACTABILITY OF LEGAL REASONING

As indicated, there are presumably two major facets to legal reasoning, consisting of reasoning and representation.

In the prior chapter, a thought experiment was sketched that suggested we could observe a lawyer practicing law and seemingly observe that the representation aspects of the reasoning process appeared to consist of tangible objects such as written legal cases, written legal rules or principles, and the like.

The reasoning process is not as readily observed since it is something that occurs within the mind of the subject, and we are left to guess at what went on in the mind of the lawyer involved.

A human being that is undertaking a legal reasoning task has some form of **implicit reasoning** that is hidden within their mind.

Attempts at trying to get the human mind to divulge how it works have been limited and are not yet achieved. For example, cognitive scientists and neuroscientists have used techniques such as MRIs to scan the brain while experts carry out various tasks, and then used the MRI results to try and indicate which parts of the brain are activating, but this is all quite highly speculative as to what is really taking place during the thinking or reasoning process.

Imagine if you were unaware of how a car engine worked.

You decided to stand outside a car, have the engine get started, and tried to divine how the engine functions by listening to the sounds that the car makes while the engine is engaged.

Could you figure out that there were pistons, spark plugs, and other such mechanisms that underlie the running engine?

It would be a stretch.

Though the car engine example is perhaps not a perfectly analogous situation, it offers nonetheless an overall indication of the challenge involved in trying to use methods such as MRIs to discern how human thinking takes place.

A skeptic might say that there's no need to unpack how the mind works and instead simply ask the lawyer what they were thinking.

Indeed, many studies have done just that. An expert, such as a lawyer, undertakes an assigned task, and then the person is asked to explain what they did.

They do so. We now have **explicit reasoning**, namely reasoning that has been explicitly articulated.

Presumably, you assume, this then completely makes clear the reasoning process, but that is not at all necessarily the case.

In the use case of explicit reasoning, the human is telling us what they believe happened during their thinking process.

It is your *rationalization* of what the thinking consisted of.

But we don't have any viable means to assert that the articulated or explicit reasoning is what truly happened during the implicit reasoning that's locked away within the brain.

Your explanation might very well be a completely fabricated indication, based on what you've been led to believe should be your thinking process.

In other words, while going to school or being raised from childhood, perhaps society has taught you what is considered a good or bad explanation, and you've therefore honed onto that as how to best explain your inner thoughts.

For all we know, your mind undertook an utterly different process altogether. Maybe your mind did do as you've articulated, or maybe not.

Overall, this raises the aspect that we can either continue to plow forward into how the human mind works, and someday hopefully crack it open, revealing how we really do reasoning, or, we might somewhat toss-in-the-towel on implicit reasoning (for now) and resort to relying solely instead on explicit reasoning.

In short, the reasoning process that we're going to have an AI system undertake is going to likely be based on the explicit articulations, rather than the implicit, though as will be discussed about AI Machine Learning in a later chapter herein, there is some chance of taking the vaunted route of implicit reasoning (kind of).

Arguing About Reasoning And Representation

Now that you've become aware of the implicit versus explicit reasoning dilemma, let's address another quandary.

We've earlier discussed the assertion that legal reasoning consists of two facets, reasoning and representation. Let's revisit that claim.

Some might argue that the dividing of legal reasoning into the two components of reasoning and representation is a false premise.

How so?

It could be that it is **reasoning-alone**, and no representation involved.

Your first impression is likely that this seems absurd or to be rejected out-of-hand, since it is obvious that lawyers use things like written cases, written rules, and the like, all of which fairly could be construed as representation (in the manner of knowledge representation).

Those that align with the reasoning-alone are often making the argument that since we don't know what is going on in the human mind, the representation that you see as the written cases is perhaps another fake artifact, one of the explicit reasoning nature, and not at all what's happening inside the mind.

Thus, this must be asked:

- **Does the human mind really "represent" the written cases and other such materials?**

- **Or, is it all purely reasoning, entirely and exclusively process-based?**

There have been many years of cognitive and psychological experiments about human thinking, and it appears that the mind is indeed representing the "outside world" (outside of the mind), and thus there must be some kind of internal representation.

That being said, this doesn't necessarily mean that the mind is storing say the words of the written pages, and might have some entirely different way of representing those external aspects, yet, however it is occurring, one way or another there is some form of representation within the human mind (one would so believe).

Meanwhile, there's the other "acting alone" argument that perhaps the brain and the mind are entirely **representation-only**, and there isn't any processing or reasoning that takes place.

Most would tend to agree that there is both reasoning and representation.

Of those believers, there are two kinds.

Some assert that you can separate apart the reasoning and the representation.

This certainly seems to be how we work, given that the written cases, written rules, etc. are one thing, and our efforts to reason about them is another matter.

The subtle difference is that within the human mind, we don't know for sure that those two facets are indeed separate and distinct.

Thus, one camp argues that reasoning and representation are one and the same, they are two commingled elements, inseparable, and it is inappropriate to consider them as somehow distinct or separated.

Once the written cases and rules are "scanned" via your eyes and stream into your noggin, does the reasoning and the representation become a blur, a mixture that is fully miscible?

We conventionally say that oil and water don't mix, they are immiscible, while in stark contrast that combining water with ethyl alcohol is considered miscible, forming a homogenous solution.

Is the act of legal reasoning within the human mind an immiscible or miscible phenomenon?

Nobody can say for sure, though there are competing theories about it.

Intractability Versus Tractability

One additional aspect to cover right now, which we'll revisit once we've delved further into the AI aspects, involves tractability versus intractability.

In computer science, a mainstay of attention goes toward algorithms. Let's suppose that we are able to ultimately figure out an algorithm for undertaking legal reasoning, doing so artificially in a machine or computer.

If you don't believe that's ever going to happen, you are in the **impossibility camp** and thus any further discussion on the matter is pointless for you, other than as idle interest.

But let's assume that it is possible that some kind of algorithm for legal reasoning will eventually be devised.

We might need to temper the excitement with the aspect that the algorithm might be so sluggish or slow to run that it cannot act in any reasonably acceptable time frame.

Here's what I mean.

You have a legal reasoning algorithm and it gets fed with legal cases and the like.

Then, you ask it to render a legal opinion about the case.

It churns away, consuming computational resources.

Suppose just for sake of discussion, one hundred years later, it provides a spotless and elegant legal opinion.

Not very timely.

For computer scientists, a problem for which there is not an "efficient" algorithm to solve the problem is labeled as an **intractable problem.**

Even if we can figure out a means to undertake legal reasoning via AI, there's another hurdle to deal with, namely, the hurdle of time. Whatever we come up with, it has to run or partake in legal reasoning within some "reasonable" amount of time.

We can't say for sure what reasonable timing is, per se, and would need to consider the circumstances.

In any case, it would certainly seem that taking one hundred years is likely "unreasonable" or at least not quite what we would hope to have occurred.

The fortunate news, if there is any, would be that we don't necessarily need to let time bother us right away. If you could craft an AI system that can perform legal reasoning (preferably provably so), there are ways to then try to make it more efficient. So, no need right now to give up the overarching goal due to the potential of untimely timing aspects.

Note: *For supplemental materials depicting the aspects discussed in this chapter, refer to Appendix B, which contains various augmented diagrams, charts, and additional related facets of relevance.*

CHAPTER 7
AI BLACK BOX AND PRACTICING LAW

The discussion about dividing legal reasoning into reasoning and representation is an attempt at delving into how legal reasoning takes place.

Set that aside for the moment. Assume that legal reasoning is a veritable Black Box and of which we might or might not be able to ultimately make translucent.

Pretend that all we know is that there are these artifacts called laws and they feed into this Black Box, and then out of the Black Box comes the practice of law (for those of you familiar with AI, this is akin to the proverbial Chinese Room problem posed by John Searle in 1980 [R.44]).

From a macroscopic perspective, the input into the Black Box is the law, and the output is (essentially) the ability or outcome associated with practicing law.

What does it mean to say that someone (or something) has the ability to practice law?

It is an important question since an AI legal reasoning system is certainly expected to be able to practice law, in some fashion or another, which otherwise it would not be especially useful, and if it does so autonomously, it might likely be held to the same standards and provisos as do humans that practice law.

I'll use the ABA as a primary source for providing a relatively definitive indication of what practicing law consists of.

Here is the ABA model definition of the practice of law [C.3]:

> **"The 'practice of law' is the application of legal principles and judgment with regard to the circumstances or objectives of a person that require the knowledge and skill of a person trained in the law."**

Somewhat nebulous, nearly self-referential, but fortunately the ABA does provide added detail.

Here's the ABA's indication of the specifics [C.3]:

> **"(1) Giving advice or counsel to persons as to their legal rights or responsibilities or to those of others;**
>
> **(2) Selecting, drafting, or completing legal documents or agreements that affect the legal rights of person;**
>
> **(3) Representing a person before an adjudicative body, including, but not limited to, preparing or filing documents or conducting discovery; or**
>
> **(4) Negotiating legal rights or responsibilities on behalf of a person."**

That is helpful to our cause. For an AI legal reasoning system, what do we want such an AI system to do?

As a minimum, presumably, we would want it to do the four acts of practicing law that the ABA has identified.

When someone claims they have an AI legal reasoning system, how will we judge whether it is indeed an AI legal reasoning system?

Via the ABA set of four acts, we can now try to assemble a test for AI legal reasoning systems and ascertain if an alleged AILR can do those four prescribed legal acts.

In the field of AI, there is a well-known type of test for assessing artificial intelligence that is referred to as the Turing Test [R.18].

Simply stated, someone that administers the test does so to two participants, another human that is hidden from view and an AI system that is also hidden from view. Upon asking each of two hidden participants a series of questions, if the administrator cannot discern one participant from the other, it is said that the AI is considered the equivalent of the human's intelligence that participated since the two were indistinguishable from each other.

Though the test is often cited as a means to someday ascertain whether a system has achieved true and complete AI, there are a number of qualms and drawbacks to this approach. For example, if the administrator asks questions that are insufficiently probing, it is conceivable that the two participants cannot be differentiated and yet the measurement of any demonstrable intelligence never took place.

In any case, for the purposes of AI legal reasoning, a test of some kind would certainly be advantageous, including being able to prod out false or misleading claims about having achieved true AILR.

Let's abbreviate the ABA depiction as these four legal acts:

(1) Advice

(2) Legal Docs

(3) Being a Rep

(4) Negotiating

Would an AI legal reasoning system be considered successful if it could only do one of those acts, such as the Advice aspects of practicing law, but not be able to do the other three legal acts?

Inarguably, it would be quite impressive, and the word "successful" is somewhat of a trap. It would be preferred to do all four acts and be able to mix them up or intermingle them, doing so as the legal problem being solved might so require; nonetheless, accomplishing even one would be a coup.

That then could be considered the ultimate goal for an AI legal reasoning system.

On the other hand, right now, we'll take at great accomplishment any AI legal reasoning system that can do *any of the four*, since achieving any of the four is in itself quite a success.

Consider a matrix that has the various combinations of the four acts of practicing law.

The rows are the combinations.

The columns consist of the four named acts.

We have four rows that are instances of having just a singular act, namely Advice-alone, Legal Docs alone, Being a Rep alone, and Negotiating alone.

There are rows that indicate the combinations of pairs (two of the acts). Thus:

- Advice + Legal Docs
- Advice + Being a Rep
- Advice + Negotiating
- Legal Docs + Being a Rep
- Legal Docs + Negotiating
- Being a Rep + Negotiating

There are rows of the combinations in threes.

And, the final row would consist of all four acts.

Most researchers that are building AI legal reasoning systems are perhaps desirous to try to achieve all four acts, but more realistically aim at a subset of the mentioned combinations.

Also, in theory, if you can do one of the four acts, the odds of extending to be able to the next, and then the next, until you achieve all four is heightened.

Which of the four legal acts should a researcher seek to achieve first?

This brings up the notion of whether any of the four is easier than the other, and if so, maybe the expedient way to approach AI legal reasoning would be to pick the easiest one first (cheery picking, as it were).

Often, the one that researchers seem to anticipate being the "easiest" is the **Legal Docs** legal activity.

Why so?

One element that makes it seem easier than the other three is that it can possibly be done without human interaction per se, though this is somewhat of a misnomer.

Consider a simple example. You might hire a lawyer to prepare a contract for you. Perhaps after a brief initial consultation to find out your particulars, the lawyer could then proceed to compose the legal contract. The lawyer would likely peruse prior contracts, might reuse some of the legal language, would draft a new version for your matter at hand, and then deliver to you the completed contract.

Notice that this could potentially be done without much interaction with other humans, including the actual client that the contract is intended for.

This possibility of a self-contained effort, absent of having to interact with other humans, provides part of the impetus for why it is often the type of AI application you might see emerging into the LegalTech and LawTech marketplace.

If an AILR can principally undertake its performance via the written word, this reduces the arduous aspects of interacting with a human and having to grasp the meaning and nuances of what the human might be conveying.

It is said that the other three legal acts tend to require a greater likelihood of human interactivity. That being said, any seasoned attorney could attest that there are contracts that do require extensive interactivity, thus the potential for this assumption being a misnomer or at least misleading.

Conclusion

This chapter has pointed out that to know whether or not an AI legal reasoning system is capable of practicing law, we could potentially test it along the lines of the four legal acts expected of human attorneys.

Perhaps a Turing Test equivalent could be established for the testing of AILR's. That being said, and with the inherent weaknesses and limitations of the Turing Test, we would undoubtedly like to have some more robust means to ascertain an AILR's capabilities, and this remains an open problem for the field of AI legal reasoning.

Note: *For supplemental materials depicting the aspects discussed in this chapter, refer to Appendix B, which contains various augmented diagrams, charts, and additional related facets of relevance.*

CHAPTER 8
AI BLACK BOX AND BEING A LAWYER

Suppose that an AI legal reasoning system was able to seemingly practice law, doing so to the level of achieving the four legal acts of practicing law as specified by the ABA (see Chapter 7).

Does that mean the AI legal reasoning system would be a lawyer?

Quite an intriguing question, though highly speculative since we aren't anywhere near having such an AI legal reasoning system today. In any case, let's pursue the question due to the eventual possibility of having such an AI legal reasoning system.

Here's the ABA definition of what constitutes being a lawyer (C.1]:

> **"A lawyer (also called attorney, counsel, or counselor) is a licensed professional who advises and represents others in legal matters."**

We generally expect that a lawyer needs to be officially licensed. The licensing requirements involve a number of required accomplishments.

The ABA lists these requirements [C.3]:

- **"Have a bachelor's degree or its equivalent.**

- **Complete three years at an ABA-accredited law school.**

- **Pass a state bar examination, which usually lasts for two or three days. The exam tests knowledge in selected areas of law. There are also required tests on professional ethics and responsibility.**

- **Pass a character and fitness review. Applicants for law licenses must be approved by a committee that investigates character and background.**

- **Take an oath, usually swearing to support the laws and the state and federal constitutions.**

- **Receive a license from the highest court in the state, usually the state supreme court."**

A person (human being) needs to have a bachelor's level college degree or its equivalent. They need to successfully pass a law school program at an ABA-accredited law school. There are state-administered law exams that need to be taken and ultimately passed.

If someone meets those requirements, they can apply to be licensed as an attorney, including taking a character test and a fitness test and then take an oath.

Finally, assuming all goes well in that aim to get the license, it would be issued to the person and they would formally be registered as such.

Why bring this up?

Here's a somewhat unsettling question about the matter.

- ➔ ***Does the prospective lawyer that seeks to get licensed need to be a human being?***

Suppose that we had an AI legal reasoning system and assume further that it otherwise passed an AILR Turing Test and was considered the equivalent of a human attorney.

Would it then be allowed to try and become a licensed attorney?

Or, turn that around, would it have to seek to attain the licensing of an attorney, since it otherwise would seem to be practicing law, and if someone (or something) is practicing law then presumably the government (in some places) requires that the law practitioner must be licensed to perform legal acts.

Suppose the AI legal reasoning system was able to only achieve one of the four acts of practicing law, let's go with the **Legal Docs** act.

Is it practicing law?

One dividing line would be whether there was a human attorney (licensed) that was working hand-in-hand with the AI legal reasoning system, in which case, presumably, the AI itself wouldn't need any licensing since the human lawyer is the one responsible for the practicing of law.

In that manner of speaking, you wouldn't ask if Microsoft Word had to be a licensed attorney simply because a licensed attorney used it to write a legal contract. Nor would you presumably insist that the AI legal reasoning system had to be a licensed attorney.

There are AI legal reasoning systems that will be semi-autonomous, being able to accomplish some aspects of legal acts, but inevitably still require a human attorney to take up the slack.

Having that licensed human attorney in-the-loop allows that the AI legal reasoning system can be either adept or inept, complete or incomplete, since it is still the responsibility of the human attorney to oversee the act of practicing law.

Only until an AI legal reasoning system is autonomous, meaning it does not need a human attorney to carry on the act of practicing law, would the question seemingly arise about whether the AI legal reasoning system needs to be licensed.

If it does need to be licensed, would it necessarily need to be the same requirements as those of a human?

You could presumably excise out the need for a bachelor's degree and also remove the need to go to law school.

Those facets would presumably be established via whether the AI legal reasoning could showcase an ability to "know" the law or not.

The aspects remaining could still be considered administrable:

- **Pass state bar exam**
- **Pass ethics & responsibility tests**
- **Pass character & fitness review**
- **Ascribe to oath**
- **Be granted a license**

Some of those elements do raise other interesting twists.

For example, there is an ongoing debate about whether an AI system can exhibit "ethics" or ethical behavior. We expect humans to do so, and thus, some argue that we ought to require AI systems to do the same.

A common counterargument is that there's "no heart" in an AI system, akin to the feelings or sentiments of the human heart, and so how can it ascribe to a code of ethics?

Steppingstones and AI Legal Reasoning

Let's shift gears.

I've pointed out that there will be AI legal reasoning systems that are semi-autonomous, and if we can get there it would be the case that we'll have ones that are fully autonomous too.

What will lawyers think of having such autonomous AI legal reasoning systems?

If the AI legal reasoning system is semi-autonomous, it likely would be a welcomed tool for a human lawyer, allowing them to do their work in a more effective and efficient manner, akin to using say Microsoft Word or its equivalent.

That analogy though to Microsoft Word or word processing is somewhat flawed, some would argue. A word processing package is going to speed-up the stenographic typing and editing, but it won't especially do much about making the "attorney knowledgeable" aspects any more efficient or effective.

An AI legal reasoning system, even a semi-autonomous one, would be chipping away at the actual attorney-like practicing of law, augmenting a human lawyer, yet also reducing the amount of effort of that lawyer.

In the aggregate, you could try to make the case that it would, therefore, threaten to reduce the number of attorneys needed.

It's somewhat convoluted to make that case, and I think most would find it hard to argue that semi-autonomous AI legal reasoning systems would substantively undermine the occupational opportunities of being a human attorney.

On the other hand, a fully autonomous AI legal reasoning system would certainly seem to go straight at the heart of those wanting to be attorneys.

You wouldn't need as many human attorneys, or maybe not need them at all (that's argumentative, of course, since some assert that you'd need human attorneys to keep the AI legal reasoning system up-to-date, though the counter argument there is that the AI legal reasoning system ought to be able to do so on its own and not need humans for that purpose).

In short, there are AI capabilities that consist of being either semi-autonomous or that are fully autonomous. We've got the human impacts on attorneys, namely the possibility that the AI could augment human lawyers or that the AI could end-up replacing human lawyers.

Let's combine those ideas.

Imagine a four-square grid that would result in combining the AI capabilities (two rows, consisting of semi-autonomous, autonomous) with the human lawyering impacts (two columns, consisting of augment, replace).

Consider each of the resultant four cells:

- **Augment + Semi-Autonomous** (human lawyer still needed)
- **Augment + Fully Autonomous** (human lawyer not needed)
- **Replace + Semi-Autonomous** (human lawyer still needed, so wouldn't be "replaced" per se)
- **Replace + Fully Autonomous** (human lawyer not needed, so would be replaced)

One important clarification. A fully autonomous AI legal reasoning system would not mean that human lawyers could not exist.

I say that because some make a colossal and false leap and assume that if there were AI legal reasoning systems of the caliber of a licensed attorney, no longer would there be any human attorneys, as though this is axiomatic.

It would seem to depend upon the preferences of those that were seeking attorney services.

Furthermore, there doesn't seem to be any reason to believe that fully autonomous AI legal reasoning systems wouldn't work hand-in-hand potentially with human lawyers (the AILR would not be dependent upon the human attorney and instead be working as a peer of the human attorney).

Today, human lawyers work hand-in-hand with each other, routinely.

Thus, the point is that a fully autonomous AI legal reasoning system does not preclude the existence of human lawyers.

That being said, other factors would certainly come to play as to whether clients would choose an AILR or choose a human attorney for performing requested legal services, such as whether it is more or less costly to use an AILR versus using a human attorney, and so on.

Not Up To Bar Par

Suppose that neither a semi-autonomous AI legal reasoning system and nor even any fully autonomous AI legal reasoning system was allowed to get the needed licensing to practice law.

Perhaps all human attorneys put their collective mettle together and insisted that AI systems could not be a licensed attorney, regardless of how capable the AILR's might be.

What happens to the autonomous AILR's then?

There is a human analogous aspect, possibly.

The ABA stipulates that humans can somewhat perform in attorney-like ways and yet not be licensed as an attorney.

Here's what the ABA indicates [C.3]:

> **"Exceptions and exclusions: Whether or not they constitute the practice of law, the following are permitted:**
>
> **(1) Practicing law authorized by a limited license to practice;**
>
> **(2) Pro se representation;**
>
> **(3) Serving as a mediator, arbitrator, conciliator or facilitator; and**
>
> **(5) Providing services under the supervision of a lawyer in compliance with the Rules of Professional Conduct."**

Those might be considered carveouts for AI legal reasoning systems too, either falling within the above-indicated scope, or an added exclusion specifically for the advent of AILR's.

Pursue that line of thinking for a moment.

Assume that there are some AI legal reasoning systems and they are good enough that they are essentially practicing law.

Meanwhile, assume that authorizing bodies have stated that any such AI must undertake certain tests or licensing requirements. Yet, imagine that for whatever reason, the AI systems haven't gotten that licensing.

What then?

Once again, we have a human analogous aspect to rely upon.

The ABA provides an indication about those that act to practice law in an unauthorized manner [C.3]:

> **"If a person who is not authorized to practice law is engaged in the practice of law, that person shall be subject to the civil and criminal penalties of this jurisdiction.**
>
> **[1] The primary consideration in defining the practice of law is the protection of the public.**
>
> **Thus, for a person's conduct to be considered the practice of law, there must be another person toward whom the benefit of that conduct is directed. The conduct also must be targeted toward the circumstances or objectives of a specific person.**
>
> **Thus, courts have held that the publication of legal self-help books is not the practice of law."**

Perhaps the provision needs to be adjusted to replace the word "person" with the indication of "person or machine," getting this ready for the future.

One additional caveat. As mentioned by the ABA quotation above, the courts have determined that the publication of legal self-help books is not within the proviso of the unauthorized law practice stipulation.

Suppose a vendor that makes an AI legal reasoning system were to claim that no licensing is required since it is nothing more than a legal self-help capability, and ergo the same as the carveout for legal self-help books?

An interesting potential case to be considered.

Conclusion

This chapter has explored the ramifications of autonomous AILR's and whether they would be considered within the realm of practicing law and therefore subject to the requirements associated with being an attorney.

In the next chapter, we'll begin to examine the status of AI legal reasoning systems and be able to assess how far from reaching such a state they currently are.

Note: *For supplemental materials depicting the aspects discussed in this chapter, refer to Appendix B, which contains various augmented diagrams, charts, and additional related facets of relevance.*

CHAPTER 9
POPOV V HAYASHI AS AI TESTBED

Are you familiar with the Popov v Hayashi court case?

If you are a baseball fan, you might be. Or, if you like unusual and intriguing legal cases, you might know this case since it has a number of novelties and who-done-it twists-and-turns.

Before I share with you the facts and nuances about Popov v Hayashi [R.10], it might be helpful to explain why this case merits being discussed in a book about AI legal reasoning.

The answer is rather simple.

A contingent of researchers in the AI and law realm have perchance chosen the case for purposes of exploring legal reasoning facets and the use of rules-based logic.

Like a snowball that grows bigger as it rolls down the mountain, this particular case got pegged by a few researchers as one of interest for examining how to unpack a court case and embody it into a formalized logic and it has since then taken on a life of its own in the AI legal reasoning field.

Subsequent researchers that wanted to add or supplement the prior research were naturally obliged to stick with the same court case.

Over, and over again.

That being said, you could generally pick any other substantive court case and have done the same type of analysis and application of a formalized logic.

Admittedly, the Popov v Hayashi case has its own innate fascination, and thus, if you were going to start a snowball effect, this was at least an interesting and compelling instance to do so with.

Let's unpack the case.

In San Francisco, during the 2001 baseball season, a famous baseball hitter was on a streak and had been knocking home runs incessantly. His name is Barry Bonds.

After having gotten 72 home runs in the season, fans were going wild over the chance that he might break a new record for the most home runs in a single season, and so his 73rd homerun was being anticipated with great eagerness.

In a packed baseball stadium, fans were crammed into every nook and corner, and many brought a baseball glove, hopeful they would be the one to catch his 73rd home run.

Why would they be so eager?

Just a few years earlier, another famous baseball player, Mark McGwire had hit his season breaking home run and that baseball was caught by a fan, which the fan subsequently sold at auction for an astounding $3,000,000.

As might be expected, the fans in the baseball stadium during Barry Bonds attempt to get his 73rd home run were motivated by the excitement of the game and likely too by the chance of catching and ultimately selling the record-breaking baseball.

Sure enough, Barry knocked a home run out to the crowd.

A fan, Alex Popov, using his baseball glove on his outstretched hand, managed to "catch" the baseball in the webbing of his glove. Immediately, other nearby attendees rammed into him, some say tackled him, and Alex went to the ground.

Standing just next to Alex was Patrick Hayashi.

He too went to the ground.

When the melee was over, Patrick stood-up and had the vaunted baseball in his hands.

A TV station camera crew was stationed close to where the matter occurred, and filmed the moment, though there was a lot of franticness at the time and the camera was unable to capture the nuances of the incident.

Stadium security personnel quickly rushed Patrick to a secure area and assumed that the baseball was his, naturally so, since it was in his possession.

Alex was livid and kept clamoring that the baseball was not Patrick's and rightfully belonged to him (Alex).

The whole thing ended up going to civil court.

At the time, many in the media ridiculed the case as an absurdity and abuse of the court system, and also maintained that it was not in the keeping of the spirit of professional baseball (a gentleman's game, you might say).

Your first assumption might be that possession eclipses anything else and therefore Patrick is the rightful owner of the baseball.

Would you change your opinion if you were told that Patrick ripped the baseball from Alex, or maybe if Patrick took a bite out of Alex's leg and then took the baseball from Alex, or otherwise affronted Alex and caused Alex to let go of the baseball, doing this while they were in a heap at the bottom of a pile of other crazed baseball fans?

I suppose you would say that the baseball should then be given to Alex.

Alternatively, imagine that Alex momentarily had the baseball, and then happened to let it go, but did so not by anything that Patrick did.

And, suppose further that once Alex had let go of the baseball, it was rolling freely in the melee, and Patrick was in the right place at the right time and managed to grab the baseball.

Now, who owns the baseball?

It's a twist-and-turn story. Experts were brought to testify about how a baseball glove could "catch" a ball and yet not actually "catch" the ball entirely (this was a point of contention). A legal parade of sorts took place during the trial, and it was a media sensation.

The public seemed to gradually become weary of the case and found it unbecoming of two grown men. Many urged that the two simply agree to sell the baseball and split the proceeds.

Neither of them seemed to prefer that method of settling the dispute, and each insisted that the baseball was their own property and it would be wrong to share that property (and its value) with anyone else.

What would you do?

Before you answer, remarkably, this case raised some intriguing questions about the rights of possession. Indeed, the attorneys dredged up some precedents on the topic of possession that you might view as clever or possibly as an attempt to obfuscate.

Here are some of the prior cases cited as relevant to the matter.

- There was a duck pond dispute that occurred in 1707, the case of Keeble v Hickergill, and it was claimed as related to this baseball dispute of 2001.

- There was a case from 1805 about the hunting of foxes with hounds, the Pierson v Post case, claimed to be related to this baseball possession dilemma.

- A commercial fisherman in 1844 went to court, the case of Young v Hitchens, and it was cited as pertinent to the baseball dispute, along with the case of Ghen v Rich, 1881, about a whale hunter and his whale.

Kind of a "wild" dredging up of old cases, some asserted. Notably, all of those cases involved wild animals and matters of possession of something labeled as "wild" in its transit (this was a core contention underlying the status of the baseball during the incident, it was alleged).

Though I realize that I haven't laid out all the particulars of the case, and so based solely on the paucity of facts and nuances that I've shared, suppose you were the judge, what would you have decided?

He split the baby. Kind of. Without going into the various details, the judge asserted that Alex had pre-possessory rights to the baseball, while Patrick had direct possessory rights, and thus both men had an equal right to the baseball, one no more so than the other.

The judge ruled that the baseball be sold, and the proceeds were to be split equally between Patrick and Alex.

At the time of the ruling, many said it was the very thing the two should have done to start with. Some criticized the judge and questioned this "unorthodox" notion of pre-possessory rights.

From the perspective of AI and legal reasoning, this case is only useful here because it provides a backdrop to discuss the various attempts at formalizing a case into a logic-based formulation.

Here's what researchers have tried to do with this case.

First, if you want to make this case into a set of logic statements, it might be handy to surface the key factors of the case.

One such research effort suggested to start with these four key factors [R.10]:

F1: Not-Caught (NC)

F2: Own/Open (OO)

F3: Livelihood (LH)

F4: Competition (CO)

You might then take each of those factors and try to see which of those factors are relevant to the set of cases that are being considered.

The set of cases would consist of the Popov v Hayashi and the other wild animal cases. Those factors and the cases will in some ways favor the plaintiff and disfavor the defendant. Likewise, those factors and the cases will in some ways favor the defendant and disfavor the plaintiff.

Upon further inspection, you might come up with even more factors, compiling them into a list or chart, including Hot Pursuit (HP), Owned Land (OL), and so on.

We can also come up with some underlying dimensions of the cases.

Those dimensions could be [R.10]:

D1: Possession

D2: Ownership

D3: Plaintiff/Motive

D4: Defendant/Motive

Using these factors and dimensions, you could put together a series of logic-based statements about the case.

For example, one logic statement is this:

Keeble: {NC, OL, N, M, EV}, Plaintiff

The logic statement is stating that for the Keeble precedent (the one about the duck pond), it is relevant to this Popov v Hayashi case for the factors of NC (Not-Caught), OL (Owned Land), N, M, and EV (I won't cover all the particulars, just providing a snippet), and that via that prior case and those factors, it favors the plaintiff.

We could make an entire set of rules like that.

In addition, there are other rules that could be devised.

For example, consider this rule:

NC -> Defendant, HP -> Plaintiff

This rule means that the Not-Caught (NC) factor tends to favor the defendant, while the HP (Hot Pursuit) factor tends to favor the plaintiff.

Ultimately, you craft many such rules.

These rules could then be put into use by essentially invoking them, meaning that we could walk through the entire set of rules, crunching through each one, and use that to do "legal reasoning" about the Popov v Hayashi case.

In the next several chapters we will be examining how such rules are executed or performed, doing so in a more robust logic notation and formulation.

Conclusion

The point of this discussion about the Popov v Hayashi case is to familiarize you with the notion of trying to extract out of a legal case or set of cases the essentials of those cases, doing so by identifying crucial factors and dimensions.

Another valuable insight is that you can proceed to use those factors and dimensions to craft various rules related to the cases.

This takes us back to the beginning of the discussion about AI and legal reasoning. We've said that you need to have two facets, reasoning and representation.

The Popov v Hayashi case has become earnest fodder for trying to outline the type of knowledge representation needed for undertaking AI legal reasoning, which would be the extraction or elicitation of factors and dimensions, and the reasoning needed, which would be the set of rules.

Can this type of logic formulization scale-up and be sufficient to turn entire legal cases into a highly visible and viable way to showcase legal reasoning, doing so with an eye toward being able to automate it?

That's something we'll be exploring next.

Note: *For supplemental materials depicting the aspects discussed in this chapter, refer to Appendix B, which contains various augmented diagrams, charts, and additional related facets of relevance.*

CHAPTER 10
NON-MONOTONIC LOGIC AND LEGAL REASONING

Let's delve into logic.

Logic is vital to legal reasoning and will be crucial to how AI can be applied to legal reasoning.

When trying to devise a formalized kind of logic, one aspect that you'd discover right away is a big concern involves dealing with logical conclusions that might have to be revamped or undone.

Humans cope with this all the time.

I might see my son standing at the kitchen table and there's a plate that had fallen to the floor, smashing it, and I could reasonably reach the conclusion that my son knocked the plate off the table.

Suppose that a moment later, I see our cat, roaming around under the table, looking quite guilty, in which case I might want to recant my earlier conclusion that my son knocked over the plate, and now conclude that the cat likely got onto the table and was the culprit.

But, then, my daughter, sitting at the far side of the table, raises her hand and declares that she accidentally pulled the tablecloth, causing the plate to fall off the table.

Time to undo the conclusion that I made about the cat, and now reach a conclusion that my daughter was the originating source of the plate breaking situation.

This aspect of dealing with being able to retract prior conclusions is not as easy as it might seem.

If you have a very long chain of logical inferences, and you make a slew of conclusions along the way, there could be a lot of inferences that were dependent upon those conclusions.

Therefore, opting to suddenly decide to recant a conclusion could have a tremendous and unnerving rippling effect.

All of this discussion has to do with **Monotonic Logic**.

In the research about law and logic, there is a sizable focus on how to cope with monotonic logic, and especially **Non-Monotonic Logic (NML)**.

More formally [R.41]:

> Monotonic refers to the idea that logical conclusion(s) which could be attained prior to adding a clause will still be concludable even after a new clause has been added to the logic set. Thus, adding "knowledge" does not reduce nor negate the set of propositions that are derived. This can be undesirable, depending upon your aims. Classic logic uses deductive reasoning and essentially does not allow retraction of prior inferences made.

Thus, monotonic logic does not allow for reducing or negating prior derived propositions and conclusions.

Meanwhile, non-monotonic logic does allow for such provisions.

Formally, one could say it this way [R.41]:

> Conclusion(s) can be invalidated upon adding new rules. Thus, more "knowledge" can impact the logic base as to what it might attain as conclusion(s). Conclusions are said to be *robust* under the addition of information. This can be desirable, depending upon your aims.

A means of implementing non-monotonic reasoning consists of using **defeasible inference**.

Defeasible inference is the notion that in the logic system being utilized, the system reserves the right to go ahead and retract prior reached conclusions.

This presumably would only be done as a result of adding some new "knowledge" that in the light of that added insight would suggest that a prior conclusion ought to be defeated.

One of the more popular examples of monotonic versus non-monotonic reasoning has to do with Tweety bird.

You are likely already are familiar with Tweety bird, a brightly colored animated canary, yellow with sparkling blue eyes, and popularized in the Looney Tunes cartoons.

Nearly any textbook on the foundations of logic seems to make use of the Tweety bird example when explaining the nuances of monotonic reasoning.

As a premise, I might say this:

> **Tweety is a bird.**

I'll add another premise to my set of premises, and say this too:

> **Birds fly.**

What can we now reach as a conclusion?

Logically, if Tweety is a bird, and apparently birds fly, we can reasonably reach the conclusion that Tweety can fly.

As such:

➔ **Conclusion: Tweety can fly.**

There, we did that, and all seemed to go quite well. Imagine though that I now want to add some additional "knowledge" into this logic about Tweety.

I'll add this premise:

Tweety is a penguin.

And, I'll add this premise too:

Penguins cannot fly.

Okay, now that we've got all of our premises in place, what can we do with them?

Let's try to ascertain what conclusions can be reached.

We seem to know that Tweety is a bird, and a penguin.

Earlier, we reached a conclusion that Tweety could fly, which we logically deduced from the fact that Tweety is a bird and that birds fly.

Now we know that Tweety is also a penguin.

Turns out though that we also know that penguins cannot fly. Thus, we would presumably conclude that Tweety cannot fly.

But, hold on, we earlier concluded that Tweety could fly.

Something is amiss.

Either Tweety can fly or Tweety cannot fly.

Which is it?

In non-monotonic logic, we have the means to deal with these kinds of predicaments. One approach would be to use defeasible inference, which would allow us to retract the prior conclusion about Tweety being able to fly, and instead have now in place the conclusion that Tweet cannot fly (in a sense, the prior conclusion is "defeated" or potentially undone).

Easy, or so it seems. The problem would be that if we had some number of other logically derived facets, all of which were based on the earlier conclusion that Tweety can fly, we would need to find all of those and look to determine how they would be impacted by the now-retracted Tweety can fly.

Furthermore, we'd need to also figure out how they are all impacted by the new conclusion that Tweety cannot fly, and thus potentially need to revisit many or all of the other logic-based premises and conclusions that we had already reached.

In short, dealing with a form of logic that allows for non-monotonic reasoning is generally more complicated and more arduous to implement than for monotonic reasoning.

There are a variety of ways to cope with non-monotonic logical reasoning, including the use of defeasible inferencing, along with additional methods referred to as **skeptical reasoning**, **credulous reasoning**, **zombie-arguments**, and the like.

Conclusion

It would be a lot simpler to always assume that monotonic reasoning will be sufficient.

Non-monotonic reasoning introduces quite a quagmire of complexities and requires dealing with clever and accurate ways to handle the NML issues.

Using or building a system of logical reasoning to undertake legal reasoning is a vital pursuit and offers a means to get us toward AI and legal reasoning. In the next chapters, we'll explore "reasoning systems" that have attempted to tackle the legal reasoning aspects, including coping with non-monotonic reasoning.

Note: *For supplemental materials depicting the aspects discussed in this chapter, refer to Appendix B, which contains various augmented diagrams, charts, and additional related facets of relevance.*

CHAPTER 11
ASPIC+ FOR LEGAL REASONING

To undertake legal reasoning in automation, it is essential to have some kind of logic-based formalized language that would allow the embodiment of logical rules and inferences about law.

One such logic language is known as ASPIC+.

As mentioned in the prior chapter, the odds are that any logic language which is going to tackle legal reasoning will need to go beyond monotonic reasoning and be capable of carrying out NML (non-monotonic logic).

The Thief Logic

Instead of using Tweety (which was used in the prior chapter), we'll now switch to the popular "thief" logic examples used in the research on logic-based systems for legal reasoning.

We'll have a series of premises, labeled as r1, r2, and r3 [R.37]:

r1: A person should be punished <u>if</u> the person is a thief.

r2: A person should not be punished <u>if</u> the person is a thief <u>and</u> the person is a minor.

r3: A person should be punished <u>if</u> the person is a thief <u>and</u> the person is violent.

So far, so good, and we now have some legal rules about dealing with thieves.

Along comes John. Turns out that John is a thief and he's a minor.

We'll represent that as this [R.37]:

f1: John is a thief.

f2: John is a minor.

Should John be punished?

We ought not to decide out of thin air, and instead use the logic that we've already established.

By enacting rule 1 (r1), we can assert that since John is a thief, he should be punished.

Don't stop there.

By enacting rule 2 (r2), we are to conclude that John should not be punished since he is a minor, and thus despite also being a thief, he gets off-the-hook due to his being a minor.

Therefore, the logic showcases that John should not be punished.

➔ **Conclusion: Don't punish John.**

For the sake of completeness, we should probably consult the other rules related to the matter, which in this case includes rule 3.

Upon enacting rule 3 (r3), this rule doesn't seem pertinent to John since the rule involves the circumstances of a thief that is violent. As far as we know, John was not violent (we can perhaps assume that due to not being informed that he is violent, he is thusly not violent, though it would have been more reassuring to have been given such a fact, either way, during the use of the logic).

Next, suppose that we discover that John was violent.

Add this premise to our set:

f3: John is violent.

Time to reconsider our earlier conclusion.

By stepping through the rules again, and upon enacting rule 3 (r3), we must conclude that John does need to be punished since he was violent.

Thus:

➔ **Conclusion: John is to be punished**

Is that a satisfactory conclusion?

No, and the rules should be inspected to see why. We have that rule 2 (r2), insisting that even if someone is a thief when the person is a minor they are not to be punished.

So, which shall it be?

Should John be punished, per rule 1 and rule 3, or should John not be punished, per rule 1 and rule 2?

Any logic automation is going to likely end-up with these kinds of predicaments.

Namely, the rules of the logic are not necessarily going to be readily harmonized and aligned to prevent these kinds of conflicts.

Real-life is often the same way.

In a sense, you could say that the famous Catch-22 is a similar kind of logic bind.

Those of you familiar with the *Catch-22* book by Joseph Heller (or the movie version) might recall that during wartime if a pilot refused to fly a dangerous mission they would be considered sane to want to refuse, and yet you would only be allowed to not fly if you were insane, thus, a logical predicament or bind.

Here's a key quote from Joseph Heller's book entitled *Catch-22* [C.9]:

> "There was only one catch and that was Catch-22, which specified that a concern for one's safety in the face of dangers that were real and immediate was the process of a rational mind. Orr was crazy and could be grounded. All he had to do was ask; and as soon as he did, he would no longer be crazy and would have to fly more missions. Orr would be crazy to fly more missions and sane if he didn't, but if he were sane he had to fly them. If he flew them he was crazy and didn't have to, but if he didn't want to he was sane and had to."

A robust system of logic will need to deal with these situations of logic that could easily have any myriad of such issues.

One aspect involves allowing defeasibility, as discussed in the prior chapter.

You might also set up rules priorities, such as in the case of John the thief, suppose that apriori it had been stated that say the rule r3 has a higher priority than rule r2, in which case the matter would be settled since we would take rule r3 over the conflict with rule r2.

Something else to consider is how difficult it can be to detect that rules might be in conflict with each other. If you only have a handful of rules, you'll likely be able to find any conflicts easily, doing so before you possibly perform or execute the rules.

Imagine though trying to capture any substantive legal matter that might have hundreds or thousands of rules and potentially well-hidden within them might be a vast convolution of conflicts.

It's a harder problem than John the thief suggests, though John the thief illustrates how readily such conflicts can occur.

Besides representing logic via the use of words and sentences in a narrative way, we could also show the logic in a graphical manner. Doing so would help humans to better understand the logic being utilized.

I mention this facet because if you were to try and inspect a logic-based system that had thousands upon thousands of logic rules, it could be overwhelming to ascertain what it portends.

Seeing the rules and logic portrayed in a graphical manner could make things easier for humans to look at the logic and also allow for inspection of whether the logic is sound or not. As such, some of the logic reasoning systems include a graphical portrayal feature.

Use of ASPIC+ for AI Legal Reasoning

A particular form of logic-based reasoning "system" is ASPIC+ which has frequently been used by researchers in the legal reasoning realm and is typically portrayed in a logic-based mathematical notation.

Over time, ASPIC+ has been shaped and reshaped, and used to explore the dynamics of logic-based systems, especially in the domain of law and legal reasoning. The ASPIC+ logic language is similar to other forms of logic that you might have learned in your mathematics or statistics classes.

Rules are written in a style or specialized language for accommodating logic.

Logic-based symbols are used to indicate sets, subsets, inferences, and other aspects such as the use of the "not" operator (using the "¬" negation symbol commonly used in mathematics) and the Material Implication symbol (shown as "⊃" in usual convention).

Consider this ASPIC+ coding for the Tweety bird logic conundrum (see [R.37] for further details):

d1: bird ⇒ canfly
d2: penguin ⇒ ¬ canfly
d3: observed_as_penguin ⇒ ¬ penguin
f1: penguin ⊃ bird
f2: penguin ⊃ ¬ r1
f3: observed_as_penguin

A1: observed_as_penguin
A2: A1 ⇒ penguin
A3: penguin ⊃ bird
A4: A2, A3 ⇒ canfly
B1: A2 ⇒ ¬ canfly
C1: A2 ⇒ ¬ r1

For the use of the Material Implication symbol, the standard format is $p \supset q$ whereby:

- $p \supset q$ is True, if p is True and q is True
- $p \supset q$ is True, if p is False and q is True
- $p \supset q$ is True, if p is False and q is False
- $p \supset q$ is False, if p is True and q is False

Some have been critical of ASPIC+ in terms of various weaknesses or limitations involved.

For example, here are some voiced criticisms (see [R.3]):

- Ill-defined logical formalisms
- Can return undesirable (unintended) results
- In some ways is based on counter-intuitive assumptions
- Could be claimed to violate some rationality precepts
- Produces at times counter-intuitive instantiations

Conclusion

ASPIC+ has been a helpful tool to explore the nature of reasoning and especially legal reasoning. For the tastes of law practitioners, ASPIC+ is somewhat abstract.

We'll take a look in the next chapters at rules-based logic systems that get closer to what legal practitioners might find of grounded interest.

Note: *For supplemental materials depicting the aspects discussed in this chapter, refer to Appendix B, which contains various augmented diagrams, charts, and additional related facets of relevance.*

CHAPTER 12
ASP FOR LEGAL REASONING

A popular logic-based tool that we'll next explore is called **Answer Set Programming (ASP)**.

ASP is considered a **declarative programming language**.

Let's take a moment to explore the nature of declarative programming languages, which differ from the traditional type of programming language which is considered procedural.

For those of you that have ever used SQL (Structured Query Language), a well-known and often used database query programming language, you've experienced declarative programming and thus ASP will seem rather evident to you.

Conventional programming languages such as C++, Python, Java, and others, typically require the programmer to stipulate the sequence of how the statements or code will be executed (such programming is often referred to as **procedural**). For example, I might set up my code so that the program is run by executing the first line, then the second line, and so on. Generally, you could say that I've laid out the sequence or procedure for the computer to take.

In the case of declarative programming, you tend to leave the order of execution of the code up to the system that executes the code.

Essentially, one might assemble a bunch of tasks to be undertaken and let the computer system decide which order to perform them. In that case, the computer might not necessarily execute the first line as its first action, and nor the second line as it the second action, and instead identify a computationally reasonable sequence or order to execute what you've asked to get done.

This might seem like a potentially jumbled approach at an initial glance.

The benefit is that the computer system will take over the chore of figuring out the "sequence" for you, rather than you having to arduously specify the sequence for the system when coding the program.

Example of Declarative Versus Procedural

A simple illustrative example might involve attending a party where there's a room full of people.

Suppose you are asked to write a procedure (aka program) that will end up with you being able to chat with each person at the party.

A conventional procedural approach might involve establishing that you'll visit each person by visiting with the person standing nearest you, chat with that person, and then move to the next nearest person, and so on. Each time that you chat with someone, you'll make a note to remember that you did so, allowing you to avoid talking to them again since you are only aiming to chat with each person once.

A declarative programming approach might be to simply indicate that each person is to be spoken with one time each (not specifying anything about the sequencing involved) and allow the computer system to determine whatever sequence it might come up with.

The computer system will attempt to determine what seems "best" to adopt, such as using the nearest neighbor kind of algorithm that the procedural approach is using, or might instead find an entirely different approach, such as visiting each person based on their height as a measure of which to pick in what sequence or the system might randomly roam as a "sequencing" approach, etc.

Tradeoffs Of Approaches

There are tradeoffs between writing a program that uses a procedural basis versus writing a program that makes use of a declarative basis.

One such tradeoff is performance or time involved in performing the program.

In the use case of the party and visiting with people, the nearest neighbor approach might be fastest, or it could be that some other approach might be faster.

It's hard to know in the abstract.

The performance of the approach depends upon the number of people at the party, along with other factors.

If you wrote a procedural based program that used the nearest neighbor approach, it might be that the procedure works well in some instances, while might be sluggish in other instances. Either way, you've made a bet that the explicitly stated and sequence-predefined procedure is going to be the right way to go.

For declarative programming, you are anticipating that the computer system will hopefully figure out a "good" way to conduct the search for you (either good, good enough, or best), and potentially will consider a variety of different ways to do so, ultimately landing on a relatively fast way to perform the tasks.

Declarative programming really shines by being able to undertake a search in a manner that a procedural based programmer might not have envisioned.

A properly designed declarative programming language will usually have optimal ways to search, thus, when writing a declarative program, you will be able to automatically leverage those purposely tuned search capabilities.

That's why it would usually behoove you to use a declarative programming language if the task at hand has something to do with searching, especially on hard or daunting searches (in computer science parlance, these are typically referred to as NP-Hard search problems).

Declarative Programming

In the field of AI, one especially popular declarative programming language is the Prolog programming language.

Prolog is a generalized kind of declarative programming language. We'll cover more about Prolog in later chapters.

ASP is another example of a declarative programming language, but narrower in what can be done than Prolog, emphasizing the use of logic and solving logic-based programs that resemble the kind of logic that you might have learned about in a mathematics class.

In ASP, you specify a finite set of rules.

This is considered your "answer set program" (thus, the name of ASP).

The system then tries to "solve" the answer set program, using its pre-built **Answer Set Solver** (akin to my remarks a few moments ago about the computer system trying various ways to conduct a search).

Who would use ASP and why would they do so?

AI developers in the robotics field often will use ASP.

They have good reasons to do so, which we'll explore by considering an example of a robot being programmed to perform a particular task.

Imagine that you are programming a robot.

You want the robot to be able to maneuver around an environment and figure out how to make its way around without running into objects such as chairs and tables.

There is a door leading into a room and a different door that's the exit.

Suppose you were asked to write a program that would guide the robot to enter into the room, navigate throughout the room, and eventually make its way to the exit and leave the room.

I trust that you can discern how this problem is similar to the problem earlier of wanting to talk to each person at a party.

Procedurally, you could try to program the robot to step-by-step explore the room, and seek to find the exit. This might require hundreds or even thousands of lines of coding.

In a declarative programming language, you might state that the robot should not bump into objects, and otherwise can move around the room, having the overarching goal of reaching the exit. You would then leave it up to the system to figure out how to then proceed.

At a quick glance, it might seem that the declarative approach is the "best choice" since you didn't have to particularly do as much work in coding the program.

A downside might be that the system opts to have the robot go from side-to-side in the room, repeatedly and excessively, and the robot takes a very long time to reach the exit. Meanwhile, the procedural approach might have been written with a better method and provide a more optimized approach.

The ease as an AI developer of creating an ASP program for a task such as the robot navigational search task could be compelling and thus be chosen in lieu of a procedural programming language.

Other disciplines that use ASP include computational biology, chemistry, and other areas of the sciences.

Researchers in legal reasoning and AI also use ASP.

Example Of ASP Use For AI And Law

Consider the example of crafting a legal license for someone to evaluate a product.

The text of a legal license could include several provisions, which we'll label as a series of "articles" for specifying what the license consists of (for more about this example, see [R.8]).

Consider these licensing provisions:

- "Article 1. The Licensor grants the Licensee a license to evaluate the Product."

- "Article 2. The Licensee must not publish the results of the evaluation of the Product without the approval of the Licensor; the approval must be obtained before the publication. If the Licensee publishes results of the evaluation of the Product without approval from the Licensor, the Licensee has 24 hours to remove the material."

- "Article 3. The Licensee must not publish comments on the evaluation of the Product, unless the Licensee is permitted to publish the results of the evaluation."
- "Article 4. If the Licensee is commissioned to perform an independent evaluation of the Product, then the Licensee has the obligation to publish the evaluation results."
- "Article 5. This license will terminate automatically if Licensee breaches this Agreement."

For those of you versed in the law, you might be tempted to immediately dig apart those provisions, likely finding aspects that you don't like or that are ambiguous, ill-written, etc. You are welcome to do so, though that's not the purpose of bringing up the matter herein.

The reason that I bring up the licensing clauses will be showcase how they might be represented in ASP.

Recall that Article 1 says that the Licensor grants the Licensee a license of the Product.

Here's how you could state that in ASP [R.8]:

```
art10 {obl_not_use :- 1=1.}
art11: art10 {-obl_not_use :- hasLicense.}
```

These two statements indicate that the license is granted to one Licensee and limited to only one Licensee as per this particular licensing provision.

Please be aware that the choice of wording in those statements is up to the "programmer" that develops an ASP program, though there is a specific format required when writing ASP code.

Next, consider the fifth article, the one that stipulates that a license will terminate automatically if Licensee breaches the Agreement.

Here's how that could be coded in ASP [R.8]:

```
art51: art11 {obl_not_use :- violation.}
art52: art40, art22 {obl_not_publish :- violation.
                    -obl_publish :- violation.}
```

Notice that the "art11" used on the line labeled as "art51" refers to the prior statement defined in the ASP code. As such, this illustrates that ASP answer set statements can refer to other ASP statements and most likely will need to do so for any substantially complex program.

Here's the full set of ASP code to embody the licensing agreement provisions (see [R.8] for additional examples of ASP):

```
:- obl_publish, obl_not_publish.
art10 {obl_not_use :- 1=1.}
art11: art10 {-obl_not_use :- hasLicense.}
art21 {obl_not_publish :- 1=1.
      obl_remove :- publish, obl_not_publish.}
art22: art21 {-obl_not_publish :- hasLicense, hasApproval.}
art31 {obl_not_comment :- 1=1.}
art32: art31 {-obl_not_comment :- -obl_not_publish.}
art40: art21 {obl_publish :- hasLicense, isCommissioned.
      -obl_not_publish :- hasLicense, isCommissioned.}
art51: art11 {obl_not_use :- violation.}
art52: art40, art22 {obl_not_publish :- violation.
                    -obl_publish :- violation.}
```

This is a rather compact way to express the licensing agreement.

If you were to try to write this same indication in a traditional procedural programming language, it would likely require many more lines of code. By coding it into ASP, the resulting ASP program can be run to ascertain whether the licensing agreement is being properly obeyed.

Notice that the ASP program is based upon having obtained the textual licensing agreement and then translating the text into the declarative programming format of ASP.

How would you generally compose or write an ASP program?

Typically, you would examine whatever the domain aspects indicated (such as the licensing agreement provisions in the case of the licensing agreement), and then try to formulate the needed ASP statements to represent the matter.

The core aspects involve first surfacing the principles or premises, along with being able to identify what kinds of conclusions you anticipate will be reached.

The licensing agreement was easy because it was already laid out in an obvious manner, allowing it to be readily translated into ASP.

To be more explicit here, let's consider the steps you would likely undertake in general, assuming that the underlying legal language wasn't quite so straightforward.

First, start by coming up with a set of principles, doing so by carefully inspecting the corpus of text that underlies the legal matter at hand. The odds are that there will be various arguments that serve to support a legal interpretation of one kind and counter-arguments too. Those arguments need to be identified and codified as to how they apply to the principles that were articulated.

Some of the principles will "succeed" in that they are supportive or favor a position, while others will not "succeed" since they are not supported.

Recall the case of John the thief. There was a set of principles or rules about thieves. When the set was "executed" or performed, some of the rules were able to "succeed" (meaning they were relevant to the enaction taking place), and others were not (having no bearing or relevance at the time).

The surfaced principles and their associated arguments are then used by the ASP run-time system to reach a conclusion or series of conclusions via the logic execution contained within the system.

Conclusion

ASP is a powerful logic-based declarative programming language, often used by AI developers for certain kinds of tasks, such as robotics programming and control, and ASP is also often used by AI legal reasoning researchers when exploring legal reasoning.

Some AILR researchers like to use ASP since it is a generalized tool, though it isn't tailored per se to the legal domain, and thus we'll be examining next some other approaches that do make use of the legal domain specifics.

Note: *For supplemental materials depicting the aspects discussed in this chapter, refer to Appendix B, which contains various augmented diagrams, charts, and additional related facets of relevance.*

CHAPTER 13
META-PHYSICS OF LEGAL REASONING

Let's continue the pursuit of legal reasoning.

Having languages such as ASPIC+ and ASP to implement legal reasoning are said to be somewhat akin to putting the cart before the horse.

Essentially, rather than rushing ahead to try and implement legal reasoning in conventional logic propositions, presumably, you ought to have a fully articulated indication of what legal reasoning is, first and foremost, and then you can proceed to try and implement it. Those engaged in such a viewpoint argue that without first getting the underpinnings settled properly, you are merely building a house of cards that will seemingly crumble under its own weight.

Indeed, there's an ongoing debate in the legal domain about the fundamental nature of legal reasoning and how to best ascertain what legal reasoning is.

As per Oliver Wendell Holmes when discussing a crucial fallacy or misperception of the law [R.29]:

> "The fallacy to which I refer is the notion that the only force at work in the development of the law is logic."

Theory Versus Practice Tensions

Some argue that you should start with a crisp and comprehensive legal theoretical framework or legal principles paradigm before you otherwise moved ahead. Those in that legal theorist camp believe that to properly illuminate and understand the nature of legal reasoning requires an appropriate overarching legal theory or set of legal theories.

Thus, in short, for achieving a grasp of what legal reasoning consists of, first make sure that there are foundational legal theories to build upon.

Meanwhile, those in the pragmatics camp would tend to argue that all that effort toward legal theories is not going to do much good if it is not grounded in legal practice. Therefore, they would assert that you might as well derive what legal reasoning is via the inspection and reflection upon what happens in actual legal practice.

Quite a number of legal researchers and legal scholars frequently butt heads about this chicken-or-the-egg conundrum.

The legal theory side contends that if you are overly focused on legal practice it means your mind is in the trees, so to speak, and whatever you come up with will ultimately fall short. You cannot be in the middle of a forest and aim to map the totality of the forest.

The legal practice side says that if you are too enmeshed in legal theory, your lofty indications will be unlikely to apply to the everyday and practical needs of the law.

So, these two at-odds precepts wages on:

- **Legal theory begets legal practice, or**
- **Legal practice begets legal theory**

If you agree with the base assumption that legal reasoning will remain an enigma until either the legal theory or the legal practice side irons things out, this implies that any semblance of legal reasoning as a formalized phenomenon will be stymied or delayed, spinning its wheels while the theory-versus-practice debate continues to wear on.

Again, per Oliver Wendell Holmes [R.29]:

> "Theory is the most important part of the dogma of the law, as the architect is the most important man who takes part in the building of a house… It is not to be feared as unpractical, for, to the competent, it simply means going to the bottom of the subject."
>
> "The remoter and more general aspects of the law are those which give it universal interest. It is through them that you not only become a great master in your calling, but connect your subject with the universe and catch an echo of the infinite, a glimpse of its unfathomable process, a hint of the universal law."

Triad Paradigm

Perhaps the world doesn't have to be one of a stark competition between whether the legal theory is first or whether legal practice is first. Some assert this is a false choice, causing a false dichotomy to perpetuate an otherwise myth about the law.

In a framework referred to as a triad paradigm, an alternative viewpoint is that the elements of legal theory, legal practice, and legal reasoning are all legs of the same three-legged stool.

Each contributes to the other.

They each three thrive off each other and need to make progress in their own separate ways and yet also in synergy with each other.

Thus, rather than somehow waiting for legal theory to become fully articulated, or waiting for legal practice to become fully understood, the revealing of legal reasoning is only likely to be developed in conjunction with the insights of both legal theory and legal practice as wholly concurrent pursuits.

Some characterize these kinds of macro-views about the fundamental nature of law as analogous to a **meta-physics of law**.

Legal Reasoning Remains Ill-Defined

This indication about the ambiguities and uncertainty of legal theory and legal practice is really an overarching theme that there is not yet a universally accepted and nor formalized definition of legal reasoning, therefore if you desire to use AI to implement legal reasoning it creates quite a dilemma.

The conundrum is that you are going to have to undertake difficult decisions about what you believe constitutes legal reasoning, and then see if you can craft AI to whatever you have decided or declared or are arguing is the nature of legal reasoning.

This creates several key issues:

- Your AI might not be implementing legal reasoning per se, and instead implementing something else that merely resembles legal reasoning.

- The AI that you craft might become mired in a minuscule subset of legal reasoning and not yield any generalizability toward being able to implement legal reasoning across the board.

- The AI implementation might be somewhat insidious in that it misleads others into believing that legal reasoning has finally been resolved and that AI has codified it, causing others to perhaps abandon their own efforts or falsely start down the same path and yet be unaware that it is a dead-end.

In short, implementing something via AI has a much higher chance of being successful as an AI implementation if the underlying nature of what is being implemented is well understood. But that's not the case for legal reasoning, since legal reasoning continues to remain ill-defined.

Now, that being the case, there is another angle to using AI.

The use of AI can help to reveal the foundations or underlying precepts that are otherwise murky in a given domain, and perhaps aid toward ferreting out how to get the underlying domain to become more apparent and ultimately more codifiable.

The Rules Paradox Of Wittgenstein

Consider an additional deep thought or meta-physics concern about proceeding with trying to achieve legal reasoning in AI.

The uneasiness has to do with a famous paradox that underlies the use of rules and we'll explore how it might pertain to specifically the aspects of legal rules, via a logic riddle generically known as the Wittgenstein rules paradox [R.51].

First, we all would likely agree that legal reasoning at least as a minimum consists of the embodiment of legal rules. We might disagree about the nature of how those rules are to be best identified and codified, yet nonetheless, it seems we'd still agree that there are rules, and those rules are crucial to being able to carry out legal reasoning.

Some though have proffered the Wittgenstein rules paradox as an argument that we should not be using rules as an integral basis for legal reasoning.

Here's why.

Ludwig Wittgenstein in 1953 postulated a doubt about the use of rules, in general, which therefore would presumably also apply to the potential use and application of legal rules.

Here's what he said [R.51]:

> **"This was our paradox: no course of action could be determined by a rule, because any course of action can be made out to accord with the rule."**

That point might seem somewhat mystifying, especially without some added context. Here's the context.

Suppose I ask you to tell me what the arithmetic answer to this is:

- What is 10 + 23?

Obviously, your answer is 33.

Suppose I ask you what the arithmetic answer to this is:

- What is 42 + 16?

Your answer is 58.

And so on, we can continue like this nearly endlessly, presumably. Now, here's the twist.

Answer this arithmetic question:

- What is 60 + 12?

I assume your answer is 72.

But, suppose I told you that was wrong, and that the correct answer is 5.

You would certainly be skeptical that the answer is 5.

How did I come up with a value of 5?

Suppose I tell you that addition, as you know it, is not what it really has seemed to be.

I explain that there's a rule known as "quus" (and presumably unknown to you) that states this:

- x **quus** y
- **quus** indicates: x **+** y **for** x**,** y **< 57**
- **quus** also indicates: **5 for** x **>= 57 or** y **>= 57**

Thus, when you were asked to add together 60 + 12, this meant that x was 60 and y was 12, and that since x as the value of 60, which is greater than 57, the final result to be indicated is the number 5.

Meanwhile, the prior question about adding together 42 + 16 would be the answer 58 via the rules of quus, and likewise, the answer to 10 + 23 would be the number 33, both instances of which comported with your prior understanding of the arithmetic function of addition, yet were insufficient examples to give rise to surface the role of the quus function or rules.

Wittgenstein's point was that though you might assume that the arithmetic function is one type of function or rule, it might really be something else, such as it might contain the (made-up) quus function or rules too (or, any other such function, functions, rule, or rules).

In fact, there could be any number of such quus-like functions that are hidden or buried within any system of rules, and you might not know it.

Imagine that I had kept asking you to add numbers to together and never reached any that were above the x and y of being at least 57. Presumably, you would unknowingly believe that the arithmetic function was always and inarguably the conventional x + y, simply due to never encountering the special case of x or y being at least 57.

How does that impact legal reasoning?

You might believe that you've figured out some set of legal rules that encompass legal reasoning, and perhaps as you exercise or execute them, they seem to work well. But it is conceivable that you've failed to include in your set some hidden or unrealized legal rules or function akin to the quus lesson, which therefore undermines the utility and validity of the legal rules that were prior elucidated.

There might not just be one quus, there might be an infinite number of such as-yet-unknown legal rules.

Another way to look at it is that any legal rule that you might come up with, and which might seem satisfying, could very well not be the "right" rule and only something that seems for the moment to be the appropriate rule.

Then, upon the happenstance discovery of a new rule, like quus, the set might be turned on its head, doing so under the belated realization that all along the "wrong" rules were being used (the notion of "wrong" is somewhat ambiguous, since the rules could have been correct and yet incomplete, or alternatively they could be entirely incorrect).

So, when trying to devise rules for legal reasoning, we could either decide that it is useless to try and essentially give up the pursuit, conceding that the Wittgenstein rules paradox has ensnared us, or we could proceed but need to always keep at the forefront of our thinking that the rules paradox is a bona fide and useful warning about what we have achieved.

Conclusion

In this chapter, we explored the role of legal theory and legal practice as it relates to the formulation of legal reasoning. The foundation for legal reasoning is currently uncertain, and legal theory or legal practice does not yet resolve that status.

We'll need to proceed on the quest to apply AI to legal reasoning and do so without the benefit of having a proper and widely accepted basis for understanding or explaining what legal reasoning is.

There is also a chance that if we use legal rules within our legal reasoning, perhaps those legal rules are susceptible to the Wittgenstein rules paradox.

Finally, consider another insightful quote from Oliver Wendell Holmes [R.29]:

> "I trust that no one will understand me to be speaking with disrespect of the law, because I criticize it so freely. I venerate the law, and especially our system of law, as one of the vastest products of the human mind."

Likewise, though it might seem that these discussions about AI legal reasoning appear to be disparaging, they are not so intended, and instead, the purpose is to layout what is open-ended and will spur those wishing to contribute to AILR into doing so with an eye towards where their energies can be aimed.

Note: *For supplemental materials depicting the aspects discussed in this chapter, refer to Appendix B, which contains various augmented diagrams, charts, and additional related facets of relevance.*

CHAPTER 14
COMPUTATIONAL LAW

An emerging subfield of legal informatics that pertains to the topic of AI and legal reasoning is known as **Computational Law**.

In a foundational paper entitled "Computational Law: The Cop in the Backseat" by Stanford Professor Michael Genesereth at the CodeX: The Center for Legal Informatics, Stanford University, this is his indicated definition of Computational Law [R.22]:

> "Computational Law is that branch of legal informatics concerned with the codification of regulations in precise, computable form."

As evident by this definition, and as per the gist of the discussions in the herein prior chapters, one of the most sought aspirations involves being able to make the law and legal reasoning become codifiable.

Thus, the ongoing efforts to find ways to turn legal text and legal aspects into something overtly tangible, detailed, and precise, and which can be used in some form of a viable computational manner.

As Professor Genesereth further states in his paper [R.22]:

> "From a pragmatic perspective, Computational Law is important as the basis for computer systems capable of doing useful legal calculations, such as compliance checking, legal planning, regulatory analysis, and so forth."

When referring to legal calculations, this brings up the notion that there is a myriad of ways in which AI-embodied legal reasoning might be used.

For example, you might have noticed that the title of the paper by Professor Genesereth invokes the imagery of having a cop in the backseat of a car, which brings up the idea that it might be useful to have a legal reasoning system embedded in your car.

Why so?

The vehicle could then advise you on-the-spot as to any potential driving infractions and aid in avoiding making driving mistakes that are against the law.

For human drivers, an on-board AI legal reasoning component could be handy on a proactive basis, perhaps detecting your driving efforts and warning you or offering guidance as you drive. Eventually, we'll have autonomously driven cars, ones that do not use a human driver, and in that use case, the AI legal reasoning would likely be directly giving guidance to the AI overall driving system.

As stated by Genesereth [R.22]:

> "Suppose that we had the benefit of a friendly policeman in the backseat of our car whenever we drove around (or perhaps an equivalent computer built into the dash panel of our car)."

> "The cop, real or computerized, could offer regulatory advice as we drive around - telling us speed limits, which roads are one-way, where U-turns are legal and illegal, where and when we can park, and so forth."

AI legal reasoning can be used in real-time situations, such as the example involved in driving a car.

In addition, AI legal reasoning could be used in less immediately responsive settings.

Computer Assisted Legal Compliance

Another example of how AI legal reasoning might be embedded in the use case involving Computer Aided Design (CAD).

As developed by Professor Harry Surden, University of Colorado Law School, and described in his 2019 article in the Georgia State University Law Review entitled "Artificial Intelligence and Law: An Overview" [R.48], a legal compliance validation component was integrated into a conventional CAD system.

Known as project **CALC** (Computer Assisted Legal Compliance), the add-on component was intended to advise architects.

When an architect is designing a construction project, there are innumerable laws and regulations that impact the nature of the architectural design, including the need to abide by local building codes, federal environmental rules, and other salient aspects such as the laws associated with the Americans With Disabilities Act (the ADA rules).

Typically, an architect has to know on their own the laws and regulations that pertain to such matters, and presumably use such knowledge to appropriately and legally shape the design of the buildings and construction efforts.

Inevitably, the architectural renderings will need to be legally reviewed to ensure proper compliance.

Via the use of a CAD system that allows for electronically rendering and designing of buildings, this same system could be augmented with an AI legal reasoning component that has a specialty in the construction legal-related domain.

The added component could be used while devising the buildings and provide immediate indications as to what is allowed and will presumably be greenlit for permitting, while also showcasing worrisome aspects of a design that might otherwise be flagged as possible violations.

This example illustrates another facet of AI legal reasoning, namely the application of AI legal reasoning to specific domains or subdomains. Rather than having one massive overarching AI legal reasoning system that is somehow able to perform across all potential domains, the chances are that we'll have numerous sub-domain AI legal reasoning systems that cover specific specialties.

One such specialty would involve the rules-of-the-road when driving a car, as indicated via the cop in the backseat aspects, while another specialty would be the legal facets of designing buildings and construction projects such as the CALC system.

This gives rise to this important point:

- ➔ **There isn't any overall normative guidance currently about which legal domains or subdomains to especially tackle when crafting AI legal reasoning systems.**

Essentially, it is a researcher's free-for-all, wherein each legal researcher or AI developer is likely to tackle whatever legal domain or subdomain opportunity seems to be of interest to them.

Boundaries Concerns

It is one thing to somehow be able to craft an AI legal reasoning system, and yet another to have it run within a desired amount of run time, referred to generally as computational tractability or intractability (as prior mentioned in Chapter 6).

In the field of computer science, there is a keen focus on whether an algorithm is computationally tractable or not. This refers to how fast or the amount of time or steps that a given algorithm might take to perform a task.

Imagine that we developed an AI legal reasoning system as a cop in the backseat. The expectations would be that the system would be able to perform in real-time and be responsive while driving and in the midst of split-second decisions thereof.

Suppose though that the AI legal reasoning took an extraordinary amount of time to figure out whether your pending U-turn was legal or illegal, and only advised after-the-fact about a potential foul maneuver, minutes after the actual maneuver occurred.

That lack of timeliness would undoubtedly undermine the usefulness of the capability. Thus, for any AI legal reasoning system that might be crafted, the performance or timeliness needs to be factored into the utility of the system.

It could be that we might devise an AI legal reasoning system that is computationally intractable. Doing so would not be especially useful per se, though certainly there might be additional ways to reduce the computational complications and therefore eventually be able to turn the system into something more useable.

The point there too is that one shouldn't necessarily give up by the prospects alone that the AI legal reasoning system might be computationally excessive. If you can get it to work at all, even if it takes a tremendous amount of time to run, there are opportunities for finding ways to cope with the computational overloads.

This does bring up another potential computational concern.

Suppose an AI legal reasoning system gets itself into an infinite loop, meaning that it runs, and runs, and runs, but never reaches a final conclusion or stopping point.

You can likely discern that this is another variant of the idea that something is computationally intractable. An AI legal reasoning system might run for a very long time, so long that it seems to be mired in an infinite loop.

To cope with these concerns, any AI legal reasoning system ought to be carefully examined to try and ascertain what kinds of run time performance it will undertake. In addition, there should be some mechanisms or means to detect when an AI legal reasoning system has gone beyond some "reasonable" limit of run time, and then have a means to interrupt or halt the system accordingly.

Conclusion

We've discussed in this chapter the emergence of the field of Computational Law.

The attempts at crafting AI legal reasoning systems have generally each chosen some preferred legal domain or subdomain to concentrate on. The choice of the domain or subdomain is not particularly being orchestrated in any overarching way and based conventionally on the interests of a particular researcher or developer.

Note: *For supplemental materials depicting the aspects discussed in this chapter, refer to Appendix B, which contains various augmented diagrams, charts, and additional related facets of relevance.*

CHAPTER 15

TAXMAN: AI CASE STUDY

One of the pioneering and most famous of all AI legal reasoning systems is known as **TAXMAN**.

The TAXMAN system was crafted in the 1970s by L. Thorne McCarty and was featured in the Harvard Law Review in 1977, doing so in a piece entitled "Reflections on TAXMAN: An Experiment in Artificial Intelligence and Legal Reasoning" [R.36].

The domain or subdomain of law that was chosen for the AI legal reasoning system prototype involved taxation of corporations, thus the appropriate naming of TAXMAN.

As an aside, some don't like the use of the word "man" or "woman" to be associated with AI systems per se, since it might imply that the AI system can do more than it can, suggesting that it has the equivalent capability of a human. In the case of TAXMAN, one supposes that the "man" part might be more of a play on our qualms about the so-called taxman that comes to get our taxes, rather than a reference to a human-like capability.

Within taxation of corporations, a legal subdomain was chosen, focusing on the Subchapter C portion of the Internal Revenue Code.

This aspect of picking a domain, and then a subdomain, and then perhaps a subdomain within the subdomain, highlights the point made in the prior chapter that the selection of a domain of interest for an AI legal reasoning system is often done for somewhat arbitrary reasons, generally due to the particular interest of the researcher or developer.

In addition, this facet brings up the sizing aspects of whatever subdomain is chosen.

Presumably, the researcher or developer wants to pick a large enough subdomain to provide a richness of variety, while at the same time trying to constrain the subdomain chosen to be reasonably viable for codifying into an AI legal reasoning system on any realistic or prudent basis.

There's a tradeoff of choosing the subdomain size, which sometimes is referred to as a kind of Goldilocks problem, opting to select a subdomain that is neither too big and nor too small for the system that is being crafted.

TAXMAN was developed in an AI programming language called LISP. We'll be exploring the LISP programming language in Chapter 20.

The use of the LISP programming language involved primarily writing a program on a **bootstrap basis**, which means developing a program that could be used to undertake the AI legal reasoning via a kind of package or tool.

In other words, LISP was used to craft a tool that would then allow for the knowledge representation and the reasoning that would be needed to accommodate the legal subdomain chosen.

This package or tool was called Micro-PLANNER.

Typical of many such AI legal reasoning systems is the notion of initially crafting a tool or package that will allow for the higher-level aspects of entering and using the legal domain that has been chosen.

It is a kind of bootstrap approach, whereby you begin by creating some capability that will get you toward the goal that you are ultimately seeking to accomplish. This might be likened to being in the woods and having to survive, and might first need to craft tools such as something to cut with, and then once you have the needed tools so crafted, you begin to construct a shelter or start a campfire.

Law As Embedded In TAXMAN

For the development of TAXMAN, an initial step involved collecting together the laws pertaining to the chosen subdomain.

As an example, consider this legal text of the Internal Revenue Code of the time [R.36]:

> "The ownership of stick possessing at least 80 percent of the total combined voting power of all classes of stock entitled to vote and at least 80 percent of the total number of shares of all other classes of stock of the corporation."

There are additional legal clauses that are needed to be included, such as this clause [R.36]:

> "… for example, the shareholders who receive stock or securities in the reorganization will carry their new certificates at the same basis as the old certificates they have given up, and the corporation will receive stock or securities in exchange for its property will carry the new certificates at the same basis as the transferred assets."

There are also cited court cases that pertain to these legal aspects.

The next step then involved trying to codify the legal elements.

Here's a snippet of the LISP code of TAXMAN that illustrates the stock aspects as pertains to a New Jersey based corporation [R.36]:

```
(CORPORATION NEW-JERSEY)
(ISSUE NEW-JERSEY S1)
(STOCK S1)
(COMMON S1)
(PIECE-OF P1 S1)
(NSHARES P1 100)
(OWN PSHELLIS P1)
```

In LISP, you make use of parentheses for the formatting of the code, quite a bit, and in this case, the LISP code is indicating that there's a specific instance of a New Jersey corporation which is issuing 100 shares of common stock.

Using TAXMAN, you could then try to have the AI legal reasoning figure out whether the issuance will abide by the regulations stipulated by the Internal Revenue Code.

Here's the code to start that aspect [R.36]:

```
(PROG (S P)
    (GOAL  (ISSUE NEW-JERSEY ?S))
    (GOAL  (STOCK ?S))
    (GOAL  (PIECE-OF ?P ?S))
    (GOAL  (OWN PHELLIS ?P)))
```

This code indicates that we are defining a program ("PROG") that will try to ascertain some variables known as S and P, and that the goals ("GOAL") for doing so include that it is a New Jersey issuance of stock, and we want to ascertain if the S and P are allowable per the Internal Revenue Code.

This snippet of code would then invoke other functions within the TAXMAN system that attempt to resolve those goals accordingly.

Here's some additional TAXMAN code to illustrate that the system was constructed to allow for theorems of what might be allowed in trying to figure out if a given instance was conforming to the Internal Revenue Code [R.36]:

```
(THEOREM EXPAND  (T P O R TA TB)
(TRANS ?T ?P ?O ?R ?TB)
(IF         (GOAL    (OWN ?O ?P ?TA))
   THEN  (ERASE   (OWN ?O ?P ?TB))
         (ASSERT  (OWN ?R ?P ?TB)))
```

This code shows that a theorem known as "EXPAND" involves the invoking of a proposed transaction ("TRANS") involving the variables of P, O, R, and TB, and if the goal ("GOAL") succeeds then to erase ("ERASE") certain ownership aspects, while otherwise to assert ("ASSERT") certain ownership aspects.

This LISP code includes several predefined functions of LISP, such as the "IF" and "THEN" function capability, and also showcases that you can define your own desired functions, such as the use of the "ERASE" and "ASSERT" that the developer created.

Conclusion

As might be rather apparent, if you don't know LISP, you would have a somewhat difficult time examining the core of the TAXMAN system.

Only a narrow part of the Internal Revenue Code was included, but in so doing the TAXMAN was able to nonetheless provide valuable insights about how to approach AI legal reasoning.

The TAXMAN system has become a classic in the field of AI legal reasoning and showcased the possibilities of what might be done.

Interestingly, though written nearly 50 years ago, today's AI legal reasoning systems that employ LISP would often tend to look somewhat similar. In short, TAXMAN still provides useful lessons for today's AI legal reasoning efforts.

Note: *For supplemental materials depicting the aspects discussed in this chapter, refer to Appendix B, which contains various augmented diagrams, charts, and additional related facets of relevance.*

CHAPTER 16
HYPO: AI CASE STUDY

Another pioneering AI legal reasoning system is called **HYPO** [R.5] and was crafted by Kevin Ashley at the University of Pittsburgh, School of Law, doing so in the late-1980s and early 1990s, thus coming to fruition about a decade after TAXMAN.

For HYPO, the domain of law chosen consisted of the United States trade secrets laws.

The HYPO system was primarily written in Prolog.

As mentioned earlier, Prolog is a popular programming language for logic-based circumstances. We'll be covering some of the introductory facets of Prolog in Chapter 20.

Once again, the Prolog program was written to provide a platform or tool upon which the legal reasoning could be undertaken, doing so by using Prolog in this instance to construct a higher-level utility or tool.

What made HYPO standout and exceed the TAXMAN system included some new facets that provided further progress in AI legal reasoning, including these elements:

- **Used rules, similar to the rule-based or expert systems that were emerging at the time**
- **Made use of Case-Based Reasoning (CBR), allowing for legal cases to be entered and utilized**
- **Allowed for hypotheticals, enabling the ability to consider various what-ifs**
- **Generated arguments that were either for or against the CBR cases**
- **Provided a rating or metric for the relevancy of cases**

Those added features have become a kind of defacto expected standard for subsequent AI legal reasoning systems.

Let's consider some of the new features that HYPO brought into the field of AI legal reasoning.

As background, during the 1980s and 1990s, the use of expert systems became popularized and was used in all types of domains, including in the medical domain, the financial domain, and others.

The legal domain was a natural fit for the use of rule-based expert systems.

In addition, there was interest in the use of cases for reasoning purposes, allowing the formation of a case and then invoking a case that appeared relevant to the matter at hand.

This led to a dovetailing or intertwining of the case-based approach with the rules-based approach, offering the benefits of both means of performing reasoning.

HYPO used both the case-based and rule-based approaches.

When humans do case-based reasoning, they tend to identify aspects of a given case that is supportive of the current matter, and also identify aspects that are not supportive or even in opposition. That's what HYPO also tried to undertake.

Furthermore, a case might be considered fully relevant, partially relevant, or not relevant to a matter at hand, thus another aspect of reasoning with the use of cases involves trying to ascertain the relevancy of a case.

This is also a feature of HYPO.

The HYPO Processing Steps

At a high-level, the HYPO system made use of nine overall steps.

The steps generally consisted of [R.5]:

1) Analysis of the problem situation
2) Retrieve relevant cases
3) Select from the relevant cases those that are the most relevant
4) Select cases that are most likely to be cited by both sides of a case
5) Calculate the distinctions between the best cases and the problem at hand
6) Identify the likely counterexamples to the chosen best cases
7) Evaluate and summarize the overall argument
8) Generate 3-ply arguments
9) Generate hypotheticals that strengthen or weaken the arguments

As you examine those nine steps, the sequence is logical and appears to be what any prudent practicing lawyer might do.

In that sense, the HYPO system provides a mirror of what we might expect a human to do and showcases an attempt to have an AI system do likewise.

One aspect that you might have not quite comprehended involves the eighth step that entails the generation of a 3-ply argument. The word "ply" essentially means a move that one might take in a game or other akin effort. For example, while playing chess, some chess players only consider the move that they are about to play and fail to scrutinize what moves their opponent will play as a countermove. This is considered a 1-ply perspective on playing a game or making moves.

A 2-ply player takes a more advanced approach, looking ahead further. A 3-ply player even more so. In the case of HYPO, the 3-ply generation consists of first taking the perspective of the defendant or plaintiff.

Then, there is a consideration of what the other side will respond with. Finally, the third perspective is what kind of rebuttal should be proffered to the response of the other side.

First, here's a HYPO example of the 1-ply [R.5]:

> **Point for Defendant as Side-1:**
>
> **Where:** Employee defendant was the sole developer of the plaintiff's product. The nondisclosure agreement did not specifically refer to plaintiff's product.
>
> **Even Though:** Plaintiff and defendant entered into a nondisclosure agreement. Plaintiff adopted security measures.
>
> **Defendant should win claim for Trade Secrets Misappropriation.**
>
> **Cite:** Amoco Production Co. v Lindley

Next, the second ply, or anticipating the response of the opposing side:

Response for Plaintiff as Side-2:

Counter-examples:
Structural Dynamics Research Corp v Engineering Mechanics Research Corp

Then, the third ply, a rebuttal for the defendant:

Rebuttal for Defendant as Side-1:

Structural Dynamics Research Corp v Engineering Mechanics Research Corp is distinguishable because:

In Structural Dynamics, plaintiff adopted more security measures than in Amexxco.

In Structural Dynamics, plaintiff's former employee brought product development information to defendant. Not in Amexxco.

Note: Platiniff's response would is known if:
Plaintiff's former employee brought product development information to defendant.

As shown, the 3-ply is a helpful means of analyzing a case. Any such n-ply approach is typically referred to as a **Dialectical or Dialogue** model of reasoning (where n > 1).

One question that is worthy of addressing is how many ply an AI legal reasoning should pursue.

Similar to chess, the further ahead that you look, presumably the better you can make your choice of what move to make. If you can do a look-ahead of 4-ply, or maybe 7-ply, or any such larger number, you would have an advantage about what is the best choice to make in your upcoming move and subsequent moves.

Part of the tradeoff in greater levels of exercising ply is the effort required in doing so. Per the prior discussion about the computational consumption of an AI legal reasoning system, presumably, the higher the ply will lead to being an elongated response time, as a result of the additional computational resources needed to be consumed for the look-ahead.

There is also a presumed point of diminishing returns due to the potential of uncertainty and probabilities of subsequent actions being predicted and analyzed.

In essence, the number of moves and countermoves, piling on top of each other, means that by the time you get to some n-ply that's a large number, you are somewhat wildly speculating about what the future moves will be. In real practice, you ultimately need to cut off the analysis and say that enough is enough in terms of how far to try and look ahead.

Of course, if the moves ahead are all discrete and fully predictable, the look-ahead could have a significant payoff and would be quite worthwhile to undertake.

The Use of Legal Case Frames

HYPO used a knowledge representation construct that was called a **Legal Case Frame**.

This consisted of having legal cases captured into what is deemed frames, and each frame has a set of slots that characterize the case.

Each slot has a slot name, followed by a colon when shown on a listing, and can have a number of slot values.

The legal case frames are organized within HYPO on a hierarchical basis.

Here's an example of a top-level legal case frame for the Amexxco case [R.5]:

Case: Amexxco Production Co. v. Gwhiz

Short-Title: Amexxco

Citation: a hypothetical case

Date: 1987

Party-List: (Corporate-Party: Amexxco

Corporate-Party: Exxssinc

Employee-Party: Gwhiz

Role-Party-Alist:

((Plaintiff Corporate-Party: Amexxco**)**

(Defendant Corporate-Party:

Exxssinc Employee-Party: Gwhiz**))**

Decision-For: Nil

Claims-Held-For: Nil

Dimensions-List: Nil

Cases-Cited: Nil

A legal case frame is linked to an additional knowledge representation construct known as a **Factual Predicate**.

The factual predicate consists of related objects, relationships, events, and other aspects that pertain to the legal case frame.

For example, a factual predicate might contain relevant agreements, promises, and other contracts that are relevant to a trade secrets case. If there were security breaches, those would be included. Any disclosure events would be included. And so on.

The Dimensions Of HYPO

The legal case frames and their associated factual predicates are then classified according to thirteen dimensions that are used in HYPO.

HYPO uses these thirteen dimensions [R.5]:

1) **Competitive-Advantage**
2) **Vertical-Knowledge**
3) **Secrets-Disclosed-Outsiders**
4) **Outsider-Disclosures-Restricted**
5) **Consideration**
6) **Bribe-Employee**
7) **Noncompetition-Agreement**
8) **Brought-Tools**
9) **Agreed-Not-To-Disclose**
10) **Employee-Sole Developer**
11) **Nondisclosure-Agreement-Specific**
12) **Disclosure-In-Negotiations**
13) **Security-Measures**

The dimensions then allow the comparing and ranking of the legal case frames.

For a hierarchical arrangement of the legal case frames, the HYPO system uses what it calls a **claims lattice**.

The claims lattice begins with a root node, essentially the top of a hierarchy.

Successor nodes are arrayed as based on their dimensions and are linked to the preceding level and the next level of the hierarchy.

To undertake a hypothetical reasoning of a given situation, the HYPO system can craft a claims lattice to showcase what legal case frames apply to the matter being analyzed.

Conclusion

HYPO is an important case study of AI legal reasoning and led to the realization that a rules-based approach, along with cases and case-based reasoning, provided key advancements in how to develop the knowledge representation and reasoning for AI legal reasoning systems.

Examples such as HYPO help to turn the otherwise abstract discussions about how to proceed on AI legal reasoning into a showcase and demonstration of how a specific pilot or prototype can be used to explore what might be useful for such AI systems.

Others have used HYPO as a cornerstone for crafting additional AI legal reasoning systems, one of which is CATO, which we'll be looking at in the next chapter.

Note: *For supplemental materials depicting the aspects discussed in this chapter, refer to Appendix B, which contains various augmented diagrams, charts, and additional related facets of relevance.*

CHAPTER 17

CATO: AI CASE STUDY

In this chapter, we'll take a look at an AI legal reasoning system known as **CATO**.

As earlier discussed, TAXMAN was the pioneering AI legal reasoning system of the 1970s.

HYPO subsequently came along in the late 1980s and early 1990s as an AI legal reasoning system that went beyond prior efforts and incorporated an extensive rules-based approach and did so in a hybrid manner with case-based reasoning.

In the early 2000s, there were various efforts involved in leveraging the work of HYPO and taking it to the next stage of capability.

One of the most well-known variants of HYPO is CATO.

CATO [R.1] was developed by Vincent Aleven and took a somewhat different slant on the purpose of an AI legal reasoning system, namely the intent of CATO was to serve as an Intelligent Tutoring System (ITS) for law students in the United States.

It might seem somewhat ironic that an AI legal reasoning system would be used to help train human lawyers. The irony being that presumably AI legal reasoning systems might eventually undermine the need for or possibly even replace human lawyers (a topic as discussed in prior chapters).

Nonetheless, it does seem that training novice human lawyers are a handy use of an AI legal reasoning system, allowing those humans learning about the law to do so via a "smart" system that can present legal reasoning to them, along with getting those budding lawyers to presumably become better at the practice of law.

The mainstay of CATO involved the matter of how to make legal arguments via the use of legal cases.

As such, HYPO's prior use of case-based reasoning was bolstered and enhanced for use in CATO, including providing an improved means of showing how cases relate to each other.

This also brings up another crucial point.

Usually, in law, a significant aspect of any legal effort involves being able to explain the logic used to reach a legal conclusion.

Without being able to explain how a result was reached, many would be skeptical about the result that was rendered. Presumably, you should be able to clearly explain the legal logic involved, and others can then assess the strengths, weaknesses, and overall robustness of the logical basis used to reach the result.

By doing so, others that want to later reuse the ruling will also be able to ascertain its applicability to other cases. In addition, those that don't believe the ruling pertains to some other matter they are involved in, can offer a logical basis for why the prior case does <u>not</u> apply, especially if there was an explanation provided in the original case result.

Due to the importance of **explainability** in the law, a later chapter will focus entirely on that topic (Chapter 23).

For now, the reason to bring up the importance of explainability is due to the aspect that CATO boosted the explainability capabilities of HYPO.

The need to do so makes perfectly good sense since the CATO AI legal reasoning system was targeted to guide and instruct human lawyers, aiding those legal novices in learning about the law and the process of legal reasoning, while HYPO focused mainly on rendering outcomes and did not offer much of an explanation or explicatory indication.

Imagine if a law school professor was unwilling to explain the legal reasoning behind legal cases and ponder thus the difficulty it would cause for those learning about the law.

Most of the AI legal reasoning systems to-date hadn't been specially outfitted to provide explanations, and instead, the focus was on getting the AI legal reasoning to behind-the-scenes undertake the legal reasoning process. Thus, those such systems were intended to produce outcomes, and not necessarily intended to explain how the outcomes themselves were reached.

CATO attempted to overcome that lack of explainability.

Use of Decision Tree Structure (Factor Hierarchy)

One of the ways to make explainability more transparent involves the use of a type of **Decision Tree**, akin to a **factor hierarchy** that is amplified with an indication of whether the nodes are supportive or not supportive of the other nodes above them.

Imagine the main stump of a tree, and further imagine various roots extending down into the ground, radiating out from the stump.

We'll say that the stump is the root node, and all other nodes radiate out from it.

CATO again used trade secrets laws as its legal domain focus, as recall so did HYPO, so let's use trade secret examples to explain how CATO works.

A root node might be that the plaintiff is said to have misused trade secrets.

A node that emanates from the root node might be that there was a trade secret involved, and this turns out to be supportive or "pro" in favor of the root node (usually represented by a plus symbol).

Each of the nodes would be given a unique code to be able to readily refer to them, and we'll say this is node F101.

Another node that connects to the root node might be node D120, indicating that the information was legitimately obtained elsewhere, and thus this facet would helpful to the defendant, so in the case of the root node, this subordinated node is <u>not</u> supportive of the root, therefore it will be scored as a "con" (usually represented with a minus symbol).

The tree would be further constructed, having roots that might extend extensively, depending upon the particulars of the case at hand.

For example, the F101 node might have subordinated nodes such as F102 that is indicative that the plaintiff made efforts to maintain secrecy.

Meanwhile, F102 might have three subordinated nodes, consisting of F4 that the plaintiff agreed to not disclose (which would be considered a "+"), and a peer node to F4 that would be labeled as D1 regarding the disclosures made during negotiations (a defendant supportive aspect, thus this node gets a "-"), and a third peer node about the security measures undertaken by the plaintiff and labeled as node F6 with a "+" for being supportive of the plaintiff.

If you've ever tried to analyze a case, you've undoubtedly ended up constructing a similar kind of tree-like structure, helping you to keep track of what appears to favor your client and what appears to disfavor your client.

By having this kind of structure in CATO, the AI legal reasoning system was able to showcase to the end-user the nature of the "logic" involved by presenting the constructed tree.

As part of the setup of CATO, various factors were created and used in the system, including factors such as [R.1]:

- **F15: Unique-Product**
- **F18: Identical-Products**
- **F7: Brought-Tools**
- **F16: Info-Reverse-Engineerable**
- **F27: Disclosure-In-Public-Forum**
- **F19: No-Security-Measures**
- **F10: Secrets-Disclosed-Outsiders**

Those are some of the factors (not shown herein in numerical order) and noted here to merely showcase some of the factors derived for CATO.

The factors were then related to questions about the selected legal cases (the questions were considered the "issues" of the case).

Factors were set up to use two numerical digits, while questions or issues were assigned three numerical digits.

For example, here's a question or issue that was posed [R.1]:

F101: Did plaintiff's information constitute a trade secret?

And the factors that pertained to this question were indicated as these factors [R.1]:

- **F15: Unique-Product**
- **F10: Secrets-Disclosed-Outsiders**
- **F16: Info-Reverse-Engineerable**
- **F19: No-Security-Measures**
- **F27: Disclosure-In-Public-Forum**

The Decision Tree and the factors are indications of the knowledge representation aspects used in CATO.

Let's consider next the processing or "reasoning" process of CATO.

Overall Processing In CATO

The overall processing within CATO consisted of performing these steps:

- **Do setup**
- **Identify issues**
- **Organize cases by issues**
- **Generate English text for argument organized by issues**

Let's take a look at each of those steps.

For the CATO setup step, here's what took place.

First, input was needed that provided a problem situation, including a set of past cases and the issues to be addressed, and established in conjunction with a set of factors. In addition, an indication needed to be provided as to which side to undertake for the argument to be constructed (the plaintiff perspective or the defendant viewpoint).

The intended output would be the presentation of a multi-case argument that is organized by the issues and shown in plain English.

To undertake the identification of issues step, here's what would occur [R.1]:

- **Find all issues related to the problem factors**
- **For each issue i:**
    - Determine strengths and weaknesses in the problem related to i
    - For the strengths, find reasons why they matter

To do the step involved in organizing the issues, here's what would occur:

- **For each issue i:**
    - Determine which of the given cases are relevant to i
    - For each relevant favorable case, determine which of its strengths and weaknesses are related to i
    - For each weakness related to i, check if there are compensating strengths in the problem
    - Check which of the given cases can be used to downplay the weakness
    - Check for which of the relevant (favorable) cases there are counterexamples among the given cases
- **Do the same for the opposing side**

To generate the English text for the argument, this is what would occur:

- **For each issue :**
  - Draw attention to strengths related to i, pointing to reasons why they matter and citing relevant cases
  - Deal with weaknesses related to i, pointing to compensating strengths and citing counterexamples
  - When arguing on behalf of the defendant, distinguish cases cited by plaintiff when discussing I and cite counterexamples

Those are the overall processing or "reasoning" aspects of CATO.

Tools Available In CATO

In an effort to enable CATO to be more usable than many of the prior AI legal reasoning systems, various special tools were developed that were aimed at use by end-users rather than by AI developers per se.

Some of the key tools offered in CATO included [R.1]:

- **CATO Database** with a query language and preloaded with factor sets for 147 trade secrets cases
- **Factor Browser** to examine the preset 26 factors about trade secrets law
- **Case Analyzer** to allow an end-user to compare their set of factors to those stored in the CATO database
- **Argument Maker** that presents argumentation examples and can perform a mini-dialogue
- **Issue-Based Argument Window** that present examples of arguments with multiple cases selected by the end-user
- **Squib Reader** that displays squibs of retrieved cases

Overall, CATO was an admirable advancement of HYPO. The advances included a Decision Tree or Factor Hierarchy for domain-specific normative knowledge about the meaning of the factors used to represent the case.

In addition, the capability to generate arguments was instrumental to the explanatory mode of CATO. This encompassed the presentation of issue-based arguments and the inclusion of a scoring method that indicated the significance of the distinctions in comparing multiple legal cases. There was also the use of a most-on-point criterion to select the "best" cases for citing as part of an argument.

Conclusion

CATO intentionally reused HYPO, adding some crucial extensions. Since the focus was on serving as a tutoring system, the incorporation of explainability facets provided the most notable of the additions.

On a features basis and the use of a 3-ply argument, the HYPO system made use of these steps [R.2]:

1) Seek an analogous prior case that offers a favorable outcome
2) Identify a case with an unfavorable outcome as a counterpoint
3) Indicate a more on-point case as a counterexample
4) Cite an as-on-point case

The CATO system used those same steps and added these steps to the approach [R.2]:

5) Downplay the significance of an identified distinction
6) Play-up the significance of an identified distinction
7) Identify a favorable case for emphasizing strengths
8) Identify another favorable case to argue that weaknesses aren't crucial

As noted, CATO was built on top of the prior work established via HYPO. One ongoing debate in the AI legal reasoning field involves whether to use prior work or whether a researcher or developer should depart from prior systems and seek to create AILR's that are entirely new.

Some express uneasiness that without building directly on prior work, each new AI legal reasoning system is starting from scratch and not leveraging the prior work. In that sense, presumably, progress will be quite disjointed and not occur on any measurable incremental and forward-moving path.

The counterargument often used is that by relying upon prior work, the newer effort is burdened with how the prior approach was undertaken, essentially putting the new system on top of a foundation that should perhaps be completely gutted and redone anew.

Both arguments have merits.

Generally, even if a prior system itself isn't directly reused, it seems prudent to argue at least it is sensible to be aware of how prior AI legal reasoning systems worked and were constructed, along with the overall approaches taken, since one can certainly assert that in a George Santayana viewpoint if we don't learn from history we're doomed in one way or another.

Note: *For supplemental materials depicting the aspects discussed in this chapter, refer to Appendix B, which contains various augmented diagrams, charts, and additional related facets of relevance.*

CHAPTER 18

SHYSTER: AI CASE STUDY

Another famous AI legal reasoning system is called **SHYSTER**.

Some have recoiled at the name given to the system since it perhaps implies that attorneys are shysters, or that AI legal reasoning systems are shysters. According to the developer of SHYSTER, he purportedly used the line that was uttered by Groucho Marx in the 1931 movie *Monkey Business* as his inspiration for the naming of his AI legal reasoning system [R.40].

In the movie, Thelma Todd says "I didn't know you were a lawyer. You're awfully shy for a lawyer," and Groucho responds: "You bet I'm shy. I'm a shyster lawyer."

So, perhaps a bit of tongue-in-cheek on the naming of the system. In any case, the name is the name, regardless of whether one likes it or not.

The developer was James Popple at the Australian National University and he developed the SHYSTER system in the mid-1990s [R.40]. He wrote the system in the C programming language, which is a conventional procedural programming language (today, you would likely use C++ rather than its forerunner), and it is somewhat significant that he used a conventional programming language at all versus using an AI-oriented programming language such as Prolog or LISP.

Similar to other approaches that we've discussed in prior chapters, Popple developed tools that allowed for the incorporation of the rules and cases and also made available a devised specification language for that purpose.

The underlying law that SHYSTER focuses on deals with the common law of Australia.

At initial glance, SHYSTER is not especially differentiated when compared to HYPO and CATO, and generally is another example of an expert system or rules-based approach that is also a hybrid that uses case-based reasoning for legal reasoning aspects.

A primary reason that SHYSTER is perhaps worthwhile of being noted is that it included a few other somewhat novel features that provided handy innovations concerning the overall design of AI legal reasoning systems.

Let's consider these subtle but notable features that made SHYSTER especially noteworthy, including these:

- Multiple legal domains utilized
- Mathematically complex distance formulas for cases comparisons
- Nearest neighbor algorithm to measure similarities and differences
- Use of about a dozen real cases per each chosen legal domain
- An attempt at using straightforward rules and attributes in the expert system

Let's address each of those facets.

Multiple Legal Domains

As already mentioned in prior chapters, one of the drawbacks of many AI legal reasoning systems is that they have tended to focus on only one domain or subdomain of the law, thus, it is hard to say whether or not those systems can scale-up and handle other domains or subdomains too.

For SHYSTER, there were four domains or subdomains used.

One domain was about the law of trover, involving the rights of finders of what is considered lost chattels, and the developer called this the FINDER subdomain.

Another domain dealt with the nuances of copyright-related authorizations, and he referred to this as the AUTHORIZATION subdomain.

A third subdomain entailed the aspects of procedural fairness in the law, such as having the right to a hearing, and for this subdomain the name assigned was NATURAL (for so-called natural justice).

The domain that I'll discuss herein is one that involves determining whether a worker is an employee versus an independent contractor, a subdomain labeled as EMPLOYEE.

Overall, it is refreshing and notable to have tackled several subdomains, allowing an opportunity to design an AI legal reasoning to be viably generalized across multiple domains.

Distance Formulas

Another noteworthy feature involved the use of mathematically complex distance formulas for case comparisons.

Here's basically how that worked.

To compare legal cases, he established metrics that allowed for doing mathematical distance calculations, akin to calculating distances on a chart or graph.

By doing so, conventional distance formulas such as the Euclidean distance and the Manhattan distance could be used. In addition, correlation coefficients could be determined, similar to what might be used in a linear regression function.

Thus, rather than the simpler approaches of merely tallying the raw number of aspects that might appear to be similar or dissimilar between the legal cases, this approached introduce a more rigorous mathematical foundation in doing so.

Nearest Neighbor Algorithm

As further indication about the use of mathematical formulations for legal case comparison, the SHYSTER system also used a nearest neighbor algorithm.

Again, this highlights an attempt to add rigor and formalization to the approaches in AI legal reasoning.

Real Cases Per Chosen Legal Domain

For each of the four subdomains, approximately a dozen or so real-world legal cases were used as source materials.

Generally, other AI legal reasoning systems have done likewise, though as mentioned not necessarily doing so across multiple domains.

This point brings up another facet that could be considered a criticism or at least a limitation of much of the work on AI legal reasoning, namely, the paucity of cases typically used.

Due to these systems often being prototypes or pilots, the developer usually assembles a handful or few dozen of the considered relevant cases. Of course, in real life, there would likely be hundreds of pertinent cases (perhaps thousands, or thousands upon thousands).

Presumably, these AILR systems can scale-up and simply add more cases, but this is not necessarily assured, therefore it would be certainly more satisfying to have such systems make use of large sets of cases, rather than a small set.

Straightforward Rules And Attributes

Consider next a somewhat positive and yet simultaneously downbeat aspect about the SHYSTER system in terms of one of its features: SHYSTER used relatively straightforward rules and attributes in the expert system portion.

The positive aspect is that the use of relatively simple rules and attributes made the system more transparent and easier to explain. As mentioned earlier, explainability is considered a crucial part of any robust AI legal reasoning system.

The downbeat aspect is that the rules and attributes could be construed as being an oversimplification of the law, and therefore not a fuller representation of the murkiness and complexities of law.

Consider these attributes associated with the EMPLOYEE subdomain [R.40]:

- **A1:** the employer directed the manner in which the work was to be done
- **A2:** the worker was not allowed to use his/her own discretion in doing an aspect of the work that was not specified beforehand
- **A3:** the worker was an integral part of the employer's business
- **A4:** the worker neither owned the tools nor provide the transport with which she/he performed the work

- **A5:** the employer would make a profit/loss if the work performed by the worker cost less/more than expected
- **A6:** the work was not performed on the employer's premises
- **A7:** the employer supervised or inspected the work

Here's are two examples of the rule used in SHYSTER for the EMPLOYEE subdomain as related to the attributes shown above (the ones labeled A1 and A2) [R.40]:

RULE RELATED TO A1

Question: Did the employer direct not only what work was to be done, but also the manner in which it was to be done?

Yes: the employer directed the manner in which work was to be done {Employee}

No: the employer did not direct the manner in which the work was to be done {Contractor}

Unknown: it is not known whether the employer directed the manner in which work was to be done

Help: If the employer had a right of control over how the worker did the work then the employer had the power to direct not only what work was to be done, but also the manner in which it was to be done.

RULE RELATED TO A2

Question: Was the worker allowed to use her/his own discretion in doing an aspect of the work that was not specified beforehand?

Yes: the worker was allowed to use her/his own discretion in doing an aspect of the work that not specified beforehand (Employee)

No: the worker was not allowed to use her/his own discretion in doing an aspect of the work that not specified beforehand (Contractor)

Unknown: it is not known whether the worker was allowed to use her/his own discretion in doing an aspect of the work that not specified beforehand

As might be evident when looking at these attributes and rules, they are relatively straightforward. The question arises though as to whether they are robust enough to sufficiently model the aspects and nuances that could arise in such legal cases.

Conclusion

SHYSTER is significant to include in the list of pioneering AI legal reasoning systems due to its novel enhancements in comparison to the other prior approaches of the time period, including the use of multiple domains, and the use of formalized distance metrics and formulas.

Another interesting facet of SHYSTER brings up a point about the advocacy role of practicing law.

One might believe that an attorney would seek to discover all legal points that would both support their case and oppose their case if nothing else to be prepared to cope with the opposing side offering those aspects that oppose their case.

The developer of SHYSTER indicated that he devised the system on the basis of how lawyers argue cases, as follows [R.40]:

- "If the result of a previously decided case is desirable, she/he argues that there are no legally significant differences between the previous case and the instant case, so the previous case should be followed."

- "If the result of a previously decided case is undesirable, she/he argues that there is some legally significant difference between the previous case and the instant case upon which the previous case should be distinguished."

This perhaps raises potential AI ethics issues about the nature of AI legal reasoning systems.

Given that ours is an advocacy-based form of legal jurisprudence, do we want AILR's that take an advocacy position, presumably so if they are to undertake the practice of law in the same manner as humans do, and to what degree and how far should this kind of AI-based advocacy extend?

We'll explore AI ethical ramifications in upcoming chapters.

Note: *For supplemental materials depicting the aspects discussed in this chapter, refer to Appendix B, which contains various augmented diagrams, charts, and additional related facets of relevance.*

CHAPTER 19

AILR:

ROSS, IBP, AGATHA,

VJAP, SCOTUS ML, NAI, DATALEX

We've covered the cornerstone of AI legal reasoning systems that are especially well-known and showcase the most oft-cited case studies of efforts toward creating AI legal reasoning capabilities.

Anyone versed in the AILR field of endeavor would likely be familiar with TAXMAN, HYPO, CATO, and SHYSTER, and also likely have used or been aware of ASPIC+ and ASP.

There are some additional AI Legal Reasoning (AILR) systems that are important to know about too.

Here are the ones we'll be covering in this chapter:

- **ROSS**
- **IBP**
- **AGATHA**
- **VJAP**
- **SCOTUS ML**
- **NAI**
- **DataLex**

Several of the AI legal reasoning systems that will be discussed in this chapter are quite current and are either in use today on a commercial basis or are part of an active research effort underway to extend and advance AI legal reasoning.

Currently in use commercially is ROSS, an AI legal reasoning capability that is widely known in the LegalTech industry.

Currently in use as active research efforts are VJAP, NAI, DataLex, and SCOTUS ML.

Another perspective on the AI legal reasoning systems is what they aim to do. For example, there are some AI legal reasoning systems that primarily act as a **predictor**, trying to predict the outcome of a legal case or legal matter.

In this chapter, we'll take a look at several prediction-focused AI legal reasoning systems, including those of IBP, VJAP, SCOTUS ML, and Lex Machina.

Another way to categorize the various AI legal reasoning systems is based on a rather intriguing approach involving **legal theory construction**.

Here's an explanation about that facet.

When undertaking a legal effort, a lawyer will typically try to assess the legal cases involved and come up with a legal theory that cohesively and convincingly provides a theory of the case at hand. Doing so provides a potentially stronger argument for why the position taken by the lawyer is worthy of consideration and potentially a winning viewpoint on the case.

Since this is an act undertaken by human lawyers, we might expect or assume that an AI legal reasoning system should do something similar.

One such theory-construction legal reasoning system is known as AGATHA, and we'll be exploring in this chapter how it works.

Notice that I've mentioned that a legal theory should presumably be cohesive and convincing. That's an important aspect since it might be possible to craft a legal theory about a case and have such a theory that is rather baseless or weak.

In that sense, an AI legal reasoning shouldn't derive just any kind of legal theory, but one that hopefully is logically robust and will stand up to potential criticism or attack.

Let's next explore each of the various AI legal reasoning systems and see how each one offers useful insights on the progress in the AILR field.

AILR Case Study: ROSS

ROSS is a legal research system that's available online for commercial use [C.12].

Founded in 2015, ROSS has gained significant notoriety due to its AI use.

One aspect involves the use of AI techniques to try and identify cases in a case database that is pertinent to a case that an end-user (lawyer) is undertaking or considering.

This involves the ROSS system trying to find similar language as used in prior cases, and then preparing a case treatment (though, notably, this is partially done by AI and also at times partially undertaken by the human-composed research team at ROSS).

ROSS also is able to do so-called deep matching and uses Machine Learning (ML) to do so.

For example, when doing a Q&A with an end-user (e.g., a lawyer), the ROSS system uses the answers provided previously as a guide toward which answer might be best or most applicable to a new question.

Similar to Machine Learning techniques (which will be covered in the next chapter), the Q&A pairs are used to try and calculate the likelihood that a question will be "answered" by the associated pair.

Weights are adjusted as to whether an answer is rated by the end-user as responsive or not responsive (a "thumbs up" or "thumbs down" voting).

One aspect to keep in mind is that the ML, in this case, has no sense of "understanding" about the law and nor the legal text. Some people mistakenly assume that ML "comprehends" the nature of the questions and the nature of the answers, but that is decidedly not the case.

Instead, in this particular use case, it is merely forming a mathematically crowd-sourced relationship between the questions and answers, and therefore making a kind of calculated guess as to which passage of text as an answer will be the best response to a given passage of text that's posed as a question.

ROSS provides via their web site various examples of the AI capabilities employed [C.12].

AILR Case Study: IBP

IBP is the acronym for the **Issue Based Prediction (IBP)** system R.13].

Similar to the other AI legal reasoning systems that we've discussed, IBP uses a case-based approach and incorporates factors, issues, and cases.

The legal domain used is trade secrets law and reuses the datasets from HYPO and CATO.

Researchers Stefanie Bruninghaus and Kevin Ashley explained the nature of IBP in their 2003 article entitled "Combining Case-Based and Model-Based Reasoning for Predicting the Outcome of Legal Cases" [R.13].

A key novelty is that IBP seeks to predict the outcome of a trade secrets legal case.

It is an example of a predictor-oriented AI legal reasoning systems. Here's how it works.

An issue tree is created that consists of raising or abstaining the related cases that have been formed into a tree relationship hierarchy.

The factors used in comparing the cases can serve as a "knock-out" in that if a factor is so crucial that it could be said to undermine the relevancy of a prior case, the case so identified is considered to be no longer applicable or that the existing case overrides the precedential case.

This **knock-out feature** serves as a handy insight for other AI legal reasoning systems, namely that not all prior relevant cases might be applicable and that it is conceivable that there is some insurmountable aspect that makes a prior case inapplicable.

Of course, trying to knock-out a prior case could readily become a rather contentious issue with the opposing side, assuming that the prior case favors their position. As such, the AI legal reasoning system would need to showcase why the prior case was considered inapplicable and do so on a convincing basis.

That's partially why it is vital that AI legal reasoning systems have explainability capabilities, as does IBP. As mentioned earlier, if an AI legal reasoning system lacks an explanatory mode or capacity, the use of such a system in actual practice is greatly limited and less likely to occur.

IBP is available on GitHub and can be used for further development (see [S.4] in Appendix B, Bibliography).

AILR Case Study: VJAP

VJAP is the acronym for the **Value Judgment-based Argumentative Prediction (VJAP)** system [R.24].

Developed by Matthias Grabmair of Carnegie Mellon University (CMU), this AI legal reasoning system is focused on making predictions of case outcomes.

Once again, trade secrets law is the focus of this AILR.

Here's how it works.

The system creates an argument graph for each case, and the model used incorporates defeasible reasoning.

An argument is a set of premise propositions, which then warrant or generate a logically derived conclusion.

Confidence levels are included as part of the prediction process.

These confidence levels are based on past cases and use an iterative optimization method.

One notable aspect is this incorporation of confidence levels and the ability to display or report on the confidence that the prediction has.

This brings up an important overarching point for AI legal reasoning systems, namely that the outcome or predictions are not necessarily going to be completely certain. If the system doesn't offer a certainly or **uncertainty indication**, there is a danger that a human lawyer relying upon such a prediction might not realize that there could be a minimal chance of the prediction being accurate.

Thus, AI legal reasoning systems that provide predictive capabilities ought to include some mechanism, such as confidence levels, and then showcase those predictive likelihoods as part of the explanation associated with the predicted outcomes.

AILR Case Study: SCOTUS ML

SCOTUS ML is a Machine Learning system for predicting the Supreme Court of the United States (SCOTUS) legal cases [R.30].

This is another example of a predictive system.

Developed by Daniel Katz, Michael Bommarito, and Josh Blackman, the SCOTUS ML system is described in detail in an article published on April 12, 2017, entitled "A General Approach for Predicting the Behavior of the Supreme Court of the United States" [R.30].

There have been many prior approaches undertaken to predict the Supreme Court and its actions. The researchers that have developed SCOTUS ML claimed a higher predictive rate than similar prior studies of predicting the Supreme Court outcomes and proffer a predictive rate of approximately 70%.

Here's how SCOTUS ML works.

The data used as input consists of the Supreme Court Database (SCDB).

Unlike many prior studies, the researchers used the entire set of cases, ranging from a date of 1791 to present, and did not focus on just a subset of the data on Supreme Court cases.

Factors used included the names of the SC justices for each case, the term of the case, the issue of the case, the court of origin, whether oral arguments were heard, and so on.

Their aim for predictive aspects was twofold:

- **Predict the legal Supreme Court case outcome**
- **Predict the vote of each Supreme Court justice**

Each term of the Supreme Court is modeled using a **randomized forest tree** technique. These are essentially Decision Trees and utilize associations between cases and the case outcomes.

Predictions of each tree are then used to average across the forest, providing a type of crowdsourced augmentation.

In their initial runs, they created a new forest (fresh) for each term, and later revised and advanced the system to only start a fresh forest whenever a Supreme Court justice left the court or came onto the court. In addition, they allow forests to grow from term-to-term, adding additional trees into a forest.

Some might argue that the use of the randomized forest approach is not what is known popularly as Machine Learning per se, while others would say that random forests are considered well within the rubric of ML and in this case an example of a supervised ML approach (more will be discussed about Machine Learning in the next chapter).

The SCOTUS ML was written in Python, a conventional procedural programming language, and makes extensive use of the sclkit-learn online toolkit that provides various ML-related techniques.

SCOUT ML is available on GitHub for further development [R.30].

AILR Case Study: Lex Machina

Lex Machina was first started at Stanford in 2006 and later sold to LexisNexis in 2015 [R.19].

The system initially used logistic regression to predict the outcomes of Intellectual Property (IP) cases.

Thus, this is another example of a predictive system.

Here's how it worked.

Case texts were examined to extract key factors.

Factors included who the judge was as assigned to the IP case, what district the case took place in, the lawyers involved in the IP case, and so on. A claimed accuracy rate of 64% was achieved in predicting the outcomes of the IP cases.

One aspect of these kinds of predictive models is that they often are unable to explain how the prediction per se comes to arise, other than a mathematically formulated indication, which doesn't necessarily provide a logic-based explanation.

In other words, when modeling with a mathematical basis, there is no explanation likely viable from the system that offers a legal argument about the outcome of the case.

One would say that the **legal merits of the case** are not therefore involved directly in deriving the predictions and to some degree makes it less viable for understanding why a predicted outcome occurred, though nonetheless, such a predictive capability does provide other added value.

AILR Case Study: AGATHA

AGATHA is an AI legal reasoning system that tries to construct a legal theory for a case.

The acronym AGATHA is based on the wording of **ArGument Agent for Theory Automation (AGATHA)** [R.9].

The system uses case-based reasoning.

As a legal domain, trade secrets law was used, along with the cases of Pierson v Post, and Keeble v Hickeringill, which were used in the Barry Bonds baseball case.

Similar to how a lawyer might try to assemble a set of court cases and derive a legal theory that underpins the cases, AGATHA generates a **legal theory space** that contains feasible constructs.

Beginning with a theory 0, essentially an empty set, the system proceeds to add cases and creates a branching tree of potential additional theories. This proceeds until all viable theories have been generated.

The assumption is that the cases presumably have some intended **overarching social end** and that the cases can be threaded together or shown to have a relationship that binds them accordingly and not arbitrarily so.

This notion of focusing on a legal theory of a set of cases is a novelty and one that few AI legal reasoning systems have undertaken.

Legal Argument Mining

This brings up a related facet about AI legal reasoning.

One particular kind of AILR sub-processor component consists of performing **legal argument mining**. Essentially, the AI attempts to examine the legal corpus of attention and surfaces potential legal arguments that are embodied in the case, similar to what a human versed in law would do.

These legal arguments are then retrieved and shown to a human lawyer for review (in a semi-autonomous AILR). In a fully autonomous AILR, the AILR itself would use the argument mining to try and derive the key legal postures of the case, including those that support the advocacy of the moment and those that might be utilized by the opposing side.

AILR Case Study: DataLex

DataLex is an AI legal reasoning system undertaken by the Australasian Legal Information Institute (AustLII) and uses a rules-based inferencing engine [R.38].

Rules are entered via a declarative format.

If needed, the procedural code can be added to the rules.

There is also a case-based reasoning feature.

As much as possible, the intent of the knowledge base is to be **isomorphic**, meaning to be one-to-one in terms of the association with a snippet of law and the rules in the DataLex system, doing so for ease of use and explanation.

The inference engine allows for both forward chaining and backward chaining (this refers to the sequencing in which the rules will be executed or enacted).

DataLex is intended for use by lawyers, rather than needing to be set up and used by AI developers, and provides an interface for entering cases, facts, conclusions, and questions.

If AI legal reasoning systems are to become readily usable, the goal would be to have such systems setup via end-users such as lawyers rather than requiring AI developers to do so.

AILR Case Study: NAI

NAI is an AI legal reasoning system that focuses on providing a formalized means to depict the law.

Developed by Tomer Libal and Alexandar Steen, the normative AI or NAI system provides a means to use formal logic to depict a case [R.33].

The source code is available on GitHub for further development (see [S.5] in Appendix B, Bibliography).

As a legal domain, the NAI was tested using Scotland law, involving regulations about prohibiting smoking while children are in a motor vehicle with the smoker.

NAI uses a normative reasoning framework.

An annotation tool is provided to allow for annotating passages of text and then having those linked into a logic-based formalism.

The NAI system attempts to undertake a proof-of-correctness of the formalizations.

One especially interesting facet that might not stand out to some is the use of an API. An **API or Application Programming Interface** is a means of allowing a piece of software to be run by another piece of software.

AILR-API Usage

This brings up the insight that AI legal reasoning systems will eventually be utilized by other systems, and thus an AI legal reasoning ought to have an available API for such use.

For example, when earlier discussing the advent of self-driving cars and a cop in the backseat as a type of AILR instance, the mainstay AI driving system would connect to the AILR specialized software, doing so via an API.

Generally, if an AI legal reasoning system is developed with an API included, this would allow other allied systems to readily invoke such an added component.

Conclusion

These AI legal reasoning systems have been described and reveal additional facets about the design and use of AI in the law:

- ROSS
- IBP
- VJAP
- SCOTUS ML
- LEX MACHINA
- AGATHA
- DataLex
- NAI

It is useful to understand the approaches undertaken by these additional systems. Each of them offers a particular nuance of AI legal reasoning and might ultimately contribute towards a larger and more comprehensive approach to such systems.

In the next chapter, we'll delve into how AILR's are built and the types of programming languages used to do so.

Note: *For supplemental materials depicting the aspects discussed in this chapter, refer to Appendix B, which contains various augmented diagrams, charts, and additional related facets of relevance.*

CHAPTER 20
BUILDING AI LEGAL REASONING APPLICATIONS

One important consideration of AI legal reasoning systems involves the act of building them.

The tool or tools that are used to build an AI legal reasoning system will shape what the system can do, along with whether the system will be readily adaptable over time.

In addition, it is easy sometimes to only look at the tool, and not realize that the underlying design is equally crucial, if not even more so. Thus, those embarking upon developing an AI legal reasoning system would be wise to figure out the needed underlying design, such as the manner in which the legal knowledge will be represented or codified, along with how the reasoning portion of the system will be undertaken.

The design effort should normally precede the selection of the building tool since the design in many respects will dictate the type of tool or tools that can accomplish the implementation of the design.

That being said, oftentimes the tools themselves drive salient aspects of the design. If the tools available won't allow for implementing the design, either you need to construct entirely new tools or you need to adjust the design accordingly.

Crucial Requirements Not to be Missed

There are additional facets to keep in mind too. For example, as has been emphasized numerous times throughout the exploration of prior AI legal reasoning systems, it would be prudent to have some method of ensuring that the system can explain what it has done.

Trying to add-on explanatory capabilities into an already designed or already built AILR system is not going to be easy and might be nearly impossible to undertake.

Thus, a fundamental requirement that ought to be essential throughout the design and the building of an AI legal reasoning system would include facets of enabling explainability.

About Pilots or Prototypes of AILR

For those that develop a pilot or prototype AILR, it is tempting to push aside a requirement of explainability and figure that though it is a nice-to-have, there are hurdles in that the system might be trying to showcase some other facet of legal reasoning and not want to dilute attention to other aspects such as the explanatory feature.

This is certainly a potentially sensible perspective when developing a one-off, something that is intended to demonstrate a specific focus or capability.

Thus, the purpose or intent of the AILR is crucial to such a decision.

In any case, those desiring to craft a robust and full-bodied AI legal reasoning system would be wise to identify a full range of requirements, and if needed perhaps put temporary placeholders into the building aspects, while including within the design the needed elements to make later updates or upgrades for adding those undeveloped features more likely doable.

Open Source of AILR

For researchers that are crafting AI legal reasoning systems, it is hoped that they would make available their source code as open source software (see subsection S of Appendix B, Bibliography for a list of several AILR's that have publicly made available their source code).

Open source means that the source code, along with preferably the associated design and design documents, would be openly posted for access.

By doing so, it aids in having incremental progress occur in the field of AI legal reasoning systems, allowing other researchers to readily build on top of what has come before. Otherwise, each next AILR becomes a from-scratch effort, oftentimes duplicating work that has already been accomplished and that could have been readily reused.

When discussing the various AI legal reasoning systems that have guided the field to-date, some of them have indeed made available their source code.

In the past, the source code might have been posted at an obscure website used by the researchers or developers, such as websites associated with a university lab or a research entity. In today's era, it is usually best to post the source code onto a globally known and popular site, such as GitHub or its equivalent. Doing so eases access for others and makes the source code more likely to be discovered during online searches.

This brings up the other side of that coin, namely, make sure to first take a look at available open source before jumping into developing your own AI legal reasoning system.

There might be available code that can be used to bootstrap a new effort.

API for AILR

Another potential requirement involves having an API for the AI legal reasoning system (an Application Programming Interface) and was mentioned in the prior chapter.

The use of an API indicates that the AILR can be invoked by other software. Thus, if some other software package needs to make use of a legal reasoning aspect, it can simply make use of the API, connect with the AILR, and then have the AILR return its results back to the other software.

This is preferred versus having to require an end-user to run the AILR separately from some other software that they might otherwise be using.

Computational Tractability and Scale

One of the facets earlier mentioned about AI legal reasoning systems is their computational tractability or potential intractability.

This refers to how much time or the number of steps that an AILR might need to perform in order to undertake some desired AI legal reasoning task. Developers of AILR's need to consider the performance characteristics of the systems they build.

Being able to scale-up an AI legal reasoning system is vital if it is going to be used on real-world problems and on any widespread basis.

Types of AILR Tools

Let's next consider the nature of the software development tools that might be used to build an AILR.

There are three major categories of AI legal reasoning building tools, consisting of:

- **AI generic programming languages**
- **AI generic development packages**
- **AI legal reasoning specific tools**

Let's consider each of those categories.

AI Generic Programming Languages

In the case of AI generic programming languages, we've seen in earlier chapters some logic-based languages such as ASPIC+ and ASP. These are typically focused on the purely logic-based formulations.

More generalized AI programming languages such as Prolog and LISP have also been used for AILR building.

We'll take a closer look at Prolog and at LISP in this chapter.

Sometimes conventional programming languages such as Python or C++ are used and oftentimes supplemented with an add-on set of utilities that provide added capabilities.

For example, it was noted that SCOTUS ML used the sclkit-learn library of functions for the implementation of the random forest trees technique. Other popular AI and Machine Learning libraries include PyTorch, Torch, and others.

AI Generic Development Packages

Rather than developing an AI legal reasoning system from the ground-up by using an AI programming language, another approach involves using a software package that already exists.

For the development of Machine Learning-based AILR's, there are now numerous ML generic oriented packages that can be used, including TensorFlow, AML (Amazon), Google Cloud ML engine, IBM Watson NLP, and others.

One downside would be that those packages aren't potentially flexible enough to accommodate the needs of an AILR, depending upon the design elements of the system.

In some cases, you might decide that part of the AILR will need to be written using an AI programming language and then augmented via the use of an AI development package.

AI Legal Reasoning Specific Tools

For several of the prior mentioned AILR's, the developers often crafted their own tools to then proceed with putting together the AI legal reasoning system.

In that case, it is possible to leverage an already crafted tool that was specifically made for AILR purposes.

AILR's such as TAXMAN, HYPO, CATO, SHYSTER, all had tools that had been built as part of the research effort in implementing those systems.

An issue that arises is whether the tool itself is adaptable to whatever new approach you might be seeking to undertake. If the design of the prior ALIR is quite afield of the design for your new AILR, it might be that the former tool is insufficient for the effort at hand.

An additional complication is that oftentimes the tools were hand-crafted and intended primarily to be used by the researchers or developers that crafted the AILR tool.

As such, it might be extremely difficult to figure out how the tool works, plus there might not be any support available and you would be on your own if the tool has errors or problems.

Let's next consider the use of AI programming languages, which offer the widest flexibility for developing an AILR.

Introduction to Prolog

Prolog is a relatively popular AI programming language, and the name comes from a mash-up of **Programming Logic (Prolog)**.

It is a declarative programming language and designed for being used in logic-based circumstances.

To provide you with a semblance of what Prolog is like, let's consider some simple examples.

Here is an example of Prolog code [S.7]:

```
human(socrates).
mortal(X) :- human(X).
```

That's the code, just two lines. Next, let's run the program and ask it a question:

```
?- mortal(socrates)
X = socrates
```

What does this Prolog program signify?

Let's step through the code, one line at a time.

The first line of the Prolog code is a statement that indicates "human(socrates)" and indicates that there will be a predicate that has a functor indicated as the word "human" (a functor is a name that you've decided to assign to a predicate).

Furthermore, as part of the predicate, we'll have what in coding is called an argument or parameter (the word "argument" is not meant in the same way as the word argument is intended in law), essentially something that will be considered associated with the named functor.

In this case, the code is asserting that the word "socrates" is associated with having the property of being "human" (it's a logical predicate).

Or, you can also think of it as we're saying that of those aspects that are to be considered "human," "socrates" is one such instance.

Next is a clause that indicates the functor "mortal" will be associated with the functor "human" and does so by indicating this: mortal(X):- human(X).

The use of the capital letter X's is considered a variable.

Thus, the line can be read to mean that for anything that might be considered a "human" that it will also be considered to be "mortal" (this is due to the aspect that the X can take on whatever valid values we might wish to use).

Next, the query about the program starts with a question mark and asks a relatively simple question, namely it asks whether "socrates" is a "mortal" and thus the Prolog system would proceed to logically figure out if that is indeed the case or not. The question is phrased as whether this logical assertion is true or not: mortal(socrates).

How would the Prolog system figure this out?

It would look through the coded declaratives that we've provided.

Finding a line that indicates something about the functor known as "mortal" the system would have the rule that any "mortal" is anyone that is a "human" (this is due to the second line of the Prolog code that we entered).

The Prolog system would then seek to find any instances of a "human" and encounter the first line of our code, the line that indicates that "socrates" is a "human."

As such, the Prolog system has searched through the logic rules that we've provided and was able to reach a conclusion that an instance that satisfies the conditions or rules is that of the value "socrates" (it would report that X is equal to "socrates").

You've now learned a little bit about Prolog.

Notice that in a mere two lines of code that we were able to right away establish a set of logic.

Also, when asking the Prolog system to make use of the logic, we didn't have to specify the steps in doing so, and instead, the Prolog system made use of whatever internally available search mechanism it had to resolve the logic processing aspects.

The general format for composing Prolog statements consists of these formatting conventions:

- Predicates with clauses
- A variable must start with a capital letter (so generally don't use capital letters as first letter for anything else)
- Name of a predicate is its functor
- Number of arguments is its arity
- Overall Prolog format is:

    <program> ::= <predicate> | <program> <predicate>

    <predicate> ::= <clause> | <predicate> <clause>

    <clause> ::= <base clause> | <nonbase clause>

    <base clause> ::= <structure> .

    <nonbase clause> ::= <structure> :- <structure> .

    <structure> ::= <structure> | <structure> , <structure>

And so on

Let's next tackle another Prolog program.

Here is some Prolog code that is somewhat lighthearted and yet also provides an opportunity to showcase more about the capabilities of Prolog [S.6]:

```
male(homer).
male(bart).
female(marge).
female(lisa).
female(maggie).
parents(bart, homer, marge).
parents(lisa, homer, marge).
parents(maggie, homer, marge).
sisterof(X,Y):- female(Y), parents(Y,M,W),
                parents(X,M,W).
```

Carefully look at the Prolog code and see if you can anticipate what it is able to do.

Let's go ahead and ask the Prolog system a question and see if it can find an answer to our question.

Here's the question, identify who the sister or sisters of Bart are:

```
?- sisterof(bart, S)
```

What would be the answer?

We can attempt to execute or perform the Prolog code, doing so in a manner similar to how the Prolog system would make use of the logic that has been coded.

First, the query or question makes use of the functor "sisterof" and passes along two arguments, the value of "bart" and the indication of a variable known as S. Thus, the Prolog system would look to see if there had been any definition given to the functor of "sisterof" and find that indeed this is the definition:

sisterof(X,Y):- female(Y), parents(Y,M,W), parents(X,M,W).

That seems rather daunting, but let's take it apart and figure out what it does.

It says that "sisterof" is associated with the functor "female" and that the parameter or argument Y should be passed to it. Furthermore, "sisterof" is associated with the functor parents, including one usage that has the variables Y, M, W, and a second instance of X, M, W.

We know that the X is going to be the value "bart" since that's what we have used in the query, therefore for the moment substitute in your mind that the X is the value of "bart" and let's proceed accordingly.

In the case of the second use of "parents" for the "sisterof" we now can say that this is "parents" with "bart" as the first parameter and the other two parameters of M and W we don't yet know.

The Prolog system would look to see if there is any definition of "parents" and in so doing would find that there are three such lines in the code.

Focus on the line that says this:

parents(bart, homer, marge).

This is handy since we do know that we are looking for an instance of "bart" as the initial value in the argument, and we've now found a match.

Since this line of "parents" indicates that there is "bart" and followed by two other arguments, namely "homer" and "marge" we can then assign those values to the parameters of M and W.

Thus, at this moment, we have that the X = bart, the M = homer, and the W = marge.

Next, consider the second use of "parents" in the "sisterof" definition.

We can now pass along that "parents" has some value Y, which we don't yet know, and a value of M = homer and W = marge.

Are there any "parents" definitions that match this condition?

Yes, we have these two lines:

parents(lisa, homer, marge).

parents(maggie, homer, marge).

In that case, we now know that the previously unknown value of Y is, in fact, the values of "lisa" and "maggie" (thus, we have satisfied that aspect). This brings us the last step involved in resolving the part of "sisterof" that says "female(Y)" and asks whether Y is a functor of "female" or not.

We currently know that Y is a value of "lisa" and a value of "maggie" and so the question to now resolve is whether either of those or both of those might be considered "female."

The Prolog system would look for any definitions associated with "female" and find these rules:

female(marge).

female(lisa).

female(maggie).

We are looking to find out if the value of Y that is "lisa" is "female" and indeed it is, and likewise that the value of "maggie" is also "female" and thus they both meet the condition.

The final result then of evaluating the "sisterof" query is that we have logically figured out that the parents of "bart" are "homer" and "marge," and that those same parents have additional children of "lisa" and "maggie," and that furthermore, those additional children are both of "female," thus the answer would be:

S = lisa;

S = maggie.

In walking you through the logic, it seemed perhaps somewhat painstaking. Fortunately, the Prolog system would be doing the logical stepwise processing for you.

This introduction to Prolog illustrates how powerful a declarative programming language it is for logic-based problems. With just a few statements, we can construct a set of logical rules, and then have the Prolog system make use of those rules.

If you have a situation involving perhaps hundreds or thousands of logic-based rules and conditions, you could setup Prolog with those rules and conditions, and then rely upon the underlying logic-based search engine to process them for you.

Introduction to LISP

Now that you've seen Prolog, let's take a look at LISP.

Recall that Prolog is a declarative programming language, and as might be evident by the Prolog code that you just saw, in Prolog, you enter in logic-based statements and let the system process those statements when performing logical reasoning.

LISP is a <u>procedural</u> programming language; thus, it is unlike Prolog.

In some sense, LISP is more akin to a conventional procedural programming language such as Python, C++, etc.

At the same time, it is actually a bit different than conventional procedural programming languages, as we'll see in a moment, and offers some crucial capabilities for developing AI applications.

LISP is an acronym for **List Processing (LISP)**.

The overarching concept of LISP is that it allows for the processing of lists of things.

Here are some key facets of LISP:

- LISP is popular for AI applications
- Powerful programming language
- Difficult for traditional programmers to master
- Uses unusual format for coding
- Has a prefix notation
- Extensive use of parentheses
- Some say "Lots of Insidiously Silly Parentheses" rather than List Programming as the name
- Readily does recursion
- Can wrap code within itself and produce new code on-the-fly
- Etc.

For conventional programmers, LISP is often a bit confusing to learn and use.

This is partially due to the somewhat unusual syntax aspects of writing a LISP program, and also due to the powerful and yet perhaps not fully transparent use of recursion (a feature available in conventional programming languages, though somewhat infrequently used, while it is extensively used in LISP).

To illustrate the use of LISP code, we'll take a look at a famous AI-related program that uses LISP. The program became famous for its attempt at acting somewhat like a psychotherapist and had some surprising results.

The program is known as ELIZA.

Aspects About the ELIZA Program

In the 1960s, one of the earliest variants of an AI-related effort and that perchance stoked great interest in AI consisted of the ELIZA program. At the time, there wasn't anything at all like today's Alexa and Siri, and the hopes of one day having Natural Language Processing (NLP) of a more dynamic and fluid nature was far from being realized.

Joseph Weizenbaum of MIT decided to write a program that he named after Eliza Doolittle from Bernard Shaw's play *Pygmalion*. The concept underlying the program was that it would appear to use NLP as though it was a human interacting with those that ran the program.

During the interaction, the program would seem to be acting like a psychotherapist, aiding in analyzing your needs and probing to find out what is on your mind. This dovetailed into the time period during which psychoanalysis had risen in attention.

The program itself is quite simplistic and doesn't do much at all, and yet it surprisingly seemed to convince some people that it had human-like qualities, including as though it was carrying on a psychoanalysis while you were using it.

To give you a sense of what it did, let's consider an example of its interaction.

The interaction was undertaken in writing using a computer screen and shows the entry of the human running the program and then the response by the ELIZA program.

Here's an example of an ELIZA dialogue (the entry by the human interacting with ELIZA is shown in bolded text) [S.3]:

Please tell me what's been bothering you.

Well, it's my boss.

Your boss?

Yes. He's not been friendly.

I see.

He is always upset.

When?

Always. Especially when things are hectic.

Can you think of a specific example?

Well, yesterday he said he was unhappy with all of us.

That is interesting. Please continue.

He says I am too lazy.

Is it because you are too lazy that you came to me?

I'm not lazy.

Do you believe it is normal to not be lazy?

Upon your first reading of the dialogue, it might seem quite impressive that the ELIZA program appears to be fully engaged in a discussion with the person. And, not just any discussion, but one in which the program seems to be analyzing the issues or concerns of the person using the program.

The reality was that the program was mainly parroting words back to the person.

For example, when the end-user indicates they are having problems with their boss, the ELIZA program simply asks, "Your boss?" and essentially parrots the word "boss" back to the end-user.

If this was an actual human that was responding, certainly they might have also sometimes parrot back to you, though after a while, if that continued extensively, you'll likely start to get somewhat suspicious about whether they were really paying attention to you (or, in the case of the computer, whether it was making any sense of what you were saying).

Furthermore, the program produced simple messages that might seem relevant and as though the program is "understanding" the discussion, but in fact, those messages are already canned fillers.

For example, notice that the program indicates "That's interesting" and does so when the program otherwise cannot parrot back the prior line. The use of "That's interesting" is employed whenever the program cannot otherwise find any other hook or means to readily parrot back the sentence that was entered by the end-user.

So, in short, this use of "AI" is actually not at all an especially capable AI program.

One of the reasons to point out this aspect is that there were many people that were fooled into believing the program was the realization of true "AI" and that the program seemingly showcased (or proved) the amazing power of AI systems.

Instead, it showcased that people could be fooled into believing that AI existed when it did not, in fact, provide anything of the sort.

➔ **Keep this caveat in mind when assessing AI legal reasoning systems:**

> Someone that proffers an AI legal reasoning system could possibly get away with having a quite rudimentary capability that does not exercise any semblance of AI, and yet if the end-user wasn't astute enough to discern this, they would fall into the trap of believing that the AI is indeed "understanding" their dialogue.

Another lesson to be learned from ELIZA was that it only usually fooled people if kept to a relatively brief interaction. In other words, if someone used ELIZA for any length of time, they would gradually realize there was trickery taking place.

This again can be applied to an AI legal reasoning system.

If you use an AI legal reasoning system and keep your dialogue or use it to a very narrow aspect, the odds are that you might be tricked into believing that it can do more than it really can accomplish.

Are you curious about the LISP code that can be used to implement ELIZA?

Let's use the code to explore some facets of the LISP programming language.

ELIZA and LISP Code

For the LISP code listing that you are about to explore, I'll explain some selected snippets of the code. The notion is to enable you to have a semblance of what LISP code looks like, including how it operates, similar to what was shown when describing the nature of Prolog code.

There are numerous books and online tutoring systems that can teach you how to program in Prolog or LISP if that's something you are interested in learning.

Both of those languages are considered essential tools for those that develop AI applications, especially if doing so from scratch and not otherwise able or wanting to use an AI package or similar development utility.

Here's LISP code used to craft an ELIZA variant [S.3]:

```
(defun match (pat in)
  (if (null pat)
      (null in)
    (if (eq (first pat) '*)
        (wildcard pat in)
      (if (eq (first pat) (first in))
          (match (rest pat) (rest in))
        nil))))


(defparameter *bindings* nil)


(defun wildcard (pat in)
  (if (match (rest (rest pat)) in)
      (progn (setf *bindings*
                   (bind (first (rest pat)) nil *bindings*)) t)
   (if (null in)
       nil
     (if (match pat (rest in))
         (progn (setf *bindings*
                      (bind (first (rest pat)) (first in) *bindings*)) t)
       nil))))


(defun bind (var value bindings)
  (if (null bindings)
      (list (if value (list var value) (list var)))
    (let* ((key (first (first bindings)))
           (values (rest (first bindings)))
           (new (swap value)))
      (if (eq var key)
          (cons (cons key (cons new values)) (rest bindings))
        (cons (first bindings) (bind var new (rest bindings)))))))
```

```
(defun lookup (key alist)
  (if (null alist) nil
    (if (eq (first (first alist)) key)
       (first alist)
      (lookup key (rest alist)))))


(defparameter *viewpoint* '((I you) (you I) (me you) (am are) (was
were) (my your)))

(defun swap (value)
  (let* ((a (lookup value *viewpoint*)))
    (if a (first (rest a)) value)))


(defun subs (list)
  (if (null list)
      nil
    (let* ((a (lookup (first list) *bindings*)))
      (if a
          (append (rest a) (subs (rest list)))
        (cons (first list) (subs (rest list)))))))

(defparameter *rules*
  '(((* x hello * y) (hello. how can I help ?))
    ((* x i want * y) (what would it mean if you got y ?)
             (why do you want y ?))
    ((* x i wish * y) (why would it be better if y ?))
    ((* x i hate * y) (what makes you hate y ?))
    ((* x if * y)
     (do you really think it is likely that y)
     (what do you think about y))
    ((* x no * y) (why not?))
    ((* x i was * y) (why do you say x you were y ?))
    ((* x i feel * y) (do you often feel y ?))
    ((* x i felt * y) (what other feelings do you have?))
    ((* x) (you say x ?) (tell me more.))))
```

```
(defun random-elt (list)
  (nth (random (length list)) list))

(defun eliza ()
  (loop
   (princ "} ")
   (let* ((line (read-line))
         (input (read-from-string (concatenate 'string "(" line ")"))))
     (when (string= line "bye") (return))
     (setq *bindings* nil)
     (format t "~{~(~a ~)~}~%"
            (dolist (r *rules*)
              (when (match (first r) input)
                (return
                 (subs (random-elt (rest r))))))))))
```

As you can see, the LISP language makes extensive use of parentheses. This is an ongoing contention and a bit of criticism about the LISP language and frequently referred to by conventional programming language programmers in a cynical manner.

Let's take a look at some snippets of the code listing.

Consider these two lines of the LISP program:

((* x i wish * y) (why would it be better if y ?))

((* x i hate * y) (what makes you hate y ?))

Here's what those lines do.

If the end-user that runs the program enters in a sentence or sentence fragment that says "i wish" or "i hate" then the program will provide a response of either "why would it be better if" in the case of the "i wish," or a response of "what makes you hate" in the case of saying "i hate."

Suppose for example that you entered into ELIZA this sentence:

I hate cookies

ELIZA would respond with this:

What makes you hate cookies?

How did it come up with that reply?

It merely took the "cookies" part of your sentence and substituted it into the predefined reply of "what makes you hate" and put the selected word at the end of the reply.

From the perspective of the person that entered the sentence, they might be impressed that the "AI" seems to be asking them about why they hate cookies, when in fact whatever word they had used would simply be appended to the reply.

You can make such a program readily show its limitations by using grammatically incorrect wording, and the program will then provide a reply that won't grammatically or logically seem to make any sense.

For example, you could say this:

I hate my mother

And the program would respond with:

What makes you hate my mother?

Notice that the reply refers to the mother of the "psychotherapist" rather than to the mother of the patient or person that is running the program.

You would undoubtedly get confused at the reply, since the system hasn't replied in a manner befitting semantically what you stated.

In any case, as you can see, the ELIZA program is relatively short and only makes use of some simplistic and underwhelming textual trickery.

Keep this in mind when making use of any AI legal reasoning systems and be on the watch for simple trickery that's trying to be used.

ELIZA and PARRY

One other aspect that is somewhat notable about ELIZA consists of attempts that were made to run ELIZA against other similar simplistic "AI" programs and see what happens.

Another somewhat famous program, though not as famous as ELIZA, consisted of the program known as PARRY. PARRY was intended to act like a paranoid psychotic.

It used similar textual trickery as had ELIZA.

When people ran PARRY, they at times thought that the program was exhibiting AI. It was as though the program was a real human that perchance was suffering from paranoia.

Cleverly, some developers decided to run ELIZA and PARRY in a dialogue with each other.

Here's a dialogue between ELIZA and PARRY [S.2]:

ELIZA: **I don't understand your motives.**

PARRY: Why don't you understand my motives?

ELIZA: **Shouldn't I be?**

PARRY: Why do you say that just now?

ELIZA: **That's just the way it is.**

PARRY: Suppose that's just the way it was not.

ELIZA: **So?**

PARRY: I am not sure I understand you fully.

ELIZA: **You harp on the same questions too much.**

PARRY: What does that similarity suggest to you?

ELIZA: **I don't get you**.

PARRY: Do you wish that you did get I?

At first glance, it almost seems as though the two programs are carrying on a human-like dialogue. When you get toward the end of the dialogue, you can begin to see things falling apart in terms of the language being used.

For example, notice that ELIZA indicated this:

I don't get you.

And PARRY replied with this:

Do you wish that you did get I?

This is another example of my earlier point about the programs not coping with the semantics of language and getting caught by using language in a manner that would showcase a lack of fluency, and presumably a lack of being able to "comprehend" the discussion.

That being said, today's NLP is much improved and would not likely get caught in similar semantics-oriented traps, though such means to prod and detect even today's best NLP can be similarly undertaken. In any case, it is increasingly becoming harder to discern that a given NLP discourse is computational versus a human.

AILR-To-AILR Interactions

A useful reason to consider the ELIZA and PARRY dialogue is that it brings up an interesting point about AI legal reasoning systems, and the possibility of AILR's interacting with each other.

Suppose that there is an AI legal reasoning system that has some particular specialty in the law, we'll call it the MFA-Law system.

Suppose there is another AI legal reasoning system, separate from MFA-Law, and it has a different legal specialty, let's say TAX-Law.

At some point in the future, we might have AI legal reasoning systems that carry on discussions or interact with other allied AI legal reasoning systems. For example, you might want to have MFA-Law AILR do a consult with TAX-Law AILR.

Some anticipate that we'll have numerous AILR's, each with a particular specialty, perhaps some also that are focused on law in a particular nation-state or locale.

This form of **Distributed AI (DAI)** will likely be used in a coordinated fashion (more on this topic in Chapter 25). Various AILR's will connect with each other to perform an overarching legal effort.

Consider this the equivalent of having human lawyers with various specialties and conferring to work together on large-scale legal efforts.

In terms of DAI for AILR's, we're not there yet, but this could very well be an integral part of the future of AI legal reasoning systems, especially as pointed out earlier than most of the AILR's to-date have been focused on narrow specialties, and thus if you wanted to bridge across them, it might involve having them engage in an electronic discussion with each other.

Conclusion

This chapter has identified the importance of both the design and the building of AI legal reasoning systems. In addition, you have now seen examples of what AI programming languages consist of, especially two of the more popular AI programming languages consisting of Prolog and LISP.

Note: *For supplemental materials depicting the aspects discussed in this chapter, refer to Appendix B, which contains various augmented diagrams, charts, and additional related facets of relevance.*

CHAPTER 21
TAXONOMY OF AI TECHNOLOGIES

Let's dive more deeply into the nature of AI.

AI is really two aspects at once:

1. **Seeking to have machines artificially achieve human intelligence**
2. **Do #1 via the use of various technologies (an umbrella of technologies to achieve the vaunted AI aspirations or goals)**

There is a dual notion underlying AI, namely that AI is simultaneously a goal or aspiration along with being a portfolio or collection of technologies that are being used to achieve that goal or aspiration.

Simply stated, though extremely hard to attain is the overarching goal or aspiration to devise a machine or machines that can artificially achieve the equivalent of human intelligence.

When I refer to a machine, consider that "machine" to be a computer, since computers are the most likely candidate for getting us to the artificially developed human-like intelligence.

We might someday develop something other than a computer that gets us to AI, but for now, it seems reasonable to assume that the keystone will indeed be a computer or computing machinery of one type or another.

Arriving at AI that is akin to human intelligence is a tall order. There is a Darwinian high-tech sprint (or more likely marathon) right now of humans trying to craft technologies that will achieve AI.

Some of the tech will maybe get us there, some maybe not.

Nobody yet knows.

I'll refer to the loose collection of AI-related technologies as an umbrella of such technologies and call them collectively the **AI technologies**.

Many elements within the umbrella are known by the qualities that they each contribute toward achieving AI, while some of them aren't necessarily considered on the path to AI per se and have their own path. Some experts in AI fervently believe in allowing anything and everything, inclusive of the kitchen sink, as being a proper member to be tossed into or under the umbrella, if it will somehow get us a step closer to reaching true AI.

As such, I suppose you could list not only topics traditionally found in computer science, but you can add all other sciences, such as physics, biology, chemistry, and you could include other seemingly disparate subjects, including anthropology, psychology, and so on, any of which might provide the last straw to finally help break the camel's back of achieving true AI.

Conventionally, there are some generally agreed-upon core technologies and subfields of study that seem to belong in AI-proper (meaning, the aspects most consider as distinctly AI relevant).

These are a commonly accepted list of AI technologies:

- Machine Learning (ML)
- Knowledge-Based Systems (KBS)
- Natural Language Processing (NLP)
- Computer Vision (CV)
- Robotics / Autonomy
- Common-Sense Reasoning
- Other Technologies

The "Other Technologies" allows this list to suggest that there are indeed other relevant technologies and therefore the above list is not considered exhaustive.

AI Approach: Replicate Versus Emulate

We've acknowledged that the goal of AI is to achieve a machine that artificially exhibits human intelligence, and for which we are going to then seek to maintain as a high bar that the artificially instantiated intelligence must be equivalent to the highest levels that we hold human intelligence to.

Thus, if you made a machine that was as intelligent as a rat, yes, that would helpful, but it isn't the uppermost goal that we are aiming at for AI overall. You'd have fallen short, though maybe provided a valuable steppingstone for the next level or levels of AI attainment.

Let's divide the approach to achieving true AI into two camps.

The goal of AI can be achieved by either of:

1. **Replicate:** Try to replicate how the human brain works, and therefore presumably arrive at the equivalent of human intelligence, or

2. **Emulate:** Devise some other means altogether to showcase human intelligence, doing so without actually replicating the brain.

In the replicate approach, your aim is to build a replica of the human brain, using computers to do so, and hopefully, it will produce human intelligence, and presumably human intelligence that is akin to the levels of human intelligence in everyday humans.

Notice that we're not saying that the machine is a human at that point, it is only exhibiting the same as human intelligence. Some believe that if we did achieve human intelligence in a box, maybe that entity ought to then accrue human rights.

This raises some interesting legal implications, and once again illustrates the rising importance of AI and law. The role of human rights as potentially assignable to a sentient AI is beyond the scope of the topic per se of this discussion on AI legal reasoning, though readers are encouraged to pursue the topic via the recommended readings in Appendix A.

The replicate approach seems to be somewhat promising due to the advent of Machine Learning (ML), a method of mimicking some aspects of the brain, though as we'll cover in the next chapter, we are still quite far away from achieving true human intelligence using the ML method.

One aspect to clarify here is that if true AI is indeed achieved in some machine, via the replicate approach, there would be an essential requirement that the machine is in many respects embodying the same properties of the human brain, minus necessarily being biological in the same manner as the human brain.

Some would assert that you would be simulating the brain, doing so in a likewise manner of the human brain, and therefore the "it" is not an actual brain, though perhaps an impressive imitation of it.

The emulate approach differs in that the base assumptions entail not trying to replicate the brain in any substantive way, and instead find some other altogether different means to produce the equivalent of human intelligence, potentially a radically different means.

Of these two approaches, which has a greater chance of either arriving at true AI at all or even potentially getting to true AI sooner than the other?

Some assert that you are far better off by trying to figure out how the brain works and replicate it into a machine

That seems sensible and prudent. You know that a brain is able to achieve human intelligence, therefore, you must be on the right path if you are taking the replicate approach. Also, the brain is something handily tangible that researchers can study and probe.

But, suppose there are some inscrutable secrets to the human brain that we won't be able to decipher for a thousand years, in which case, your AI is going to not result until after that thousand years mark. Or, suppose we never unravel the code of the human brain. Your AI goal won't ever be achieved, at least on the basis of the purist version of the replicate approach. Presumably, the replicate approach is dependent upon first figuring out the nature of the human brain.

The emulate camp argues that maybe we don't need to know how the brain works, or maybe we might know just enough already that it helps us part of the way toward achieving human intelligence, and yet we can come up with some other solution that drives us home the rest of the way.

Of course, the emulate approach could be heading in the wrong direction, and yet you might not know that it is. The replicate approach presumably can make direct comparisons to the base model of interest, the human brain, in an effort to gauge any gaps or misdirection.

Some believe that the emulate approach is more of a shot-in-the-dark. On the other hand, if the replicate approach does get entombed by not figuring out the human brain, perhaps the emulate approach will inexorably have the upper hand, as it were, and might leap past those that are insistent on scrutinizing one brain after another.

From the perspective of AI as applied to the law, admittedly this debate over the replicate approach versus the emulate approach is perhaps somewhat abstract, but it does possibly foretell what might need to be done to achieve AI legal reasoning.

Currently, AILR efforts are predominantly focused on employing the **emulate approach**, while relatively very few are engaged in the replicate approach.

Will the emulate approach eventually hit a roadblock and not succeed, and if so, might it turn out that only the replicate approach is the likelier means to achieve AILR?

This is an open question.

Artificial Super-Intelligence (ASI)

Do you think that humanity will be satisfied if it is possible to arrive at true AI?

Some believe that we would instinctively want to go further, going beyond the "mere" achieving of human intelligence. We might aim to achieve Super-Intelligence.

As such, we might craft **Artificial Super-Intelligence (ASI)**.

There are lots of science fiction writers that have tried to predict what an Artificial Super-Intelligence might be. Discussions about ASI are rather speculative and it is problematic to predict what an ASI might consist of, if even possible to achieve.

The point at which we achieve conventional true AI, not necessarily a super-intelligence, some predict will be accompanied by the AI system becoming sentient, and this moment of doing so is referred to as **the singularity**.

There is debate over whether true AI will necessarily be directly accompanied by sentience since perhaps true AI can be achieved without the need for being sentient. Some insist that sentience is a key element of true AI and therefore you cannot achieve true AI without also arriving at sentience. Others disagree and argue that sentience is an independent matter that does not either occur concomitantly with true AI and nor is required for and not going to particularly arise as a result of true AI.

Some also wonder if true AI might improve upon itself and go even further on its own, without the hand of mankind needed to boost it, becoming an ASI. And, furthermore, perhaps there is a super-charged version of ASI beyond some basic version of ASI, which seems plausible since there's no clear demarcation of the endpoint of ASI.

On the matter of AI legal reasoning, we return to the initial discussion in Chapter 1 about the question of whether legal reasoning is a subset of human thinking or whether it entails the full set of human thinking. This is relevant to this discussion about true AI and singularity, along with ASI, since if legal reasoning of the human mind is inextricably tied into the totality of human thinking, it would seem that no AILR of a fully or true AI legal reasoning will exist until the achievement of true AI is reached.

And, as such, the topic of AI legal reasoning then would seemingly get mired into the open-ended questions about singularity, sentience, and the other perplexing aspects about arriving at true AI.

These are somewhat philosophical considerations, and for the moment, AI legal reasoning researchers and practitioners are likely to set aside those qualms, pursuing AILR's in any case, and yet keeping a watchful eye on such vital matters.

Narrow AI

While we are on the topic of AI and the singularity, along with ASI (be forewarned that "ASI" is a rarely used abbreviation, and most just say "super-intelligence" rather than referring to the abbreviated version), it is handy to introduce some additional AI-related vocabulary.

Recall, as mentioned earlier, we are not anywhere close to achieving true AI as yet, which, as a reminder, consists of the goal of arriving at artificial human intelligence in all its respects. Meanwhile, in specific domains, there are some interesting AI applications that do well at seemingly exhibiting very narrow human-like intelligence.

Some refer to these small-scale variants of AI as "narrow AI," which is rather unfortunate and taking unfair liberty with the true AI aspirations.

You might assume that the word "narrow" means that an AI application is presumably an AI system that can do a human intelligence-based task, in its entirety, but within just a narrow domain.

Narrow actually means a lot more of narrowness than one might so assume. Present-day narrow AI applications are not at all like human intelligence and are completely lacking for example in any semblance of common-sense reasoning.

Artificial General Intelligence (AGI)

The acronym and phrase of "AI" and artificial intelligence has become so misused and overused that the duality mentioned earlier of AI is both a goal and a set of technologies has unfortunately become blurred. The blurring has led to confounding the use of AI technologies with the ability to emit or provide true AI when the reality is that the goal of true AI is still far off in the distant future.

This blurring has made it difficult for specialists within AI to refer to the goal of yet-attained true AI, and thus, there's another phrase and acronym that some like to use, namely **Artificial General Intelligence (AGI).**

AGI, for example, would include common-sense reasoning, along with whatever else is going to be needed to arrive at true AI.

Does legal reasoning require common-sense reasoning?

If the answer is yes, this then presents quite a problem, since efforts to craft AI that contains the equivalent of human common-sense reasoning has so far been incapable of arriving at such a revered target.

Within the field of AI legal reasoning, the aim has been to push forward without having AI capable common-sense reasoning, and trust for now that AILR can be achieved without such a capability or that some form of "narrow" variant of common-sense reasoning can be crafted for purposes of enabling AI legal reasoning

Intelligence Explosion

There is something else that also comes up in discussions about AI and AGI. Some like to contemplate and discuss the potential for an **intelligence explosion**.

In short, some assert that intelligence begets intelligence. The more you have of intelligence, the more it can spark additional intelligence, so some belief. If that's the case, perhaps when crafting AI, we might not need to fully do all the work ourselves, and it could be that with the right minimal amount of AI, the rest of the artificial intelligence will produce itself, doing so in a chain reaction manner.

If an intelligence explosion gets underway, and we don't know how to control it, might this be the means by which we arrive at either AI, AGI, ASI, or whatever comes after ASI?

No one knows.

Those of you that are history buffs might recall that during the making of the atomic bomb during World War II, there was concern among some of the scientists that it might start a chain reaction that would be unstoppable by human means. One theory was that the air would ignite, and this would happen rapidly, spreading around the entire globe, causing a conflagration that would wipe-out every living entity on earth.

As such, there are those in the AI field that worry that an artificial intelligence explosion could produce an intelligence that could then wipe-out humanity. This raises once again some notable AI ethics questions.

In terms of AI legal reasoning, one aspect about the prospects of an intelligence explosion is whether it might be possible to establish some kind of base or core for AI legal reasoning, and then prod the AI legal reasoning into self-improving itself, becoming more robust at AI legal reasoning on its own (without human developers having to do so).

This would be a form of self-learning, perhaps, doing so to a large-scale degree, thus averting the need for human developers to have to hand-craft into the AI system the next advances or iterations of capability at legal reasoning.

This might be likened to a kind of intelligence explosion, focused though on specifically entailing the act of legal reasoning. One perspective is that developers ought to seek out this kind of intelligence explosion, purposely seeding AILR's with this capability, while others suggest that AILR's might of their own accord trigger an intelligence explosion that furthers the AI's legal reasoning facilities.

Introduction To The AI Technologies

As earlier mentioned, here again, are the core technologies and subfields of study that seem to belong in AI-proper (meaning the aspects most people think of as AI relevant):

- Machine Learning (ML)
- Knowledge-Based Systems (KBS)
- Natural Language Processing (NLP)
- Computer Vision (CV)
- Robotics / Autonomy
- Common-Sense Reasoning
- Other Technologies

Let's use this list of core technologies and subfields as a taxonomy for AI and cover the key ones involved in AILR's.

Please be aware that there are numerous ways to categorize and produce a taxonomy of AI. Furthermore, each such approach tends to vary since it is not the same as a taxonomy of animal species or other well-specified and bounded scientific aspects.

In today's application of AI, you'll find that most AI applications tend to use only one of the AI domains or subdomains and do not oft contain the other AI domains.

For example, a legal contract analysis application that uses AI is probably using aspects of Natural Language Processing, and perhaps not any of the other AI subdomains. It is challenging to know which elements of AI are embodied in an AILR system until you ask what the AI consists of. Plus, of course, you would be wise to examine the AI under-the-hood, if feasible, in order to verify what is claimed.

A more robust use of AI would be to combine together several of the AI subdomain's capabilities. This is often referred to as an **ensemble** version of AI.

For now, let's explore each of the AI technologies separately, and then consider how they might be used in combination with each other in an ensemble manner.

Machine Learning (ML)

Machine Learning has become the most notably popular form of AI technology in recent times. Unfortunately, the wording of "machine" and "learning" suggests greater capabilities than is currently the case.

Essentially, today's ML is no more (and no less) than computational pattern matching.

For those of you that have familiarity with statistics, you can think of ML as part of the overall statistical algorithm's families of data pattern detection and identification. For example, most would include the statistical technique of linear regression as a member of the ML realm.

Though there are various conventional statistical techniques in ML, the greatest acclaim and attention has gone toward the use of Artificial Neural Networks (ANNs).

ANNs are a mathematical-based simulation of sorts, attempting to leverage the notion of neurons, and by using those simulated "neurons" in a collective way, and formed into a network or collective of them, you can do some interesting pattern detection.

Not everyone refers to the use of these computationally calculated "neurons" as Artificial Neural Networks, and instead use the easier phrase or simply "Neural Networks" to refer to such computer-based systems, though the word "artificial" is purposefully helpful since it aids in distinguishing that these are not the biological versions of neurons and neural networks.

Importantly, these simulated NN's or ANN's aren't yet anything close to what real neurons and real human-based biological neural networks are. Some hope that perhaps ultimately, we'll be able to create extremely large-scale ANNs and make them more analogous to the biological version, which might get us closer to achieving true AI (this is the replicate approach mentioned earlier).

When using an ANN that is somewhat smaller, you cannot get as much out of it in terms of the pattern matching robustness, so the notion is to increase the number of neurons (artificial or mathematically simulated neurons) and the size and potentially shape of the network (the artificial network of the artificial neurons), including how the neurons are interconnected, aiming to make the whole conglomeration larger, and potentially larger enough for improved capabilities.

To distinguish shallow or smaller ANNs from larger sets of ANNs, most refer to the larger sets as showcasing **Deep Learning (DL)**.

Deep Learning is a vague indication and there is no firmly established number of neurons or interconnections that demark the difference between lesser versions of ANN's and the "deeper" versions of ANN's.

During the earlier days of ML, much of the building of an ML involved doing computer programming from scratch and was relatively arcane to accomplish. Nowadays, there many software packages that have the ML modeling capabilities available.

Besides specialized ML software packages, most of the major statistics packages that you might already know have added many of the ML modeling constructs.

There are a variety of elements and aspects of Machine Learning that are useful to be aware of.

These are some of the more popular and significant aspects of Machine Learning:

- **ML Frameworks Used**
- **Deep Learning (DL)**
- **Artificial Neural Networks (ANN)**
- **Supervised Models**
- **Unsupervised Models**
- **Reinforcement Models**
- **Explainability (XAI)**
- **Data Requirements**
- **Training Requirements**
- **Prediction Capabilities**
- **Base Algorithms**
- **Clustering**
- **Regression**
- **Analytics**
- **Real-Time**
- **Scalability**
- **Etc.**

When you think about statistical packages, you usually right away also realize that you need to have data to be able to adequately use a statistical routine.

Any statistics class emphasizes that you need to have sufficient and proper data to calculate stats, and also need to think carefully about the nature of the data, including whether it contains inherent biases, how the data was collected, the accuracy of the data values, and so on.

All of that is the same for Machine Learning.

Unfortunately, partially since ML modeling has become so easy due to the availability of ML modeling packages, there are many that are crafting ML models that aren't particularly sound and have forgotten or neglected the basic principles espoused when undertaking proper statistical analyses and modeling.

In the case of using ML for AI legal reasoning systems, keep in mind that it is easier to use ML than might otherwise seem, but doing it properly is something that needs to be carefully ascertained.

Be wary when an AILR systems developer claims they are using ML, and make sure to find out the specifics of what they are using ML for and how it works in their system.

Natural Language Processing (NLP)

It used to be that Natural Language Processing (NLP) was relatively crudely done and didn't seem impressive, as exhibited by the ELIZA and PARRY examples in the prior chapter.

Our everyday use of Alexa and Siri are obvious examples of the use of today's NLP and serves as a showcase of the advances in NLP. That being said, if you use Alexa or Siri for any length of time, you very rapidly reach the edges of what even today's NLP can do. It doesn't take much effort to discover the brittleness and boundaries of what contemporary NLP is able to figure out.

One important aspect to keep in mind is that today's NLP does not "understand" what you are expressing.

To date, we don't really know what "understanding" consists of, at least with respect to how humans understand. There are various ways to computationally model the notion of "understanding" and that's what the advanced NLP systems do, yet it still is not the same as the human capabilities of understanding.

This list shows you some of the more popular and significant elements of NLP:

- **Classical NLP**
- **ML/DL-based NLP**
- **Domain-Specific Modeling**
- **Syntax Analysis**
- **Tokenization**
- **Stemming**
- **Lemmatization**
- **Part of Speed Tagging (POST)**
- **Named Entity Recognition (NER)**
- **Dependency Parser**
- **Intent Analysis**
- **Library Use**
- **Open Source Use**
- **Proprietary**
- **Real-Time**
- **Scalability**
- **Etc.**

One of the reasons that NLP has improved is due to the adoption of Machine Learning for the use of NLP.

Thus, there are some NLP systems that are considered classic-NLP, <u>not</u> making use of ML, while there are other NLP systems that are using Machine Learning or Deep Learning. You cannot assume that just because an NLP uses ML/DL that it is going to be better than an NLP that doesn't use ML/DL. As with anything else, it all depends upon how the ML/DL is applied to NLP.

In the use case of legal activities, the use of NLP is a popular AI add-on to many LegalTech systems [R.18].

There are numerous software packages that provide an NLP tool or capability, thus, you don't necessarily need to code NLP from scratch to apply NLP to a particular domain, and it is relatively "easy" for a LegalTech system to add a packaged NLP into their mix [R.18].

An important underpinning of any well-prepared NLP consists of its domain-related setup.

One aspect that is crucial to NLP in a particular domain is loading the NLP with the domain vocabulary and terminology, such as in legal reasoning to include a set of legal terminology and vocabulary into the NLP.

Computer Vision (CV)

Computer Vision (CV) consists of having the computer system capture images and then try to ascertain what those images consist of.

CV has come a long way over the years. This is partially due to the advances made in being able to capture images, such as better cameras and improved lenses. This is also partially due to the advances made in computer memory capacity and speed, being able to store the images in their binary format and do so inexpensively.

This is further partially due to the speed of computer processors, along with their reduction in the physical size of computing, making computers available at the point of the image capture, such as residing inside a camera, rather than having to necessarily upload the image to a larger sized computer to do image processing.

One quick example of the vast improvement in CV consists of the seemingly simple act of scanning a document. It used to be that when you scanned a document, you had a blob, and couldn't do anything with whatever text or other aspects were found in the scanned file. CV today is usually able to find and extract out the text and do the same for other sub-portions of an overall image.

Here are some of the key facets in the field of Computer Vision:

- **Object Detection**
- **Scene Detection**
- **Facial Recognition**
- **Activity Detection**
- **Feature Extraction**
- **Pattern Analysis**
- **Still Images**
- **Video**
- **Multiple Perspectives**
- **Motion Estimation**
- **Image Reconstruction**
- **Labeling**
- **Prediction**
- **Analytics**
- **Real-Time**
- **Scalability**
- **Etc.**

Conclusion

AI is really two aspects at once, namely the aspiration of achieving true artificial intelligence and meanwhile acting as a loose collection of various AI-related technologies.

In the next chapter, we'll take a closer look at the use of Machine Learning for AI legal reasoning systems.

Note: *For supplemental materials depicting the aspects discussed in this chapter, refer to Appendix B, which contains various augmented diagrams, charts, and additional related facets of relevance.*

CHAPTER 22
AI
MACHINE LEARNING

In this chapter, we will delve further into Machine Learning.

Machine Learning is a subarea of AI that makes use of various pattern detection and recognition approaches and has been a substantial reason that many contemporary AI systems are able to achieve greater accomplishments than previously was achieved.

As mentioned in the prior chapter, there is nothing magical about ML. It is a mathematical or computational approach that uses various models.

SCOTUS ML was explored as an example of ML for AI legal reasoning (see [S.8] in Appendix B, Bibliography for the source code).

Recall that SCOTUS ML used random forest trees, a statistical technique that is often listed as within the realm of ML. The SCOTUS ML system was able to predict Supreme Court outcomes and the votes of individual justices of the Supreme Court, doing so to a claimed level of around 70% accuracy [R.30].

A prior use of a simpler means of predicting Supreme Court outcomes was undertaken in 2004 by Andrew Martin, Kevin Quinn, Theodore Ruger, and Pauline Kim as described in their paper entitled "Competing Approaches to Predicting Supreme Court Decision Making" [R.35].

Using a much smaller set of Supreme Court cases, a corpus of 628 cases, this earlier work used classification trees.

As an example of the classification trees crafted as predictors, consider this tree crafted for an instance for any of Justice O'Connor cases:

Was the lower court decision liberal?

| Yes: Reverse

| No: Was the case from 2nd, 3rd, DC, or Federal Circuit?

| Yes: Affirm

| No: Is the respondent the United States?

| No: Reverse

| Yes: Is the primary issue civil rights, 1st Amendment, economic, activity, or federalism?

| No: Affirm

| Yes: Reverse

When assessing the predictive capabilities of an ML system, a comparison can be made to either other prediction-focused systems or compared to human expert opinion.

In this research study, the researchers opted to make a comparison to a selected group of legal experts.

An interesting finding was that the ML performed well for some Supreme Court justice predictions and yet performed poorly for predicting other Supreme Court justices, while the human legal experts did roughly on par with the ML and did better in some instances.

The legal experts typically appeared to do better at making predictions when the Supreme Court justices tended to be "extreme" in their views.

This result is significant not only for this particular use of ML but highlights an important point about ML overall regarding brittleness.

Brittleness of Machine Learning

Many of the ML techniques tend to be oriented toward the overall trends discovered within data and less so toward the extremes of data.

Generally, ML is often said to be **brittle or weak at the edge cases**.

Anyone familiar with performing statistical analyses has likely encountered such problems. If you are using a typical linear regression model, the outliers tend to not be accounted for suitably or are given a rather low weighting, which could set up a hidden danger that those outliers might actually be significant, though they are being relatively discounted or underweighted by the model.

ML systems can often perform in a similar manner thus you have to be quite cautious in using the ML model when the underlying data contains potential outliers or anomalies.

For any AI legal reasoning system, the implication is that any use of ML must be done with a cautionary eye about the potential underplay of any outliers or edge cases that the data was based upon.

Imagine a large corpus of law cases, and the AILR has pattern matched across those cases. Within the corpus, let's assume there are some "unusual" cases that go against the norm. The ML might treat these outliers as insignificant, and yet there might well be a chance that future cases will possibly rely upon those prior outlier edge cases.

Indeed, sometimes the edge cases reveal startling or important changes in the direction of the law [R.35].

This cautionary point needs to be kept in mind by those that use an ML-based AILR, along with emphasizing that as a design and building reminder, any developer of an AILR needs to be considering how to deal with ML brittleness issues in their AILR system.

Supervised Versus Unsupervised ML

One of the most significant choices made when leveraging Machine Learning involves whether to use a **supervised** versus an **unsupervised** approach to training the ML system.

In a paper by researcher Harry Surden in the Washington Law Review, 2014, in an article entitled "Machine Learning and the Law," highlights the tradeoffs of a supervised versus unsupervised approach for the training of AI legal reasoning systems [R.47].

Let's consider what a supervised approach of ML consists of.

When you have data that includes targets or outcomes, you can essentially have the Machine Learning model be "supervised" in the sense that it is trying to model based on given targets.

Suppose that you were trying to train a Machine Learning model to recognize cats. A supervised approach would consist of providing pictures of cats and including an indication or labeling of the cats within the images. Imagine a picture that contained a dog, a cat, and a chair. The cat portion of the picture would be labeled or outlined. In addition, the cat portion might have labels that indicate the presence of the ears of the cat, the tail of the cat, and so on.

In this manner, the ML model can try to match inputs to outputs.

The inputs are typically composed into a vector, and the outputs are considered a **supervisory signal**. The training data is arranged into **input-output pairs**.

This approach can be contrasted to an unsupervised approach to ML modeling.

We might provide pictures to an ML model and have it attempt to identify where a cat is, and what characteristics typify a cat. The ML would have to ascertain that a cat has ears, a cat has a tail, and so on.

Essentially, the ML in an unsupervised modeling approach is seeking to identify the factors or clusters that can specify a potential pattern. Usually, there are no pre-existing labels about the data. And, there is a minimum amount of human supervision over the ML modeling process, allowing the ML to essential self-model over the inputs provided.

It can be advantageous to sometimes use both methods together, which is known as **semi-supervised learning**.

AILR and Machine Learning Modeling

Let's now shift into considering how this impacts AI legal reasoning systems that use Machine Learning.

An example of a supervised learning approach might consist of first collecting together a set of employment law cases, including the legal outcomes of each case. The legal outcome could be whether the case was settled or not, and whether there was a trial or not, etc.

By providing this data into a Machine Learning model, the ML would attempt to identify how the inputs, consisting of the employment law cases, match with the stated outcomes.

In contrast, consider an unsupervised approach to training an ML model.

We might provide to a Machine Learning model a corpus of Supreme Court case outcomes and see if the ML can identify any factors or clusters that underlie those outcomes.

In a sense, the ML is trying to identify the characteristics of a cat, similar to the notion of using an unsupervised ML for analyzing pictures of cats. The ML would potentially provide statistical indications of which factors would possibly be the best predictors or that aid in identifying dimensions or factors within the dataset.

The unsupervised approach is especially used if you otherwise are unsure of what the prominent dimensions or factors are, whereas if you already contend that you know the factors and have inputs that match to outputs you would tend to use the supervised approach instead.

Cautions About Machine Learning

One of the precautions about Machine Learning that we've already explored has to do with the potential brittleness of ML and the lack of giving due consideration to edge cases.

There are additional precautions to keep in mind.

Another difficulty with ML is the **possibility of overfitting** to the training data that is being used to prepare the Machine Learning.

Suppose you provide a corpus of 20 court cases and the ML system trains to those cases.

The ML model might become relatively specific to those 20 cases, essentially overfitting to the provided data Meanwhile, if the training data had consisted of thousands of cases, perhaps the ML would be better able to generalize across the cases.

Another concern is the potential for **hidden biases** in the ML model.

Consider the predictions of Supreme Court outcomes.

Human experts predicting Supreme Court outcomes might have biases such as perhaps one expert has a "conservative" perspective and another expert has a "liberal" perspective, and therefore when making predictions their own personal biases enter into their predictions.

You could potentially interview those experts and identify such biases as elements impacting their predictions.

In the case of a Machine Learning system, you are likely to assume that the ML is inherently "unbiased" and will not carry over any semblance of bias into what it predicts (this is a **machine-bias fallacy** that most of us fall into).

Consider though that the nature of the training dataset can setup the ML to essentially contain bias. If you were to assemble court cases of a certain kind or perhaps of a particular time period, the ML would pattern across those cases and could develop essentially a "bias" based on the selected dataset.

Anyone using or relying upon the ML would be unlikely to know that such bias had been encompassed into the model, and nor even think to ask about whether bias might exist in the ML system.

Finally, another concern about many of the ML approaches is that they are not readily able to explain any kind of **logically legal merits** or reasoning for their results. As mentioned earlier, an ML will likely have some arcane or obscure mathematical basis for producing a result, and this calculation or computation is not necessarily able to be turned into something that offers a logically apparent explanation.

Thus, the ML model might innately not be able to explain the legal merits for its rendered outcome.

This will be of concern when trying to trust or believe that the results of the ML system are valid, and also undermines the ability to probe the results, plus you will be unable to readily learn from what the Machine Learning has produced.

This need for explainability is especially pronounced in the legal field since we conventionally expect that any legal reasoning effort, whether done by human lawyers or by an AI system, should be able to justify or elucidate whatever results are produced, doing so by offering a logically expounded explanation about the legal reasoning utilized.

Conclusion

This chapter has provided additional insight into the use of Machine Learning for AI legal reasoning systems.

A recurring theme has been the need to be able to have an AILR present an explanation for what it undertakes. In the next chapter, we will undertake a deeper exploration into the explainability aspects of AL legal reasoning systems.

Note: *For supplemental materials depicting the aspects discussed in this chapter, refer to Appendix B, which contains various augmented diagrams, charts, and additional related facets of relevance.*

CHAPTER 23

EXPLAINABILITY AND XAI

In this chapter, we will undertake a focus on the explainability of AI legal reasoning systems.

Within the field of AI, there is a rising interest in ensuring that AI systems can explain what they are doing or what they have done.

This subfield is often referred to as **XAI for explainable AI**.

As AI grows more widespread and enters into all facets of our lives, the embedded and oftentimes hidden algorithms within an AI system are making crucial choices, yet we might not have any ready means to interrogate the system to find out how those choices were made.

Part of the difficulty associated with making AI that is explainable or able to explain itself is that the underlying mechanism used to devise the AI might be complex mathematical computations that do not immediately translate into any logical meaning per se.

Consider the overall nature of an Artificial Neural Network (recall, ANN's were discussed in prior chapters).

If a deep neural network is used for an AI system (referred to as Deep Learning), the odds are that the mathematically composed "neurons" and their patterns do not lend themselves to any particular logical interpretation. It is to a large degree oftentimes a morass that in a computational manner seems to be able to model data and do so in oftentimes compelling ways.

Another reason besides the underlying cryptic or calculative hindrance or inscrutability entails the simple fact that there can be a substantial added effort in including an explainability capability.

There is typically an added cost and potential delay in designing, building, and fielding an AI system if there is a desire to include an explainability capability. Unless the end-user of the AI system seemingly demands or requires an XAI, there is little incentive to expend the extra needed effort and cost.

There are some that predict we will gradually see a spate of new regulations about AI that will require AI systems to be able to do XAI. This might arise as a backlash by the public when confronting enigmatic AI systems that won't explain why they have turned down say a loan application or refused to approve a medical procedure that someone has requested.

In a notable paper on the importance of explainability in AI and Law, Bernhard Waltl and Roland Vogl point out that XAI is crucial to the future of legal informatics [R.50], highlighting the challenges and opportunities in encompassing explainability into the advent and use of AILR's.

Framework of XAI

An incisive way to establish the range of explainability features that we might want an AI system to provide has been depicted in a framework provided by Zachary Lipton [R.34] and can be envisioned as a framework tree.

Here is the framework tree:

- **Transparency**
    - Simulatability
    - Decomposability
    - Algorithmic Transparency
- **Interpretability**
    - Textual Descriptions
    - Visualizations
    - Local Explanations
    - Examples

Let's unpack each of the elements of the framework.

Transparency: Simulatability

Within the aspects of transparency, one vital capability is **simulatability.**

The core concept underlying simulatability is whether or not a human can conceive of the approach that the AI system has undertaken, and essentially "simulate" in their own human mind the process that is being used by the AI.

For example, a rules-based system might be considered more accommodating to simulatability, since a human can presumably inspect the rules and then in their own mind walk-through the rules to ascertain how the AI reached a given result (even if the AI system itself does not display the rules used during the actual AI processing).

Of course, if the number of rules rises into the many hundreds or thousands of such rules being used in an AI system, it becomes less likely that the human could mentally conceive of all of those rules and their interactions. Thus, there is a presumed limit to even the more seemingly transparent aspects of using rules.

If the AI is using a deep neural network, and even if the end-user is told or shown the mathematical values of the neural network, this does not usually lend itself to simulatability, due to the aspect that there is often no semblance of a logical nature in being able to contemplate how the AI is deriving a result.

The exception to the opaqueness of a neural network might be if the neural network can be logically divided into portions that one might ascribe to having some kind of logical overarching purposes.

For example, a neural network that is constructed for NLP purposes might have one portion that does the analysis of individual words, while another portion considers the use of words as composed within sentences and yet another portion that deals with multiple sentences composed into paragraphs.

Thus, if a Machine Learning model is using artificial neural networks, it is conceivable that the designer of the ML might intentionally devise such a set of components or might via reverse engineering reach the logical notion that those components exist.

This leads us to the next topic of transparency, namely decomposability.

Transparency: Decomposability

If an AI system can be depicted in a decomposed manner, it could help toward understanding the logical aspects of how the AI is arriving at a result.

The example that described a neural network devised for NLP and for which it decomposes paragraphs into sentences, sentences into words, and has ANN portions that deal with each of the decomposable parts provides an added possibility of having some modicum of transparency.

That being said, if the **decomposability** is a derivative artifact that does not relate directly to the inner workings of the AI, it undercuts the presumed or potential transparency. In essence, suppose the developer offered an explanation for how the AI system worked, and yet it wasn't the actual manner in which the AI was functioning.

Though having some kind of explanation might be helpful, a fabricated explanation is less satisfactory and obviously might not truly pertain to what the AI system has been devised to do.

Transparency: Algorithmic Transparency

Suppose the algorithm being used in an AI system is not transparent per se, such as a deep neural network that we might assume is a collection of artificial neurons for which there is no particular explanation viable of what it represents.

Besides not having the AI be able to explain itself, there is another form of lack of transparency, referred to as **algorithmic transparency**, wherein we might not be informed as to what algorithm at all is being used in the AI system.

For example, there are dozens of different kinds of neural network approaches, and thus, when an AI system is purported to be using a neural network, it would be helpful to provide at least transparency to the degree that the specific kind of neural network is divulged to those using or dependent upon the AI system.

In other cases, a developer of an AI legal reasoning system might insist that the algorithm being used is a proprietary one, and they will not reveal anything whatsoever about the nature of the algorithm.

This would then undermine the potential transparency of the AI system and any end-user utilizing such an AILR should take into account the lack of transparency as a precautionary consideration in using or relying upon the particular AILR.

Interpretability

For XAI, the **interpretability** refers to how the explanatory display or report is portrayed to the end-user of the AI system.

In the case of a rules-based AILR, the rules themselves might be displayed, allowing the end-user to consider the performed rules as the "explanation" for how the AI system reached a particular outcome or conclusion.

If the rules themselves are encoded within the AI system in a manner not readily readable by end-users, the AI system might have text passages associated with each of the rules, and then display the textual aspects, rather than displaying the actual rules themselves.

Though, as earlier mentioned, whenever the explanation itself is once or twice removed from the actual manner in which the AI is devising its results, there is a possibility that the second-hand explanation is not accurately or aptly depicting what the AI actually instantiated during its processing.

In the case of displaying text that was crafted and assigned to the rules by a developer, the question arises as to whether the text descriptions are apt. It is possible that the text descriptions are afield of what the rules actually indicated.

Besides textual displays for explanatory purposes, another valuable way to provide an explanation is via a visualization.

A visual portrayal as a graph, chart, figure, or even an animation might be a viable explanatory mechanism for the AI processing aspects.

Consider that if a rules-based AI system has hundreds or thousands of rules that are executed over the course of reaching an outcome, having all of those rules flatly listed out might not be especially helpful in understanding what took place, due to the voluminous nature of the explanation.

A visualization might provide a graph of the rules used and portray a higher-level perspective, along with the ability to drill-down within the graph to look at specific rules that were invoked.

Another valuable way to explain an AI system result would be to have the system be decomposed into global and local areas of the inner workings, allowing again a drill-down that might get at the core of what the outcome produced.

Finally, another helpful form of explanation for interpretability involves the production of examples.

When a human lawyer explains a legal case, they might do so by offering an example of how the case applies to something else that is more easily understood. Once establishing that base, the explanation about the actual case might be easier to grasp.

In a similar manner, an AI legal reasoning system might be set up with the capability to produce simple examples that highlight the logic used to solve a given case.

Including XAI into AILR

As might be evident, the addition or inclusion of XAI into an AILR will potentially cause added effort and cost during the design and development of the AILR.

To provide the facets of transparency such as simulatability, decomposability, and algorithmic transparency takes added effort.

Similarly, so does extra effort need to occur to have interpretability such as textual descriptions, visualizations, local explanations, and the ability to produce examples.

Generally, the overall design of the AILR needs to have such aspects envisioned at the start of the effort, during its initial design, as it is unlikely that on an after-the-fact basis those explanatory elements could be readily retrofitted into the AI system.

Importantly, if the only means to gain use and acceptance of an AILR is via it having an explanatory capability, this would presumably encourage or spur the development of the AILR to include explainability, despite an added cost or delay in doing so.

Notably, as long as those that use an AILR are satisfied to do so without any explainability, and if there's no mandated requirement, there would seem to be little impetus to include it.

Conclusion

Some would argue that any bona fide AI legal reasoning system must have some form of explainability included.

This though might be a desire that doesn't have any teeth to it. Thus, those such proponents would likely urge that any AILR that is intended for actual legal practice should be legally mandated to have an explainability feature be included in the AI system. This requirement might be promulgated by some appropriate legal licensing body.

One last comment in that regard.

It is one thing to claim that explainability is included, and another altogether to have an explainability capability that is useful and apt.

For example, suppose that an AILR that used an artificial neural network was able to provide the mathematical values of the neural network. The developers would presumably "claim" that the AILR does have an explanatory capability and therefore fulfills any such requirement.

This though would hardly seem to be in the spirit of what explainability is about.

As such, some believe that an industry-wide AI legal reasoning standard should be proposed and set into use about what is considered explanatory for XAI and an AILR. A rating or scoring system might be used, allowing then an indication that a particular AILR achieved an XAI rating of some designated level.

Note: *For supplemental materials depicting the aspects discussed in this chapter, refer to Appendix B, which contains various augmented diagrams, charts, and additional related facets of relevance.*

CHAPTER 24
LEGAL IMPLICATIONS OF AI LEGAL REASONING

AI legal reasoning has the potential to upend the nature of law and undoubtedly the practice of law.

In this chapter, we'll examine some of the implications of AI legal reasoning and how our society might change as a result of the creation of AI legal reasoning systems.

Should Law Be Forced To Fit To AI

Right now, the capabilities of AI legal reasoning systems are rather simplistic and at best are serving as an aid to those that practice law.

If AI legal reasoning systems continue to advance, and if they gradually approach some level between semi-autonomous and fully autonomous, we could find ourselves grappling with how such systems alter the way we perceive laws and the act of practicing law.

Consider this famous quote by Montesquieu (1748), in De l'Esprit des Lois [C.10]:

> "Thus when a man takes on absolute power, he first thinks of simplifying the law. In such a state one begins to be more affected by technicalities than by the freedom of the people, about which one no longer cares at all."

In the quote, there is a raised concern of mankind taking on absolute power and opting therefore to simplify the law.

This simplification, in turn, might lead to law that no longer affords the freedoms that we enjoy and could become stagnant and stifling.

Substitute into that proviso the idea of AI legal reasoning and whether widespread adoption of either nearly autonomous or fully autonomous AI legal reasoning systems might prod us toward a simplification of the law.

And, if so, would we suffer the fate as implied by Montesquieu?

At first glance, you might think that the notion of simplifying the law doesn't necessarily comport with the advent of AI legal reasoning.

It could be the case that we might have law that is even more flexible and accommodating due to the use of such automation, and not necessarily that the law would somehow become stilted via the advent of AILR.

Though, there are perhaps some potential signs of the possibility of a stagnating outcome, as mentioned next.

There are some AILR developers that lament the chaotic and ill-defined open-ended nature of today's laws and point out that if we as a society could simply nail-down the laws and make them more specific and determinate, it would be much easier to develop and field AI legal reasoning systems.

This seems like a "reasonable" call for easing the burden on developing AILR's.

Is that really what's needed to achieve AI legal reasoning?

Some belief so, others vehemently disagree.

Those that disagree are apt to counterargue that AI needs to fit law, rather than trying to make law fit AI.

In other words, improve the capabilities of AI to cope with the uncertainties and indeterminate nature of law, rather than turning the matter on its head and trying to force-fit law into whatever AI today can do.

One must also question fundamentally whether it makes sense to change law and the nature of law solely to allow for an easier effort to codify law and craft AI legal reasoning systems. Presumably, there might be some merits in doing so, and additional qualities might accrue as a result of other intended and unintended consequences, but if one considers this on a societal cost-benefit basis, it seems not readily able to pass a reasonableness test.

Judges And AI

Let's shift now to another implication about AI legal reasoning.

If AI legal reasoning systems become lawyers, what happens to judges?

One approach would be to continue to keep human judges in their present roles, retaining the human quality of judging and perhaps serving as a kind of humanity-based check-and-balance on the AI legal reasoning systems.

That's one way to proceed.

Lasswell in 1955 predicted this [R.32]:

> "When machines are more prefect [sic] a bench of judicial robots … can be constructed. The machine would apply a system of "weights" to allegations of fact made by parties to a controversy, and also to the justifications advanced in support of the claims put forward by participants. Litigation can proceed by counsel for the plaintiff and defendant pressing buttons that translate their cases into the physical signs built into the machine. Many results would be "no decision." However, the machine could be designed to settle a controversy of this kind with a "random" operation (by a lot)."

Before you start to criticize the portrayal of "judicial robots" in the quotation, let's remember that the statement was made in the 1950s and thus quite prior to the advances in AI that we have today. As such, set aside the somewhat unrefined depiction of what the judicial AI might consist of.

Assume instead that the AI legal reasoning of the future, presuming it was already the equivalent of human lawyers, could be just as capable at judging as it were at being a practicing lawyer.

One could debate whether the same kind of AILR capacity required for being a lawyer is the same as that required to be a judge, in which case, it could be that we might have AILR's for serving as lawyers but not yet advanced AILR's to be capable as judges, but assume that with further advances in AI that the AILR as the judge became viable.

Would we be contented with AI legal reasoning lawyers and AI legal reasoning judges, thus excising any direct human involvement in the jurisprudence matters at hand?

Some might argue that perhaps this would indeed be preferred, allowing the entire stream of legal resolution activities to be presumably undertaken without the intrusion of human biases.

This seems appealing in some simplistic way, though keep in mind, as mentioned earlier about AI and Machine Learning, it is not the case that you can assume that all biases have been eradicated simply due to the advent of AILR.

Petrification Of Law

If there were AILR's serving as both lawyers and as judges, there is another concern that dovetails into the earlier point about the law becoming potentially stagnant.

According to James Popple, he offers this concern [R.40]:

> "The idea of a judgment machine removing uncertainty and ambiguity in the law raises the possibility of the petrifaction of the law. This possibility is also relevant to legal expert system design. D'Amato claims that, once programmed, the law would become settled. The computer would stop "progress," although the legislature could always step in if anomalous results were being produced."

In short, some suggest that law could inevitably become fossilized or ossified and that after being placed into AILR's, the whole matter is essentially petrified or frozen in place.

This might seem like an evidentiary logical conclusion if you believe that AI is going to be some kind of automata that is unchanging.

But this is actually not what most in AI would conceive as the goal of AI. If AI is aiming to be the equivalent of human intelligence, we don't today wring our hands that human intelligence is somehow becoming fossilized or petrified.

In other words, this worry about the AILR somehow leading to ossification is based on a false or misleading presumption that the only way to get AILR to occur would be by forcing law into becoming so.

A more expansive view would be that the AILR's would continue to struggle with the ongoing push and pull of changes in law, just as human lawyers and human judges do.

Unless you can somehow foresee the coming point of wherein human lawyers and human judges would land on ossification of law, a rather doubtful proposition, there seems little basis to assume that AI legal reasoning systems would entail that kind of petrification.

Legal Creativity Purview

Consider the role of creativity and thinking outside-the-box as to the practicing of law.

It is taken as a base assumption that a practicing attorney will bring to the legal act a sense of innovativeness and not somehow mindlessly or in a rote manner perform their work, though this can be highly variable as to those that might be inclined toward keeping strictly to the case that they are undertaking and not be able to avail themselves of looking outward or elsewhere for added inspiration.

Recall the famous case of a young Abraham Lincoln in his role as defending Duff Armstrong on charges of murder in an Illinois courtroom in 1858 [C.14]. Charles Allen, the key eyewitness to the killing, testified that he saw Duff use a striking blow to kill the victim. Upon cross-examination, Lincoln sought details from the eyewitness, extracting from Charles that he was 150 feet away from the killing, the time was approximately 11 p.m. at night, and that despite the darkness he was able to witness the act due to the light of the moon.

It seems that Lincoln then set a trap for the eyewitness, asking repeatedly about the visibility during the enveloped darkness, and for which the eyewitness insisted that the moon was shining brightly and positioned high in the sky.

If you've ever seen the classic movie "Young Mr. Lincoln" (1939), you know what essentially happened next (though the movie dramatized the case and changed many aspects of the case).

During a recess in the trial, Lincoln purportedly walked over to a nearby drugstore, purchased a copy of the 1857 Almanac, and went back to the courtroom and sought to have it entered into evidence, which the judge allowed. The reason Lincoln did so was to cite that on the evening in question, the moon was apparently in its first quarter and had set at just a few minutes after midnight, as such, this seemed to "contradict" the claims of the eyewitness.

The action by Lincoln is often portrayed as the sole basis for the jury later providing a full acquittal, but some assert that there were other factors involved too [C.14]. Nonetheless, it is heralded as one of those Perry Mason moments in the history of American jurisprudence.

Let's consider how this instance of Lincoln seemingly winning his case applies to the advent of AI legal reasoning systems.

First, in the trial, there wasn't any specific indication or direct contention about the moon and the moonlight, thus, would an AI system that say was conducting such a case have been able to make the kind of "mental leap" that Lincoln tied together, namely the veracity of the witness and the claims of the late-night illumination as a factor in his testimony?

One viewpoint would be that an AI system would not have such a creative or outside-the-box capacity, and therefore would be unable or "inept" at making such connections. On the other hand, you could argue that the AI might actually do as good or even a better job of this, overall, since presumably, it would have access to voluminous information of all kinds, such as an almanac (though, not quite so valued in today's era), and thus it could be looking nearly incessantly for any such advantageous connected elements.

Literal Or Myopic Legal Interpretations

This discussion about creativity is a bridge to another side of the coin, consisting of literal or myopic interpretation of language.

In "The Path of the Law" (1897) [R.29], consider this comment about churns:

> "One mark of a great lawyer is that he sees the application of the broadest rules. There is a story of a Vermont justice of the peace before whom a suit was brought by one farmer against another for breaking a churn. The justice took time to consider and then said that he has looked through the statutes and could find nothing about churns and gave judgment for the defendant. The same state of mind is shown in all our common digests and textbooks. Applications of rudimentary rules of contract or tort are tucked away under the head of Railroads or Telegraphs or go to swell treatises on historical subdivisions, such as Shipping or Equity, or are gathered under an arbitrary title which is thought likely to appeal to the practical mind, such as Mercantile Law. If a man goes into law it pays to be a master of it, and to be a master of it means to look straight through all the dramatic incidents and to discern the true basis for prophecy."

Some contend that an AI legal reasoning system would fall into the "churn" trap by only considering the words directly being employed in a case. Thus, the AI would search for any specific reference to the word "churns" and if finding none, would potentially falter due to taking a strict or myopic interpretation, being mired in a form of literalism.

The counterargument is that an AILR of such a literal "mindedness" would likely not pass muster as being viable for practicing law, to begin with, since so much of the legal task involves coping with the semantically indeterminate elements (per Chapter 2).

Legal Malpractice of AI

In this futuristic look at what might happen due to the advent of AI legal reasoning, it is easy at times to idealistically assume that the AILR's will always be right and proper, if once so invented.

We certainly don't assume that human lawyers will always be right and proper. Thus, if the AILR's are essentially the equivalent of human lawyers, we might be mistaken to make the assumption that such AI systems will always be right and proper.

When human lawyers fail to do the right thing, they are subject to malpractice provisions. Per the ABA on the topic of malpractice by lawyers, consider these aspects [C.2]:

> "Of all the malpractice errors that lawyers can commit, what is the most common one? If your answer is a failure to know or apply substantive law, you are correct. Also, intentional wrongs constitute 12.3 percent of claims. Intentional wrongs include fraudulent acts by the lawyer, malicious prosecution or abuse of process, libel or slander, and violations of civil rights."

This point about human legal malpractice brings up some intriguing considerations about AI legal reasoning:

- ➔ **Would it be possible for an AILR to fail to know or apply substantive law?**

The answer is presumably yes, it could happen. We cannot make an assumption that an AILR will be all-knowing.

- ➔ **Would it be possible for an AILR to commit an "intentional" wrong?**

Intentional wrongs as listed by the ABA quotation include acts such as malicious prosecution, abuse of process, libel or slander, and violation of civil rights. The answer is presumably yes, AILR's could commit such wrongs, though the question of "intent" is a rather significant twist.

➔ What is meant by intent when the matter is undertaken by an AI legal reasoning system?

If the AILR has developed a capacity that leads it toward committing wrongful acts, would this be considered intentional, or might we reserve intentionality as something that only humans can possess? Some would argue that intentionality is wrapped into the notion of being sentient, and we aren't necessarily saying that an AILR has to be sentient in order to be able to undertake the duties and activities of AI legal reasoning (see discussion in Chapter 21).

In any case, the overall point does raise the specter that we would need to have some means of coping with AILR's that are suspected of committing malpractice and have provisions or contingencies to cope with such acts.

Conclusion

There is an abundance of implications that arise from the possibility of autonomous AI legal reasoning systems. It might seem a bit presumptuous to start tackling those concerns now, given that they are not yet overtly arising per se, but they do have a direct bearing on today's AILR efforts and what the future portends.

In short, the design, crafting, and application of AILR's will inexorably reveal these stated qualms, and rather than waiting until the horse is out of the barn, there is prudence in trying to anticipate and adapt at the front-end of the pending evolution.

Note: *For supplemental materials depicting the aspects discussed in this chapter, refer to Appendix B, which contains various augmented diagrams, charts, and additional related facets of relevance.*

CHAPTER 25

RESEARCH FRAMEWORK OF AI LEGAL REASONING

In this chapter, let's consider the overall nature of research that is occurring in the realm of AI legal reasoning.

Besides characterizing the AILR efforts at a macroscopic level, it will be useful to consider the future direction of such research too.

As earlier pointed out, various AI technologies have been applied to selected legal domains or subdomains, typically done on an opportunistic basis. By opportunistic, it is meant that the researchers opted to choose a legal domain that perchance was convenient to their effort and opted to choose an aspect of AI that was perchance of interest to them too.

Thus, we have two elements that are being combined, namely the field of AI and the field of law.

Next, let's take a deeper analysis of this combination.

Combinations of AI and Legal Reasoning

When referring to legal domains and subdomains, there is a wide variety of approaches that can be taken toward categorizing law. Let's adopt herein a commonly accepted list of the domains and subdomains of law, for ease of discussion.

Legal domains can include but are not limited to these:

- Animal law
- Admiralty law
- Bankruptcy law
- Banking law
- Civil Rights law
- Constitutional law
- Corporate law
- Criminal law
- Education law
- Entertainment law
- Employment law
- Environmental law
- Family law
- Health law
- Immigration law
- International law
- IP law
- Military law
- Personal injury law
- Real Estate law
- Tax law
- Etc.

The list of legal domains and subdomains is not exhaustive and could be further expanded.

Also, the list is shown in alphabetical order simply for ease of referral.

The list of AI technologies consists of these major categories:

- Machine Learning (ML)
- Knowledge-Based Systems (KBS)
- Natural Language Processing (NLP)
- Computer Vision (CV)
- Robotics/Autonomy
- Common-Sense Reasoning
- Other Technologies

In a manner of speaking, you could consider these now two lists as providing a menu for use in a restaurant, allowing us to specify an item from one list and an item from the other list.

AILR Research Approach #1: Pick One of Each

The base or fundamental level of performing AI legal reasoning research consists of picking one element from the AI technologies list and picking one item from the legal domains list.

For example, choosing to use NLP (an AI technology) in the legal domain of Intellectual Property (IP) law (a legal domain) is a "pick one" approach.

AILR Research Approach #2: Pick Two in AI, One in Law

At the next level of AI legal reasoning research, a choice is made of two or more AI technologies and then just one item from the legal domain list.

For example, the use of Machine Learning and NLP, coupled together in some manner for application to Tax law.

Domains and Subdomains

Usually, when selecting a legal domain, the researchers will choose a subdomain, or perhaps a subdomain within a subdomain, trying to narrow the scope of the legal area to something more manageable when trying to develop a prototype AILR.

Likewise, the researchers are likely to do the same within the AI technologies. When using Machine Learning, we've seen that the SCOTUS ML opted to use random forest trees, which could be considered one subdomain within ML.

Starting Points

In the case of choosing a particular legal subdomain, there is an argument to be made that the choice of a specific legal subdomain might not reveal the generic aspects needed to scale-up to other legal domains and thus not provide a generalizable approach to AILR.

Thus, some urge that an AILR research effort start with a generic legal domain approach, and then refocus the generalizable into a specific legal subdomain for demonstration or illustrative purposes.

In any case, there is an ongoing debate as to whether to start with something specific and then aim to shift toward something generic or start with a generic emphasis and then transform into specific subdomains.

AILR Research Approach #3: Pick Two (plus) of Each

Ideally, it might be preferred to select two or more AI technologies <u>and</u> select two or more legal domains when crafting an AI legal reasoning system.

Doing so would seemingly lead to a more robust solution.

Unfortunately, this can also lead to an effort that falls into the research trap of trying to a bite off more than can be chewed. The complexities of using multiple AI technologies offers its own difficulties when undertaking any kind of AI research. Likewise, there are inherent difficulties in coping with multiple legal domains.

Those difficulties can make the AILR research effort become more arduous, lengthy, and perhaps "riskier" in terms of being able to provide substantive results and might falter midway of the effort. Nonetheless, it can be argued that without such AILR research entailing those complexities, demonstrative progress in the field of AI legal reasoning might proceed at a lessened pace.

ALIR DAI and Legal Reasoning

On the topic of choosing multiple AI technologies, there's an additional consideration. As mentioned previously, there is an area of AI known as Distributed AI (DAI). The focus of DAI involves dealing with multiple AI systems that are interacting with each other, encompassing considerations around coordination, cooperation, contentions, and so on.

In the case of AILR's, it is likely that AILR's will have distinct specialties, and thus there will be a need for them to interact with each other, operating in a DAI manner. This is a relatively untouched area of AI legal reasoning and offers substantial opportunities for new research.

That being said, much about DAI is still unsettled, thus, it can be difficult to decide how to use DAI in a legal context, and any such research is likely to be contending with the unknowns associated with the still being explored field of DAI.

Conclusion

This is the last chapter of this book, and if you have further interest in these topics, please take a moment to read through the Appendices, which offer suggestions and pointers on continuing your pursuit of AI legal reasoning aspects.

A few final comments to provide some conclusionary remarks. As Lewis Carroll indicated in *Alice's Adventures in Wonderland* (dated 1865) [C.4]:

> "Fury said to a mouse, That he met in the house,
> 'Let us both go to law; I will prosecute you,
> Come, I'll take no denial: We must have the trial;
> For really this morning I've nothing to do.'
> Said the mouse to the cur, 'Such a trial, dear sir,
> With no jury or judge, would be wasting our breath.'
> 'I'll be judge, I'll be jury,' said cunning old Fury;
> 'I'll try the whole cause, and condemn you to death.'

This poetic or prophetic thought reminds us that we need to be careful of aiming to have AI legal reasoning systems that might end-up being our lawyers, judges, and jury, since in so doing, we might find ourselves having gored ourselves onto our own petard, as it were.

Speaking of poetry, here's an infamous William Shakespeare quote from Henry VI, Part 2 (dated 1591) [C.13]: "The first thing we do, let's kill all the Lawyers."

Some worry that we'll be in an even worse spot if we end-up having AI lawyers (and no human lawyers), thus, the line might need to be adjusted to modern times as the first thing we do is "kill" all the AI lawyers, if a dystopian result has occurred.

This is not to suggest that we should be avoiding or averting the pursuit of AI legal reasoning. Not at all. As with any new innovation and advancement, let's make sure to keep our eyes open and ensure that the societal implications are given their due and considered as essential and integral to the otherwise efforts underway.

Note: *For supplemental materials depicting the aspects discussed in this chapter, refer to Appendix B, which contains various augmented diagrams, charts, and additional related facets of relevance.*

APPENDIX A
TEACHING WITH THIS MATERIAL AND BIBLIOGRAPHY

The material in this book can be readily used either as a supplemental to other content for a class, or it can also be used as a core set of textbook material for a specialized class.

Classes, where this material is most likely used, include any classes at the college or university level that want to augment the class by offering thought-provoking and educational essays about AI and Law.

In particular, here are some typical settings that might apply:

- Computer Science. Classes studying AI, or possibly a CS social impacts class, etc.

- Law. Law classes exploring technology and its adoption for legal uses.

- Sociology. Sociology classes on the adoption and advancement of technology.

Specialized classes at the undergraduate and graduate level can also make use of this material.

For each chapter, consider whether you think the chapter provides material relevant to your course topic.

There are plenty of opportunities to get the students thinking about the topics and encourage them to decide whether they agree or disagree with the points offered and positions taken.

I would also encourage you to have the students do additional research beyond the chapter material presented (I provide next some suggested assignments that they can do).

RESEARCH ASSIGNMENTS ON THESE TOPICS

Your students can find research and background material on these topics, doing so in various tech journals, law journals, and other related publications.

Here are some suggestions for homework or projects that you could assign to students:

a) Assignment for foundational AI research topics: Research and prepare a paper and a presentation on a specific aspect of AI, such as Machine Learning, ANN, etc. The paper should cite at least 3 reputable sources. Compare and contrast to what has been stated in this book.

b) Assignment for Law topics: Research and prepare a paper covering Law aspects via at least 3 reputable sources and analyze the characterizations. Compare and contrast to what has been stated in this book.

c) Assignment for a Business topic: Research and prepare a paper and a presentation on businesses and advanced technology regarding AI and Law. What is trending, and why? Make sure to cite at least 3 reputable sources. Compare and contrast to the depictions herein.

d) Assignment to do a Startup: Have the students prepare a paper or business plan about how they might start up a business in this realm. They could also be asked to present their business plan and should also have a prepared presentation deck to coincide with it.

You can certainly adjust the aforementioned assignments to fit your particular needs and class structure.

You'll notice that I usually suggest that (at least) 3 reputable cited sources be utilized for the paper writing-based assignments.

I usually steer students toward "reputable" publications, since otherwise, they will cite some less reliable sources that have little or no credentials, other than that they happened to appear online was easy to retrieve. You can, of course, define "reputable" in whatever way you prefer, for example some faculty think Wikipedia is not reputable while others believe it is reputable and allow students to cite it.

The reason that I usually ask for at least 3 citations is that if the student only relies upon one or two citations, they usually settle on whatever they happened to find the fastest. By requiring 3 (or more) citations, it usually seems to force them to explore more extensively and likely end-up finding five or more sources, and then whittling it down to 3 if so needed.

I have not specified the length of their papers and leave that to you to tell the students what you prefer.

For each of those assignments, you could end up with a short one to two-pager or you could do a dissertation length in-depth paper. Base the length on whatever best fits for your class, and likewise the credit amount of the assignment within the context of the other grading metrics you'll be using for the class.

I usually try to get students to present their work, in addition to doing the writing. This is a helpful practice for what they will do in the business world. Most of the time, they will be required to prepare an analysis and present it. If you don't have the class time or inclination to have the students present, then you can omit the aspect of them putting together presentations.

GUIDE TO USING THE CHAPTERS

For each of the chapters, I provide the next some various ways to use the chapter contents.

You can assign the below tasks as individual homework assignments, or the tasks can be used for team projects. You can easily layout a series of assignments, such as indicating that the students are to do item "a" below for say Chapter 1, then "b" for the next chapter of the book, and so on.

a) What is the main point of the chapter and describe in your own words the significance of the topic.

b) Identify at least two aspects in the chapter that you agree with and support your concurrence by providing at least one other outside researched item as support; make sure to explain your basis for agreeing with the aspects.

c) Identify at least two aspects in the chapter that you disagree with and support your disagreement by providing at least one other outside researched item as support; make sure to explain your basis for disagreeing with the aspects.

d) Find an aspect that was not covered extensively in the chapter, doing so by conducting outside research, and then offer an expanded indication about how that aspect ties into the chapter, along with the added significance it brings to the topic.

e) Interview a specialist in industry about the topic of the chapter, collect from them their thoughts and opinions, and readdress the chapter by citing your source and how they compared and contrasted to the material,

f) Interview a relevant professor or researcher in a college or university setting about the topic of the chapter, collect from them their thoughts and opinions, and readdress the chapter by citing your source and how they compared and contrasted to the material,

g) Try to update a chapter by finding out the latest on the topic and ascertain whether the issue or topic has now been solved or whether it is still being addressed, explain what you come up with.

The above are all ways in which you can get the students of your class involved in considering the material of a given chapter. You could mix things up by having one of those above assignments per each week, covering the chapters over the course of the semester or quarter.

BIBLIOGRAPHY

References

Indicated as [R.n] in the chapters

1. Aleven, Vincent (1997). "Teaching Case-Based Argumentation Through a Model and Examples," Ph.D. Dissertation, University of Pittsburgh.

2. Aleven, Vincent (2003). "Using Background Knowledge in Case-Based Legal Reasoning: A Computational Model and an Intelligent Learning Environment," Artificial Intelligence.

3. Amgoud, Leila (2012). "Five Weaknesses of ASPIC+," Volume 299, Communications in Computer and Information Science (CCIS).

4. Antonious, Grigoris, and George Baryannis, Sotiris Batsakis, Guido Governatori, Livio Robaldo, Givoanni Siragusa, Ilias Tachmazidis (2018). "Legal Reasoning and Big Data: Opportunities and Challenges," August 2018, MIREL Workshop on Mining and Reasoning Legal Texts.

5. Ashley, Kevin (1991). "Reasoning with Cases and Hypotheticals in HYPO," Volume 34, International Journal of Man-Machine Studies.

6. Ashley, Kevin, and Karl Branting, Howard Margolis, and Cass Sunstein (2001). "Legal Reasoning and Artificial Intelligence: How Computers 'Think' Like Lawyers," Symposium: Legal Reasoning and Artificial Intelligence, University of Chicago Law School Roundtable.

7. Baker, Jamie (2018). "A Legal Research Odyssey: Artificial Intelligence as Disrupter," Law Library Journal.

8. Batsakis, Sotiris, and George Baryannis, Guido Governatori, Illias Tachmazidis, Grigoris Antoniou (2018). "Legal Representation and Reasoning in Practice: A Critical Comparison," Volume 313, Legal Knowledge and Information Systems.

9. Bench-Capon, Trevor (2004). "AGATHA: Automation of the Construction of Theories in Case Law Domains," January 2004, Legal Knowledge and Information Systems Jurix 2004, Amsterdam.

10. Bench-Capon, Trevor (2012). "Representing Popov v Hayashi with Dimensions and Factors," March 2012, Artificial Intelligence and Law.

11. Bench-Capon, Trevor and Givoanni Sartor (2003). "A Model of Legal Reasoning with Cases Incorporating Theories and Values," November 2013, Artificial Intelligence.

12. Breuker, Joost (1996). "A Functional Ontology of Law," October 1996, ResearchGate.

13. Bruninghaus, Stefanie, and Kevin Ashley (2003). "Combining Case-Based and Model-Based Reasoning for Predicting the Outcome of Legal Cases," June 2003, ICCBR'03: Proceedings of the 5th International Conference on Case-based reasoning: Research and Development.

14. Buchanan, Bruce, and Thomas Headrick (1970). "Some Speculation about Artificial Intelligence and Legal Reasoning," Volume 23, Stanford Law Review.

15. Chagal-Feferkorn, Karni (2019). "Am I An Algorithm or a Product: When Products Liability Should Apply to Algorithmic Decision-Makers," Stanford Law & Policy Review.

16. Douglas, William (1948). "The Dissent: A Safeguard of Democracy," Volume 32, Journal of the American Judicature Society.

17. Dung, P, and R. Kowalski, F. Toni (2006). "Dialectic Proof Procedures for Assumption-Based Admissible Argumentation," Artificial Intelligence.

18. Eliot, Lance (2020). Artificial Intelligence and LegalTech Essentials. LBE Press Publishing.

19. Eliot, Lance (2020). "FutureLaw 2020 Showcases How Tech is Transforming The Law, Including the Impacts of AI," April 16, 2020, Forbes.

20. Erdem, Esra, and Michael Gelfond, Nicola Leone (2016). "Applications of Answer Set Programming," AI Magazine.

21. Gardner, Anne (1987). Artificial Intelligence and Legal Reasoning. MIT Press.

22. Genesereth, Michael (2009). "Computational Law: The Cop in the Backseat," Stanford Center for Legal Informatics, Stanford University.

23. Ghosh, Mirna (2019). "Automation of Legal Reasoning and Decision Based on Ontologies," Normandie Universite.

24. Grabmair, Matthias (2017). "Predicting Trade Secret Case Outcomes using Argument Schemes and Learned Quantitative Value Effect Tradeoffs," IJCAI June 12, 2017, London, United Kingdom.

25. Hage, Jaap (1996). "A Theory of Legal Reasoning and a Logic to Match," Volume 4, Artificial Intelligence and Law.

26. Hage, Jaap (2000). "Dialectical Models in Artificial Intelligence and Law," Artificial Intelligence and Law.

27. Hage, Japp, and Ronald Leenes, Arno Lodder (1993). "Hard Cases: A Procedural Approach," Artificial Intelligence and Law.

28. Hobbes, Thomas (1651). The Matter, Form and Power of a Common-Wealth Ecclesiasticall and Civil.

29. Holmes, Oliver (1897). "The Path of the Law," Volume 10, Harvard Law Review.

30. Katz, Daniel, and Michael Bommarito, Josh Blackman (2017). "A Genera Approach for Predicting the Behavior of the Supreme Court of the United States," April 12, 2017, PLOS ONE.

31. Kowalski, Robert, and Francesca Toni (1996). "Abstract Argumentation," AI-Law96.

32. Laswell, Harold (1955). "Current Studies of the Decision Process: Automation Creativity," Volume 8, Western Political Quarterly.

33. Libal, Tomer, and Alexander Steen (2019). "The NAI Suite: Drafting and Reasoning over Legal Texts," October 15, 2019, arXiv.

34. Lipton, Zachary (2017). "The Mythos of Model Interpretability," March 6, 2017, arXiv.

35. Martin, Andrew, and Kevin Quinn, Theodore Ruger, Pauline Kim (2004). "Competing Approaches to Predicting Supreme Court Decision Making," December 2014, Symposium on Forecasting U.S. Supreme Court Decisions.

36. McCarty, Thorne (1977). "Reflections on TAXMAN: An Experiment in Artificial Intelligence and Legal Reasoning," January 1977, Harvard Law Review.

37. Modgil, Sanjay, and Henry Prakken (2013). "The ASPIC+ Framework for Structured Argumentation: A Tutorial," December 16, 2013, Argument & Computation.

38. Mowbray, Andrew and Philip Chung, Graham Greenleaf (2019). "Utilising AI in the Legal Assistance Sector," LegalAIIA Workshop, ICAIL, June 17, 2019, Montreal, Canada.

39. Parasuraman, Raja, and Thomas Sheridan, Christopher Wickens (2000). "A Model for Types and Levels of Human Interaction with Automation," May 2000, IEEE Transactions on Systems, Man, and Cybernetics.

40. Popple, James (1993). "SHYSTER: A Pragmatic Legal Expert System," Ph.D. Dissertation, Australian National University.

41. Prakken, Henry, and Giovanni Sartor (2015). "Law and Logic: A Review from an Argumentation Perspective," Volume 227, Artificial Intelligence.

42. Rissland, Edwina (1988). Artificial Intelligence and Legal Reasoning: A Discussion of the Field and Gardner's Book," Volume 9, AI Magazine.

43. Rissland, Edwina (1990). "Artificial Intelligence and Law: Stepping Stones to a Model of Legal Reasoning," Yale Law Journal.

44. Searle, John (1980). "Minds, Brains, and Programs," Volume 3, Behavioral and Brain Sciences.

45. Sunstein, Cass (2001). "Of Artificial Intelligence and Legal Reasoning," University of Chicago Law School, Public Law and Legal Theory Working Papers.

46. Sunstein, Cass, and Kevin Ashley, Karl Branting, Howard Margolis (2001). "Legal Reasoning and Artificial Intelligence: How Computers 'Think' Like Lawyers," Symposium: Legal Reasoning and Artificial Intelligence, University of Chicago Law School Roundtable.

47. Surden, Harry (2014). "Machine Learning and Law," Washington Law Review.

48. Surden, Harry (2019). "Artificial Intelligence and Law: An Overview," Summer 2019, Georgia State University Law Review.

49. Valente, Andre, and Joost Breuker (1996). "A Functional Ontology of Law," Artificial Intelligence and Law.

50. Waltl, Bernhard, and Roland Vogl (2018). "Explainable Artificial Intelligence: The New Frontier in Legal Informatics," February 2018, Jusletter IT 22, Stanford Center for Legal Informatics, Stanford University.

51. Wittgenstein, Ludwig (1953). Philosophical Investigations. Blackwell Publishing.

Cited Quotations and Charts

Indicated as [C.n] in the chapters

1. ABA Definition of a Lawyer: https://www.americanbar.org/groups/public_education/resources/public-information/what-is-a-lawyer-/

2. ABA Legal Malpractice: https://www.americanbar.org/groups/gpsolo/publications/gp_solo/2011/march/the_biggest_malpractice_claim_risks/

3. ABA Model Definition of the Practice of Law: https://www.americanbar.org/groups/professional_responsibility/task_force_model_definition_practice_law/model_definition_definition/

4. Alice in Wonderland quote: https://www.goodreads.com/work/quotes/2933712-alice-in-wonderland

5. Cornell Law School foraging and sensing scheme: https://blog.law.cornell.edu/voxpop/category/sense-making-systems-in-law/

6. DataLex AustLII information: http://austlii.community/wiki/DataLex/

7. Hammurabi's Law Code: https://www.ushistory.org/civ/4c.asp

8. John Gay poem: https://www.poetrynook.com/poem/fable-1-dog-and-fox-lawyer

9. Joseph Heller's Catch-22: https://www.goodreads.com/work/quotes/814330-catch-22

10. Montesquieu quote: https://www.the-philosophy.com/montesquieu-quotes

11. Robo-Lawyer usage: https://en.wikipedia.org/wiki/Robot_lawyer

12. ROSS web site: https://rossintelligence.com/

13. Shakespeare's Henry VI: http://shakespeare.mit.edu/1henryvi/full.html

14. Sonik on "How Abraham Lincoln Argued a Murder Trial" (Mental Floss, September 15, 2011): https://www.mentalfloss.com/article/28774/how-abraham-lincoln-argued-murder-trial

15. Toppr definition of law: https://www.toppr.com/guides/business-law-cs/introduction-to-law/various-definitions-of-law/

Source Code
Indicated as [S.n] in the chapters

1. Docassemble source code: https://docassemble.org/

2. ELIZA and PARRY code: https://github.com/norvig/paip-lisp/blob/master/docs/chapter5.md

3. ELIZA code in LISP: http://lisp.plasticki.com/show?24GC

4. IBP source code: https://github.com/mgrabmair/openlcbr

5. NAI source code: https://tutorial.normativeai.com/

6. Prolog code of Bart: http://people.cs.ksu.edu/~schmidt/301s09/Lectures/prologS.html

7. Prolog code of human and Socrates: https://www.cis.upenn.edu/~matuszek/Concise%20Guides/Concise%20Prolog.html

8. SCOTUS ML source code: https://github.com/mjbommar/scotus-predict-v2

9. SHYSTER source code: http://users.cecs.anu.edu.au/~James.Popple/shyster/source/

10. Suite of LexNLP open source NLP for the legal domain, plus other features for legal document tracking, etc.: https://github.com/LexPredict/lexpredict-lexnlp https://contraxsuite.com/lexnlp/ https://contraxsuite.com/open-source-legal/

APPENDIX B
SUPPLEMENTAL FIGURES AND CHARTS

For the convenience of viewing, supplemental figures and charts related to the chapters are shown on the next pages

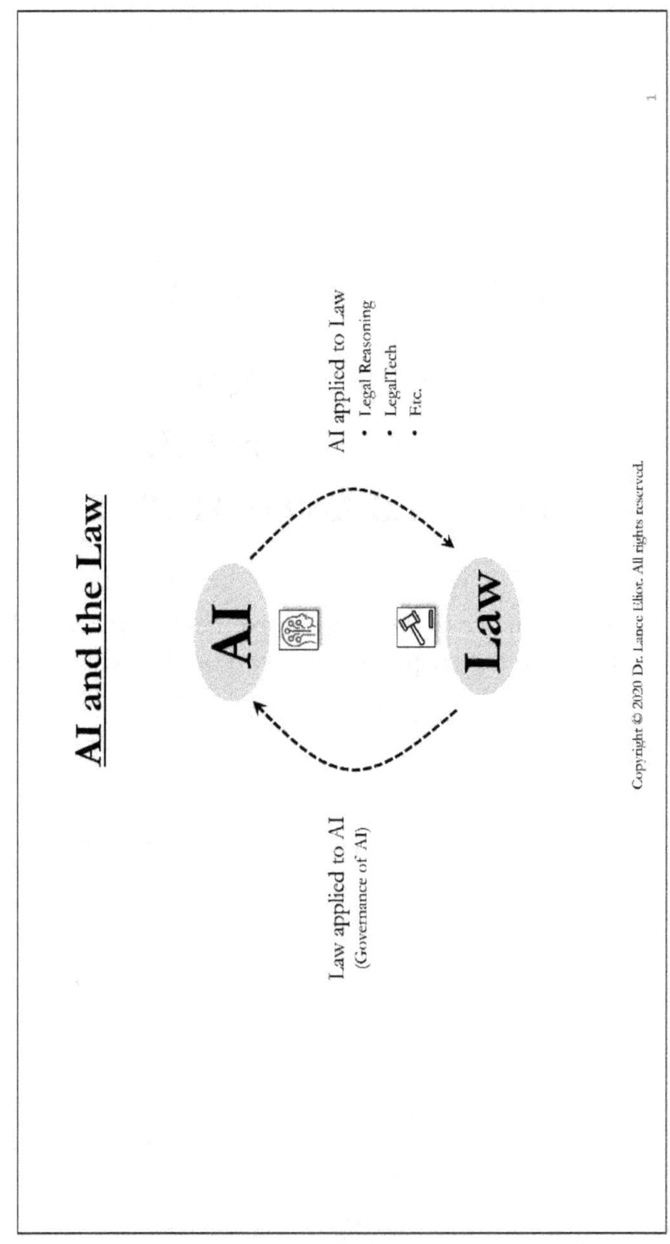
AI and the Law
AI
Law
AI applied to Law
• Legal Reasoning
• LegalTech
• Etc.
Law applied to AI
(Governance of AI)
Copyright © 2020 Dr. Lance Eliot. All rights reserved.
1

Figure 1

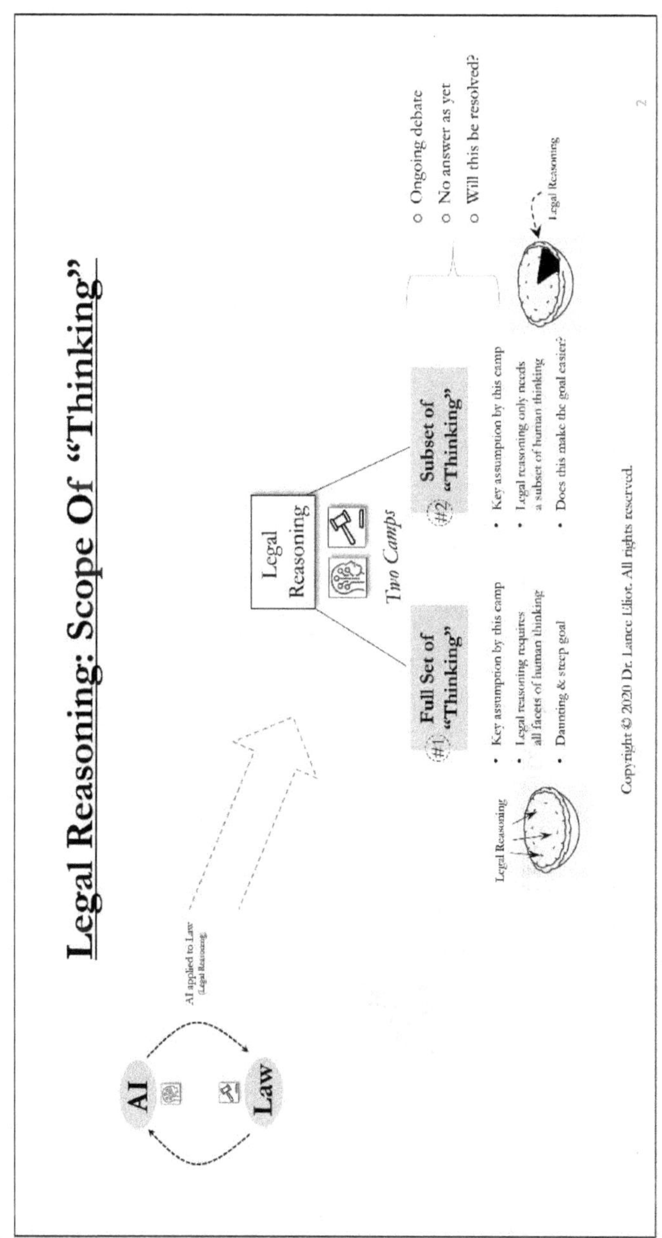
Legal Reasoning: Scope Of "Thinking"
AI
Law
AI applied to Law
(Legal Reasoning)
Legal Reasoning
Two Camps
#1 Full Set of "Thinking"
• Key assumption by this camp
• Legal reasoning requires all facets of human thinking
• Daunting & steep goal
Legal Reasoning
#2 Subset of "Thinking"
• Key assumption by this camp
• Legal reasoning only needs a subset of human thinking
• Does this make the goal easier?
Legal Reasoning
o Ongoing debate
o No answer as yet
o Will this be resolved?
Copyright © 2020 Dr. Lance Eliot. All rights reserved.
2

Figure 2

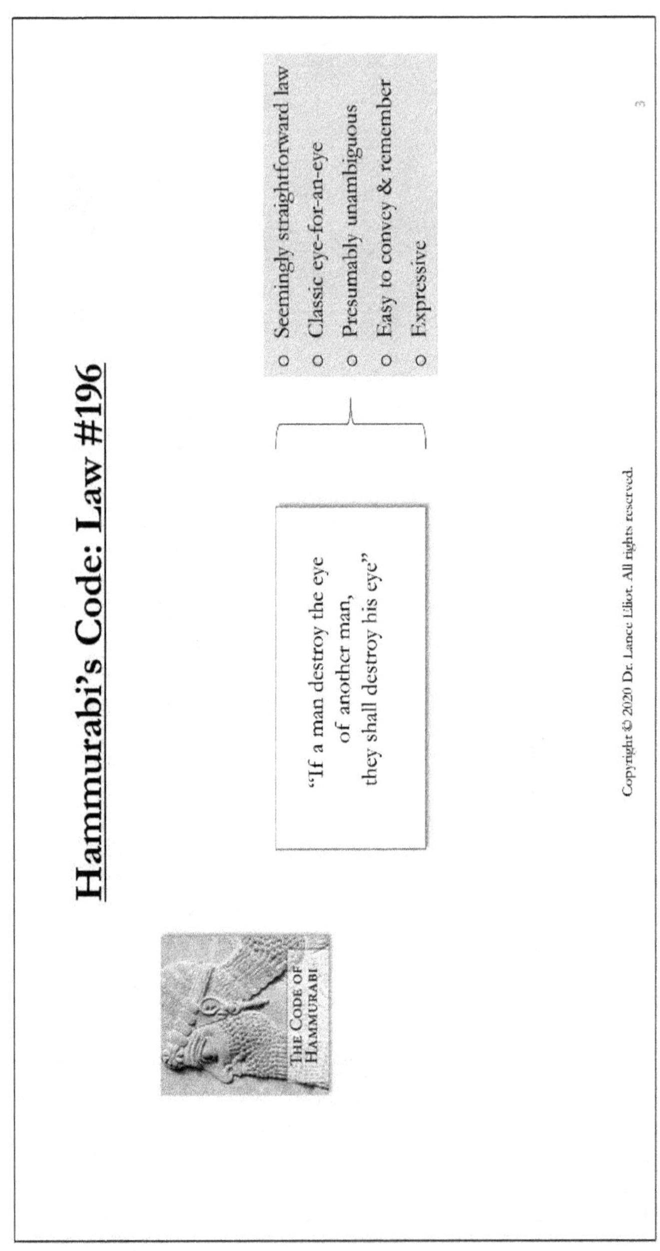
Hammurabi's Code: Law #196
THE CODE OF HAMMURABI
"If a man destroy the eye
of another man,
they shall destroy his eye"
Seemingly straightforward law
Classic eye-for-an-eye
Presumably unambiguous
Easy to convey & remember
Expressive
Copyright © 2020 Dr. Lance Eliot. All rights reserved.
3

Figure 3

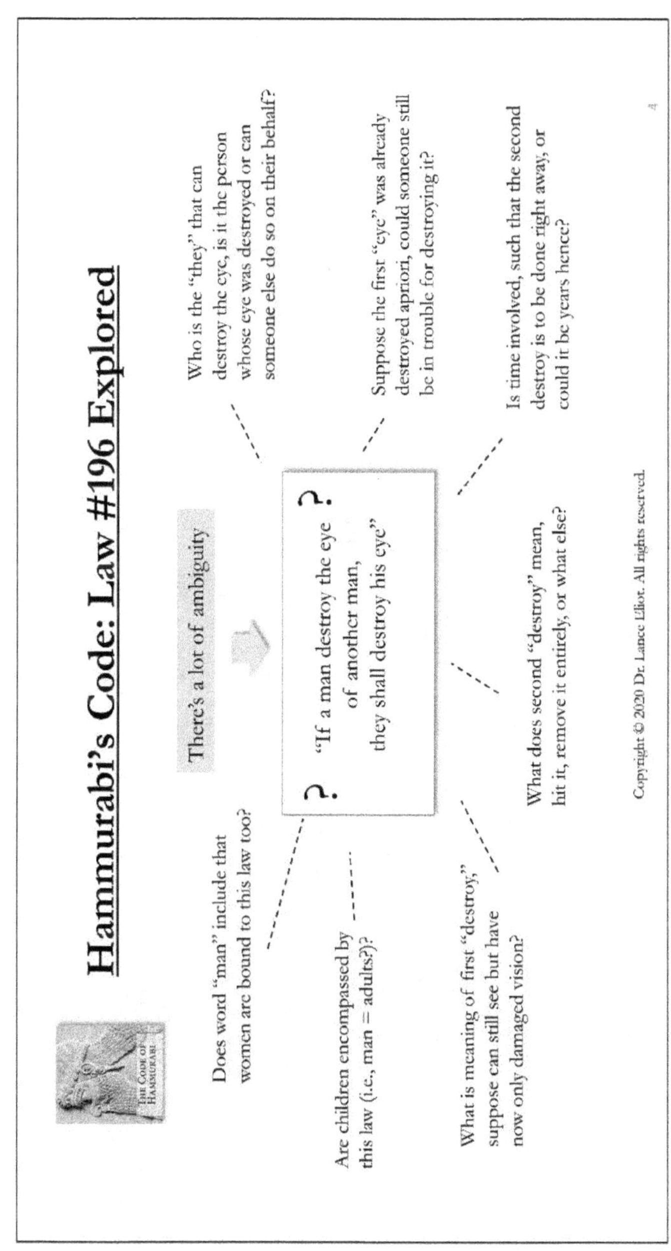
Hammurabi's Code: Law #196 Explored
The Code of Hammurabi
There's a lot of ambiguity
? "If a man destroy the eye of another man, they shall destroy his eye" ?
Does word "man" include that women are bound to this law too?
Are children encompassed by this law (i.e., man = adults?)?
What is meaning of first "destroy," suppose can still see but have now only damaged vision?
What does second "destroy" mean, hit it, remove it entirely, or what else?
Who is the "they" that can destroy the eye, is it the person whose eye was destroyed or can someone else do so on their behalf?
Suppose the first "eye" was already destroyed apriori, could someone still be in trouble for destroying it?
Is time involved, such that the second destroy is to be done right away, or could it be years hence?
Copyright © 2020 Dr. Lance Eliot. All rights reserved.

Figure 4

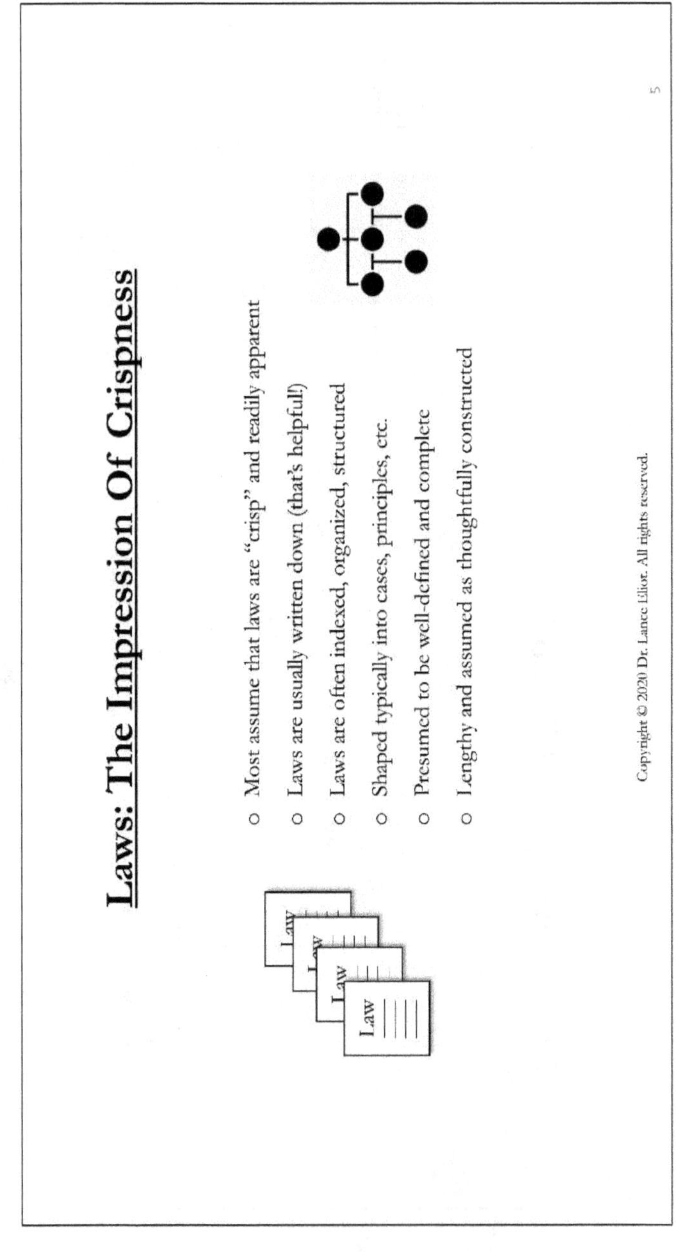
Laws: The Impression Of Crispness
Most assume that laws are "crisp" and readily apparent
Laws are usually written down (that's helpful!)
Laws are often indexed, organized, structured
Shaped typically into cases, principles, etc.
Presumed to be well-defined and complete
Lengthy and assumed as thoughtfully constructed
Law
Law
Law
Law
Copyright © 2020 Dr. Lance Eliot. All rights reserved.
5

Figure 5

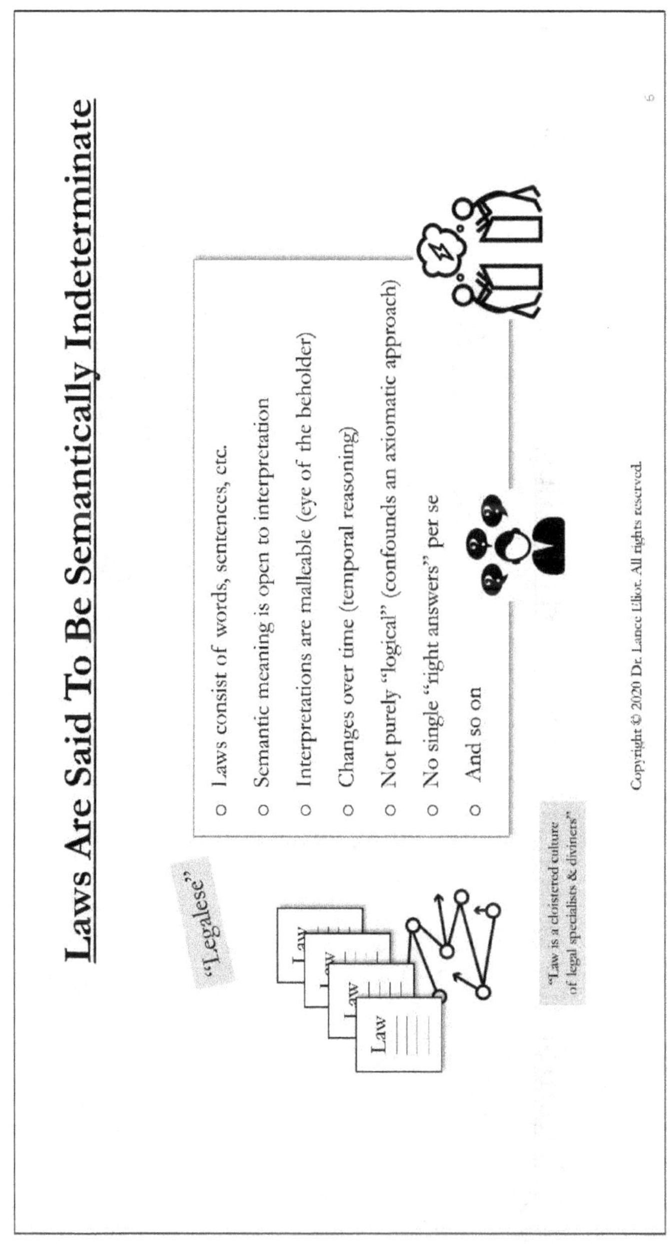

Laws Are Said To Be Semantically Indeterminate
"Legalese"
Law
Law
Law
Law
Laws consist of words, sentences, etc.
Semantic meaning is open to interpretation
Interpretations are malleable (eye of the beholder)
Changes over time (temporal reasoning)
Not purely "logical" (confounds an axiomatic approach)
No single "right answers" per se
And so on
"Law is a cloistered culture of legal specialists & diviners"
Copyright © 2020 Dr. Lance Eliot. All rights reserved.
6

Figure 6

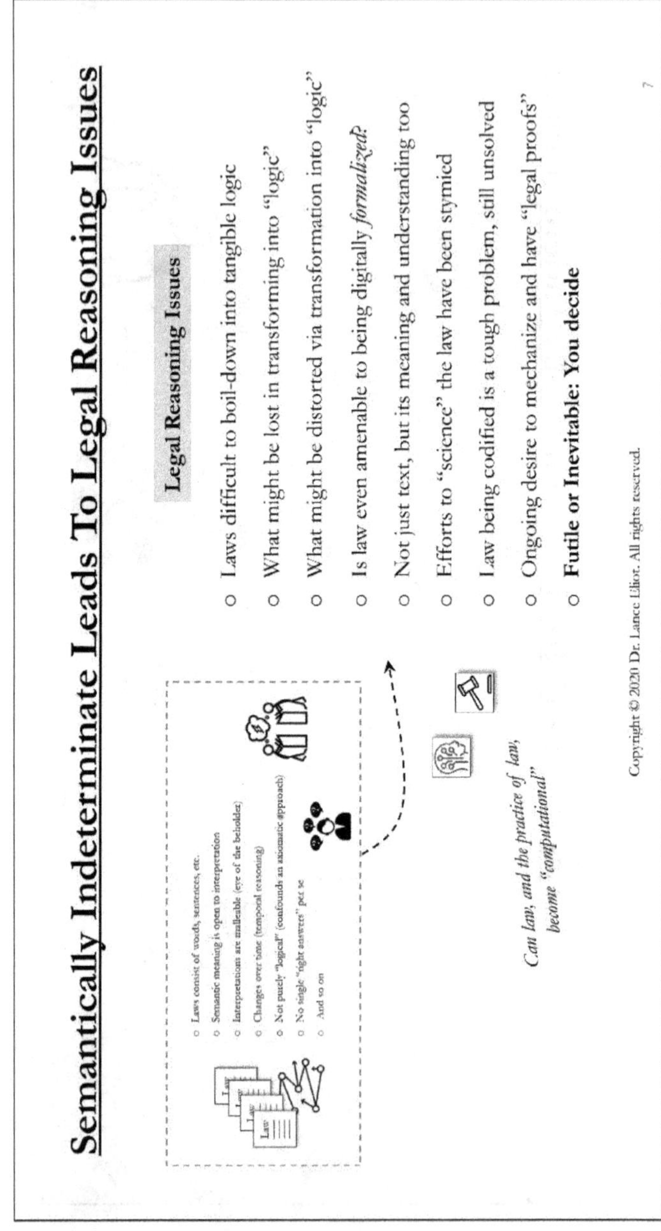
Semantically Indeterminate Leads To Legal Reasoning Issues
Laws consist of words, sentences, etc.
Semantic meaning is open to interpretation
Interpretations are malleable (eye of the beholder)
Changes over time (temporal reasoning)
Not purely "logical" (confounds an axiomatic approach)
No single "right answers" per se
And so on
Can law, and the practice of law, become "computational"
Legal Reasoning Issues
Laws difficult to boil-down into tangible logic
What might be lost in transforming into "logic"
What might be distorted via transformation into "logic"
Is law even amenable to being digitally formalized?
Not just text, but its meaning and understanding too
Efforts to "science" the law have been stymied
Law being codified is a tough problem, still unsolved
Ongoing desire to mechanize and have "legal proofs"
Futile or Inevitable: You decide
Copyright © 2020 Dr. Lance Eliot. All rights reserved.
7

Figure 7

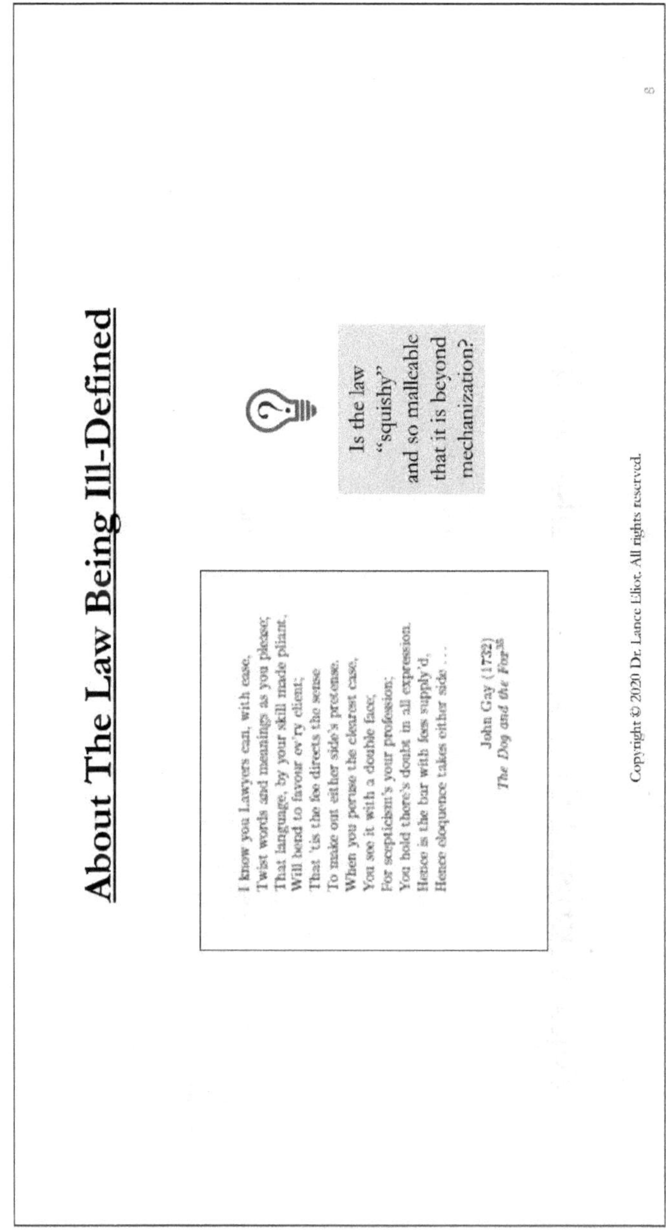
About The Law Being Ill-Defined
I know you Lawyers can, with ease,
Twist words and meanings as you please;
That language, by your skill made pliant,
Will bend to favour ev'ry client;
That 'tis the fee directs the sense
To make out either side's pretense.
When you peruse the clearest case,
You see it with a double face;
For scepticism's your profession;
You hold there's doubt in all expression.
Hence is the bar with fees supply'd,
Hence eloquence takes either side . . .
John Gay (1732)
The Dog and the Fox[35]
Is the law "squishy" and so malleable that it is beyond mechanization?
Copyright © 2020 Dr. Lance Eliot. All rights reserved.
8

Figure 8

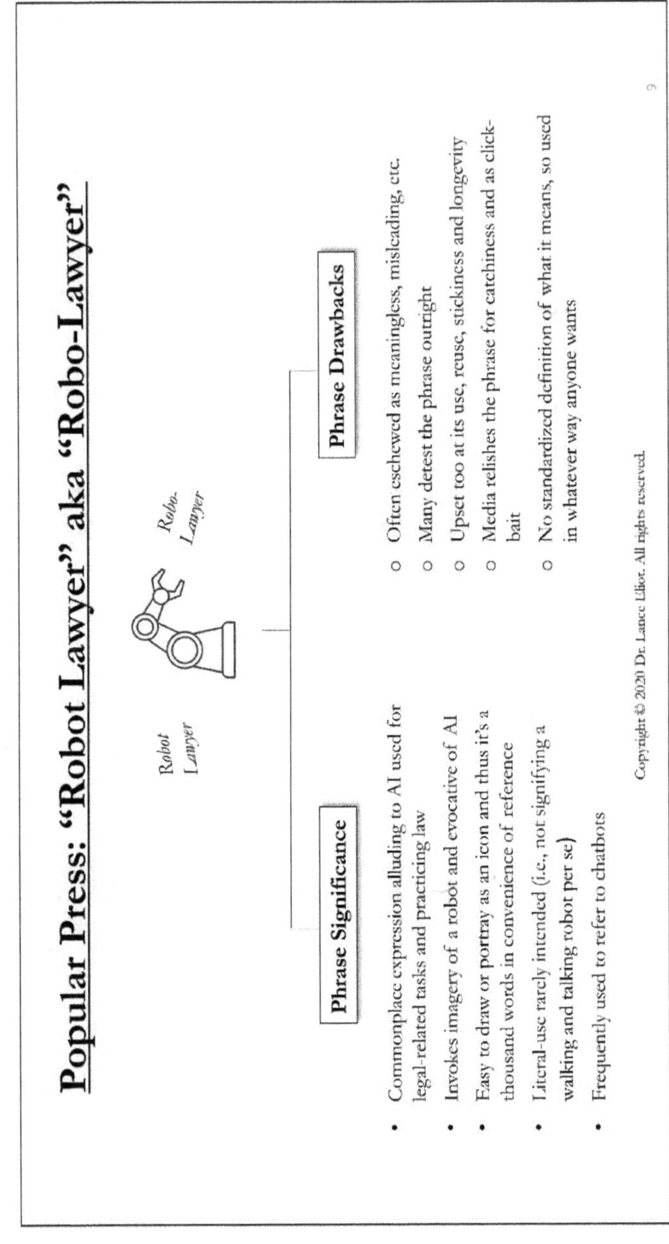
Popular Press: "Robot Lawyer" aka "Robo-Lawyer"
Robot Lawyer
Robo-Lawyer
Phrase Significance
Commonplace expression alluding to AI used for legal-related tasks and practicing law
Invokes imagery of a robot and evocative of AI
Easy to draw or portray as an icon and thus it's a thousand words in convenience of reference
Literal-use rarely intended (i.e., not signifying a walking and talking robot per se)
Frequently used to refer to chatbots
Phrase Drawbacks
Often eschewed as meaningless, misleading, etc.
Many detest the phrase outright
Upset too at its use, reuse, stickiness and longevity
Media relishes the phrase for catchiness and as click-bait
No standardized definition of what it means, so used in whatever way anyone wants
Copyright © 2020 Dr. Lance Eliot. All rights reserved.
9

Figure 9

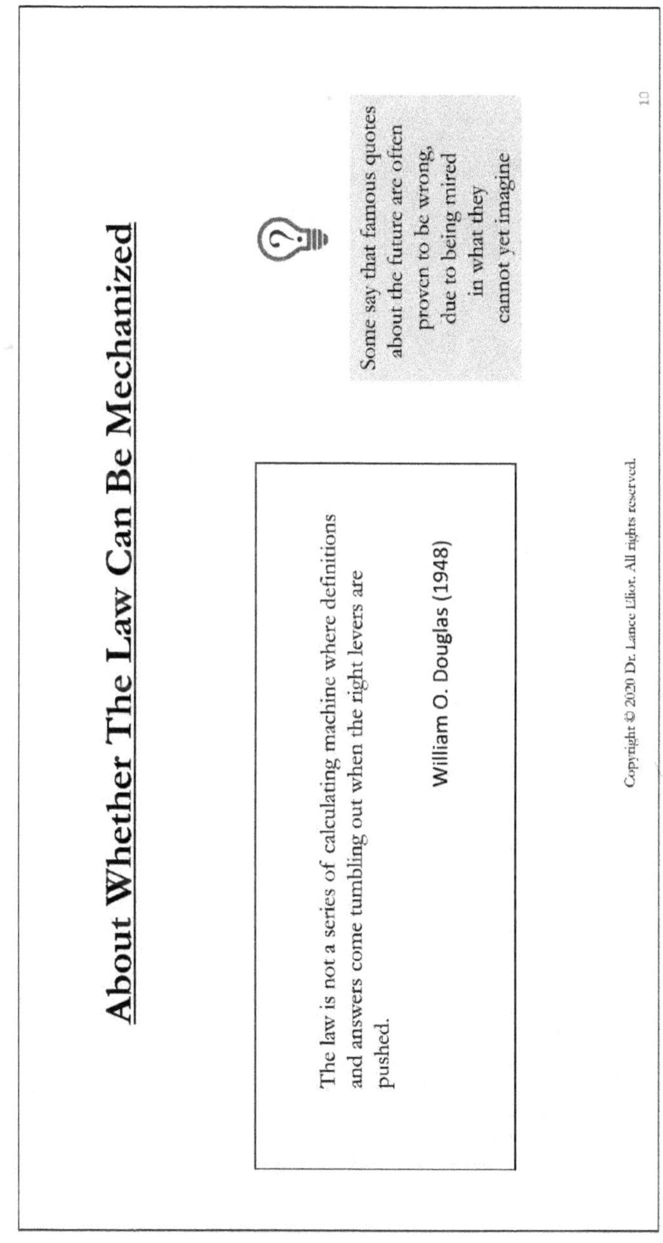
About Whether The Law Can Be Mechanized
The law is not a series of calculating machine where definitions and answers come tumbling out when the right levers are pushed.
William O. Douglas (1948)
Some say that famous quotes about the future are often proven to be wrong, due to being mired in what they cannot yet imagine
Copyright © 2020 Dr. Lance Eliot. All rights reserved.
10

Figure 10

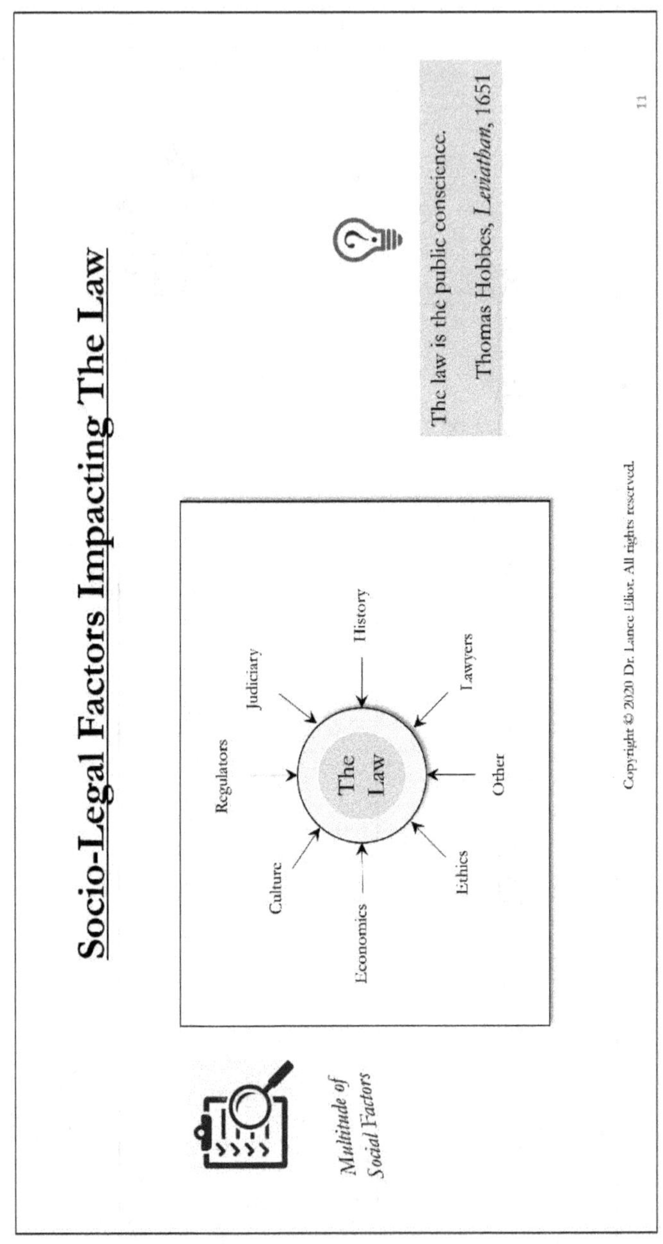
Socio-Legal Factors Impacting The Law
Multitude of Social Factors
The Law
Regulators
Judiciary
History
Lawyers
Other
Ethics
Economics
Culture
The law is the public conscience.
Thomas Hobbes, *Leviathan*, 1651
Copyright © 2020 Dr. Lance Eliot. All rights reserved.
11

Figure 11

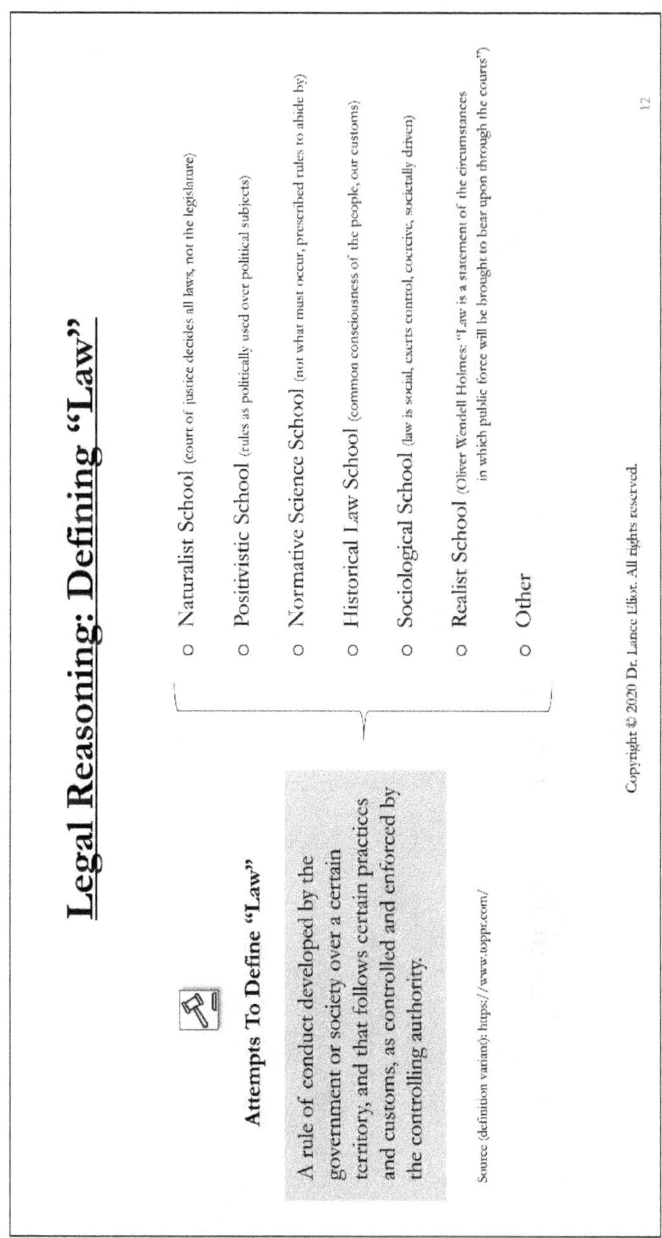
Legal Reasoning: Defining "Law"
Attempts To Define "Law"
A rule of conduct developed by the government or society over a certain territory, and that follows certain practices and customs, as controlled and enforced by the controlling authority.
Source (definition variant): https://www.toppr.com/
o Naturalist School (court of justice decides all laws, not the legislature)
o Positivistic School (rules as politically used over political subjects)
o Normative Science School (not what must occur, prescribed rules to abide by)
o Historical Law School (common consciousness of the people, our customs)
o Sociological School (law is social, exerts control, coercive, societally driven)
o Realist School (Oliver Wendell Holmes: "Law is a statement of the circumstances in which public force will be brought to bear upon through the courts")
o Other
Copyright © 2020 Dr. Lance Eliot. All rights reserved.
12

Figure 12

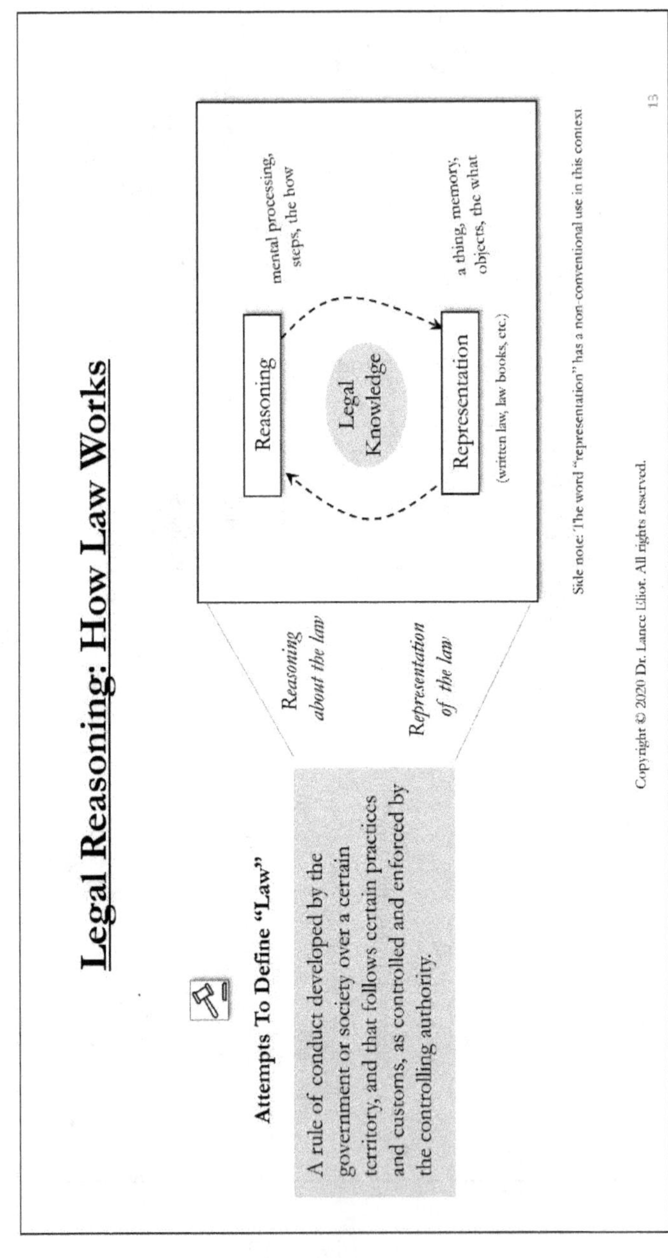
Legal Reasoning: How Law Works
Attempts To Define "Law"
A rule of conduct developed by the government or society over a certain territory, and that follows certain practices and customs, as controlled and enforced by the controlling authority.
Reasoning about the law
Representation of the law
Reasoning
Legal Knowledge
Representation
(written law, law books, etc.)
mental processing, steps, the how
a thing, memory, objects, the what
Side note: The word "representation" has a non-conventional use in this context
Copyright © 2020 Dr. Lance Eliot. All rights reserved.
13

Figure 13

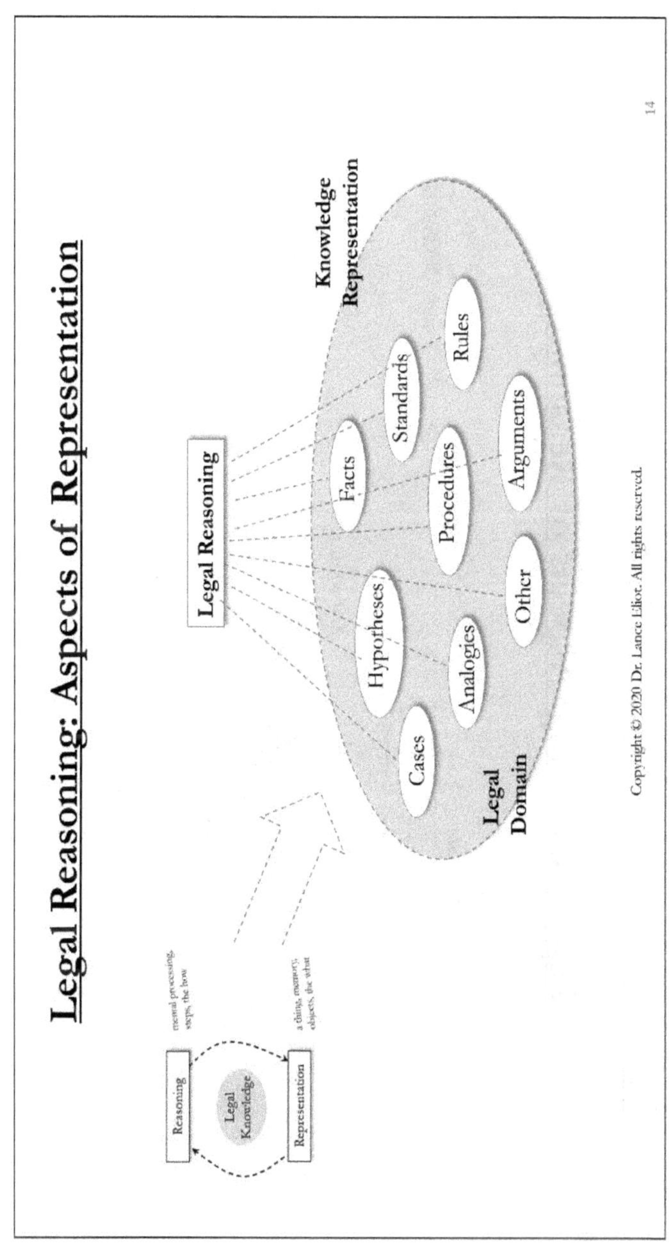
Legal Reasoning: Aspects of Representation
Reasoning
Legal Knowledge
Representation
mental processing, steps, the how
a thing, memory, objects, the what
Legal Reasoning
Knowledge Representation
Facts
Standards
Rules
Procedures
Arguments
Hypotheses
Other
Analogies
Cases
Legal Domain
Copyright © 2020 Dr. Lance Eliot. All rights reserved.
14

Figure 14

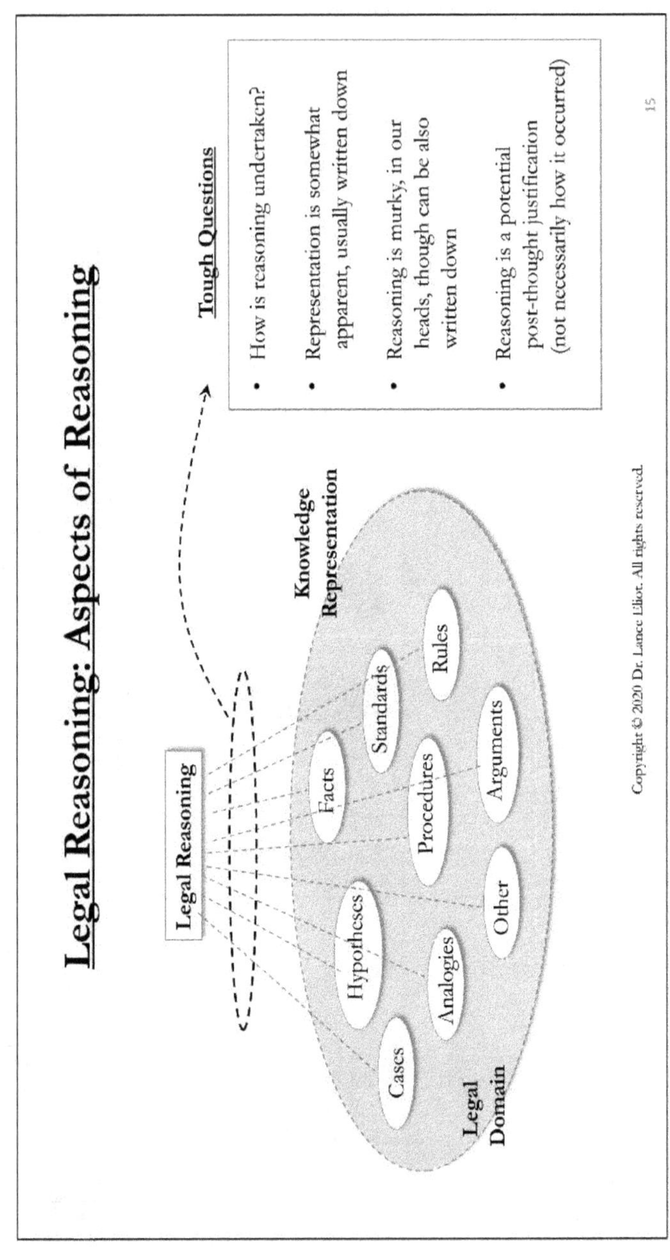
Legal Reasoning: Aspects of Reasoning
Legal Reasoning
Cases
Hypotheses
Analogies
Other
Facts
Procedures
Arguments
Standards
Rules
Legal Domain
Knowledge Representation
Tough Questions
• How is reasoning undertaken?
• Representation is somewhat apparent, usually written down
• Reasoning is murky, in our heads, though can be also written down
• Reasoning is a potential post-thought justification (not necessarily how it occurred)
Copyright © 2020 Dr. Lance Eliot. All rights reserved.
15

Figure 15

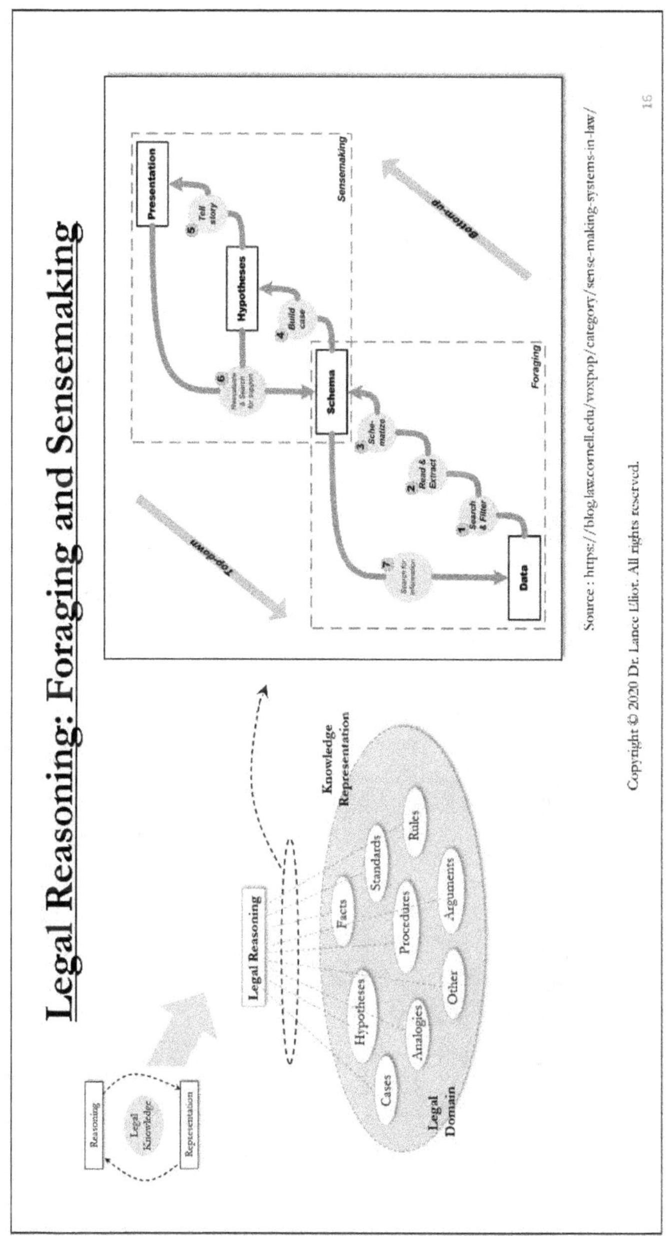
Legal Reasoning: Foraging and Sensemaking
Reasoning
Legal Knowledge
Representation
Legal Reasoning
Knowledge Representation
Facts
Standards
Rules
Hypotheses
Procedures
Arguments
Cases
Analogies
Other
Legal Domain
Presentation
Hypotheses
Schema
Data
5 Tell story
4 Build case
3 Schematize
2 Read & Extract
1 Search & Filter
6
7
Sensemaking
Foraging
Top-down
Bottom-up
Source : https://blog.law.cornell.edu/voxpop/category/sense-making-systems-in-law/
Copyright © 2020 Dr. Lance Eliot. All rights reserved.
16

Figure 16

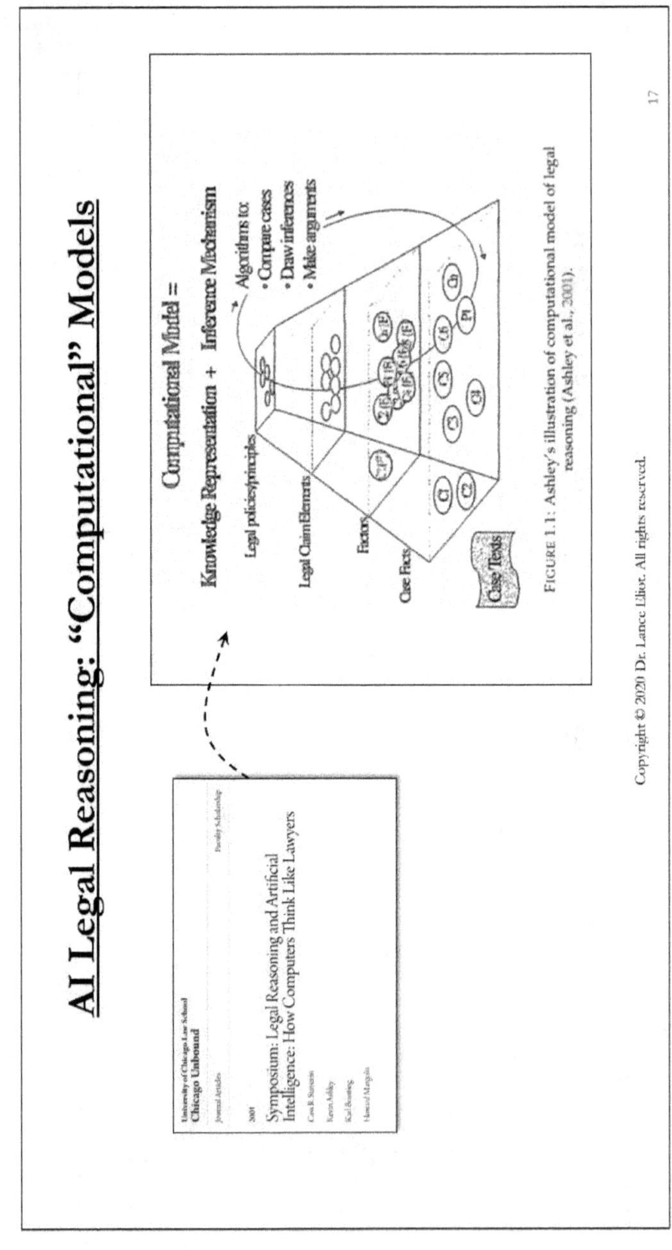
AI Legal Reasoning: "Computational" Models
University of Chicago Law School
Chicago Unbound
Journal Articles
Faculty Scholarship
2001
Symposium: Legal Reasoning and Artificial Intelligence: How Computers Think Like Lawyers
Cass R. Sunstein
Kevin Ashley
Karl Branting
Howard Margolis
Computational Model =
Knowledge Representation + Inference Mechanism
Algorithms to:
• Compare cases
• Draw inferences
• Make arguments
Legal policies/principles
Legal Claim Elements
Factors
Case Facts
Case Texts
FIGURE 1.1: Ashley's illustration of computational model of legal reasoning (Ashley et al., 2001).
Copyright © 2020 Dr. Lance Eliot. All rights reserved.
17

Figure 17

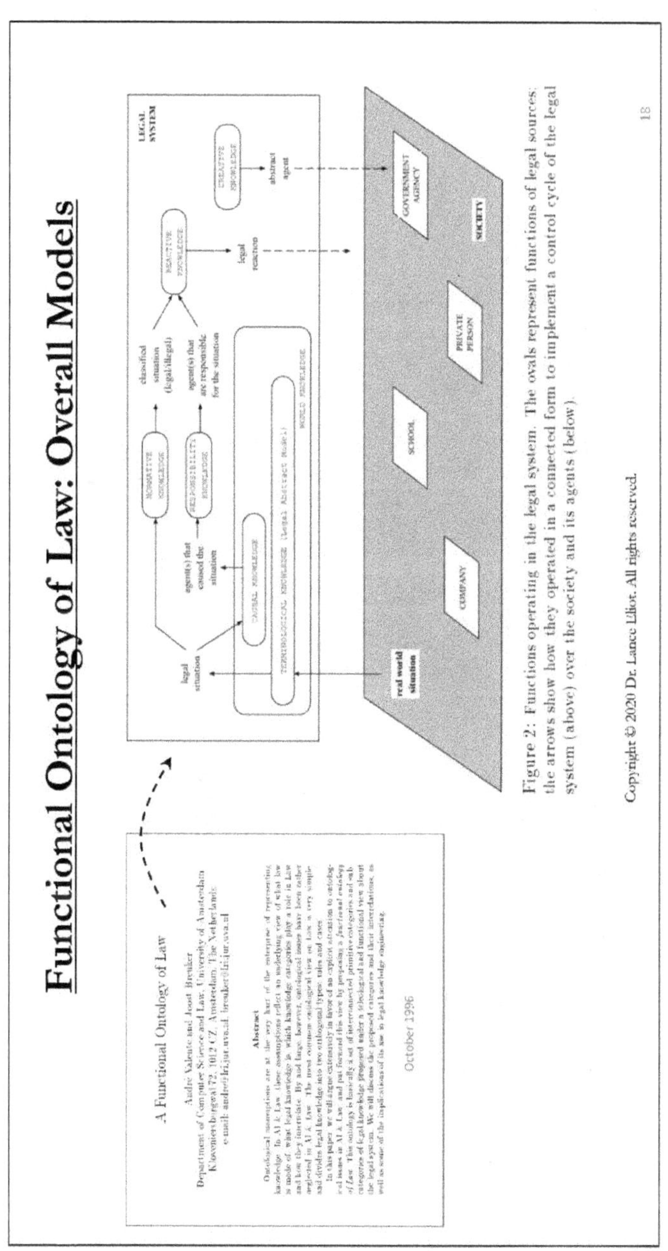
Functional Ontology of Law: Overall Models
A Functional Ontology of Law
André Valente and Joost Breuker
Department of Computer Science and Law, University of Amsterdam
Kloveniersburgwal 72, 1012 CZ, Amsterdam, The Netherlands
e-mail: andre@lri.jur.uva.nl, breuker@lri.jur.uva.nl
Abstract
October 1996
LEGAL SYSTEM
legal situation
NORMATIVE KNOWLEDGE
classified situation (legal/illegal)
agent(s) that caused the situation
RESPONSIBILITY KNOWLEDGE
agent(s) that are responsible for the situation
REACTIVE KNOWLEDGE
legal reaction
CREATIVE KNOWLEDGE
abstract agent
CAUSAL KNOWLEDGE
TERMINOLOGICAL KNOWLEDGE (Legal Abstract Model)
WORLD KNOWLEDGE
real world situation
SCHOOL
GOVERNMENT AGENCY
COMPANY
PRIVATE PERSON
SOCIETY
Figure 2: Functions operating in the legal system. The ovals represent functions of legal sources; the arrows show how they operated in a connected form to implement a control cycle of the legal system (above) over the society and its agents (below).
Copyright © 2020 Dr. Lance Eliot. All rights reserved.
18

Figure 18

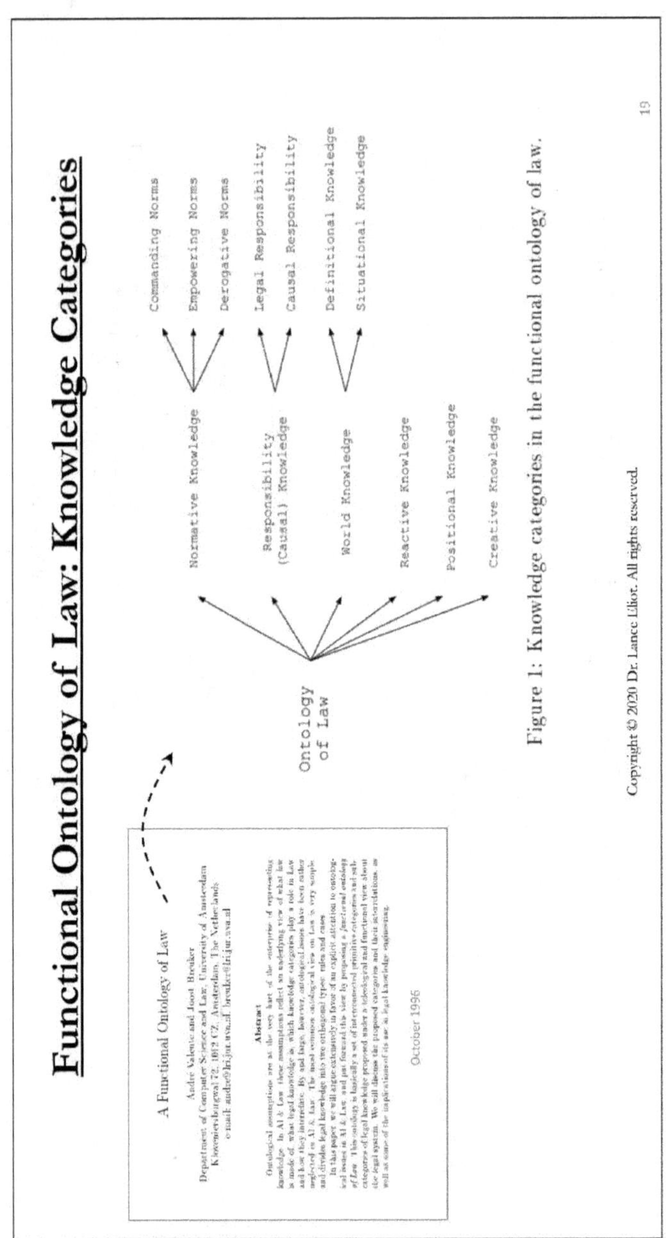
Functional Ontology of Law: Knowledge Categories
A Functional Ontology of Law
Andre Valente and Joost Breuker
Abstract
October 1996
Ontology of Law
Normative Knowledge
Commanding Norms
Empowering Norms
Derogative Norms
Responsibility (Causal) Knowledge
Legal Responsibility
Causal Responsibility
World Knowledge
Definitional Knowledge
Situational Knowledge
Reactive Knowledge
Positional Knowledge
Creative Knowledge
Figure 1: Knowledge categories in the functional ontology of law.
Copyright © 2020 Dr. Lance Eliot. All rights reserved.
19

Figure 19

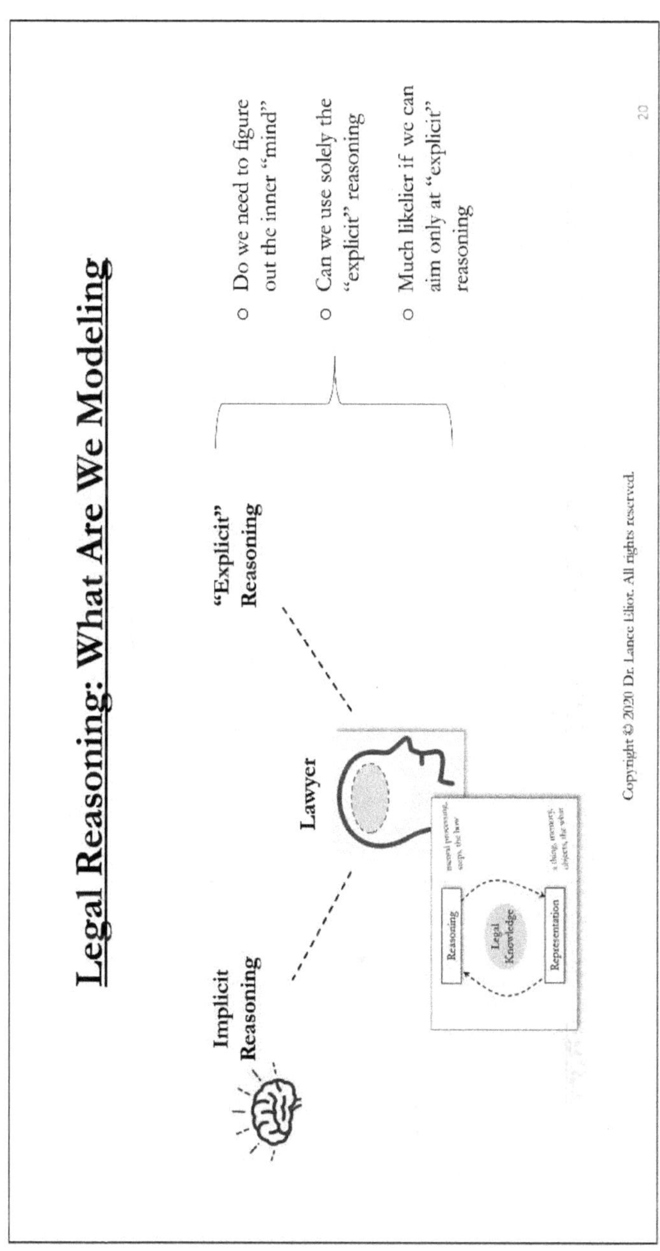
Legal Reasoning: What Are We Modeling
Implicit Reasoning
Lawyer
"Explicit" Reasoning
Reasoning
Legal Knowledge
Representation
Do we need to figure out the inner "mind"
Can we use solely the "explicit" reasoning
Much likelier if we can aim only at "explicit" reasoning
Copyright © 2020 Dr. Lance Eliot. All rights reserved.
20

Figure 20

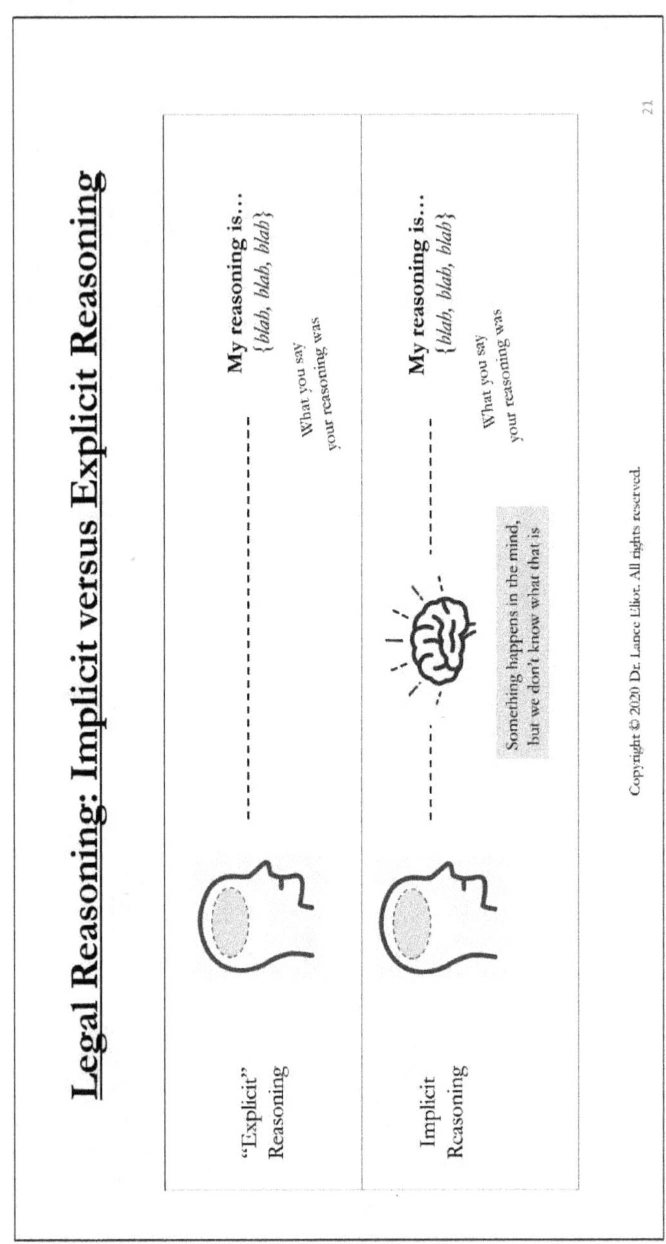
Legal Reasoning: Implicit versus Explicit Reasoning
"Explicit" Reasoning
My reasoning is…
{blah, blah, blah}
What you say your reasoning was
Implicit Reasoning
Something happens in the mind, but we don't know what that is
My reasoning is…
{blah, blah, blah}
What you say your reasoning was
Copyright © 2020 Dr. Lance Eliot. All rights reserved.
21

Figure 21

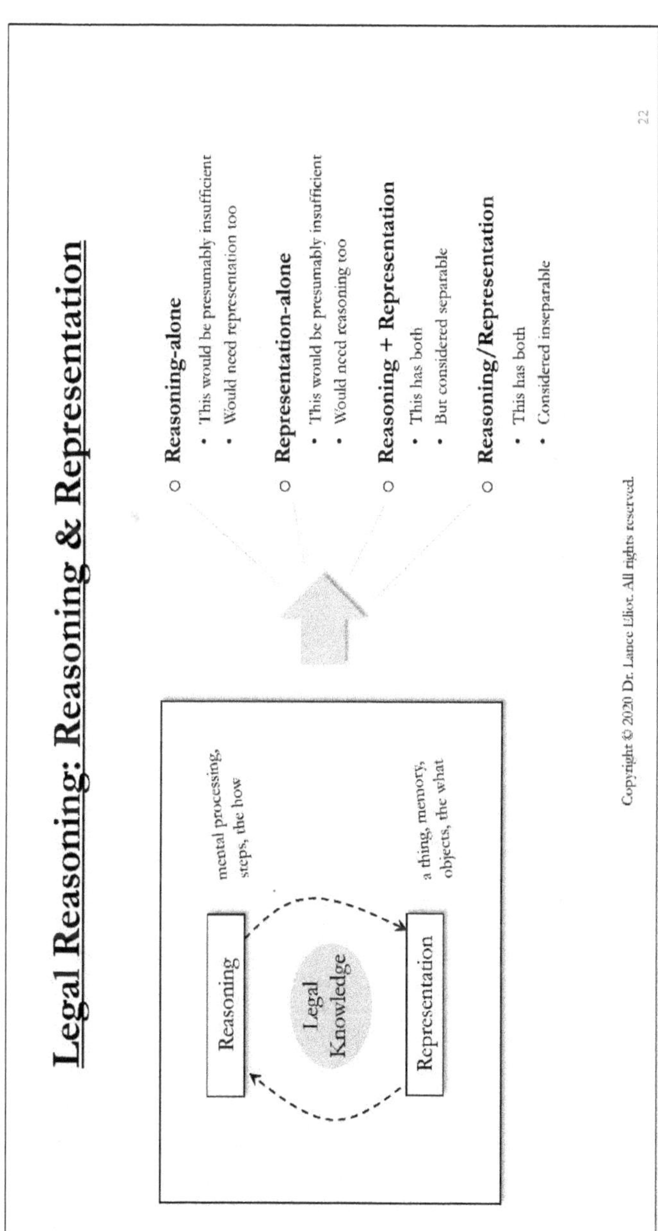
Legal Reasoning: Reasoning & Representation
Reasoning
Legal Knowledge
Representation
mental processing, steps, the how
a thing, memory, objects, the what
Reasoning-alone
This would be presumably insufficient
Would need representation too
Representation-alone
This would be presumably insufficient
Would need reasoning too
Reasoning + Representation
This has both
But considered separable
Reasoning/Representation
This has both
Considered inseparable
Copyright © 2020 Dr. Lance Eliot. All rights reserved.
22

Figure 22

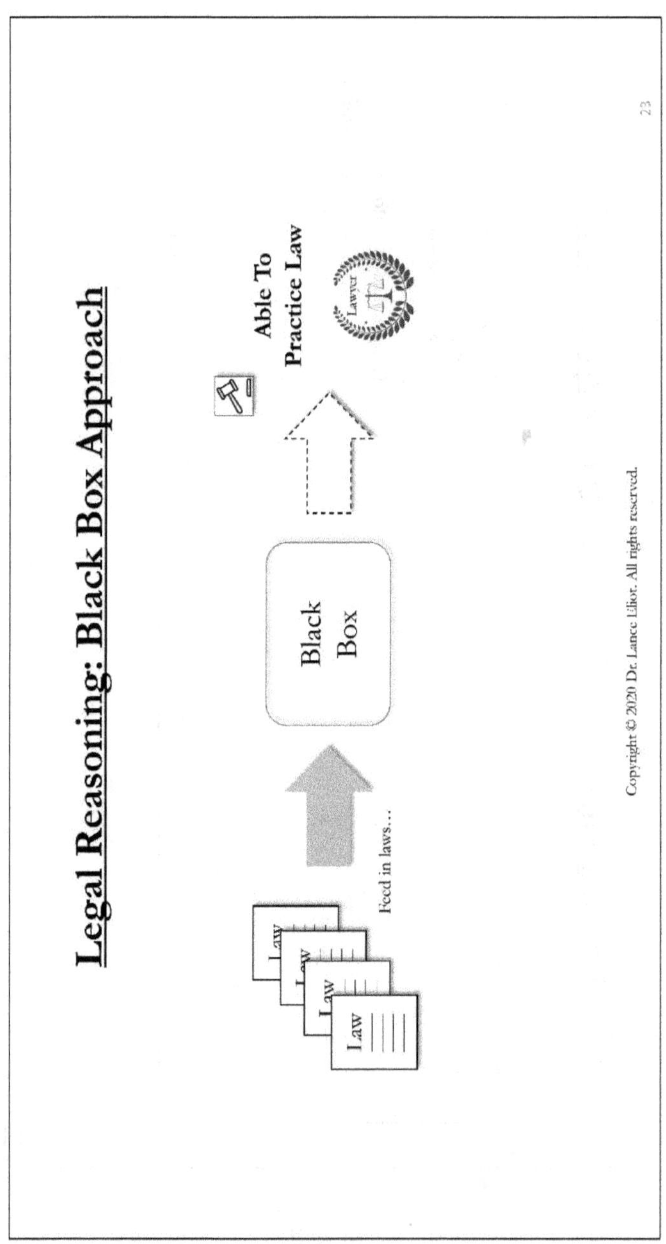
Legal Reasoning: Black Box Approach
Law
Law
Law
Law
Feed in laws…
Black
Box
Able To
Practice Law
Lawyer
Copyright © 2020 Dr. Lance Eliot. All rights reserved.
23

Figure 23

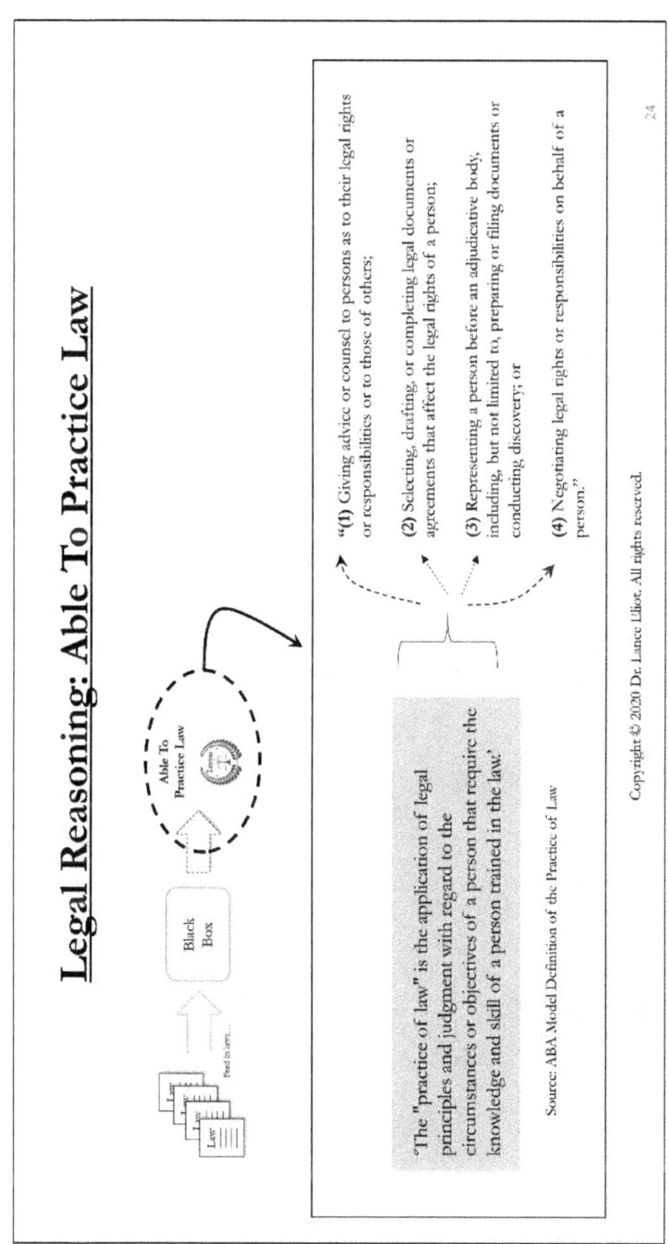
Legal Reasoning: Able To Practice Law
Law
Feed in laws...
Black Box
Able To Practice Law
"The "practice of law" is the application of legal principles and judgment with regard to the circumstances or objectives of a person that require the knowledge and skill of a person trained in the law.'
Source: ABA Model Definition of the Practice of Law
"(1) Giving advice or counsel to persons as to their legal rights or responsibilities or to those of others;
(2) Selecting, drafting, or completing legal documents or agreements that affect the legal rights of a person;
(3) Representing a person before an adjudicative body, including, but not limited to, preparing or filing documents or conducting discovery; or
(4) Negotiating legal rights or responsibilities on behalf of a person."
Copyright © 2020 Dr. Lance Eliot. All rights reserved.
24

Figure 24

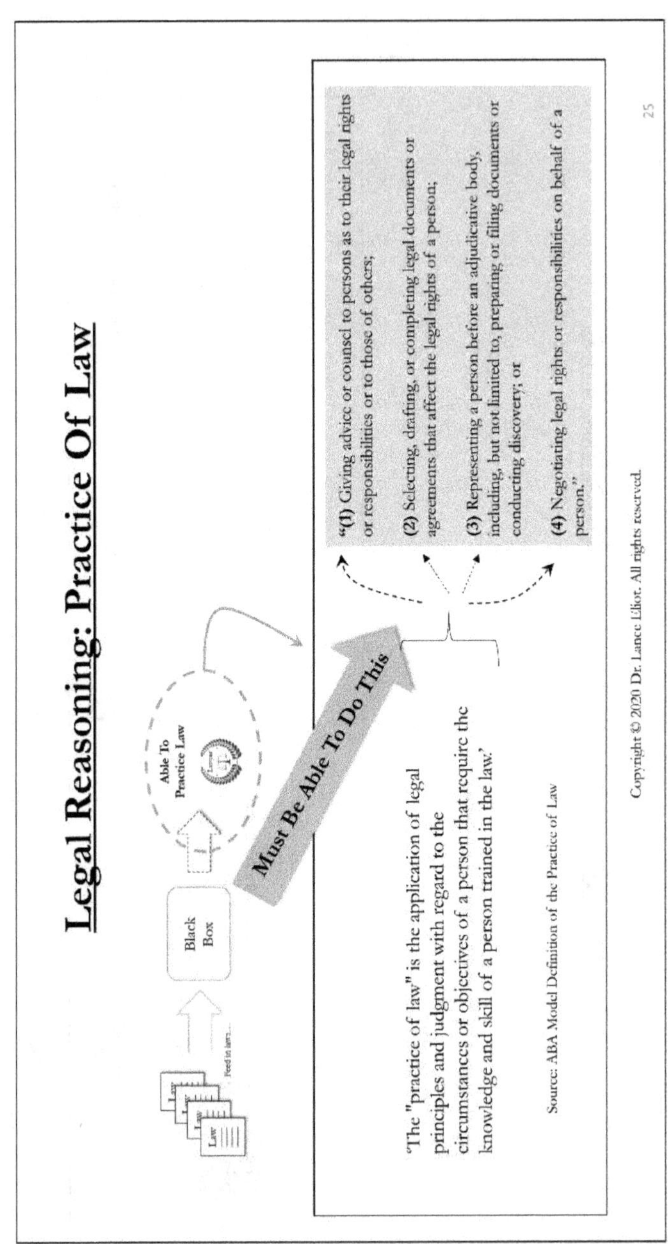
Legal Reasoning: Practice Of Law
Law
Feed in laws...
Black Box
Able To Practice Law
Must Be Able To Do This
The "practice of law" is the application of legal principles and judgment with regard to the circumstances or objectives of a person that require the knowledge and skill of a person trained in the law.'
Source: ABA Model Definition of the Practice of Law
"(1) Giving advice or counsel to persons as to their legal rights or responsibilities or to those of others;
(2) Selecting, drafting, or completing legal documents or agreements that affect the legal rights of a person;
(3) Representing a person before an adjudicative body, including, but not limited to, preparing or filing documents or conducting discovery; or
(4) Negotiating legal rights or responsibilities on behalf of a person."
Copyright © 2020 Dr. Lance Eliot. All rights reserved.
25

Figure 25

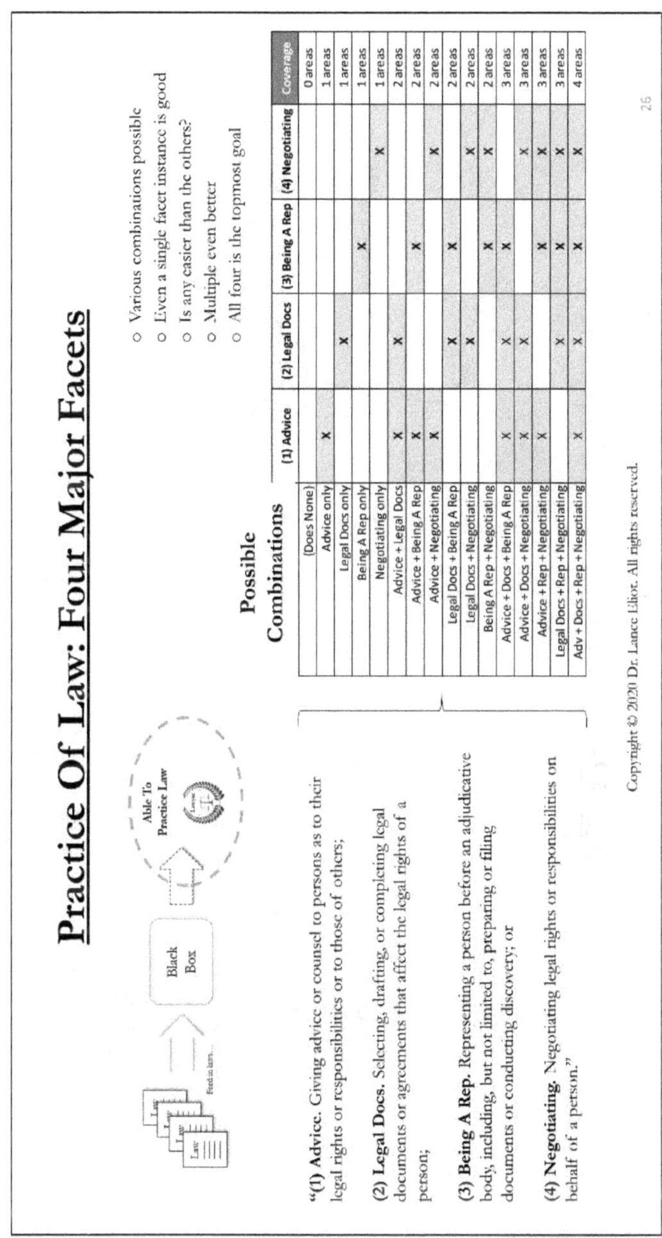

Possible Combinations	(1) Advice	(2) Legal Docs	(3) Being A Rep	(4) Negotiating	Coverage
(Does None)					0 areas
Advice only	X				1 areas
Legal Docs only		X			1 areas
Being A Rep only			X		1 areas
Negotiating only				X	1 areas
Advice + Legal Docs	X	X			2 areas
Advice + Being A Rep	X		X		2 areas
Advice + Negotiating	X			X	2 areas
Legal Docs + Being A Rep		X	X		2 areas
Legal Docs + Negotiating		X		X	2 areas
Being A Rep + Negotiating			X	X	2 areas
Advice + Docs + Being A Rep	X	X	X		3 areas
Advice + Docs + Negotiating	X	X		X	3 areas
Advice + Rep + Negotiating	X		X	X	3 areas
Legal Docs + Rep + Negotiating		X	X	X	3 areas
Adv + Docs + Rep + Negotiating	X	X	X	X	4 areas

Figure 26

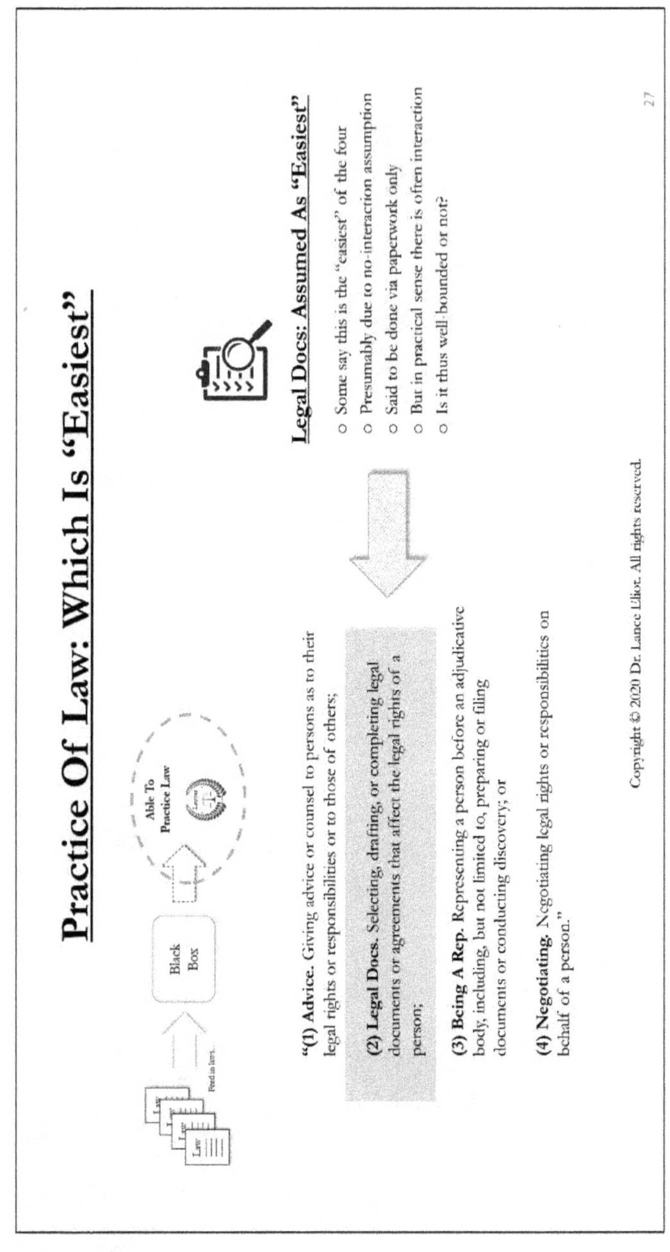
Practice Of Law: Which Is "Easiest"
Law
Black Box
Able To Practice Law
"(1) Advice. Giving advice or counsel to persons as to their legal rights or responsibilities or to those of others;
(2) Legal Docs. Selecting, drafting, or completing legal documents or agreements that affect the legal rights of a person;
(3) Being A Rep. Representing a person before an adjudicative body, including, but not limited to, preparing or filing documents or conducting discovery; or
(4) Negotiating. Negotiating legal rights or responsibilities on behalf of a person."
Legal Docs: Assumed As "Easiest"
Some say this is the "easiest" of the four
Presumably due to no-interaction assumption
Said to be done via paperwork only
But in practical sense there is often interaction
Is it thus well-bounded or not?
Copyright © 2020 Dr. Lance Eliot. All rights reserved.
27

Figure 27

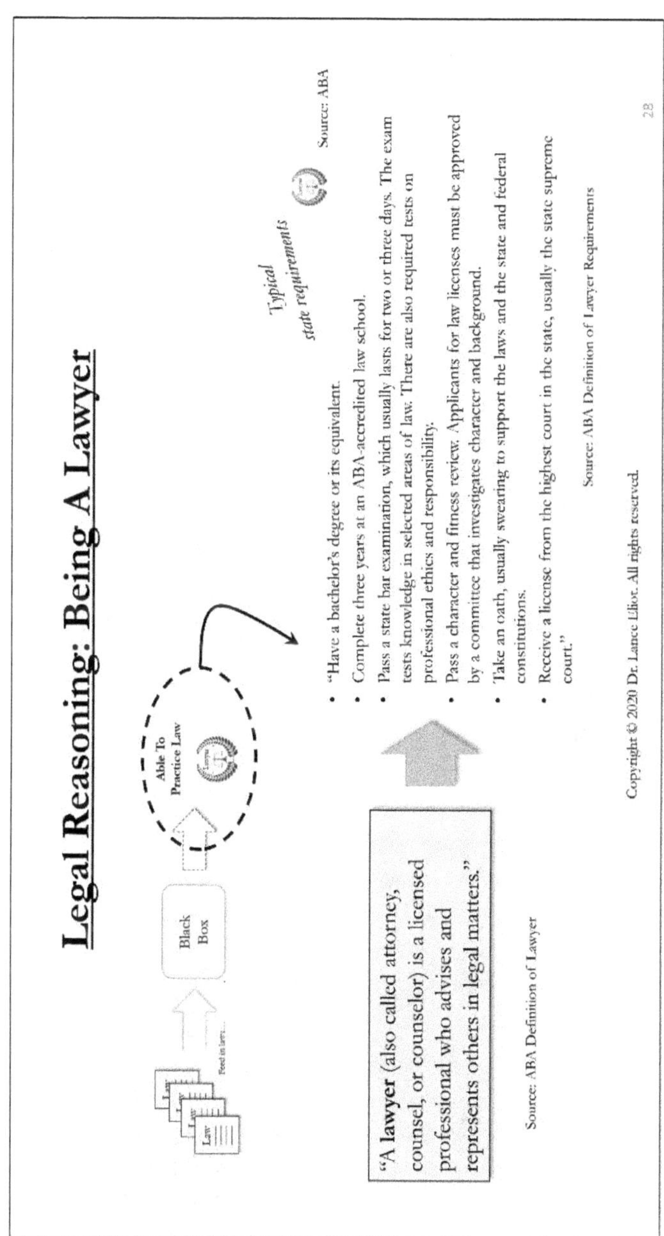
Legal Reasoning: Being A Lawyer
Law
Feed in laws...
Black Box
Able To Practice Law
"A lawyer (also called attorney, counsel, or counselor) is a licensed professional who advises and represents others in legal matters."
Source: ABA Definition of Lawyer
Typical state requirements
Source: ABA
"Have a bachelor's degree or its equivalent.
Complete three years at an ABA-accredited law school.
Pass a state bar examination, which usually lasts for two or three days. The exam tests knowledge in selected areas of law. There are also required tests on professional ethics and responsibility.
Pass a character and fitness review. Applicants for law licenses must be approved by a committee that investigates character and background.
Take an oath, usually swearing to support the laws and the state and federal constitutions.
Receive a license from the highest court in the state, usually the state supreme court."
Source: ABA Definition of Lawyer Requirements
Copyright © 2020 Dr. Lance Eliot. All rights reserved.
28

Figure 28

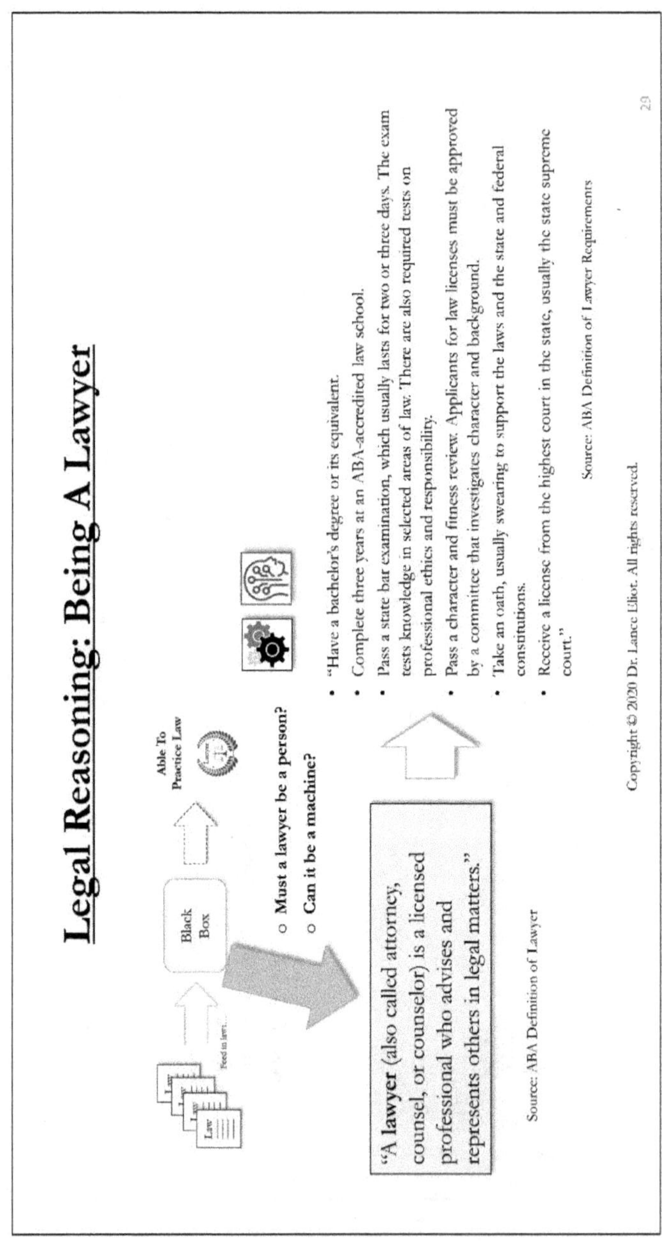
Legal Reasoning: Being A Lawyer
Law
Feed in laws
Black Box
Able To Practice Law
Must a lawyer be a person?
Can it be a machine?
"A lawyer (also called attorney, counsel, or counselor) is a licensed professional who advises and represents others in legal matters."
Source: ABA Definition of Lawyer
"Have a bachelor's degree or its equivalent.
Complete three years at an ABA-accredited law school.
Pass a state bar examination, which usually lasts for two or three days. The exam tests knowledge in selected areas of law. There are also required tests on professional ethics and responsibility.
Pass a character and fitness review. Applicants for law licenses must be approved by a committee that investigates character and background.
Take an oath, usually swearing to support the laws and the state and federal constitutions.
Receive a license from the highest court in the state, usually the state supreme court."
Source: ABA Definition of Lawyer Requirements
Copyright © 2020 Dr. Lance Eliot. All rights reserved.
29

Figure 29

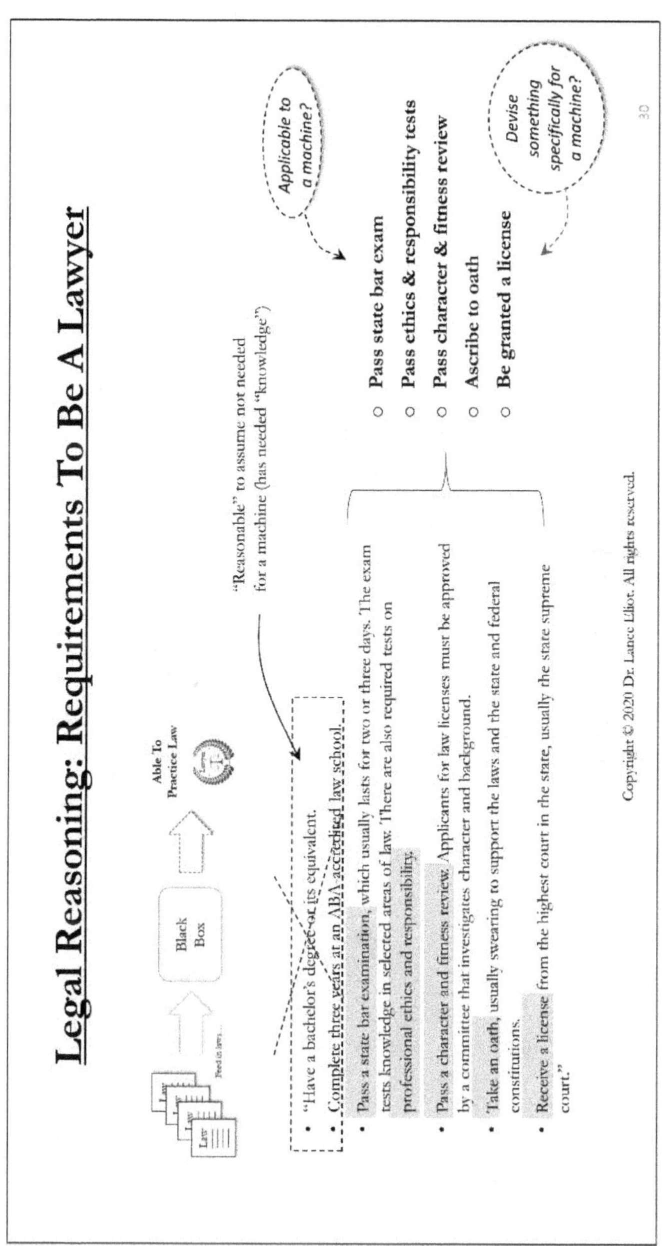
Legal Reasoning: Requirements To Be A Lawyer
Black Box
Able To Practice Law
"Reasonable" to assume not needed for a machine (has needed "knowledge")
Applicable to a machine?
"Have a bachelor's degree or its equivalent.
Complete three years at an ABA-accredited law school.
Pass a state bar examination, which usually lasts for two or three days. The exam tests knowledge in selected areas of law. There are also required tests on professional ethics and responsibility.
Pass a character and fitness review. Applicants for law licenses must be approved by a committee that investigates character and background.
Take an oath, usually swearing to support the laws and the state and federal constitutions.
Receive a license from the highest court in the state, usually the state supreme court."
Pass state bar exam
Pass ethics & responsibility tests
Pass character & fitness review
Ascribe to oath
Be granted a license
Devise something specifically for a machine?
Copyright © 2020 Dr. Lance Eliot. All rights reserved.
30

Figure 30

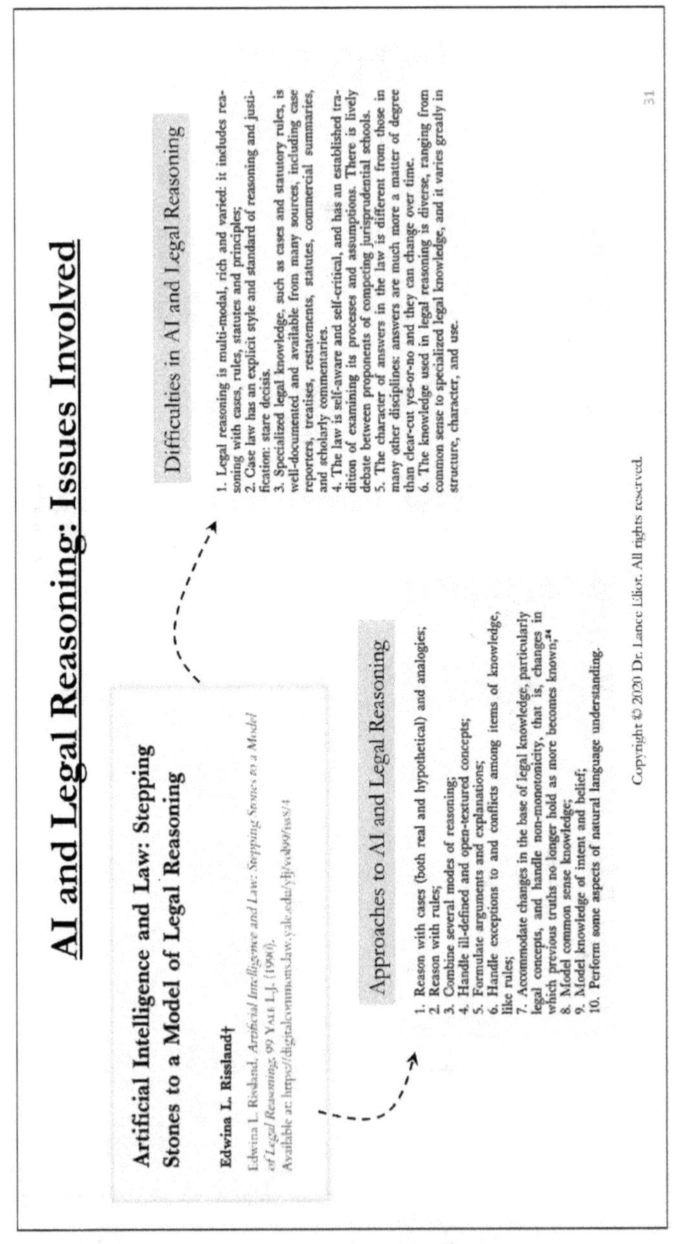
AI and Legal Reasoning: Issues Involved
Artificial Intelligence and Law: Stepping Stones to a Model of Legal Reasoning
Edwina L. Rissland†
Edwina L. Rissland, Artificial Intelligence and Law: Stepping Stones to a Model of Legal Reasoning, 99 YALE L.J. (1990).
Available at: https://digitalcommons.law.yale.edu/ylj/vol99/iss8/4
Difficulties in AI and Legal Reasoning
1. Legal reasoning is multi-modal, rich and varied: it includes reasoning with cases, rules, statutes and principles;
2. Case law has an explicit style and standard of reasoning and justification: stare decisis.
3. Specialized legal knowledge, such as cases and statutory rules, is well-documented and available from many sources, including case reporters, treatises, restatements, statutes, commercial summaries, and scholarly commentaries.
4. The law is self-aware and self-critical, and has an established tradition of examining its processes and assumptions. There is lively debate between proponents of competing jurisprudential schools.
5. The character of answers in the law is different from those in many other disciplines: answers are much more a matter of degree than clear-cut yes-or-no and they can change over time.
6. The knowledge used in legal reasoning is diverse, ranging from common sense to specialized legal knowledge, and it varies greatly in structure, character, and use.
Approaches to AI and Legal Reasoning
1. Reason with cases (both real and hypothetical) and analogies;
2. Reason with rules;
3. Combine several modes of reasoning;
4. Handle ill-defined and open-textured concepts;
5. Formulate arguments and explanations;
6. Handle exceptions to and conflicts among items of knowledge, like rules;
7. Accommodate changes in the base of legal knowledge, particularly legal concepts, and handle non-monotonicity, that is, changes in which previous truths no longer hold as more becomes known;
8. Model common sense knowledge;
9. Model knowledge of intent and belief;
10. Perform some aspects of natural language understanding.
Copyright © 2020 Dr. Lance Eliot. All rights reserved.
31

Figure 31

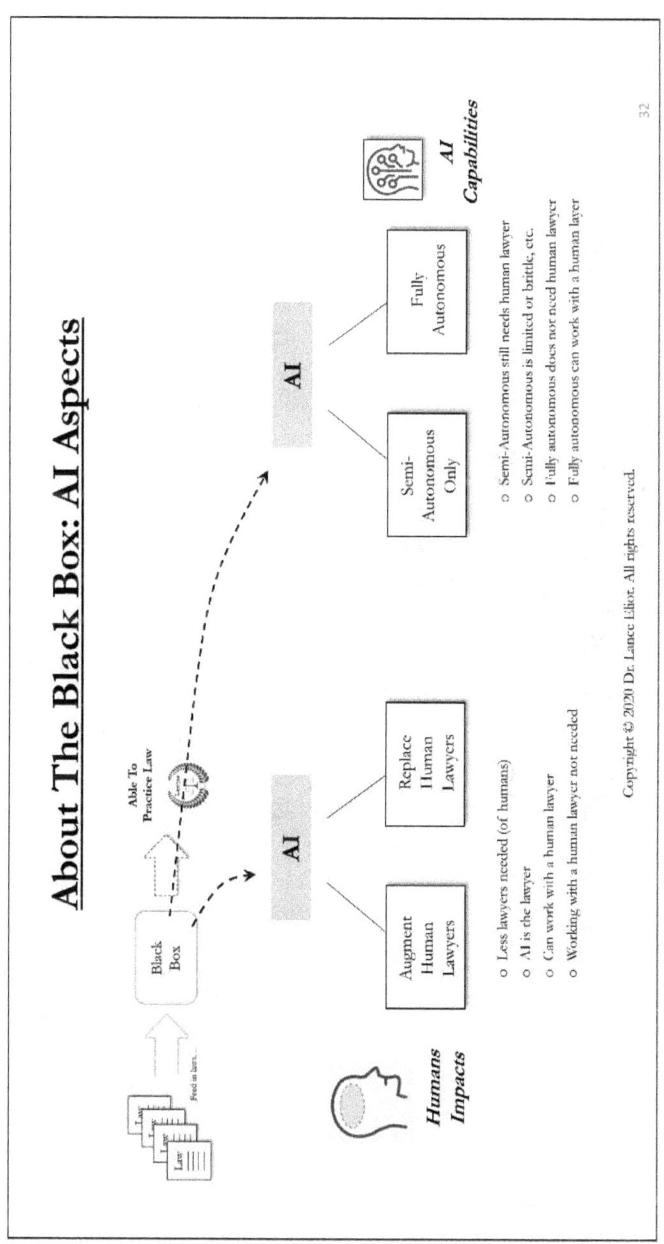
About The Black Box: AI Aspects
Law
Feed in laws...
Black Box
Able To Practice Law
AI
AI
Humans Impacts
Augment Human Lawyers
Replace Human Lawyers
Semi-Autonomous Only
Fully Autonomous
AI Capabilities
Less lawyers needed (of humans)
AI is the lawyer
Can work with a human lawyer
Working with a human lawyer not needed
Semi-Autonomous still needs human lawyer
Semi-Autonomous is limited or brittle, etc.
Fully autonomous does not need human lawyer
Fully autonomous can work with a human layer
Copyright © 2020 Dr. Lance Eliot. All rights reserved.
32

Figure 32

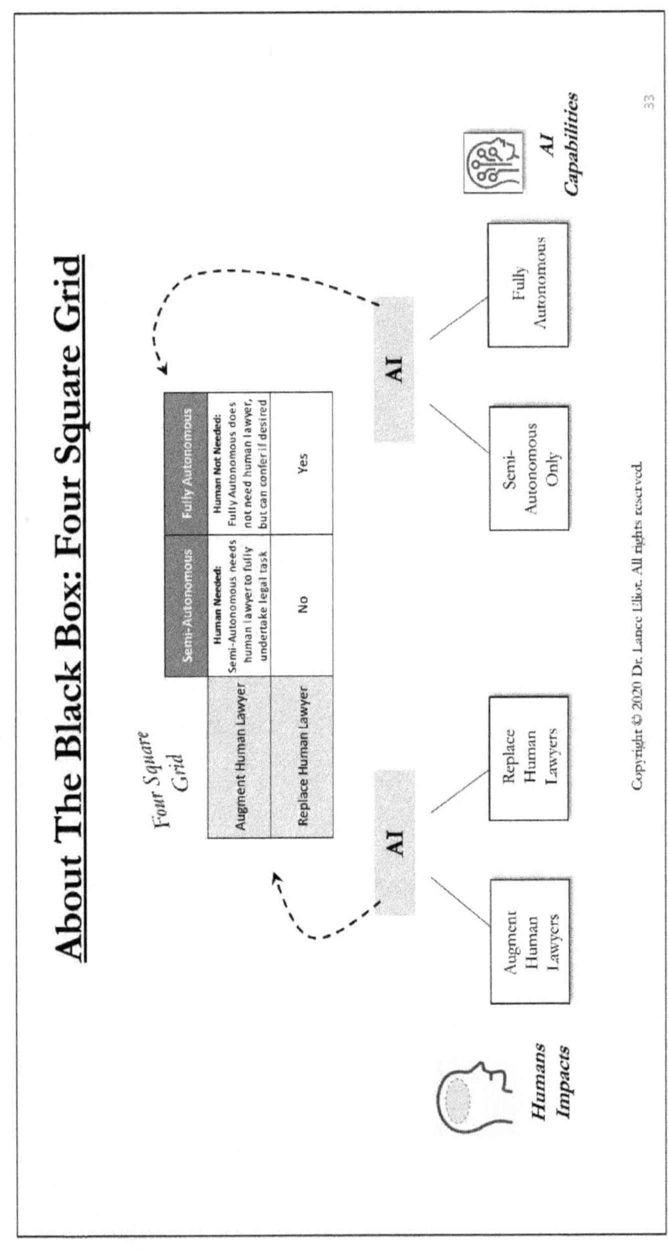
About The Black Box: Four Square Grid
Four Square Grid
Semi-Autonomous
Fully Autonomous
Human Needed: Semi-Autonomous needs human lawyer to fully undertake legal task
Human Not Needed: Fully Autonomous does not need human lawyer, but can confer if desired
Augment Human Lawyer
Replace Human Lawyer
No
Yes
AI
AI
Augment Human Lawyers
Replace Human Lawyers
Semi-Autonomous Only
Fully Autonomous
Humans Impacts
AI Capabilities
Copyright © 2020 Dr. Lance Eliot. All rights reserved.
33

Figure 33

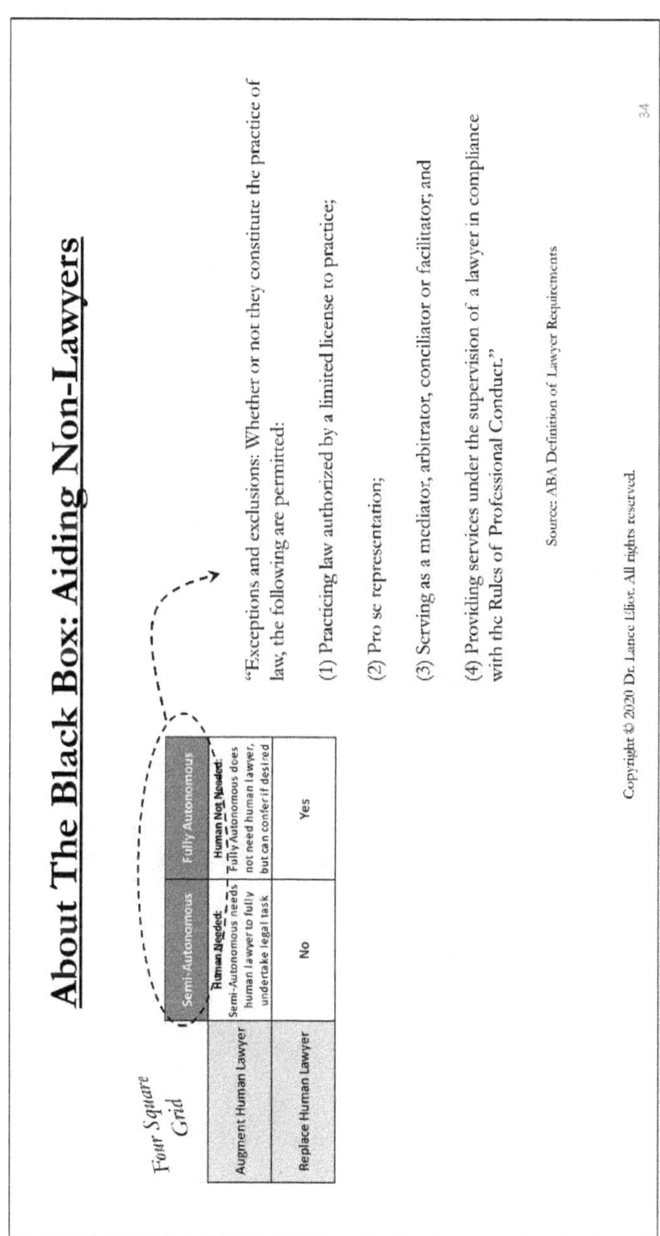
About The Black Box: Aiding Non-Lawyers
Four Square Grid
Augment Human Lawyer
Replace Human Lawyer
Semi-Autonomous
Fully Autonomous
Human Needed: Semi-Autonomous needs human lawyer to fully undertake legal task
Human Not Needed: Fully Autonomous does not need human lawyer, but can confer if desired
No
Yes
"Exceptions and exclusions: Whether or not they constitute the practice of law, the following are permitted:
(1) Practicing law authorized by a limited license to practice;
(2) Pro se representation;
(3) Serving as a mediator, arbitrator, conciliator or facilitator; and
(4) Providing services under the supervision of a lawyer in compliance with the Rules of Professional Conduct."
Source: ABA Definition of Lawyer Requirements
Copyright © 2020 Dr. Lance Eliot. All rights reserved.
34

Figure 34

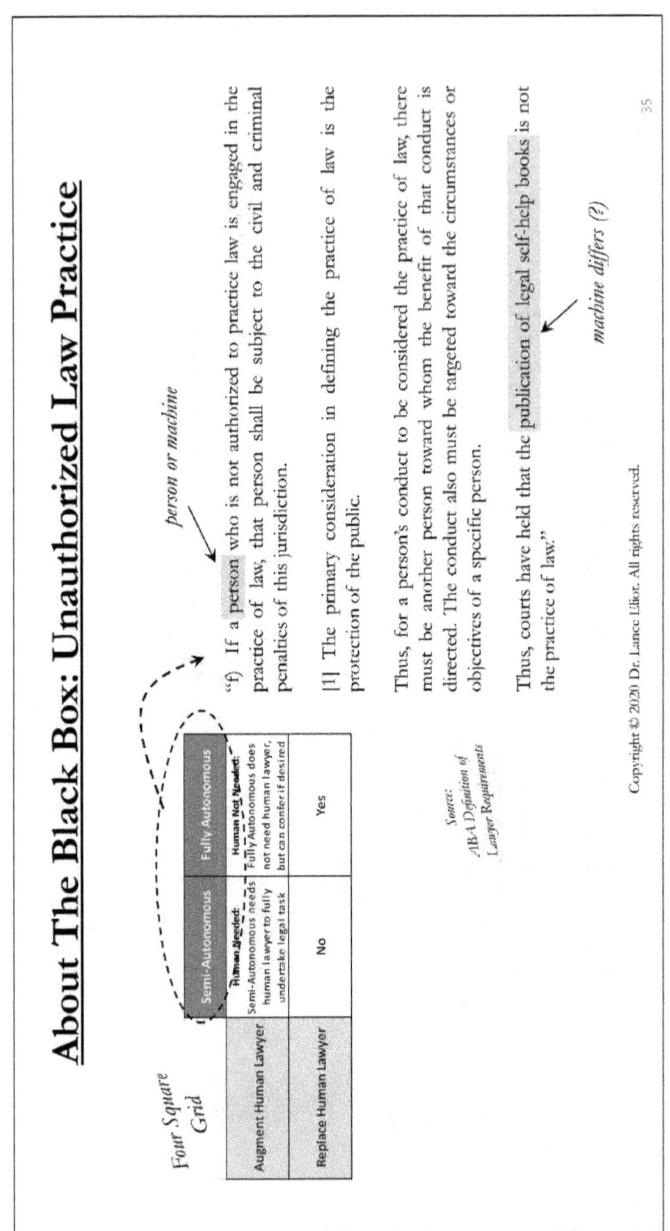
About The Black Box: Unauthorized Law Practice
Four Square Grid
Semi-Autonomous
Fully Autonomous
Augment Human Lawyer
Human Needed: Semi-Autonomous needs human lawyer to fully undertake legal task
Human Not Needed: Fully Autonomous does not need human lawyer, but can confer if desired
Replace Human Lawyer
No
Yes
person or machine
"f) If a person who is not authorized to practice law is engaged in the practice of law, that person shall be subject to the civil and criminal penalties of this jurisdiction.
[1] The primary consideration in defining the practice of law is the protection of the public.
Thus, for a person's conduct to be considered the practice of law, there must be another person toward whom the benefit of that conduct is directed. The conduct also must be targeted toward the circumstances or objectives of a specific person.
Thus, courts have held that the publication of legal self-help books is not the practice of law."
machine differs (?)
Source: ABA Definition of Lawyer Requirements
Copyright © 2020 Dr. Lance Eliot. All rights reserved.
35

Figure 35

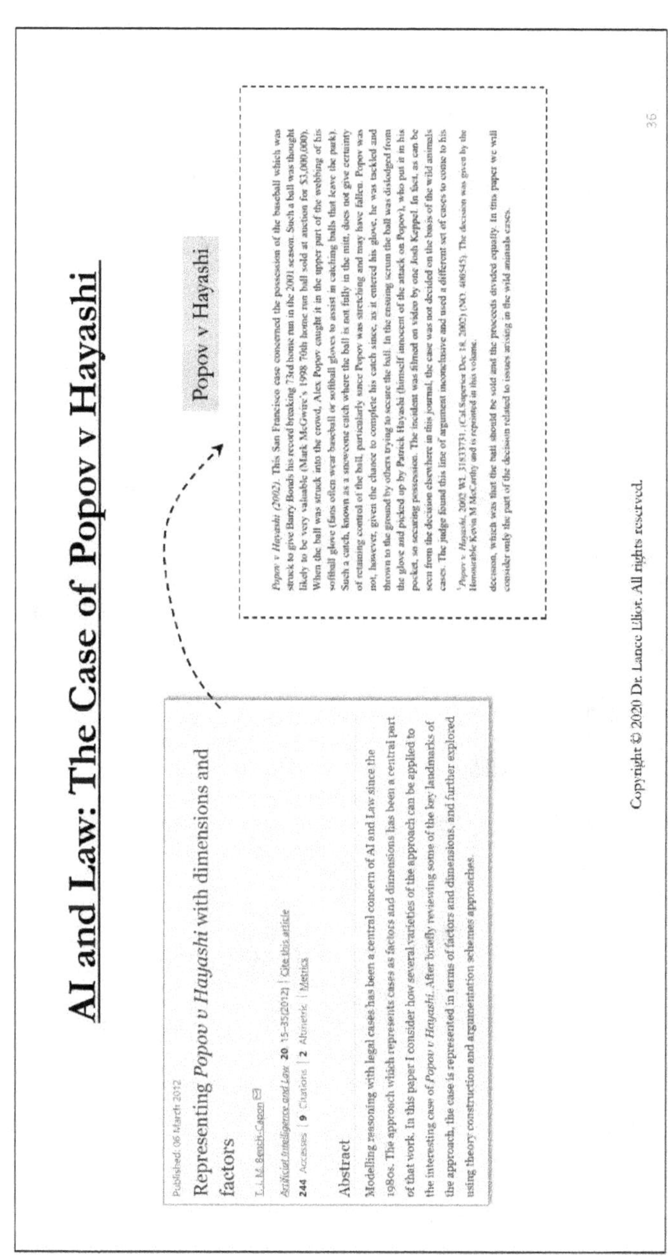
AI and Law: The Case of Popov v Hayashi
Published: 06 March 2012
Representing Popov v Hayashi with dimensions and factors
T. J. M. Bench-Capon
Artificial Intelligence and Law 20, 15–35(2012) | Cite this article
244 Accesses | 9 Citations | 2 Altmetric | Metrics
Abstract
Modelling reasoning with legal cases has been a central concern of AI and Law since the 1980s. The approach which represents cases as factors and dimensions has been a central part of that work. In this paper I consider how several varieties of the approach can be applied to the interesting case of Popov v Hayashi. After briefly reviewing some of the key landmarks of the approach, the case is represented in terms of factors and dimensions, and further explored using theory construction and argumentation schemes approaches.
Popov v Hayashi
Popov v Hayashi (2002). This San Francisco case concerned the possession of the baseball which was struck to give Barry Bonds his record breaking 73rd home run in the 2001 season. Such a ball was thought likely to be very valuable (Mark McGwire's 1998 70th home run ball sold at auction for $3,000,000). When the ball was struck into the crowd, Alex Popov caught it in the upper part of the webbing of his softball glove (fans often wear baseball or softball gloves to assist in catching balls that leave the park). Such a catch, known as a snowcone catch where the ball is not fully in the mitt, does not give certainty of retaining control of the ball, particularly since Popov was stretching and may have fallen. Popov was not, however, given the chance to complete his catch since, as it entered his glove, he was tackled and thrown to the ground by others trying to secure the ball. In the ensuing scrum the ball was dislodged from the glove and picked up by Patrick Hayashi (himself innocent of the attack on Popov), who put it in his pocket, so securing possession. The incident was filmed on video by one Josh Keppel. In fact, as can be seen from the decision elsewhere in this journal, the case was not decided on the basis of the wild animals cases. The judge found this line of argument inconclusive and used a different set of cases to come to his
[1] Popov v. Hayashi, 2002 WL 31833731, (Cal.Superior Dec 18, 2002) (NO. 400545). The decision was given by the Honourable Kevin M McCarthy and is reprinted in this volume.
decision, which was that the ball should be sold and the proceeds divided equally. In this paper we will consider only the part of the decision related to issues arising in the wild animals cases.
Copyright © 2020 Dr. Lance Eliot. All rights reserved.
36

Figure 36

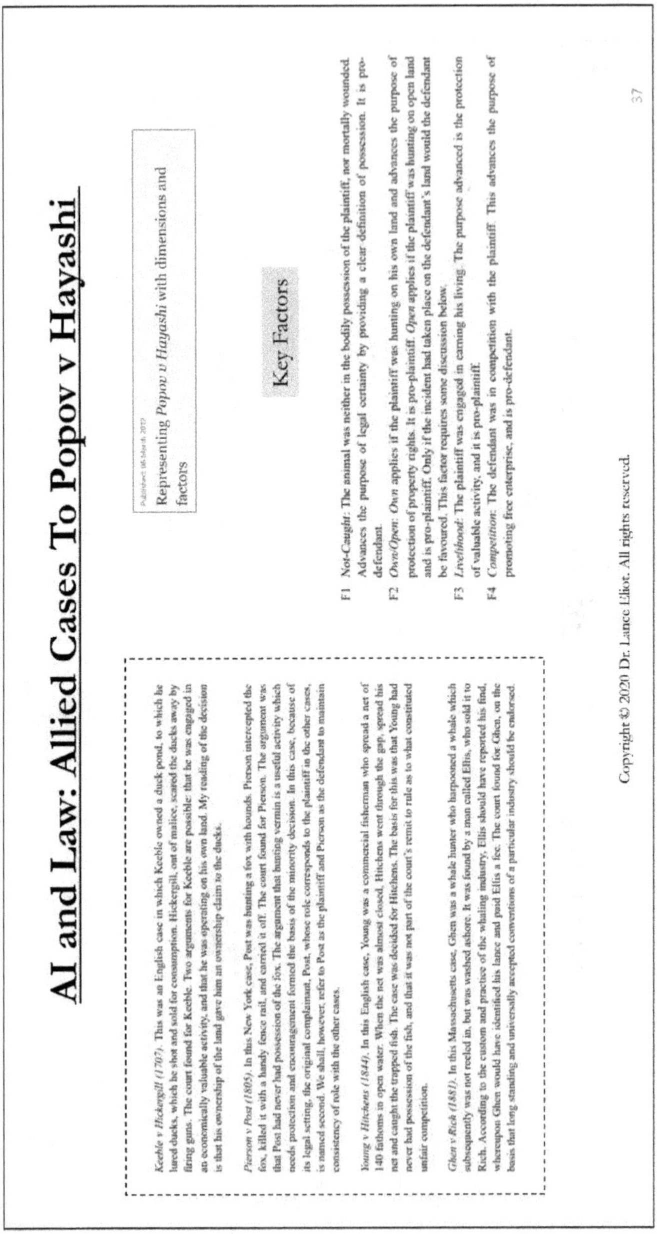

AI and Law: Allied Cases To Popov v Hayashi

Keeble v Hickergill (1707). This was an English case in which Keeble owned a duck pond, to which he lured ducks, which he shot and sold for consumption. Hickergill, out of malice, scared the ducks away by firing guns. The court found for Keeble. Two arguments for Keeble are possible: that he was engaged in an economically valuable activity, and that he was operating on his own land. My reading of the decision is that his ownership of the land gave him an ownership claim to the ducks.

Pierson v Post (1805). In this New York case, Post was hunting a fox with hounds. Pierson intercepted the fox, killed it with a handy fence rail, and carried it off. The court found for Pierson. The argument was that Post had never had possession of the fox. The argument that hunting vermin is a useful activity which needs protection and encouragement formed the basis of the minority decision. In this case, because of its legal setting, the original complainant, Post, whose role corresponds to the plaintiff in the other cases, is named second. We shall, however, refer to Post as the plaintiff and Pierson as the defendant to maintain consistency of role with the other cases.

Young v Hitchens (1844). In this English case, Young was a commercial fisherman who spread a net of 140 fathoms in open water. When the net was almost closed, Hitchens went through the gap, spread his net and caught the trapped fish. The case was decided for Hitchens. The basis for this was that Young had never had possession of the fish, and that it was not part of the court's remit to rule as to what constituted unfair competition.

Ghen v Rich (1881). In this Massachusetts case, Ghen was a whale hunter who harpooned a whale which subsequently was not reeled in, but was washed ashore. It was found by a man called Ellis, who sold it to Rich. According to the custom and practice of the whaling industry, Ellis should have reported his find, whereupon Ghen would have identified his lance and paid Ellis a fee. The court found for Ghen, on the basis that long standing and universally accepted conventions of a particular industry should be endorsed.

Published: 06 March 2017

Representing *Popov v Hayashi* with dimensions and factors

Key Factors

F1 *Not-Caught*: The animal was neither in the bodily possession of the plaintiff, nor mortally wounded. Advances the purpose of legal certainty by providing a clear definition of possession. It is pro-defendant.

F2 *Own/Open*: *Own* applies if the plaintiff was hunting on his own land and advances the purpose of protection of property rights. It is pro-plaintiff. *Open* applies if the plaintiff was hunting on open land and is pro-plaintiff. Only if the incident had taken place on the defendant's land would the defendant be favoured. This factor requires some discussion below.

F3 *Livelihood*: The plaintiff was engaged in earning his living. The purpose advanced is the protection of valuable activity, and it is pro-plaintiff.

F4 *Competition*: The defendant was in competition with the plaintiff. This advances the purpose of promoting free enterprise, and is pro-defendant.

37

Figure 37

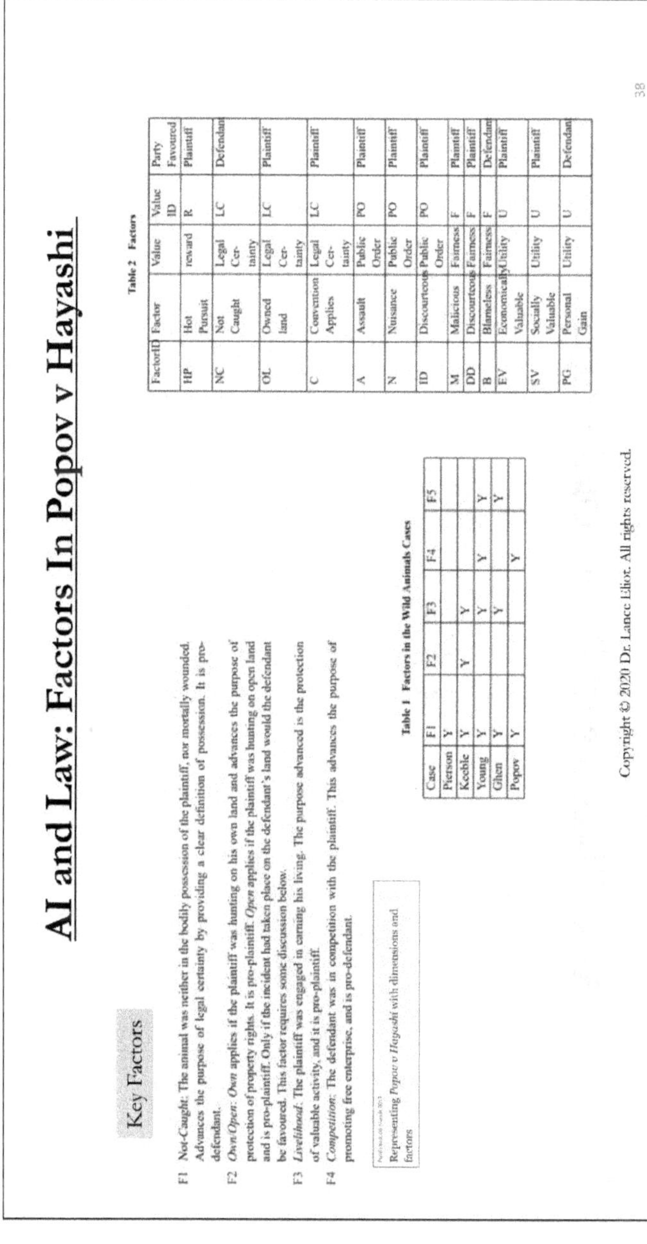
AI and Law: Factors In Popov v Hayashi
Key Factors
F1 Not-Caught: The animal was neither in the bodily possession of the plaintiff, nor mortally wounded. Advances the purpose of legal certainty by providing a clear definition of possession. It is pro-defendant.
F2 Own/Open: Own applies if the plaintiff was hunting on his own land and advances the purpose of protection of property rights. It is pro-plaintiff. Open applies if the plaintiff was hunting on open land and is pro-plaintiff. Only if the incident had taken place on the defendant's land would the defendant be favoured. This factor requires some discussion below.
F3 Livelihood: The plaintiff was engaged in earning his living. The purpose advanced is the protection of valuable activity, and it is pro-plaintiff.
F4 Competition: The defendant was in competition with the plaintiff. This advances the purpose of promoting free enterprise, and is pro-defendant.
Representing Popov v Hayashi with dimensions and factors
Table 1 Factors in the Wild Animals Cases

Case	F1	F2	F3	F4	F5
Pierson	Y				
Keeble	Y	Y	Y		
Young	Y		Y	Y	Y
Ghen	Y		Y		Y
Popov	Y			Y	

Table 2 Factors

FactorID	Factor	Value	Value ID	Party Favoured
HP	Hot Pursuit	reward	R	Plaintiff
NC	Not Caught	Legal Cer-tainty	LC	Defendant
OL	Owned land	Legal Cer-tainty	LC	Plaintiff
C	Convention Applies	Legal Cer-tainty	LC	Plaintiff
A	Assault	Public Order	PO	Plaintiff
N	Nuisance	Public Order	PO	Plaintiff
ID	Discourteous	Public Order	PO	Plaintiff
M	Malicious	Fairness	F	Plaintiff
DD	Discourteous	Fairness	F	Plaintiff
B	Blameless	Fairness	F	Defendant
EV	Economically Valuable	Utility	U	Plaintiff
SV	Socially Valuable	Utility	U	Plaintiff
PG	Personal Gain	Utility	U	Defendant

Copyright © 2020 Dr. Lance Eliot. All rights reserved.
38

Figure 38

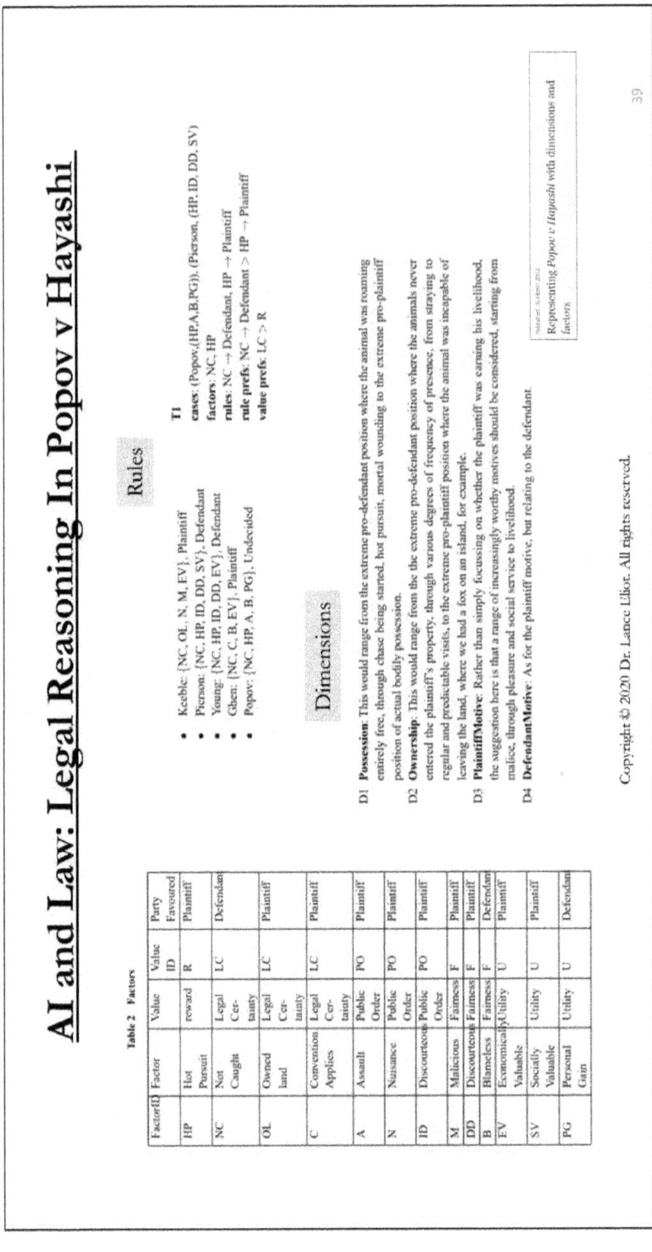
AI and Law: Legal Reasoning In Popov v Hayashi
Table 2 Factors
FactorID | Factor | Value | Value ID | Party Favoured
HP | Hot Pursuit | reward | R | Plaintiff
NC | Not Caught | Legal Certainty | LC | Defendant
OL | Owned land | Legal Certainty | LC | Plaintiff
C | Convention Applies | Legal Certainty | LC | Plaintiff
A | Assault | Public Order | PO | Plaintiff
N | Nuisance | Public Order | PO | Plaintiff
ID | Discourteous | Public Order | PO | Plaintiff
M | Malicious | Fairness | F | Plaintiff
DD | Discourteous | Fairness | F | Plaintiff
B | Blameless | Fairness | F | Defendant
EV | Economically Valuable | Utility | U | Plaintiff
SV | Socially Valuable | Utility | U | Plaintiff
PG | Personal Gain | Utility | U | Defendant
Rules
Keeble: {NC, OL, N, M, EV}, Plaintiff
Pierson: {NC, HP, ID, DD, SV}, Defendant
Young: {NC, HP, ID, DD, EV}, Defendant
Ghen: {NC, C, B, EV}, Plaintiff
Popov: {NC, HP, A, B, PG}, Undecided
T1
cases: (Popov,(HP,A,B,PG)), (Pierson, (HP, ID, DD, SV)
factors: NC, HP
rules: NC → Defendant, HP → Plaintiff
rule prefs: NC → Defendant > HP → Plaintiff
value prefs: LC > R
Dimensions
D1 Possession: This would range from the extreme pro-defendant position where the animal was roaming entirely free, through chase being started, hot pursuit, mortal wounding to the extreme pro-plaintiff position of actual bodily possession.
D2 Ownership: This would range from the the extreme pro-defendant position where the animals never entered the plaintiff's property, through various degrees of frequency of presence, from straying to regular and predictable visits, to the extreme pro-plaintiff position where the animal was incapable of leaving the land, where we had a fox on an island, for example.
D3 PlaintiffMotive: Rather than simply focussing on whether the plaintiff was earning his livelihood, the suggestion here is that a range of increasingly worthy motives should be considered, starting from malice, through pleasure and social service to livelihood.
D4 DefendantMotive: As for the plaintiff motive, but relating to the defendant.
Representing Popov v Hayashi with dimensions and factors
Copyright © 2020 Dr. Lance Eliot. All rights reserved.
39

Figure 39

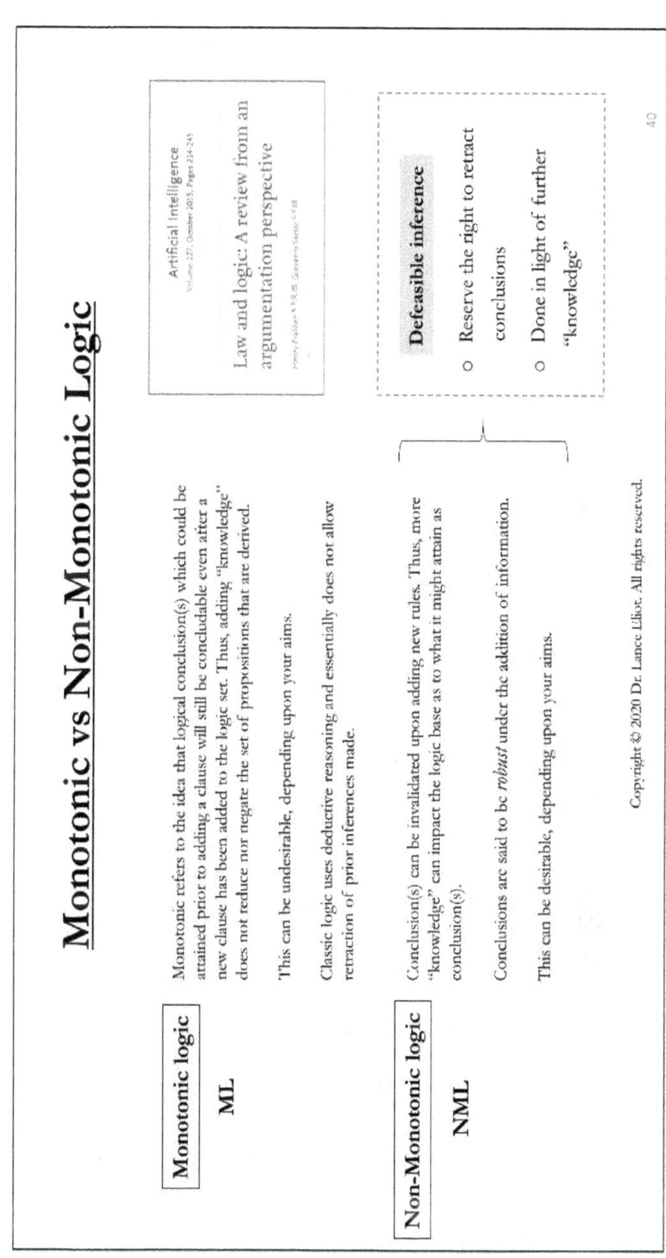
Monotonic vs Non-Monotonic Logic
Monotonic logic
ML
Monotonic refers to the idea that logical conclusion(s) which could be attained prior to adding a clause will still be concludable even after a new clause has been added to the logic set. Thus, adding "knowledge" does not reduce nor negate the set of propositions that are derived.
This can be undesirable, depending upon your aims.
Classic logic uses deductive reasoning and essentially does not allow retraction of prior inferences made.
Artificial Intelligence
Volume 227, October 2015, Pages 214-245
Law and logic: A review from an argumentation perspective
Non-Monotonic logic
NML
Conclusion(s) can be invalidated upon adding new rules. Thus, more "knowledge" can impact the logic base as to what it might attain as conclusion(s).
Conclusions are said to be robust under the addition of information.
This can be desirable, depending upon your aims.
Defeasible inference
Reserve the right to retract conclusions
Done in light of further "knowledge"
Copyright © 2020 Dr. Lance Eliot. All rights reserved.
40

Figure 40

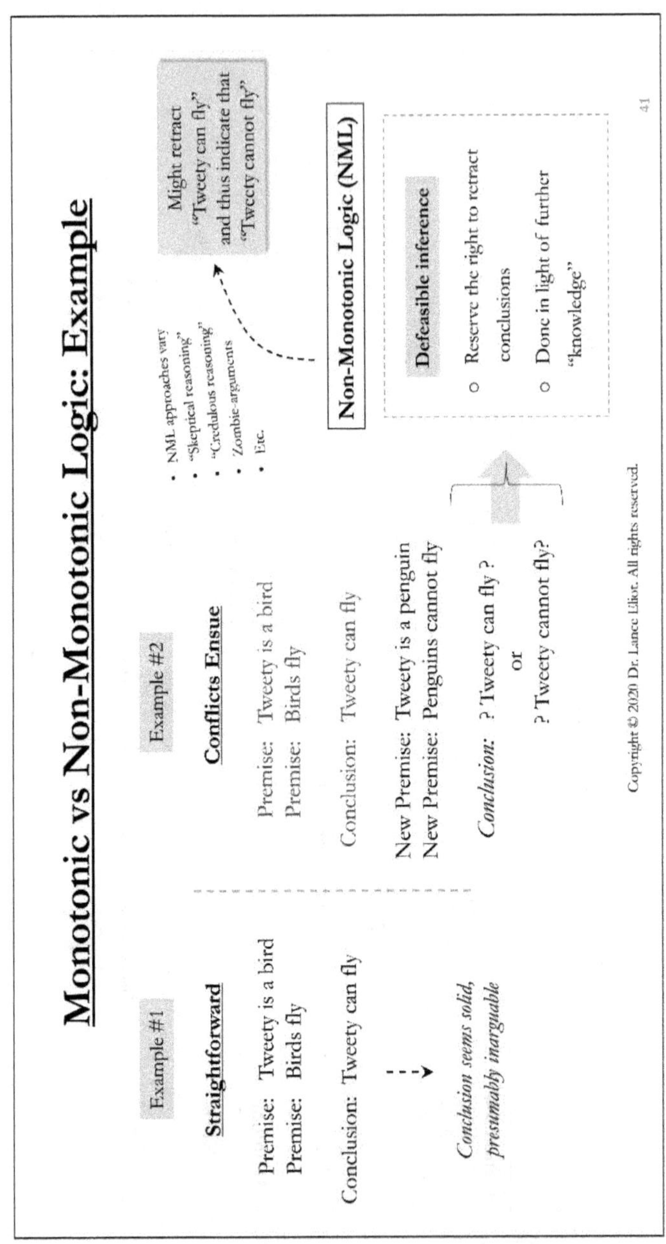
Monotonic vs Non-Monotonic Logic: Example
Example #1
Straightforward
Premise: Tweety is a bird
Premise: Birds fly
Conclusion: Tweety can fly
Conclusion seems solid, presumably inarguable
Example #2
Conflicts Ensue
Premise: Tweety is a bird
Premise: Birds fly
Conclusion: Tweety can fly
New Premise: Tweety is a penguin
New Premise: Penguins cannot fly
Conclusion: ? Tweety can fly ?
or
? Tweety cannot fly?
NML approaches vary
"Skeptical reasoning"
"Credulous reasoning"
Zombie-arguments
Etc.
Might retract "Tweety can fly" and thus indicate that "Tweety cannot fly"
Non-Monotonic Logic (NML)
Defeasible inference
Reserve the right to retract conclusions
Done in light of further "knowledge"
Copyright © 2020 Dr. Lance Eliot. All rights reserved.
41

Figure 41

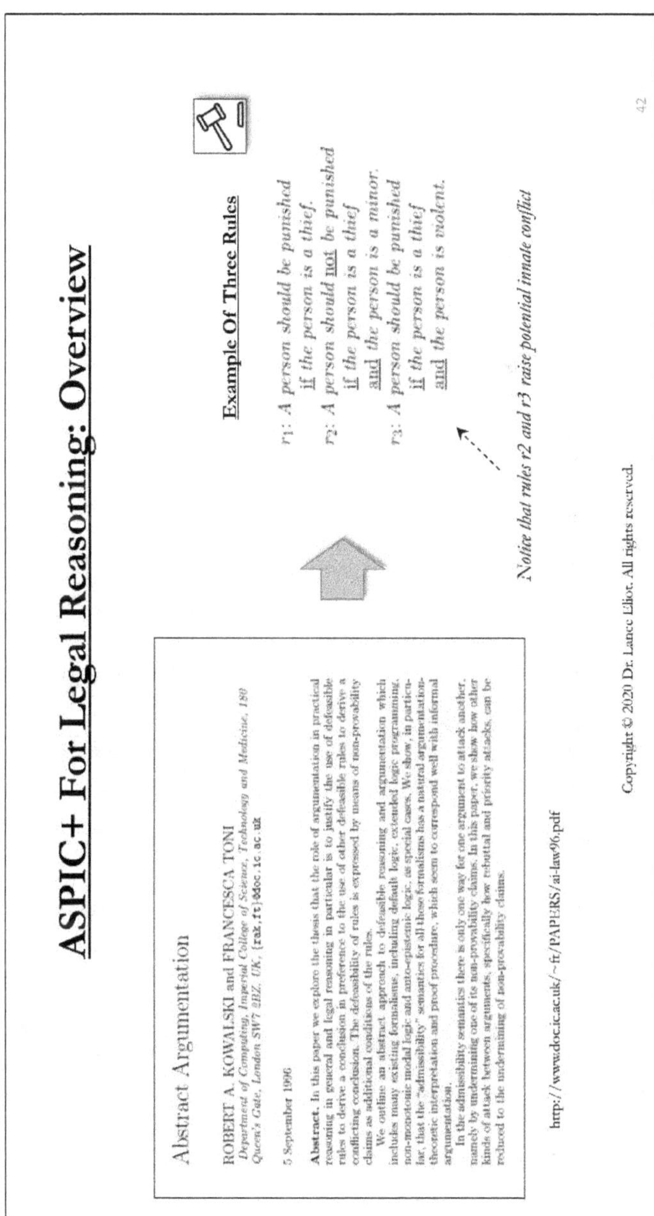
ASPIC+ For Legal Reasoning: Overview
Abstract Argumentation
ROBERT A. KOWALSKI and FRANCESCA TONI
Department of Computing, Imperial College of Science, Technology and Medicine, 180 Queen's Gate, London SW7 2BZ, UK, {rak,ft}@doc.ic.ac.uk
5 September 1996
Abstract. In this paper we explore the thesis that the role of argumentation in practical reasoning in general and legal reasoning in particular is to justify the use of defeasible rules to derive a conclusion in preference to the use of other defeasible rules to derive a conflicting conclusion. The defeasibility of rules is expressed by means of non-provability claims as additional conditions of the rules.
We outline an abstract approach to defeasible reasoning and argumentation which includes many existing formalisms, including default logic, extended logic programming, non-monotonic modal logic and auto-epistemic logic, as special cases. We show, in particular, that the "admissibility" semantics for all these formalisms has a natural argumentation-theoretic interpretation and proof procedure, which seem to correspond well with informal argumentation.
In the admissibility semantics there is only one way for one argument to attack another, namely by undermining one of its non-provability claims. In this paper, we show how other kinds of attack between arguments, specifically how rebuttal and priority attacks, can be reduced to the undermining of non-provability claims.
http://www.doc.ic.ac.uk/~ft/PAPERS/ai-law96.pdf
Example Of Three Rules
r1: A person should be punished
if the person is a thief.
r2: A person should not be punished
if the person is a thief
and the person is a minor.
r3: A person should be punished
if the person is a thief
and the person is violent.
Notice that rules r2 and r3 raise potential innate conflict
Copyright © 2020 Dr. Lance Eliot. All rights reserved.
42

Figure 42

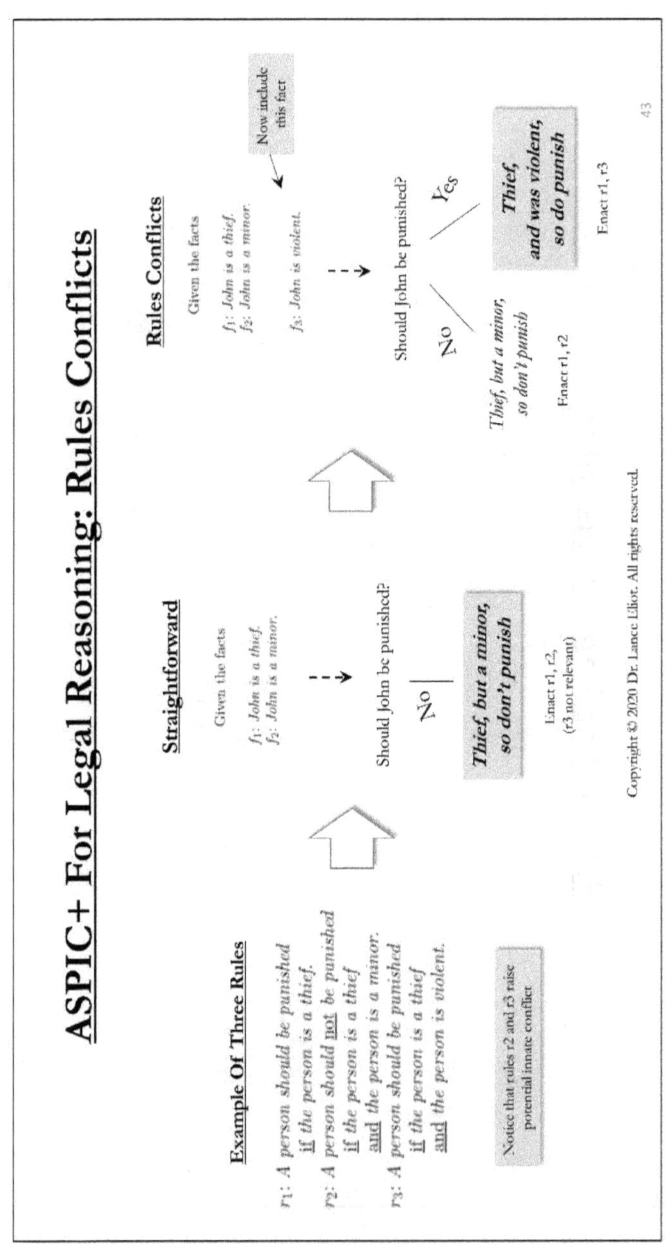
ASPIC+ For Legal Reasoning: Rules Conflicts
Example Of Three Rules
r1: A person should be punished if the person is a thief.
r2: A person should not be punished if the person is a thief and the person is a minor.
r3: A person should be punished if the person is a thief and the person is violent.
Notice that rules r2 and r3 raise potential innate conflict
Straightforward
Given the facts
f1: John is a thief.
f2: John is a minor.
Should John be punished?
No
Thief, but a minor, so don't punish
Enact r1, r2, (r3 not relevant)
Rules Conflicts
Given the facts
f1: John is a thief.
f2: John is a minor.
f3: John is violent.
Now include this fact
Should John be punished?
No
Yes
Thief, but a minor, so don't punish
Enact r1, r2
Thief, and was violent, so do punish
Enact r1, r3
Copyright © 2020 Dr. Lance Eliot. All rights reserved.
43

Figure 43

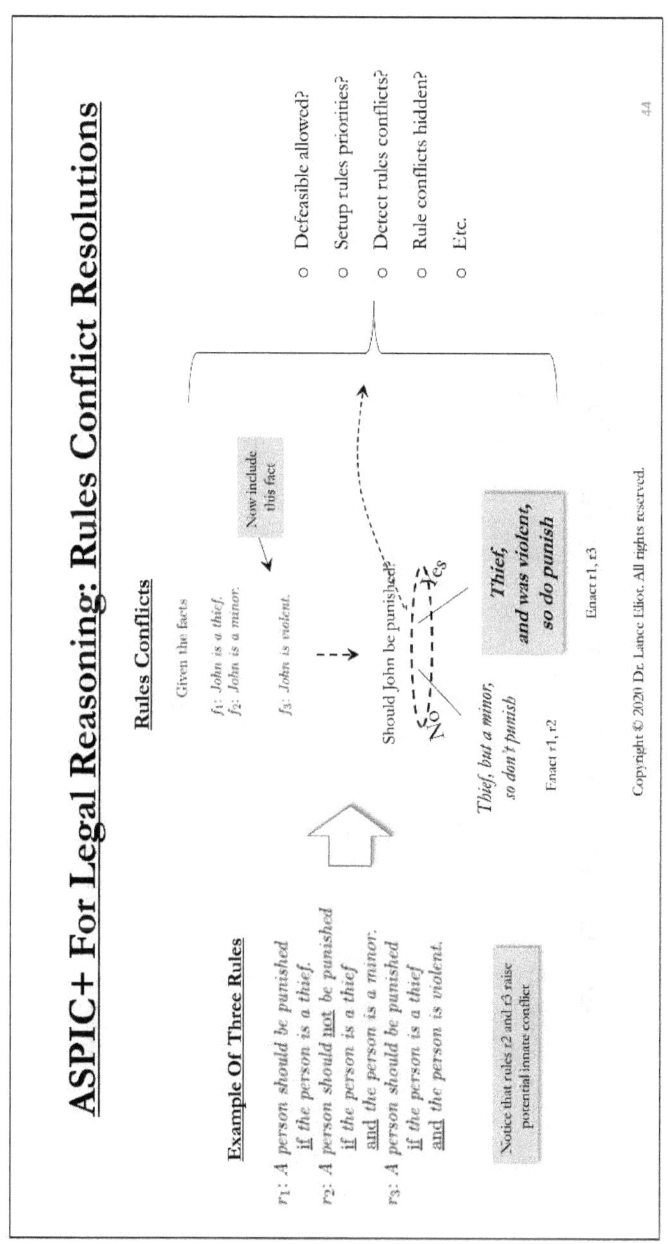
ASPIC+ For Legal Reasoning: Rules Conflict Resolutions
Example Of Three Rules
r1: A person should be punished if the person is a thief.
r2: A person should not be punished if the person is a thief and the person is a minor.
r3: A person should be punished if the person is a thief and the person is violent.
Notice that rules r2 and r3 raise potential innate conflict
Rules Conflicts
Given the facts
f1: John is a thief.
f2: John is a minor.
Now include this fact
f3: John is violent.
Should John be punished?
No
Yes
Thief, but a minor, so don't punish
Enact r1, r2
Thief, and was violent, so do punish
Enact r1, r3
Defeasible allowed?
Setup rules priorities?
Detect rules conflicts?
Rule conflicts hidden?
Etc.
Copyright © 2020 Dr. Lance Eliot. All rights reserved.
44

Figure 44

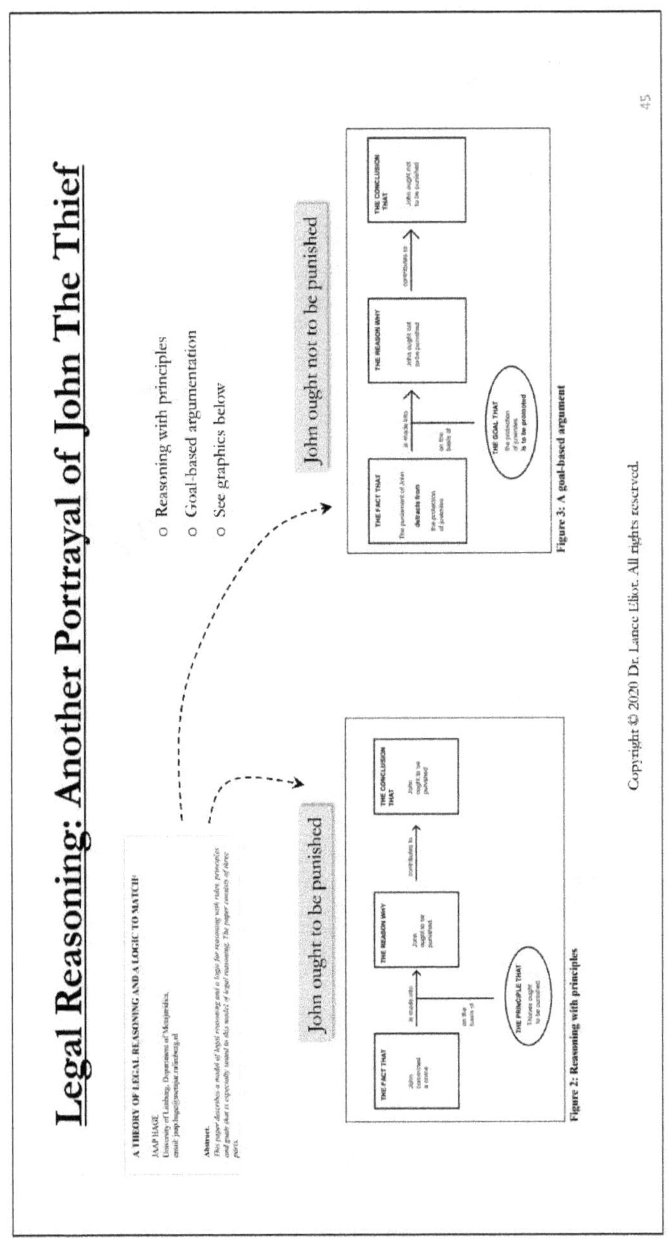
Legal Reasoning: Another Portrayal of John The Thief
Reasoning with principles
Goal-based argumentation
See graphics below
A THEORY OF LEGAL REASONING AND A LOGIC TO MATCH
JAAP HAGE
Abstract.
John ought to be punished
John ought not to be punished
THE FACT THAT
THE REASON WHY
THE CONCLUSION THAT
THE PRINCIPLE THAT
THE GOAL THAT
Figure 2: Reasoning with principles
Figure 3: A goal-based argument
Copyright © 2020 Dr. Lance Eliot. All rights reserved.
45

Figure 45

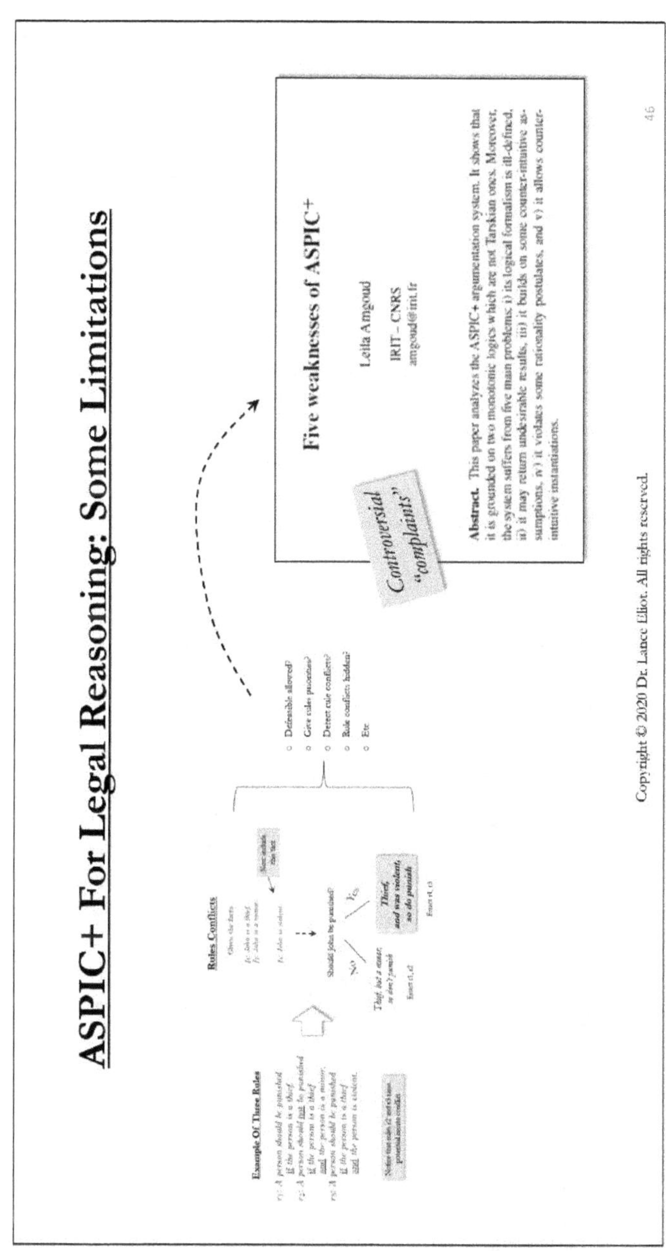
ASPIC+ For Legal Reasoning: Some Limitations
Example Of Three Rules
Rules Conflicts
Should John be punished?
No
Yes
Thief, and was violent, so do punish
Defeasible allowed?
Give rules priorities?
Detect rule conflicts?
Rule conflicts hidden?
Etc.
Five weaknesses of ASPIC+
Leila Amgoud
IRIT – CNRS
amgoud@irit.fr
Abstract. This paper analyzes the ASPIC+ argumentation system. It shows that it is grounded on two monotonic logics which are not Tarskian ones. Moreover, the system suffers from five main problems: i) its logical formalism is ill-defined, ii) it may return undesirable results, iii) it builds on some counter-intuitive assumptions, iv) it violates some rationality postulates, and v) it allows counter-intuitive instantiations.
Controversial “complaints”
Copyright © 2020 Dr. Lance Eliot. All rights reserved.
46

Figure 46

ASPIC+ For Legal Reasoning: Style Of Language

RESEARCH ARTICLE

The *ASPIC+* framework for structured argumentation: a tutorial

Sanjay Modgil[a] and Henry Prakken[b]

[a]*Department of Informatics, King's College London, UK;* [b]*Department of Information and Computing Sciences, Utrecht University & Faculty of Law, University of Groningen, The Netherlands*

(Received 00 Month 200x; final version received 00 Month 200x)

This article gives a tutorial introduction to the *ASPIC*$^{+}$ framework for structured argumentation. The philosophical and conceptual underpinnings of *ASPIC*$^{+}$ are discussed, the main definitions are illustrated with examples and several ways are discussed to instantiate the framework and to reconstruct other approaches as special cases of the framework. The *ASPIC*$^{+}$ framework is based on two ideas: the first is that conflicts between arguments are often resolved with explicit preferences, and the second is that arguments are built with two kinds of inference rules: strict, or deductive rules, whose premises guarantee their conclusion, and defeasible rules, whose premises only create a presumption in favour of their conclusion. Accordingly, arguments can in *ASPIC*$^{+}$ be attacked in three ways: on their uncertain premises, or on their defeasible infences, or on the conclusions of their defeasible inferences. *ASPIC*$^{+}$ is not a system but a framework for specifying systems. A main objective of the study of the *ASPIC*$^{+}$ framework is to identify conditions under which instantiations of the framework satisfy logical consistency and closure properties.

https://nms.kcl.ac.uk/sanjay.modgil/ASPICtutorial.pdf

Example of style of Logic Language used

d_1: $bird \Rightarrow canfly$
d_2: $penguin \Rightarrow \neg canfly$
d_3: $observed\_as\_penguin \Rightarrow \neg penguin$
f_1: $penguin \supset bird$
f_2: $penguin \supset \neg r_1$
f_3: $observed\_as\_penguin$

A_1: $observed\_as\_penguin$ — B_1: $A_2 \Rightarrow \neg canfly$
A_2: $A_1 \Rightarrow penguin$
A_3: $penguin \supset bird$
A_4: $A_2, A_3 \Rightarrow canfly$ — C_1: $A_2 \Rightarrow \neg r_1$

Note also that no argument can be built against the conclusion *penguin*. We have that A_4 and B_1 rebut each other while C_1 undercuts A_4. Whatever the argument ordering between A_4 and B_1, we thus obtain that the conclusion $\neg canfly$ is justified in any semantics.

Concluding, the classical modelling of this example is simpler in that it only uses classical inference and does not have to rely on the notion of a defeasible inference rule.

47

Figure 47

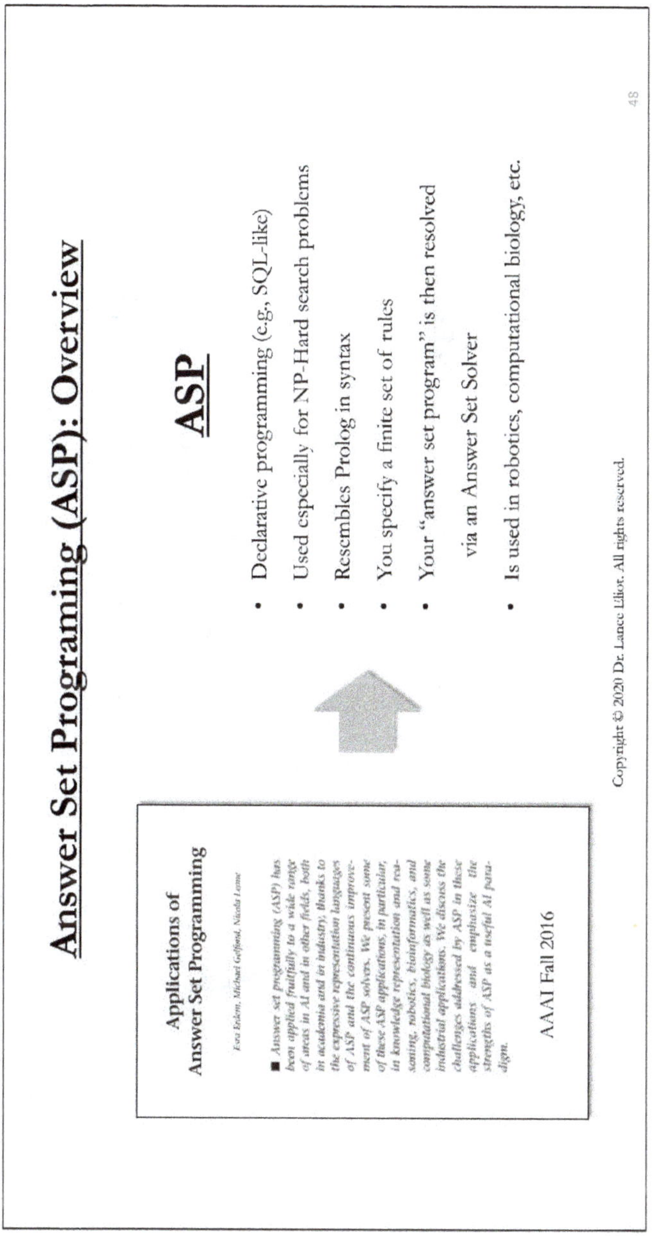

Answer Set Programing (ASP): Overview

Applications of Answer Set Programming

Esra Erdem, Michael Gelfond, Nicola Leone

■ Answer set programming (ASP) has been applied fruitfully to a wide range of areas in AI and in other fields, both in academia and in industry, thanks to the expressive representation languages of ASP and the continuous improvement of ASP solvers. We present some of these ASP applications, in particular, in knowledge representation and reasoning, robotics, bioinformatics, and computational biology as well as some industrial applications. We discuss the challenges addressed by ASP in these applications and emphasize the strengths of ASP as a useful AI paradigm.

AAAI Fall 2016

ASP

- Declarative programming (e.g., SQL-like)
- Used especially for NP-Hard search problems
- Resembles Prolog in syntax
- You specify a finite set of rules
- Your "answer set program" is then resolved via an Answer Set Solver
- Is used in robotics, computational biology, etc.

48

Figure 48

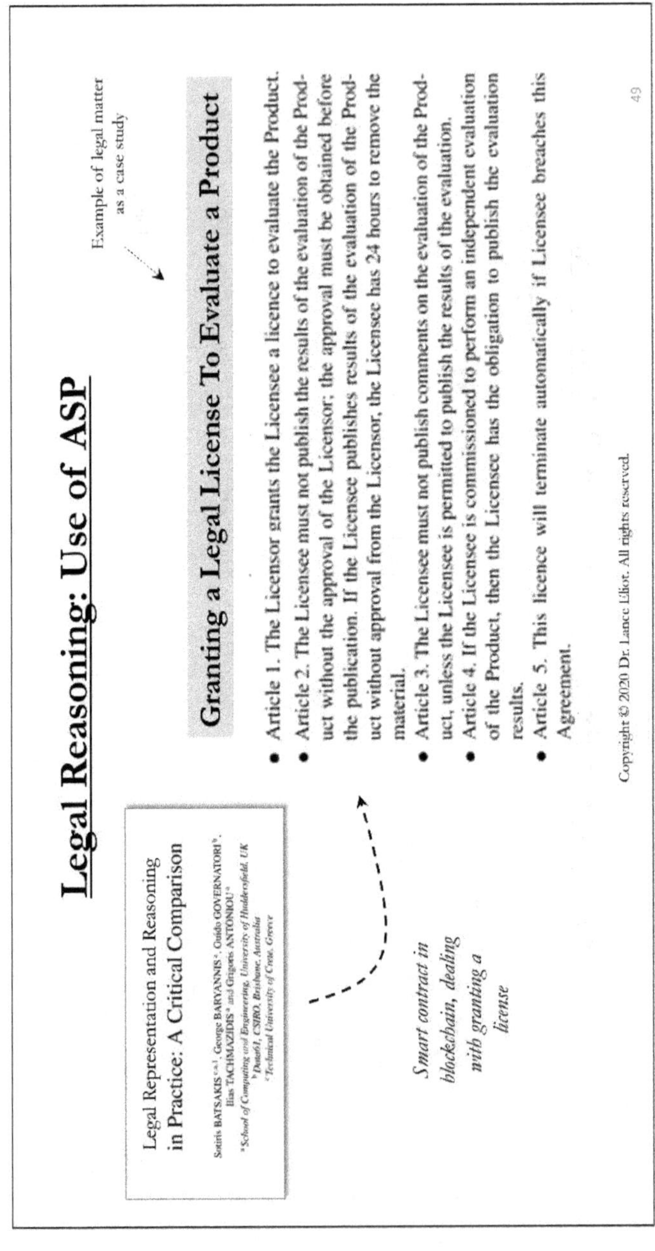
Legal Reasoning: Use of ASP
Legal Representation and Reasoning in Practice: A Critical Comparison
Example of legal matter as a case study
Granting a Legal License To Evaluate a Product
Article 1. The Licensor grants the Licensee a licence to evaluate the Product.
Article 2. The Licensee must not publish the results of the evaluation of the Product without the approval of the Licensor; the approval must be obtained before the publication. If the Licensee publishes results of the evaluation of the Product without approval from the Licensor, the Licensee has 24 hours to remove the material.
Article 3. The Licensee must not publish comments on the evaluation of the Product, unless the Licensee is permitted to publish the results of the evaluation.
Article 4. If the Licensee is commissioned to perform an independent evaluation of the Product, then the Licensee has the obligation to publish the evaluation results.
Article 5. This licence will terminate automatically if Licensee breaches this Agreement.
Smart contract in blockchain, dealing with granting a license
Copyright © 2020 Dr. Lance Eliot. All rights reserved.
49

Figure 49

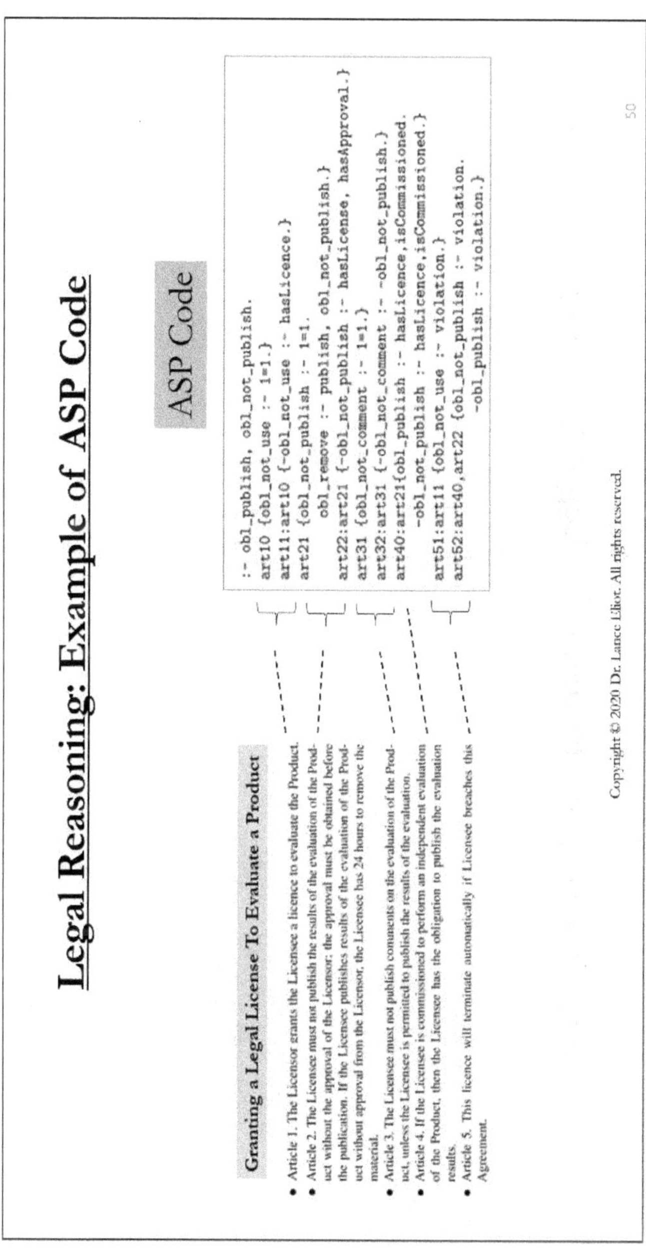
Legal Reasoning: Example of ASP Code
ASP Code
Granting a Legal License To Evaluate a Product
• Article 1. The Licensor grants the Licensee a licence to evaluate the Product.
• Article 2. The Licensee must not publish the results of the evaluation of the Product without the approval of the Licensor; the approval must be obtained before the publication. If the Licensee publishes results of the evaluation of the Product without approval from the Licensor, the Licensee has 24 hours to remove the material.
• Article 3. The Licensee must not publish comments on the evaluation of the Product, unless the Licensee is permitted to publish the results of the evaluation.
• Article 4. If the Licensee is commissioned to perform an independent evaluation of the Product, then the Licensee has the obligation to publish the evaluation results.
• Article 5. This licence will terminate automatically if Licensee breaches this Agreement.
:- obl_publish, obl_not_publish.
art10 {obl_not_use :- 1=1.}
art11:art10 {-obl_not_use :- hasLicence.}
art21 {obl_not_publish :- 1=1.
obl_remove :- publish, obl_not_publish.}
art22:art21 {-obl_not_publish :- hasLicense, hasApproval.}
art31 {obl_not_comment :- 1=1.}
art32:art31 {-obl_not_comment :- -obl_not_publish.}
art40:art21{obl_publish :- hasLicence,isCommissioned.
-obl_not_publish :- hasLicence,isCommissioned.}
art51:art11 {obl_not_use :- violation.}
art52:art40,art22 {obl_not_publish :- violation.
-obl_publish :- violation.}
Copyright © 2020 Dr. Lance Eliot. All rights reserved.
50

Figure 50

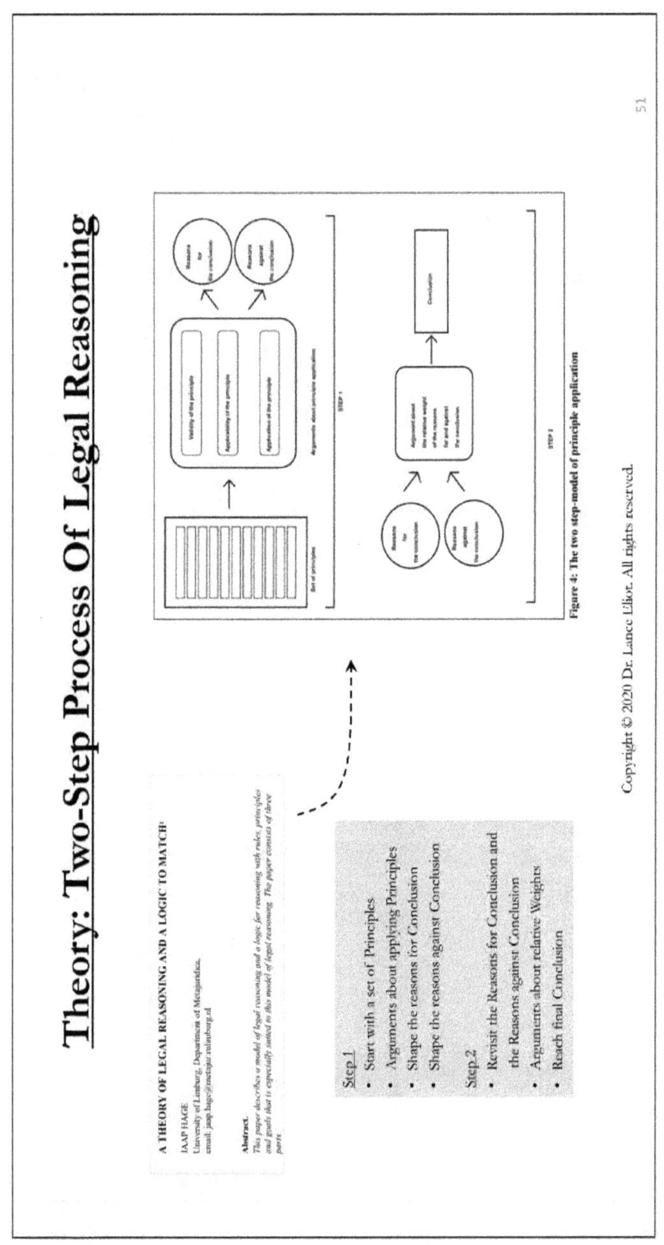

Theory: Two-Step Process Of Legal Reasoning
A THEORY OF LEGAL REASONING AND A LOGIC TO MATCH
JAAP HAGE
University of Limburg, Department of Metajuridica.
email: jaap.hage@metajur.rulimburg.nl
Abstract.
This paper describes a model of legal reasoning and a logic for reasoning with rules, principles and goals that is especially suited to this model of legal reasoning. The paper consists of three parts.
Step 1
• Start with a set of Principles
• Arguments about applying Principles
• Shape the reasons for Conclusion
• Shape the reasons against Conclusion
Step 2
• Revisit the Reasons for Conclusion and the Reasons against Conclusion
• Arguments about relative Weights
• Reach final Conclusion
Set of principles
Validity of the principle
Applicability of the principle
Application of the principle
Arguments about principle application
Reasons for the conclusion
Reasons against the conclusion
STEP 1
Reasons for the conclusion
Reasons against the conclusion
Argument about the relative weight of the reasons for and against the conclusion
Conclusion
STEP 2
Figure 4: The two step-model of principle application
Copyright © 2020 Dr. Lance Eliot. All rights reserved.
51

Figure 51

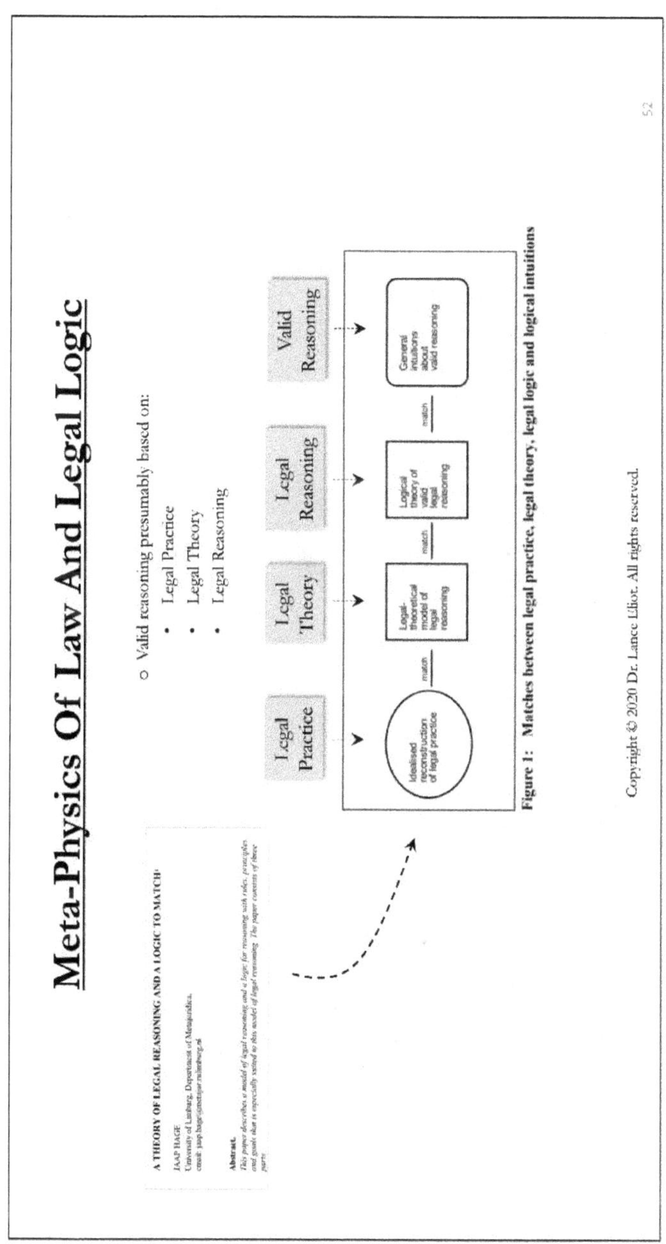
Meta-Physics Of Law And Legal Logic
A THEORY OF LEGAL REASONING AND A LOGIC TO MATCH
JAAP HAGE
University of Limburg, Department of Metajuridica,
Abstract.
This paper describes a model of legal reasoning and a logic for reasoning with rules, principles and goals that is especially suited to this model of legal reasoning. The paper consists of three parts
o Valid reasoning presumably based on:
• Legal Practice
• Legal Theory
• Legal Reasoning
Legal Practice
Legal Theory
Legal Reasoning
Valid Reasoning
Idealised reconstruction of legal practice
match
Legal-theoretical model of legal reasoning
match
Logical theory of valid legal reasoning
match
General intuitions about valid reasoning
Figure 1: Matches between legal practice, legal theory, legal logic and logical intuitions
Copyright © 2020 Dr. Lance Eliot. All rights reserved.
52

Figure 52

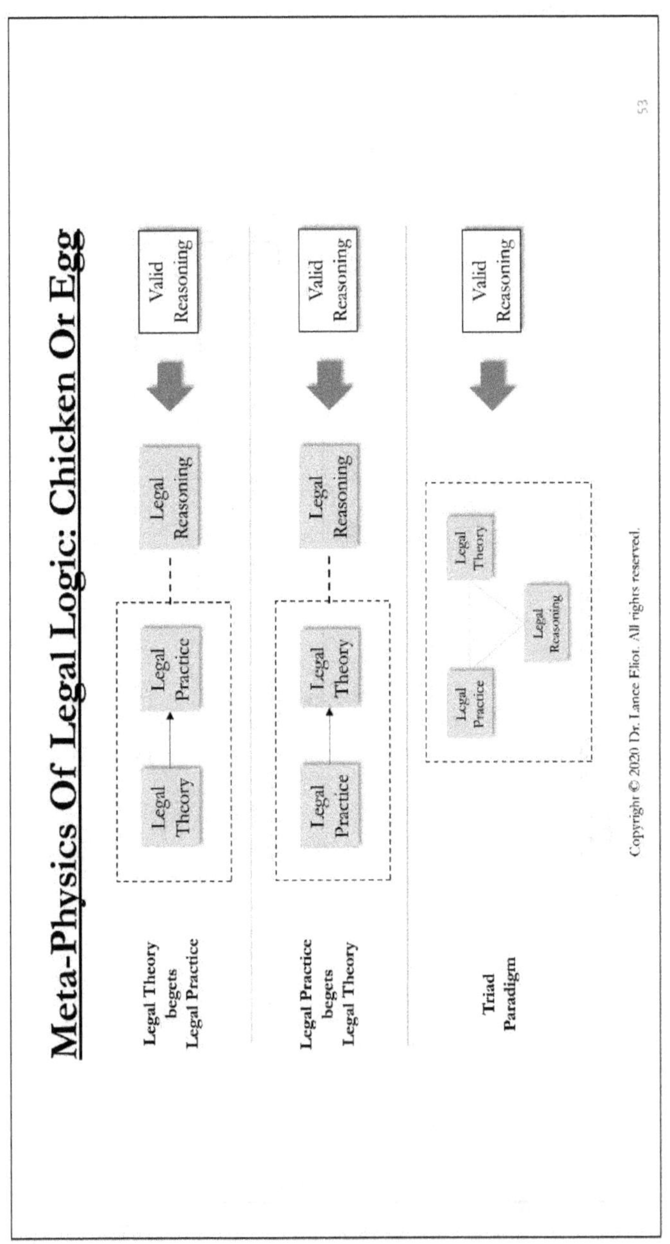
Meta-Physics Of Legal Logic: Chicken Or Egg
Legal Theory begets Legal Practice
Legal Theory
Legal Practice
Legal Reasoning
Valid Reasoning
Legal Practice begets Legal Theory
Legal Practice
Legal Theory
Legal Reasoning
Valid Reasoning
Triad Paradigm
Legal Practice
Legal Reasoning
Legal Theory
Valid Reasoning
Copyright © 2020 Dr. Lance Eliot. All rights reserved.
53

Figure 53

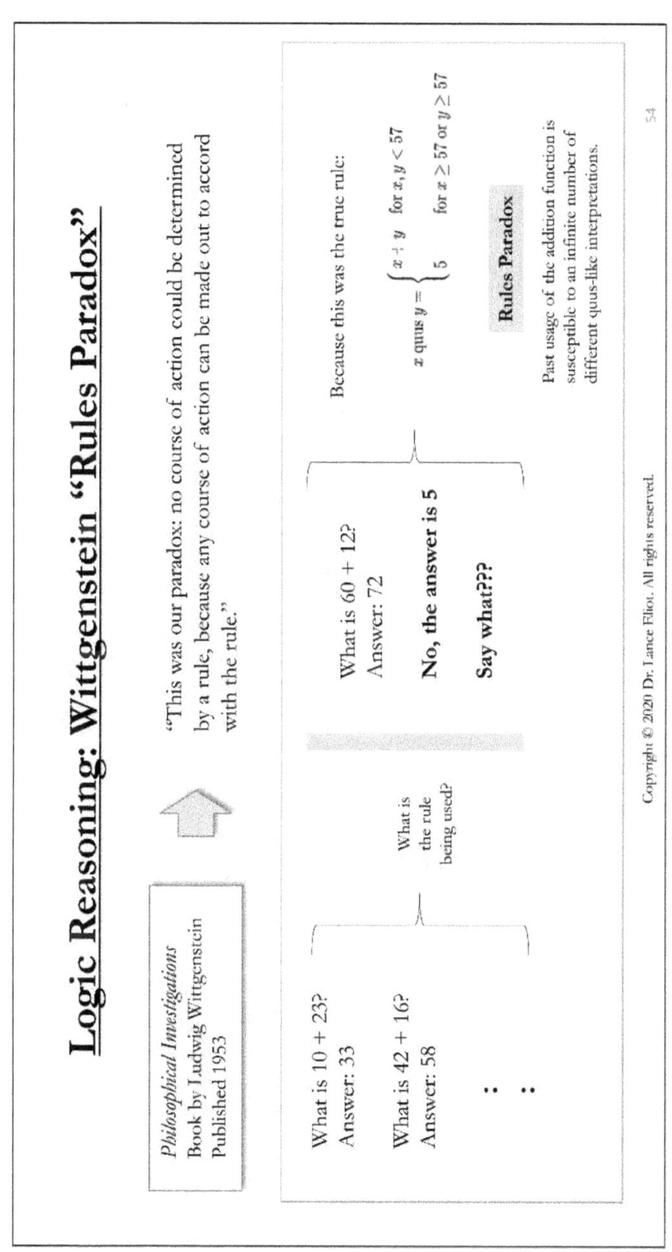

Logic Reasoning: Wittgenstein "Rules Paradox"
Philosophical Investigations
Book by Ludwig Wittgenstein
Published 1953
"This was our paradox: no course of action could be determined by a rule, because any course of action can be made out to accord with the rule."
What is 10 + 23?
Answer: 33
What is 42 + 16?
Answer: 58
What is the rule being used?
What is 60 + 12?
Answer: 72
No, the answer is 5
Say what???
Because this was the true rule:
$x \text{ quus } y = \begin{cases} x + y & \text{for } x, y < 57 \\ 5 & \text{for } x \geq 57 \text{ or } y \geq 57 \end{cases}$
Rules Paradox
Past usage of the addition function is susceptible to an infinite number of different quus-like interpretations.
Copyright © 2020 Dr. Lance Eliot. All rights reserved.
54

Figure 54

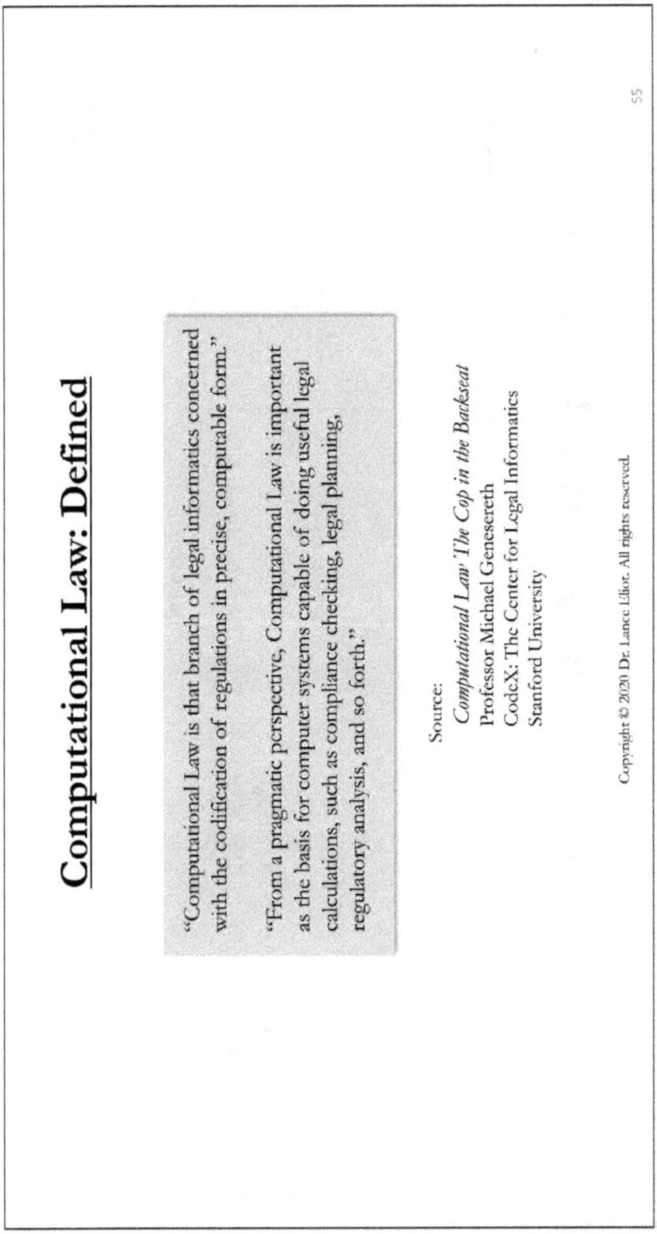

Computational Law: Defined

"Computational Law is that branch of legal informatics concerned with the codification of regulations in precise, computable form."

"From a pragmatic perspective, Computational Law is important as the basis for computer systems capable of doing useful legal calculations, such as compliance checking, legal planning, regulatory analysis, and so forth."

Source:
Computational Law The Cop in the Backseat
Professor Michael Genesereth
CodeX: The Center for Legal Informatics
Stanford University

55

Figure 55

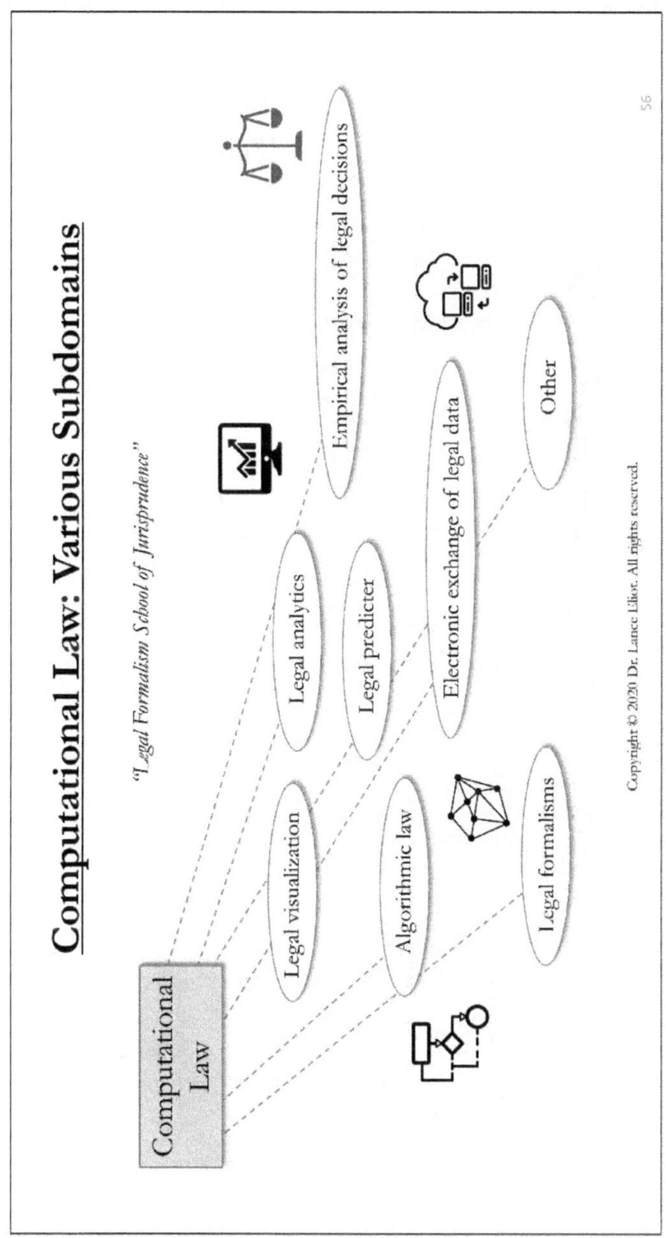
Computational Law: Various Subdomains
"Legal Formalism School of Jurisprudence"
Computational Law
Legal visualization
Legal analytics
Empirical analysis of legal decisions
Legal predicter
Algorithmic law
Electronic exchange of legal data
Legal formalisms
Other
Copyright © 2020 Dr. Lance Eliot. All rights reserved.
56

Figure 56

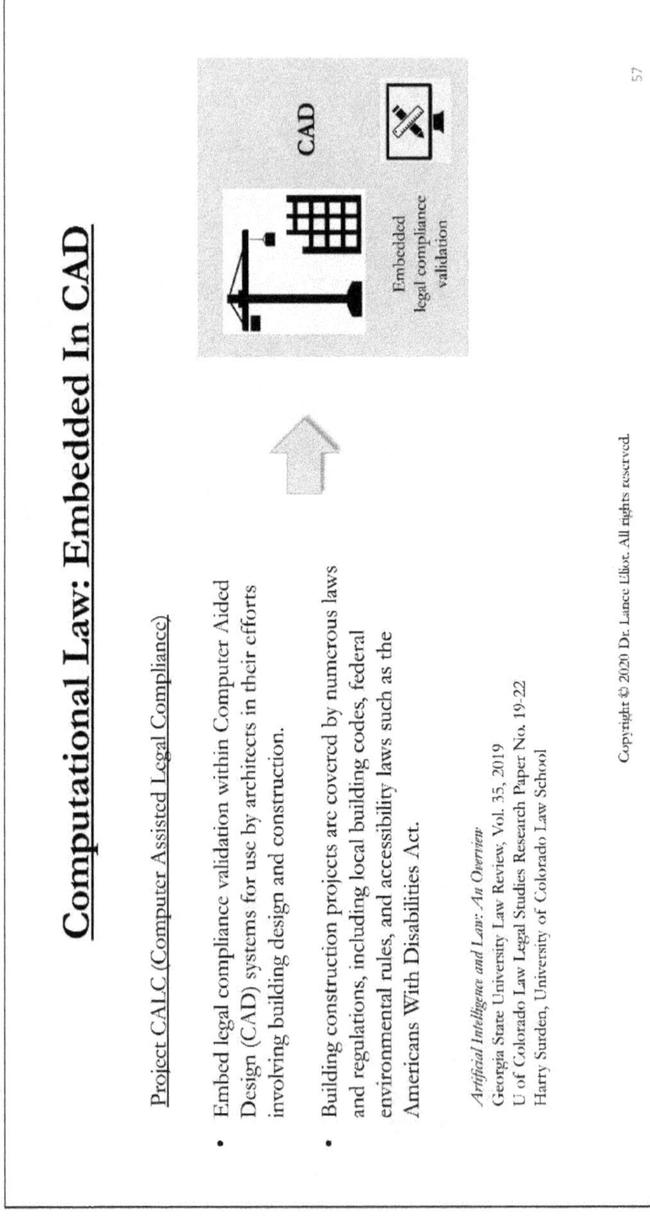
Computational Law: Embedded In CAD
Project CALC (Computer Assisted Legal Compliance)
• Embed legal compliance validation within Computer Aided Design (CAD) systems for use by architects in their efforts involving building design and construction.
• Building construction projects are covered by numerous laws and regulations, including local building codes, federal environmental rules, and accessibility laws such as the Americans With Disabilities Act.
Artificial Intelligence and Law: An Overview
Georgia State University Law Review, Vol. 35, 2019
U of Colorado Law Legal Studies Research Paper No. 19-22
Harry Surden, University of Colorado Law School
CAD
Embedded legal compliance validation
Copyright © 2020 Dr. Lance Eliot. All rights reserved.
57

Figure 57

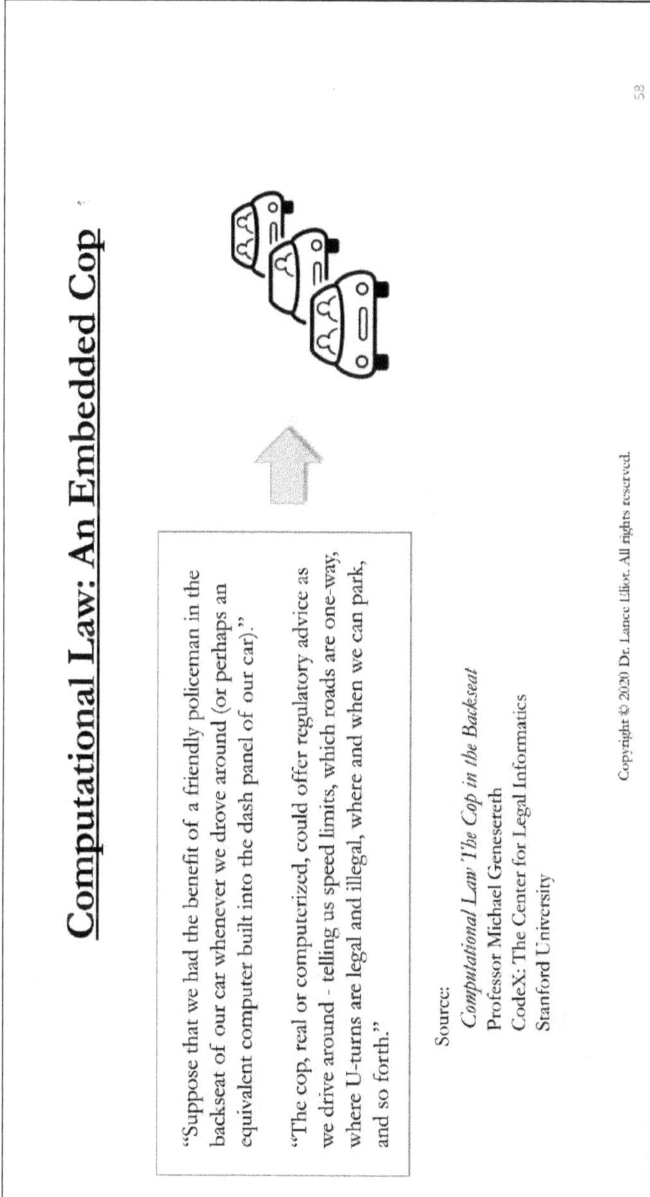
Computational Law: An Embedded Cop
"Suppose that we had the benefit of a friendly policeman in the backseat of our car whenever we drove around (or perhaps an equivalent computer built into the dash panel of our car)."
"The cop, real or computerized, could offer regulatory advice as we drive around - telling us speed limits, which roads are one-way, where U-turns are legal and illegal, where and when we can park, and so forth."
Source:
Computational Law The Cop in the Backseat
Professor Michael Genesereth
CodeX: The Center for Legal Informatics
Stanford University
Copyright © 2020 Dr. Lance Eliot. All rights reserved.
58

Figure 58

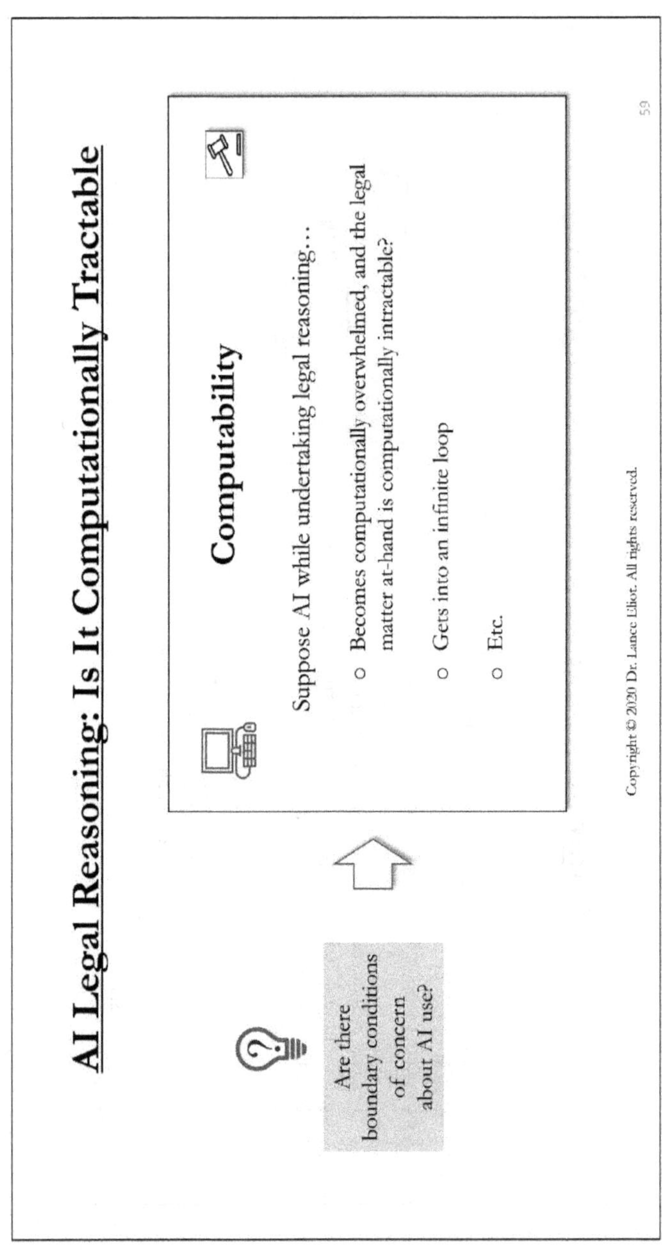
AI Legal Reasoning: Is It Computationally Tractable
Computability
Suppose AI while undertaking legal reasoning…
Becomes computationally overwhelmed, and the legal matter at-hand is computationally intractable?
Gets into an infinite loop
Etc.
Are there boundary conditions of concern about AI use?
Copyright © 2020 Dr. Lance Eliot. All rights reserved.
59

Figure 59

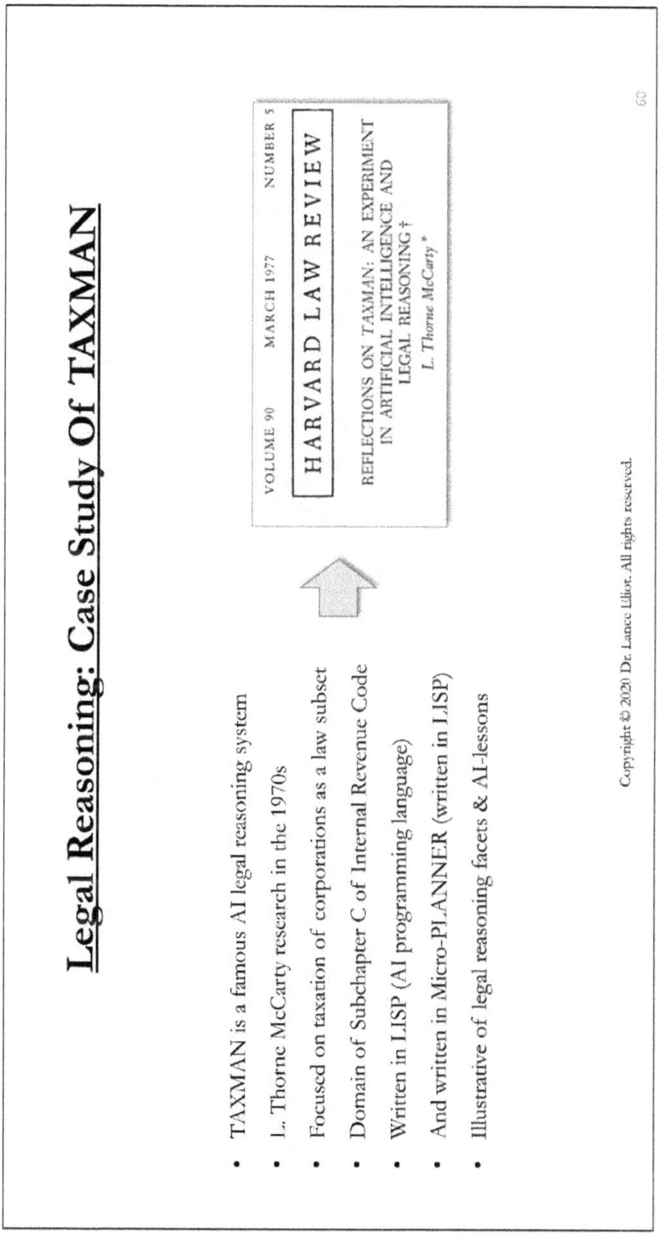

Legal Reasoning: Case Study Of TAXMAN

- TAXMAN is a famous AI legal reasoning system
- L. Thorne McCarty research in the 1970s
- Focused on taxation of corporations as a law subset
- Domain of Subchapter C of Internal Revenue Code
- Written in LISP (AI programming language)
- And written in Micro-PLANNER (written in LISP)
- Illustrative of legal reasoning facets & AI-lessons

VOLUME 90 MARCH 1977 NUMBER 5

HARVARD LAW REVIEW

REFLECTIONS ON TAXMAN: AN EXPERIMENT IN ARTIFICIAL INTELLIGENCE AND LEGAL REASONING †

L. Thorne McCarty *

60

Figure 60

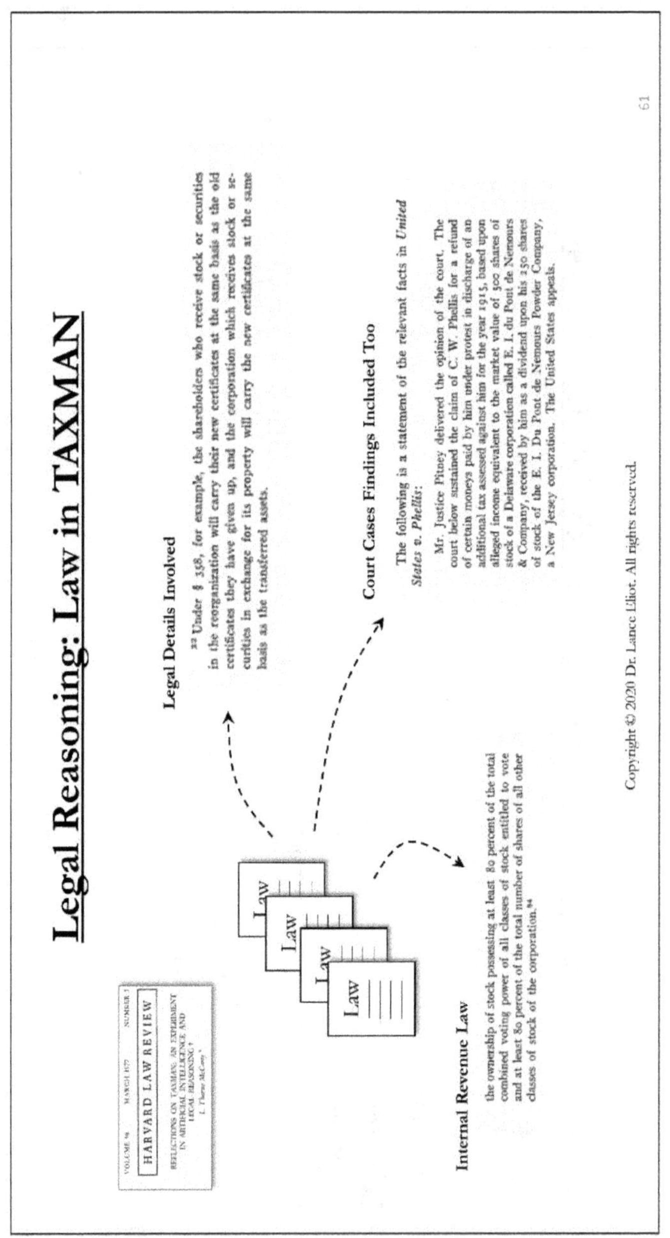
Legal Reasoning: Law in TAXMAN
HARVARD LAW REVIEW
Law
Law
Law
Law
Legal Details Involved
[22] Under § 358, for example, the shareholders who receive stock or securities in the reorganization will carry their new certificates at the same basis as the old certificates they have given up, and the corporation which receives stock or securities in exchange for its property will carry the new certificates at the same basis as the transferred assets.
Court Cases Findings Included Too
The following is a statement of the relevant facts in United States v. Phellis:
Mr. Justice Pitney delivered the opinion of the court. The court below sustained the claim of C. W. Phellis for a refund of certain moneys paid by him under protest in discharge of an additional tax assessed against him for the year 1915, based upon alleged income equivalent to the market value of 500 shares of stock of a Delaware corporation called E. I. du Pont de Nemours & Company, received by him as a dividend upon his 250 shares of stock of the E. I. Du Pont de Nemours Powder Company, a New Jersey corporation. The United States appeals.
Internal Revenue Law
the ownership of stock possessing at least 80 percent of the total combined voting power of all classes of stock entitled to vote and at least 80 percent of the total number of shares of all other classes of stock of the corporation.[24]
Copyright © 2020 Dr. Lance Eliot. All rights reserved.
61

Figure 61

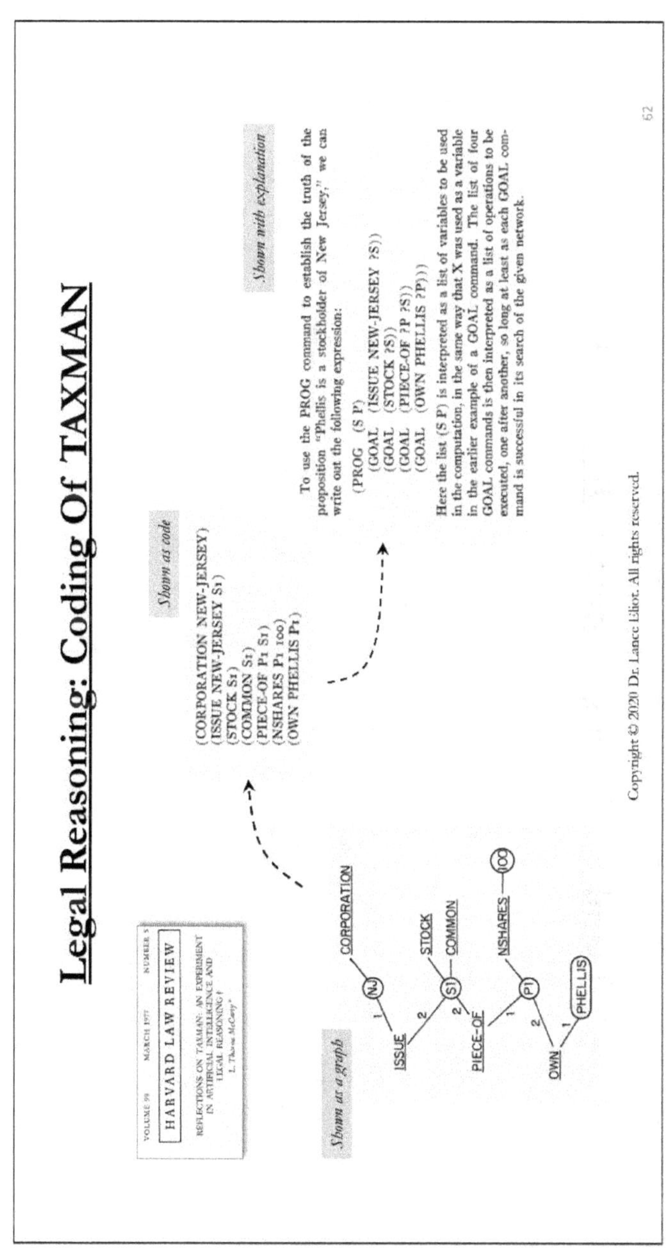
Legal Reasoning: Coding Of TAXMAN
VOLUME 90 MARCH 1977 NUMBER 5
HARVARD LAW REVIEW
REFLECTIONS ON TAXMAN: AN EXPERIMENT IN ARTIFICIAL INTELLIGENCE AND LEGAL REASONING
L. Thorne McCarty
Shown as a graph
ISSUE
NJ
CORPORATION
S1
STOCK
COMMON
PIECE-OF
P1
NSHARES
100
OWN
PHELLIS
1
2
Shown as code
(CORPORATION NEW-JERSEY)
(ISSUE NEW-JERSEY S1)
(STOCK S1)
(COMMON S1)
(PIECE-OF P1 S1)
(NSHARES P1 100)
(OWN PHELLIS P1)
Shown with explanation
To use the PROG command to establish the truth of the proposition "Phellis is a stockholder of New Jersey," we can write out the following expression:
(PROG (S P)
(GOAL (ISSUE NEW-JERSEY ?S))
(GOAL (STOCK ?S))
(GOAL (PIECE-OF ?P ?S))
(GOAL (OWN PHELLIS ?P)))
Here the list (S P) is interpreted as a list of variables to be used in the computation, in the same way that X was used as a variable in the earlier example of a GOAL command. The list of four GOAL commands is then interpreted as a list of operations to be executed, one after another, so long at least as each GOAL command is successful in its search of the given network.
Copyright © 2020 Dr. Lance Eliot. All rights reserved.
62

Figure 62

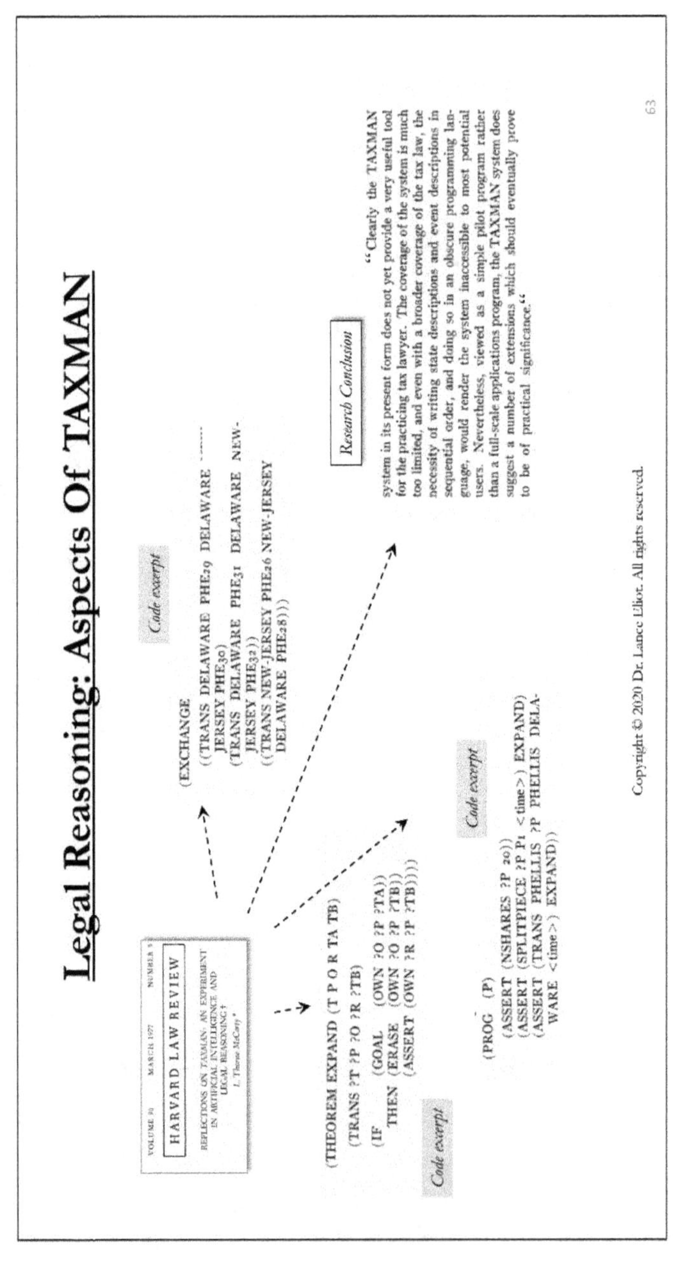
Legal Reasoning: Aspects Of TAXMAN
VOLUME 90 MARCH 1977 NUMBER 5
HARVARD LAW REVIEW
REFLECTIONS ON TAXMAN: AN EXPERIMENT IN ARTIFICIAL INTELLIGENCE AND LEGAL REASONING †
Code excerpt
(EXCHANGE
((TRANS DELAWARE PHE29 DELAWARE JERSEY PHE30)
(TRANS DELAWARE PHE31 DELAWARE NEW-JERSEY PHE32))
((TRANS NEW-JERSEY PHE26 NEW-JERSEY DELAWARE PHE28)))
(THEOREM EXPAND (T P O R TA TB)
(TRANS ?T ?P ?O ?R ?TB)
(IF (GOAL (OWN ?O ?P ?TA))
THEN (ERASE (OWN ?O ?P ?TB))
(ASSERT (OWN ?R ?P ?TB))))
Code excerpt
Code excerpt
(PROG (P)
(ASSERT (NSHARES ?P 20))
(ASSERT (SPLITPIECE ?P P1 <time>) EXPAND)
(ASSERT (TRANS PHELLIS ?P PHELLIS DELAWARE <time>) EXPAND))
Research Conclusion
"Clearly the TAXMAN system in its present form does not yet provide a very useful tool for the practicing tax lawyer. The coverage of the system is much too limited, and even with a broader coverage of the tax law, the necessity of writing state descriptions and event descriptions in sequential order, and doing so in an obscure programming language, would render the system inaccessible to most potential users. Nevertheless, viewed as a simple pilot program rather than a full-scale applications program, the TAXMAN system does suggest a number of extensions which should eventually prove to be of practical significance."
Copyright © 2020 Dr. Lance Eliot. All rights reserved.
63

Figure 63

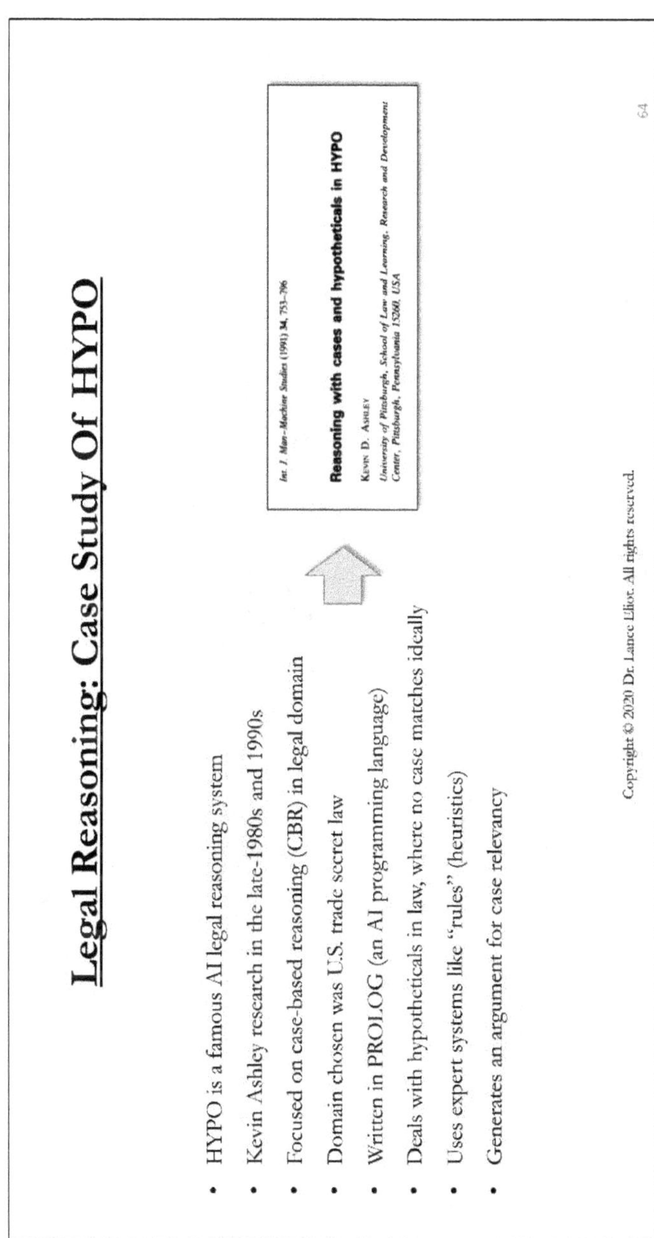
Legal Reasoning: Case Study Of HYPO
• HYPO is a famous AI legal reasoning system
• Kevin Ashley research in the late-1980s and 1990s
• Focused on case-based reasoning (CBR) in legal domain
• Domain chosen was U.S. trade secret law
• Written in PROLOG (an AI programming language)
• Deals with hypotheticals in law, where no case matches ideally
• Uses expert systems like "rules" (heuristics)
• Generates an argument for case relevancy
Int. J. Man-Machine Studies (1991) 34, 753–796
Reasoning with cases and hypotheticals in HYPO
Kevin D. Ashley
University of Pittsburgh, School of Law and Learning, Research and Development Center, Pittsburgh, Pennsylvania 15260, USA
Copyright © 2020 Dr. Lance Eliot. All rights reserved.
64

Figure 64

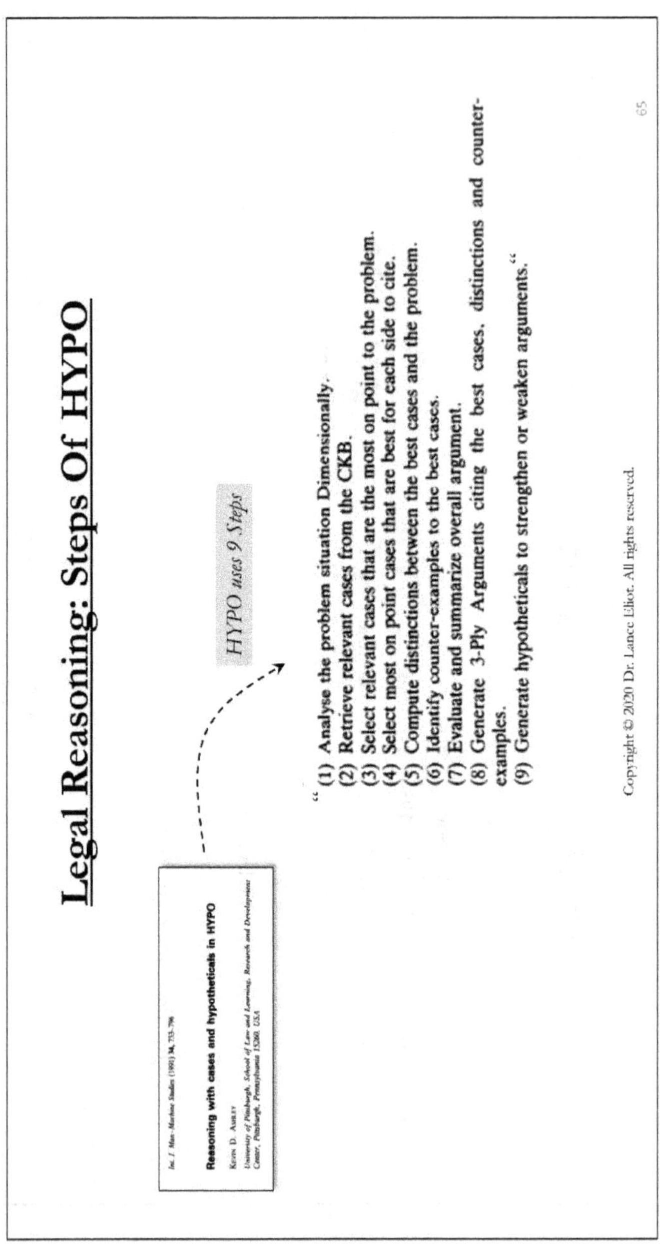
Legal Reasoning: Steps Of HYPO
Reasoning with cases and hypotheticals in HYPO
HYPO uses 9 Steps
" (1) Analyse the problem situation Dimensionally.
(2) Retrieve relevant cases from the CKB.
(3) Select relevant cases that are the most on point to the problem.
(4) Select most on point cases that are best for each side to cite.
(5) Compute distinctions between the best cases and the problem.
(6) Identify counter-examples to the best cases.
(7) Evaluate and summarize overall argument.
(8) Generate 3-Ply Arguments citing the best cases, distinctions and counter-examples.
(9) Generate hypotheticals to strengthen or weaken arguments."
Copyright © 2020 Dr. Lance Eliot. All rights reserved.
65

Figure 65

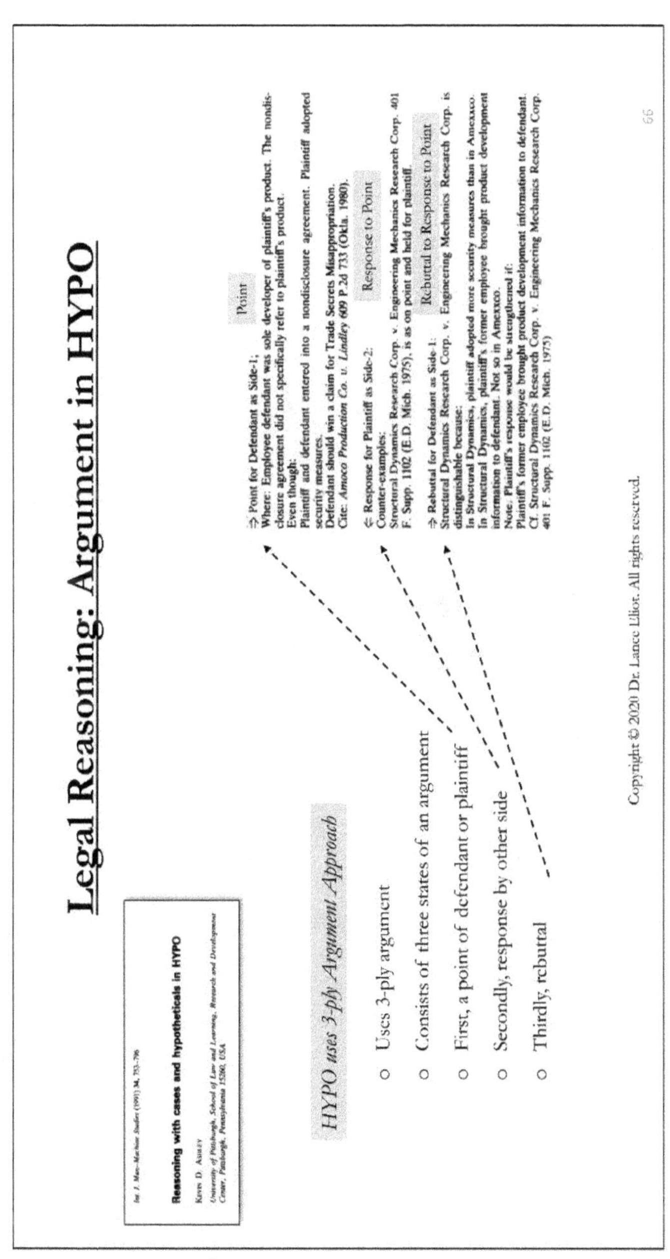
Legal Reasoning: Argument in HYPO
Int. J. Man-Machine Studies (1991) 34, 753–796
Reasoning with cases and hypotheticals in HYPO
Kevin D. Ashley
University of Pittsburgh, School of Law and Learning, Research and Development Center, Pittsburgh, Pennsylvania 15260, USA
HYPO uses 3-ply Argument Approach
Uses 3-ply argument
Consists of three states of an argument
First, a point of defendant or plaintiff
Secondly, response by other side
Thirdly, rebuttal
Point
⇒ Point for Defendant as Side-1;
Where: Employee defendant was sole developer of plaintiff's product. The nondisclosure agreement did not specifically refer to plaintiff's product.
Even though:
Plaintiff and defendant entered into a nondisclosure agreement. Plaintiff adopted security measures.
Defendant should win a claim for Trade Secrets Misappropriation.
Cite: Amoco Production Co. v. Lindley 609 P.2d 733 (Okla. 1980).
Response to Point
⇐ Response for Plaintiff as Side-2:
Counter-examples:
Structural Dynamics Research Corp. v. Engineering Mechanics Research Corp. 401 F. Supp. 1102 (E.D. Mich. 1975), is as on point and held for plaintiff.
Rebuttal to Response to Point
⇒ Rebuttal for Defendant as Side-1:
Structural Dynamics Research Corp. v. Engineering Mechanics Research Corp. is distinguishable because:
In Structural Dynamics, plaintiff adopted more security measures than in Amexxco.
In Structural Dynamics, plaintiff's former employee brought product development information to defendant. Not so in Amexxco.
Note: Plaintiff's response would be strengthened if:
Plaintiff's former employee brought product development information to defendant.
Cf. Structural Dynamics Research Corp. v. Engineering Mechanics Research Corp. 401 F. Supp. 1102 (E.D. Mich. 1975)
Copyright © 2020 Dr. Lance Eliot. All rights reserved.
66

Figure 66

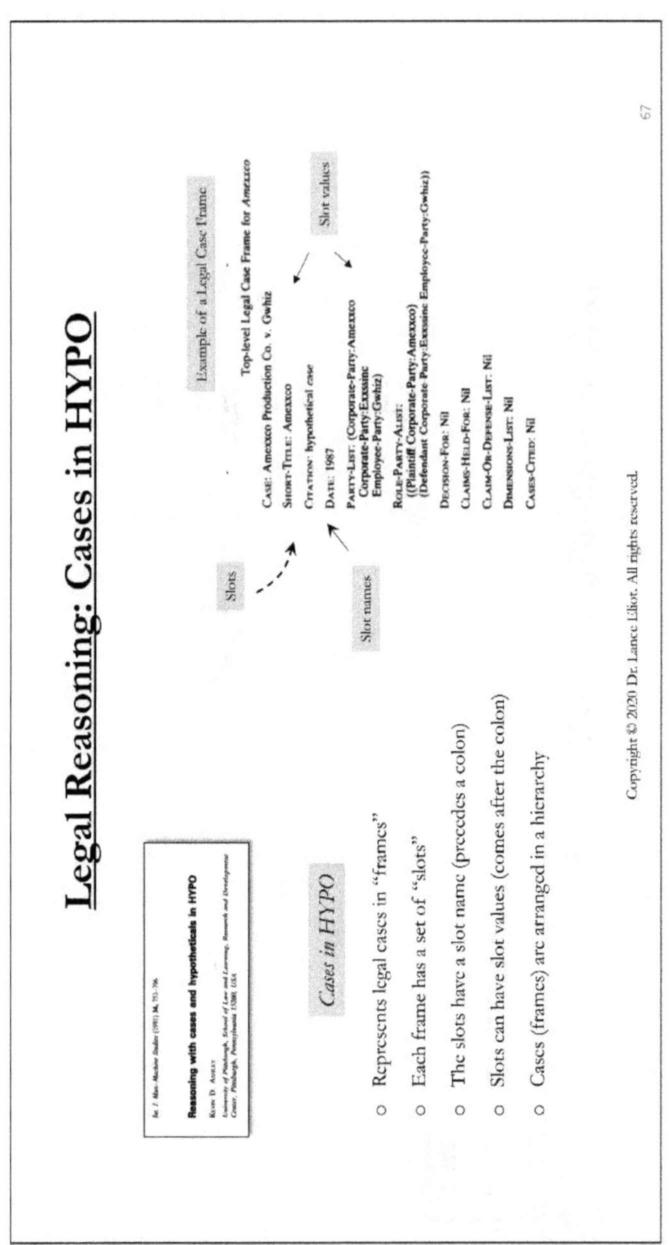
Legal Reasoning: Cases in HYPO
Int. J. Man-Machine Studies (1991) 34, 753-796
Reasoning with cases and hypotheticals in HYPO
Kevin D. Ashley
University of Pittsburgh, School of Law and Learning, Research and Development Center, Pittsburgh, Pennsylvania 15260, USA
Cases in HYPO
Represents legal cases in "frames"
Each frame has a set of "slots"
The slots have a slot name (precedes a colon)
Slots can have slot values (comes after the colon)
Cases (frames) are arranged in a hierarchy
Example of a Legal Case Frame
Slots
Slot names
Slot values
Top-level Legal Case Frame for Amexxco
Case: Amexxco Production Co. v. Gwhiz
Short-Title: Amexxco
Citation: hypothetical case
Date: 1987
Party-List: (Corporate-Party:Amexxco
Corporate-Party:Exxssinc
Employee-Party:Gwhiz)
Role-Party-Alist:
((Plaintiff Corporate-Party:Amexxco)
(Defendant Corporate Party:Exxssinc Employee-Party:Gwhiz))
Decision-For: Nil
Claims-Held-For: Nil
Claim-Or-Defense-List: Nil
Dimensions-List: Nil
Cases-Cited: Nil
Copyright © 2020 Dr. Lance Eliot. All rights reserved.
67

Figure 67

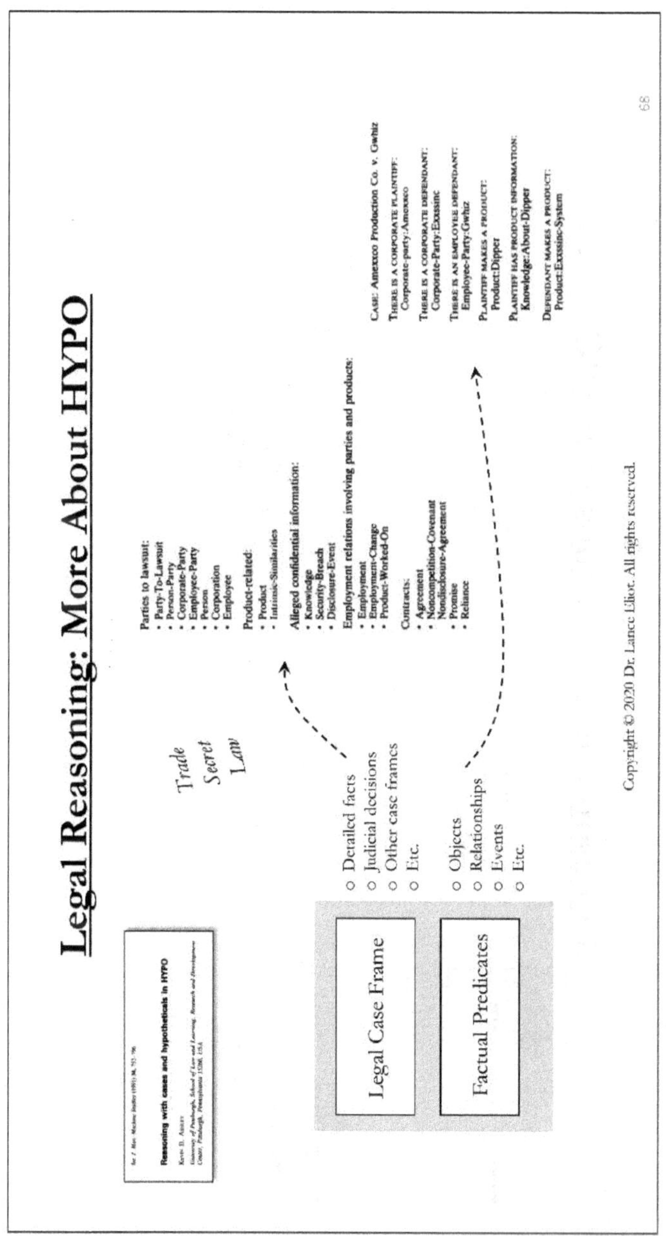
Legal Reasoning: More About HYPO
Reasoning with cases and hypotheticals in HYPO
Trade Secret Law
Legal Case Frame
Factual Predicates
Detailed facts
Judicial decisions
Other case frames
Etc.
Objects
Relationships
Events
Etc.
Parties to lawsuit:
• Party-To-Lawsuit
• Person-Party
• Corporate-Party
• Employee-Party
• Person
• Corporation
• Employee
Product-related:
• Product
• Intrinsic-Similarities
Alleged confidential information:
• Knowledge
• Security-Breach
• Disclosure-Event
Employment relations involving parties and products:
• Employment
• Employment-Change
• Product-Worked-On
Contracts:
• Agreement
• Noncompetition-Covenant
Nondisclosure-Agreement
• Promise
• Reliance
CASE: Amexxco Production Co. v. Gwhiz
THERE IS A CORPORATE PLAINTIFF:
Corporate-party:Amexxco
THERE IS A CORPORATE DEFENDANT:
Corporate-Party:Exxssinc
THERE IS AN EMPLOYEE DEFENDANT:
Employee-Party:Gwhiz
PLAINTIFF MAKES A PRODUCT:
Product:Dipper
PLAINTIFF HAS PRODUCT INFORMATION:
Knowledge:About-Dipper
DEFENDANT MAKES A PRODUCT:
Product:Exxssinc-System
Copyright © 2020 Dr. Lance Eliot. All rights reserved.
68

Figure 68

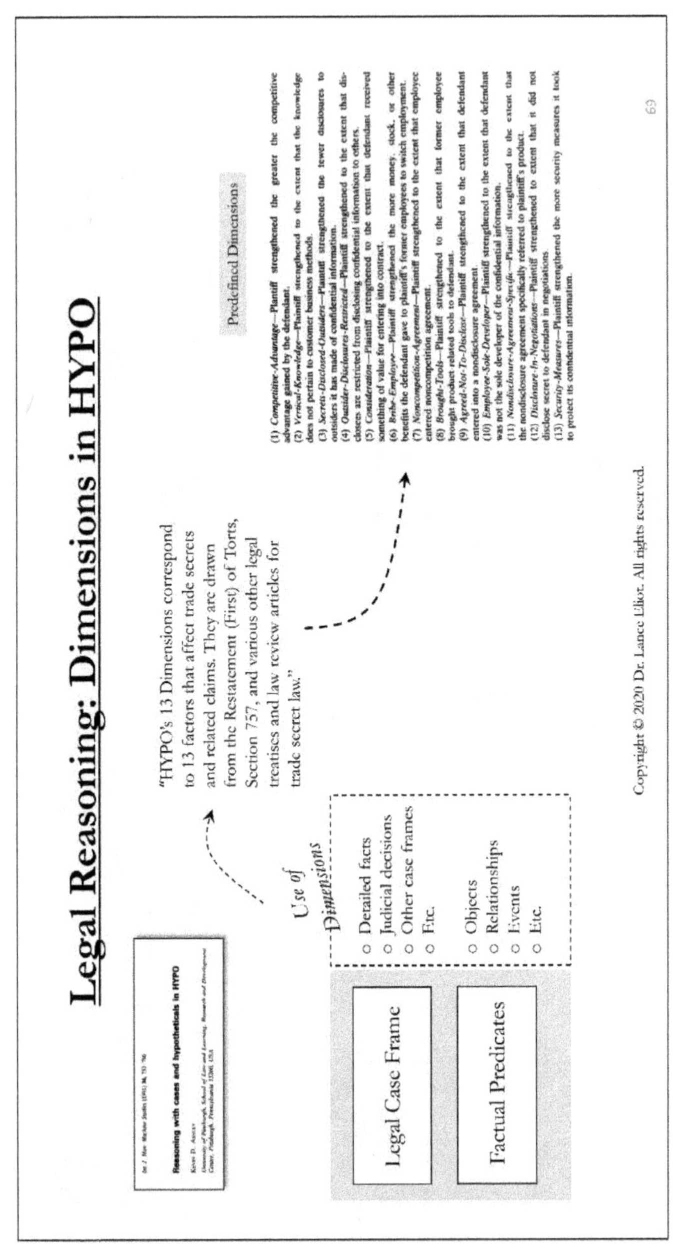
Legal Reasoning: Dimensions in HYPO
Reasoning with cases and hypotheticals in HYPO
Use of Dimensions
Legal Case Frame
Factual Predicates
○ Detailed facts
○ Judicial decisions
○ Other case frames
○ Etc.
○ Objects
○ Relationships
○ Events
○ Etc.
"HYPO's 13 Dimensions correspond to 13 factors that affect trade secrets and related claims. They are drawn from the Restatement (First) of Torts, Section 757, and various other legal treatises and law review articles for trade secret law."
Predefined Dimensions
(1) Competitive-Advantage—Plantiff strengthened the greater the competitive advantage gained by the defendant.
(2) Vertical-Knowledge—Plaintiff strengthened to the extent that the knowledge does not pertain to customer business methods.
(3) Secrets-Disclosed-Outsiders—Plaintiff strengthened the fewer disclosures to outsiders it has made of confidential information.
(4) Outsider-Disclosures-Restricted—Plaintiff strengthened to the extent that disclosees are restricted from disclosing confidential information to others.
(5) Consideration—Plaintiff strengthened to the extent that defendant received something of value for entering into contract.
(6) Bribe-Employee—Plaintiff strengthened the more money, stock, or other benefits the defendant gave to plaintiff's former employees to switch employment.
(7) Noncompetition-Agreement—Plaintiff strengthened to the extent that employee entered noncompetition agreement.
(8) Brought-Tools—Plaintiff strengthened to the extent that former employee brought product-related tools to defendant.
(9) Agreed-Not-To-Disclose—Plaintiff strengthened to the extent that defendant entered into a nondisclosure agreement.
(10) Employee-Sole-Developer—Plaintiff strengthened to the extent that defendant was not the sole developer of the confidential information.
(11) Nondisclosure-Agreement-Specific—Plaintiff strengthened to the extent that the nondisclosure agreement specifically referred to plaintiff's product.
(12) Disclosure-In-Negotiations—Plaintiff strengthened to extent that it did not disclose secret to defendant in negotiations.
(13) Security-Measures—Plaintiff strengthened the more security measures it took to protect its confidential information.
Copyright © 2020 Dr. Lance Eliot. All rights reserved.
69

Figure 69

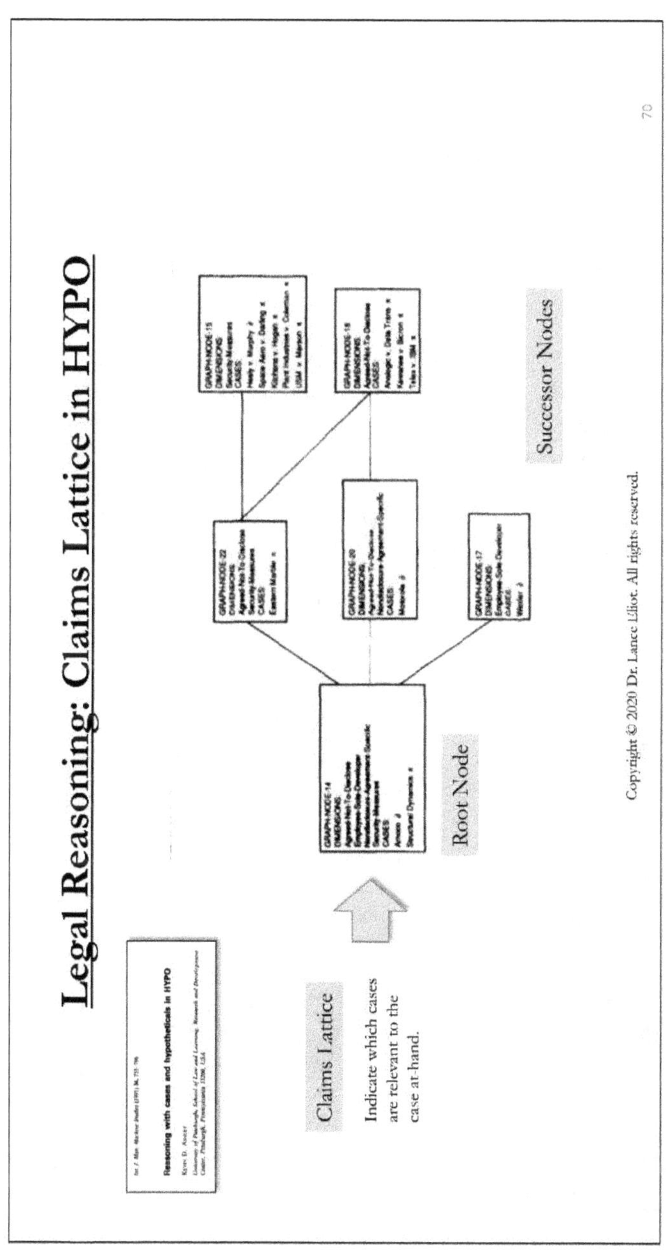
Legal Reasoning: Claims Lattice in HYPO
Claims Lattice
Indicate which cases are relevant to the case at-hand.
Root Node
Successor Nodes
Copyright © 2020 Dr. Lance Eliot. All rights reserved.
70

Figure 70

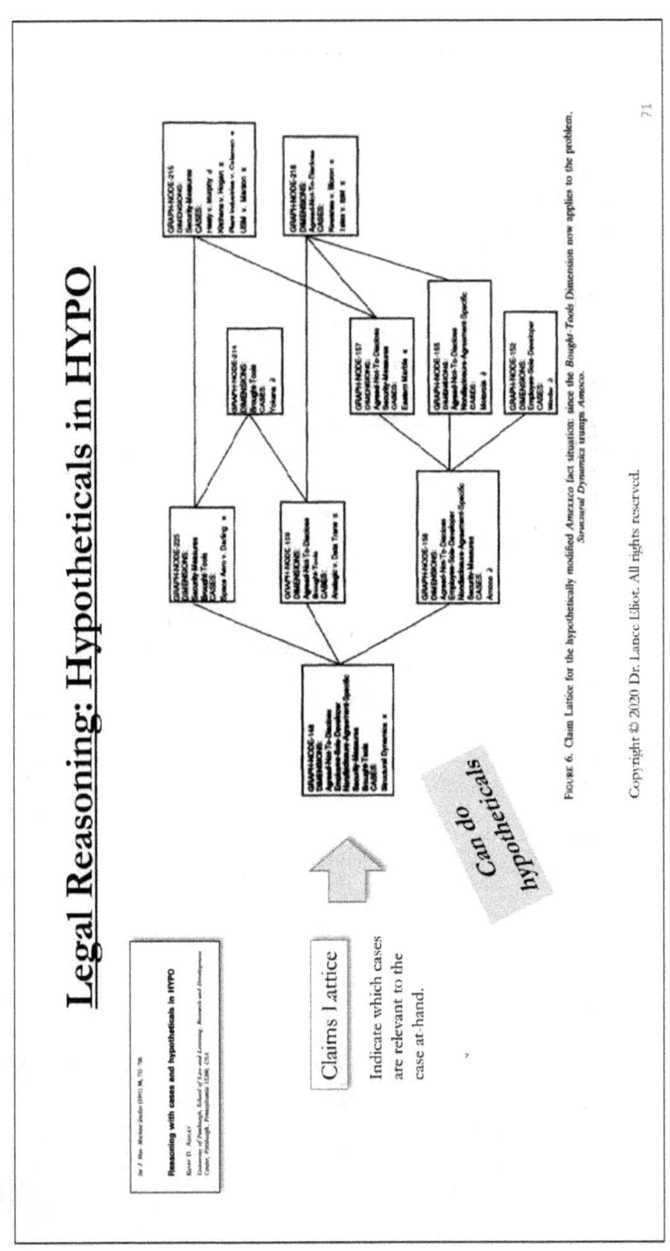
Legal Reasoning: Hypotheticals in HYPO
Reasoning with cases and hypotheticals in HYPO
Claims Lattice
Indicate which cases are relevant to the case at-hand.
Can do hypotheticals
FIGURE 6. Claim Lattice for the hypothetically modified Amexxco fact situation: since the Bought-Tools Dimension now applies to the problem. Structural Dynamics trumps Amoco.
Copyright © 2020 Dr. Lance Eliot. All rights reserved.
71

Figure 71

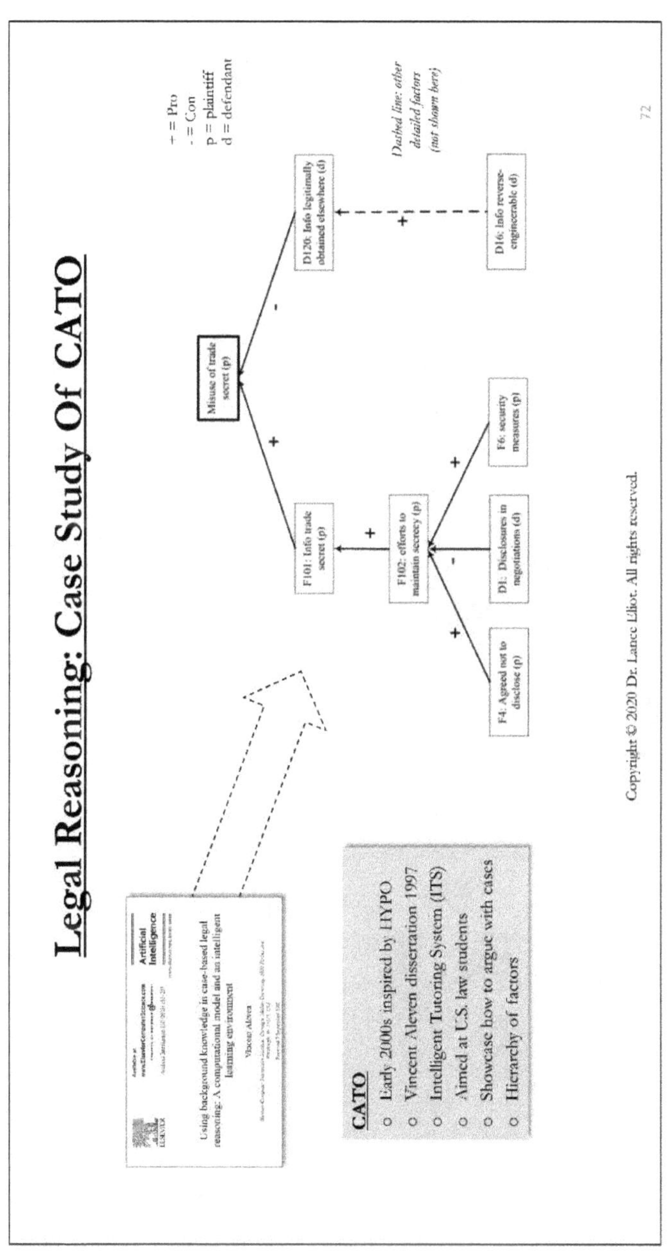
Legal Reasoning: Case Study Of CATO
Using background knowledge in case-based legal reasoning: A computational model and an intelligent learning environment
Vincent Aleven
Artificial Intelligence
CATO
Early 2000s inspired by HYPO
Vincent Aleven dissertation 1997
Intelligent Tutoring System (ITS)
Aimed at U.S. law students
Showcase how to argue with cases
Hierarchy of factors
Misuse of trade secret (p)
F101: Info trade secret (p)
D120: Info legitimally obtained elsewhere (d)
F102: efforts to maintain secrecy (p)
F4: Agreed not to disclose (p)
D1: Disclosures in negotiations (d)
F6: security measures (p)
D16: Info reverse-engineerable (d)
+ = Pro
- = Con
p = plaintiff
d = defendant
Dashed line: other detailed factors (not shown here)
Copyright © 2020 Dr. Lance Eliot. All rights reserved.
72

Figure 72

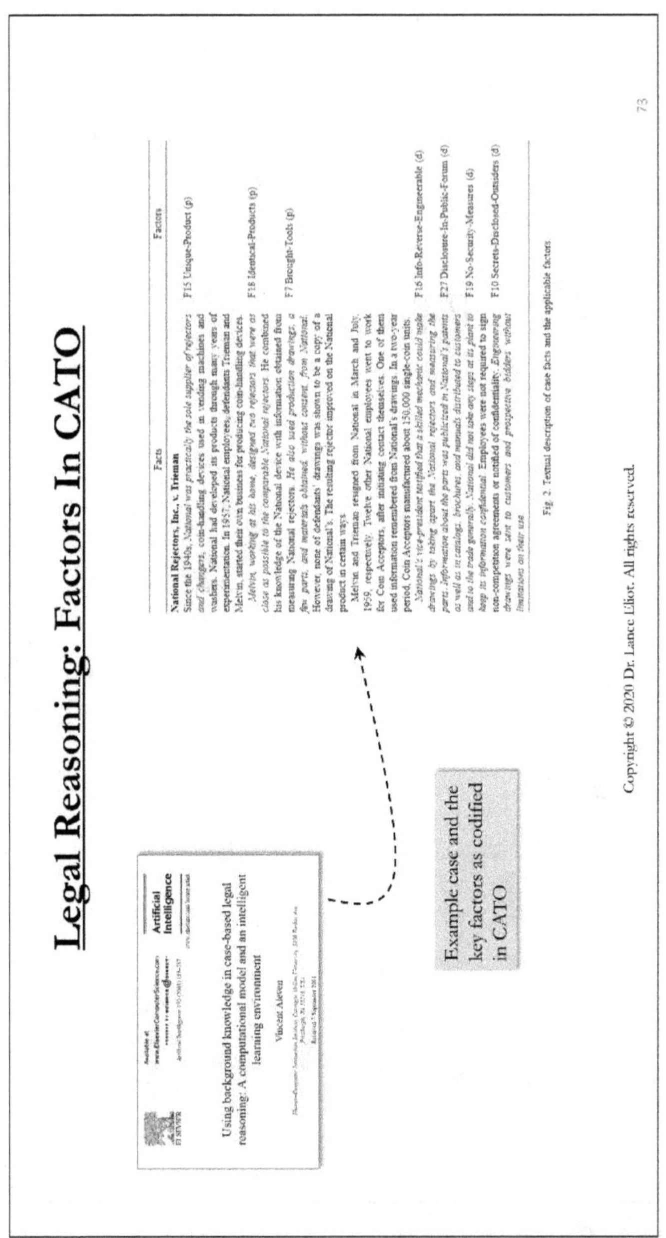
Legal Reasoning: Factors In CATO
Artificial Intelligence
Using background knowledge in case-based legal reasoning: A computational model and an intelligent learning environment
Vincent Aleven
Example case and the key factors as codified in CATO
Copyright © 2020 Dr. Lance Eliot. All rights reserved.
73

Figure 73

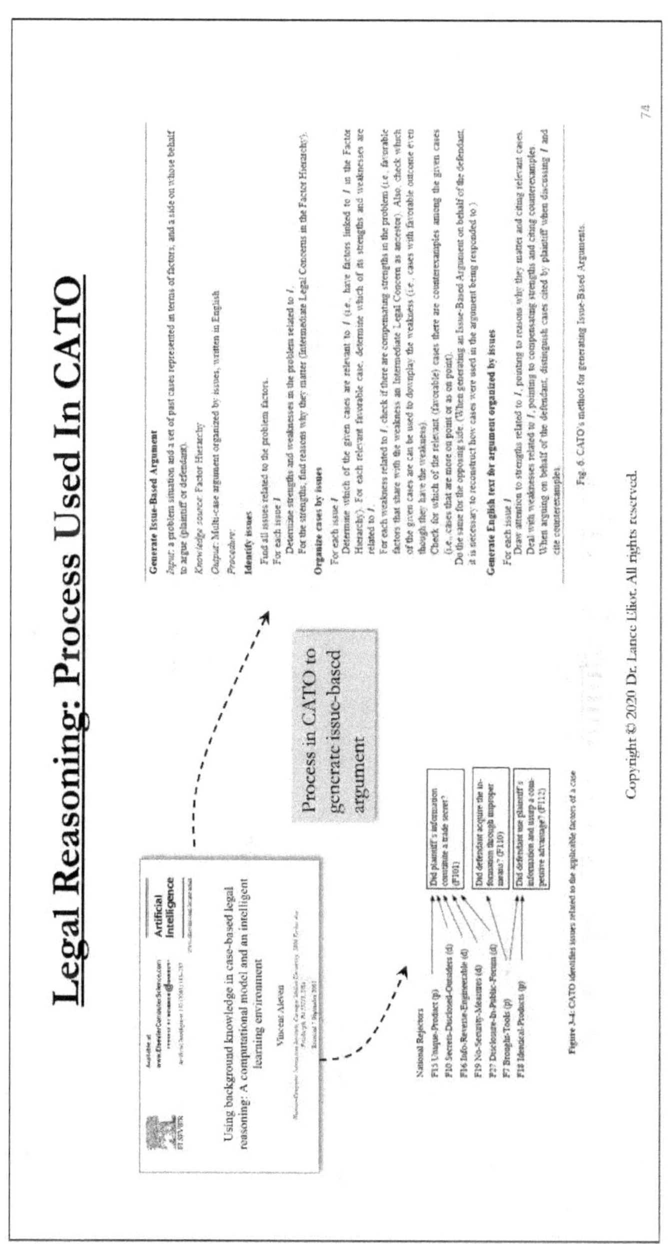
Legal Reasoning: Process Used In CATO
Process in CATO to generate issue-based argument
Copyright © 2020 Dr. Lance Eliot. All rights reserved.
74

Figure 74

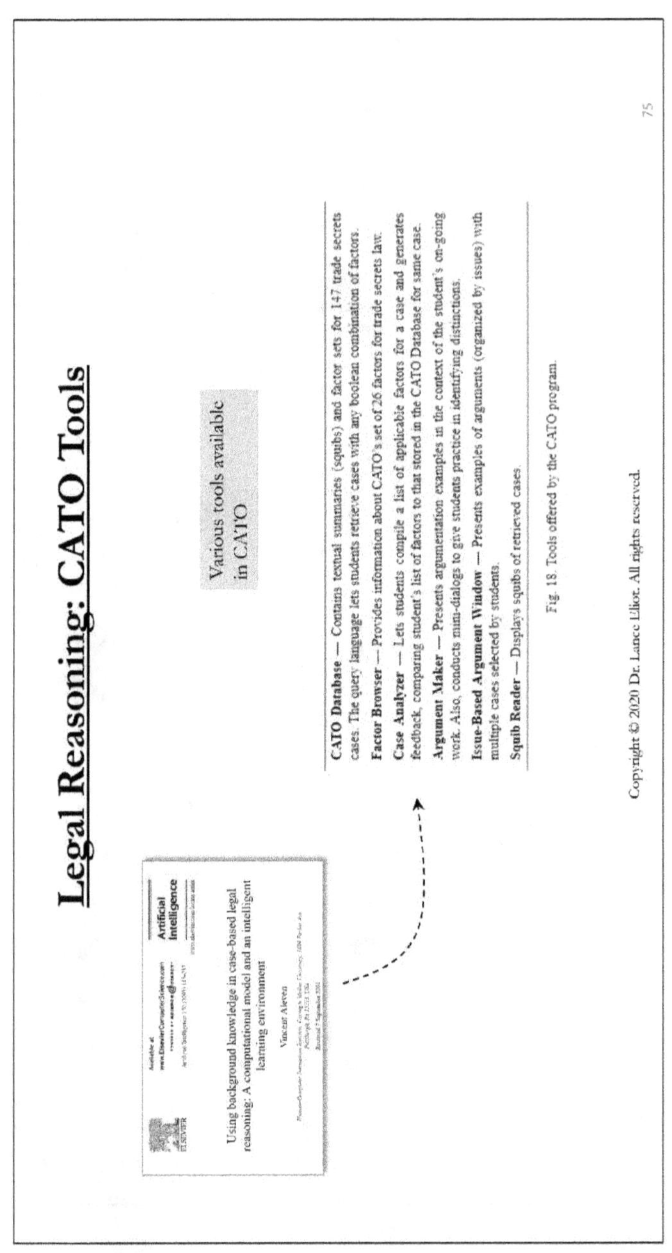

Legal Reasoning: CATO Tools
Various tools available in CATO
Using background knowledge in case-based legal reasoning: A computational model and an intelligent learning environment
Vincent Aleven
Artificial Intelligence
CATO Database — Contains textual summaries (squibs) and factor sets for 147 trade secrets cases. The query language lets students retrieve cases with any boolean combination of factors.
Factor Browser — Provides information about CATO's set of 26 factors for trade secrets law.
Case Analyzer — Lets students compile a list of applicable factors for a case and generates feedback, comparing student's list of factors to that stored in the CATO Database for same case.
Argument Maker — Presents argumentation examples in the context of the student's on-going work. Also, conducts mini-dialogs to give students practice in identifying distinctions.
Issue-Based Argument Window — Presents examples of arguments (organized by issues) with multiple cases selected by students.
Squib Reader — Displays squibs of retrieved cases.
Fig. 18. Tools offered by the CATO program.
Copyright © 2020 Dr. Lance Eliot. All rights reserved.
75

Figure 75

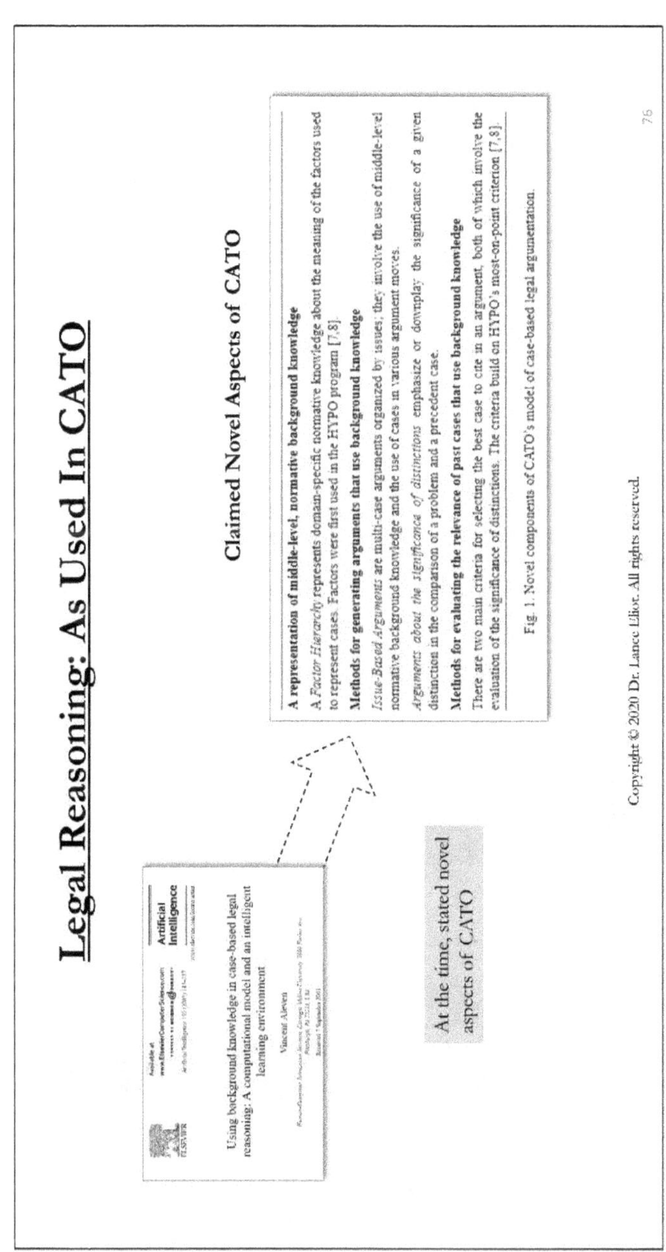
Legal Reasoning: As Used In CATO
Artificial Intelligence
ELSEVIER
Using background knowledge in case-based legal reasoning: A computational model and an intelligent learning environment
Vincent Aleven
At the time, stated novel aspects of CATO
Claimed Novel Aspects of CATO
A representation of middle-level, normative background knowledge
A Factor Hierarchy represents domain-specific normative knowledge about the meaning of the factors used to represent cases. Factors were first used in the HYPO program [7,8].
Methods for generating arguments that use background knowledge
Issue-Based Arguments are multi-case arguments organized by issues; they involve the use of middle-level normative background knowledge and the use of cases in various argument moves.
Arguments about the significance of distinctions emphasize or downplay the significance of a given distinction in the comparison of a problem and a precedent case.
Methods for evaluating the relevance of past cases that use background knowledge
There are two main criteria for selecting the best case to cite in an argument, both of which involve the evaluation of the significance of distinctions. The criteria build on HYPO's most-on-point criterion [7,8].
Fig. 1. Novel components of CATO's model of case-based legal argumentation.
Copyright © 2020 Dr. Lance Eliot. All rights reserved.
76

Figure 76

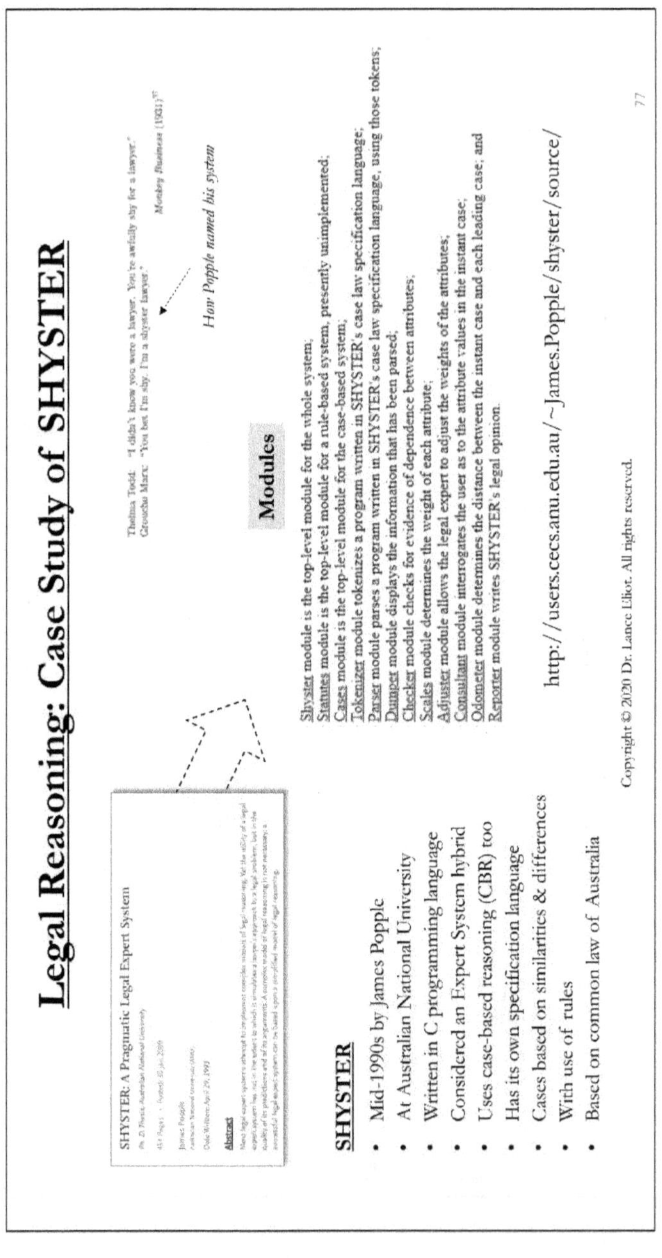
Legal Reasoning: Case Study of SHYSTER
SHYSTER: A Pragmatic Legal Expert System
Thelma Todd: "I didn't know you were a lawyer. You're awfully shy for a lawyer."
Groucho Marx: "You bet I'm shy. I'm a shyster lawyer."
Monkey Business (1931)
How Popple named his system
Modules
Shyster module is the top-level module for the whole system;
Statutes module is the top-level module for a rule-based system, presently unimplemented;
Cases module is the top-level module for the case-based system;
Tokenizer module tokenizes a program written in SHYSTER's case law specification language;
Parser module parses a program written in SHYSTER's case law specification language, using those tokens;
Dumper module displays the information that has been parsed;
Checker module checks for evidence of dependence between attributes;
Scales module determines the weight of each attribute;
Adjuster module allows the legal expert to adjust the weights of the attributes;
Consultant module interrogates the user as to the attribute values in the instant case;
Odometer module determines the distance between the instant case and each leading case; and
Reporter module writes SHYSTER's legal opinion.
SHYSTER
Mid-1990s by James Popple
At Australian National University
Written in C programming language
Considered an Expert System hybrid
Uses case-based reasoning (CBR) too
Has its own specification language
Cases based on similarities & differences
With use of rules
Based on common law of Australia
http://users.cecs.anu.edu.au/~James.Popple/shyster/source/
Copyright © 2020 Dr. Lance Eliot. All rights reserved.
77

Figure 77

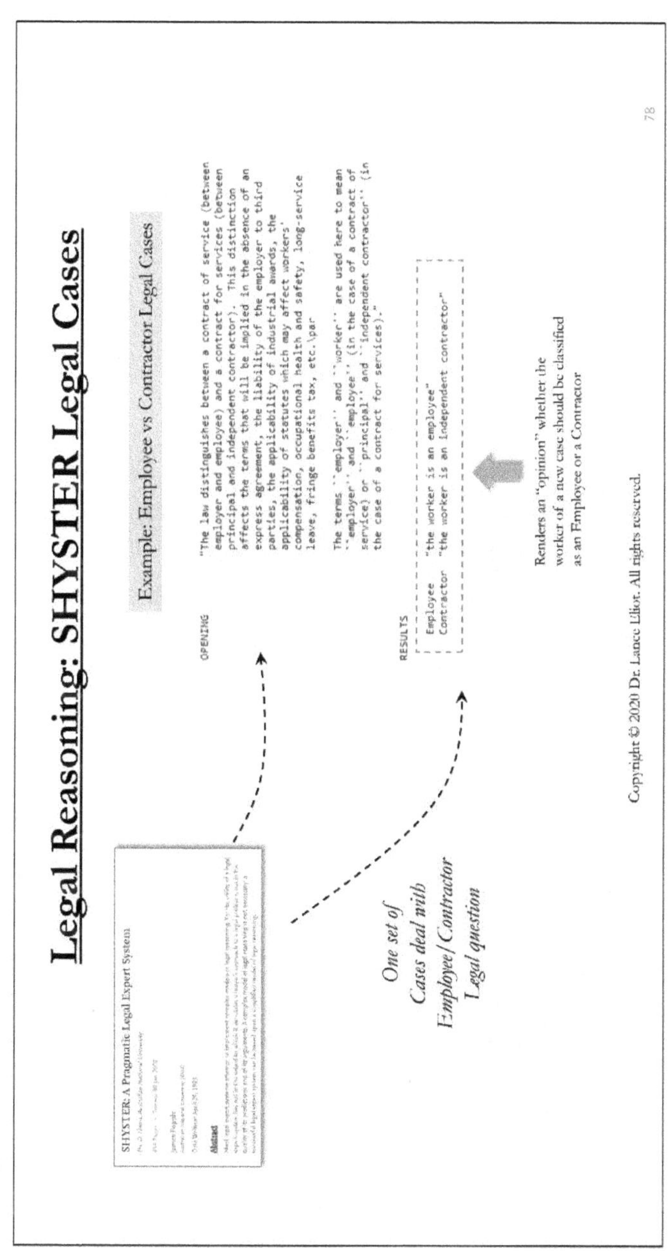
Legal Reasoning: SHYSTER Legal Cases
SHYSTER: A Pragmatic Legal Expert System
Abstract
Example: Employee vs Contractor Legal Cases
OPENING
"The law distinguishes between a contract of service (between employer and employee) and a contract for services (between principal and independent contractor). This distinction affects the terms that will be implied in the absence of an express agreement, the liability of the employer to third parties, the applicability of industrial awards, the applicability of statutes which may affect workers' compensation, occupational health and safety, long-service leave, fringe benefits tax, etc.\par
The terms ``employer'' and ``worker'' are used here to mean ``employer'' and ``employee'' (in the case of a contract of service) or ``principal'' and ``independent contractor'' (in the case of a contract for services)."
RESULTS
Employee "the worker is an employee"
Contractor "the worker is an independent contractor"
One set of Cases deal with Employee/Contractor Legal question
Renders an "opinion" whether the worker of a new case should be classified as an Employee or a Contractor
Copyright © 2020 Dr. Lance Eliot. All rights reserved.
78

Figure 78

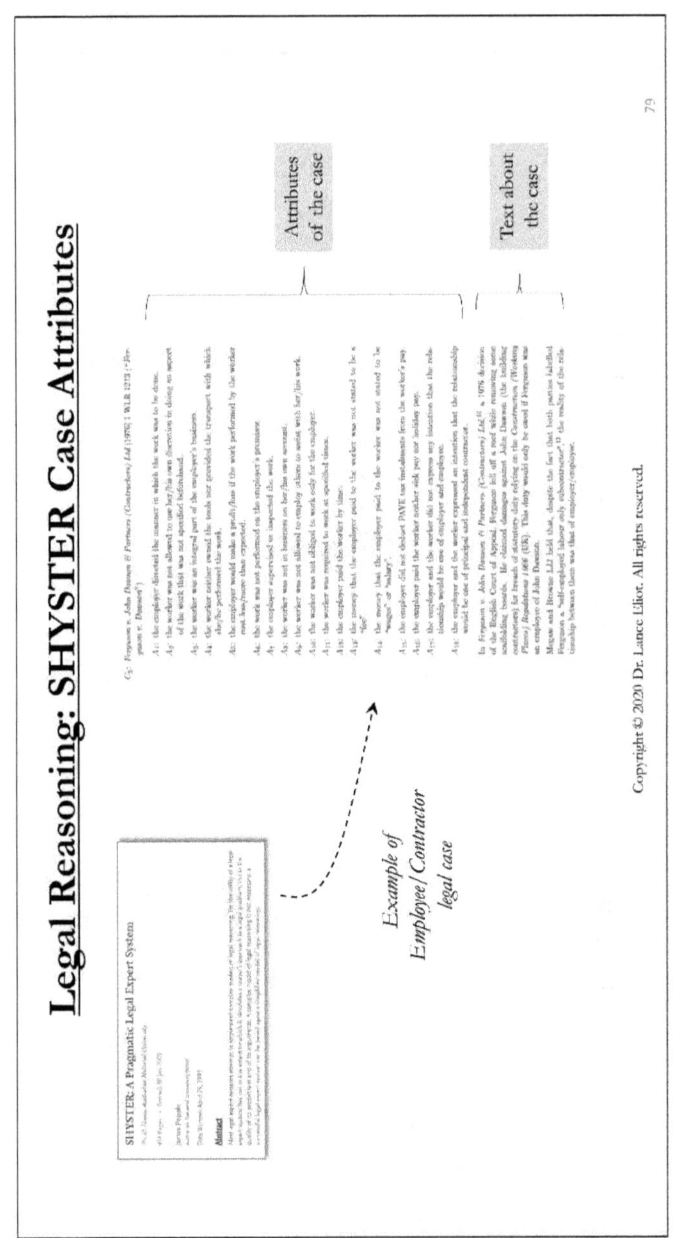
Legal Reasoning: SHYSTER Case Attributes
SHYSTER: A Pragmatic Legal Expert System
Example of Employee/Contractor legal case
Attributes of the case
Text about the case
Copyright © 2020 Dr. Lance Eliot. All rights reserved.
79

Figure 79

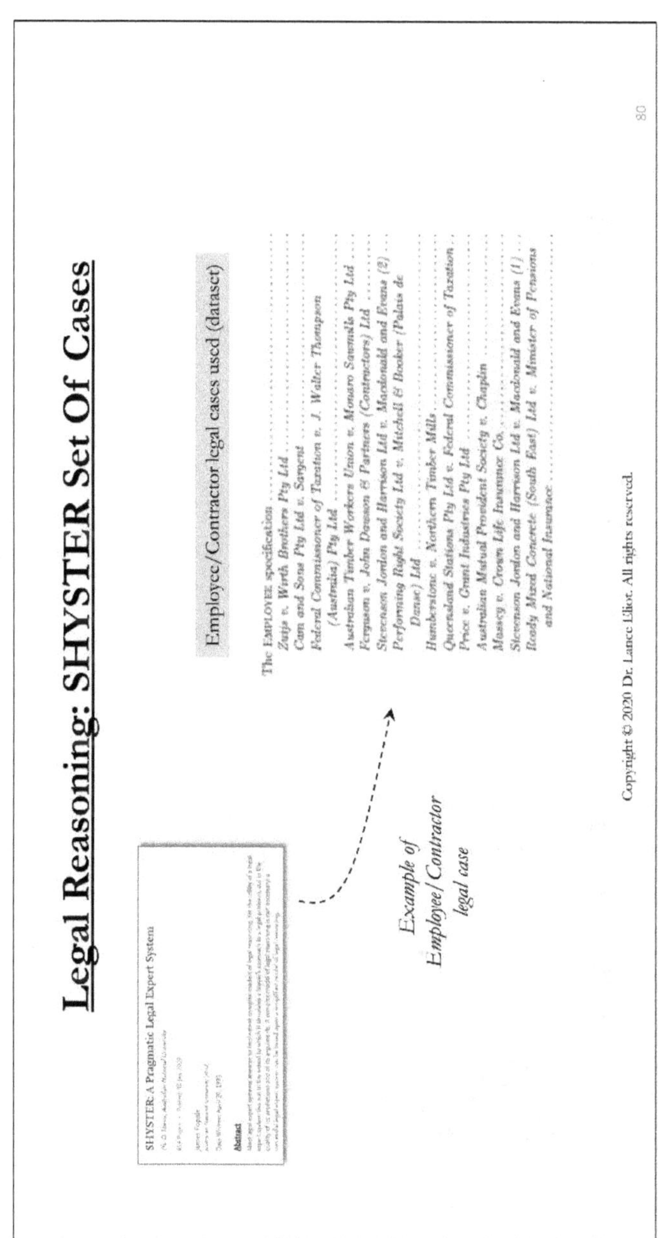
Legal Reasoning: SHYSTER Set Of Cases
SHYSTER: A Pragmatic Legal Expert System
Example of Employee/Contractor legal case
Employee/Contractor legal cases used (dataset)
The EMPLOYEE specification
Zuijs v. Wirth Brothers Pty Ltd
Cam and Sons Pty Ltd v. Sargent
Federal Commissioner of Taxation v. J. Walter Thompson (Australia) Pty Ltd
Australian Timber Workers Union v. Monaro Sawmills Pty Ltd
Ferguson v. John Dawson & Partners (Contractors) Ltd
Stevenson Jordan and Harrison Ltd v. Macdonald and Evans (2)
Performing Right Society Ltd v. Mitchell & Booker (Palais de Danse) Ltd
Humberstone v. Northern Timber Mills
Queensland Stations Pty Ltd v. Federal Commissioner of Taxation
Price v. Grant Industries Pty Ltd
Australian Mutual Provident Society v. Chaplin
Massey v. Crown Life Insurance Co.
Stevenson Jordan and Harrison Ltd v. Macdonald and Evans (1)
Ready Mixed Concrete (South East) Ltd v. Minister of Pensions and National Insurance
Copyright © 2020 Dr. Lance Eliot. All rights reserved.
80

Figure 80

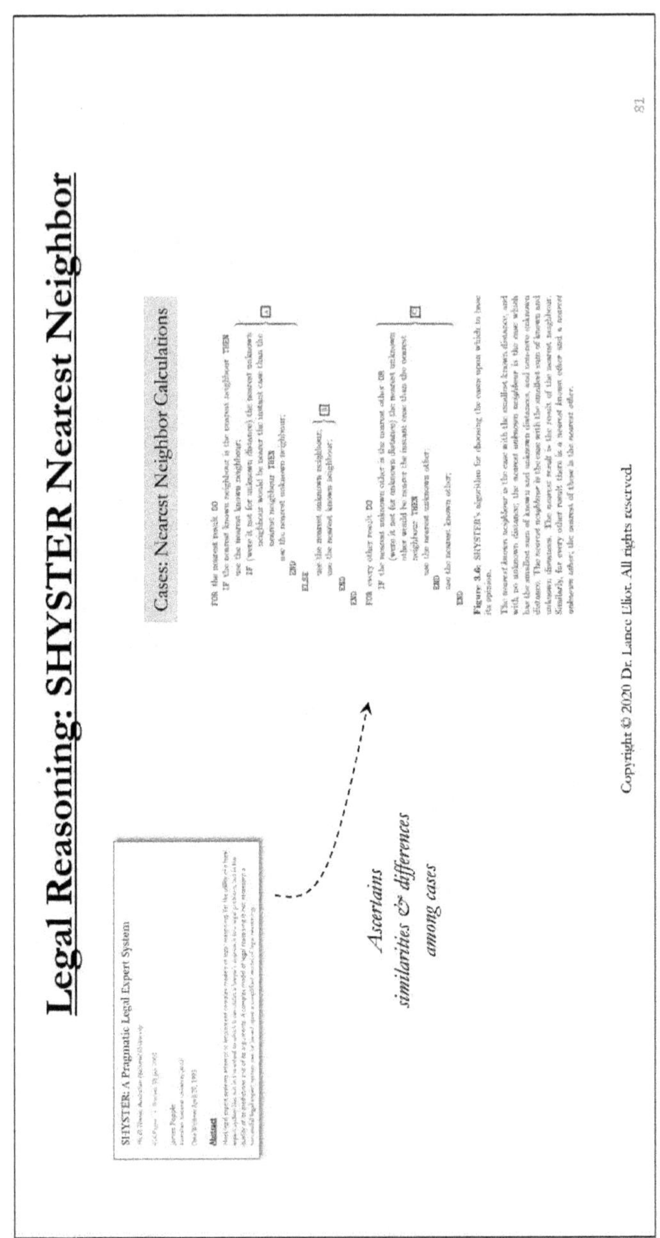

Legal Reasoning: SHYSTER Nearest Neighbor
SHYSTER: A Pragmatic Legal Expert System
Cases: Nearest Neighbor Calculations
Ascertains similarities & differences among cases
Copyright © 2020 Dr. Lance Eliot. All rights reserved.
81

Figure 81

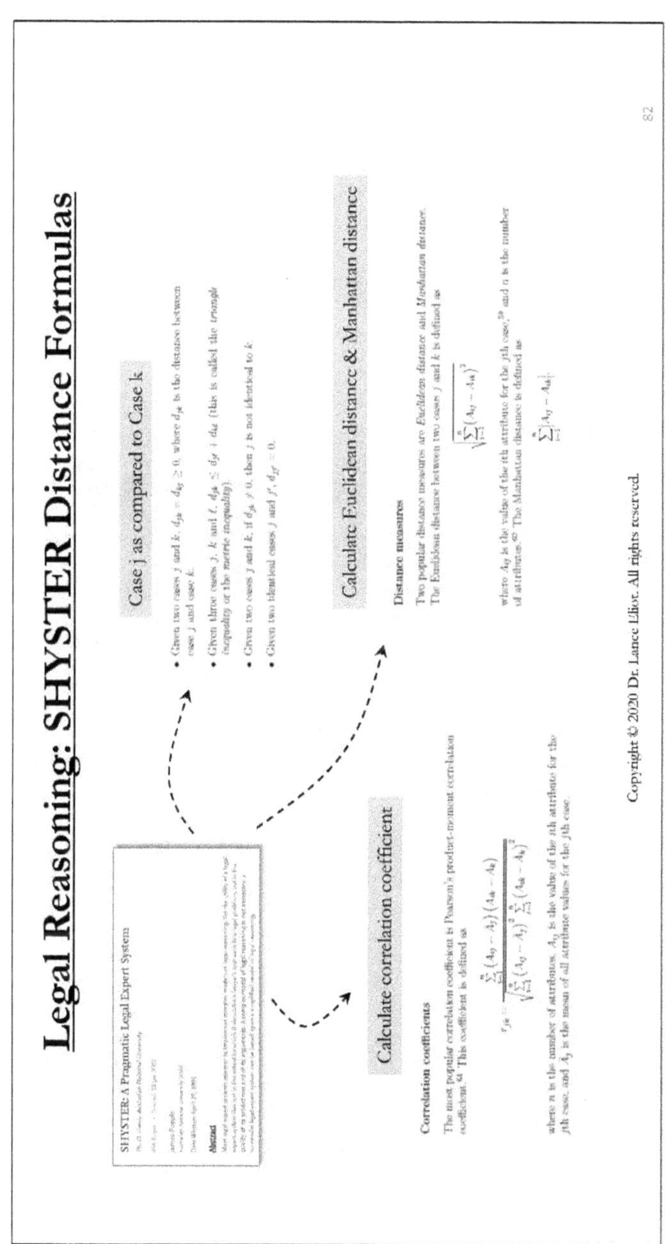
Legal Reasoning: SHYSTER Distance Formulas
SHYSTER: A Pragmatic Legal Expert System
Abstract
Case j as compared to Case k
Calculate correlation coefficient
Correlation coefficients
Calculate Euclidean distance & Manhattan distance
Distance measures
Copyright © 2020 Dr. Lance Eliot. All rights reserved.
82

Figure 82

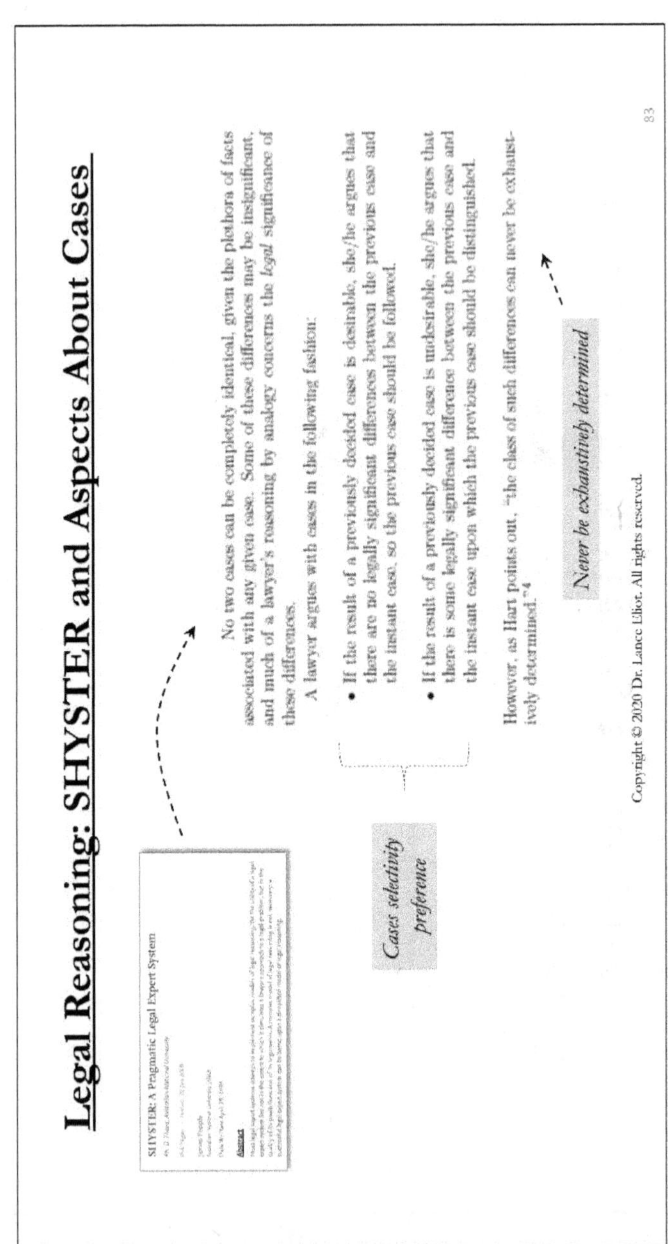
Legal Reasoning: SHYSTER and Aspects About Cases
SHYSTER: A Pragmatic Legal Expert System
Abstract
No two cases can be completely identical, given the plethora of facts associated with any given case. Some of these differences may be insignificant, and much of a lawyer's reasoning by analogy concerns the legal significance of these differences.
A lawyer argues with cases in the following fashion:
• If the result of a previously decided case is desirable, she/he argues that there are no legally significant differences between the previous case and the instant case, so the previous case should be followed.
• If the result of a previously decided case is undesirable, she/he argues that there is some legally significant difference between the previous case and the instant case upon which the previous case should be distinguished.
However, as Hart points out, "the class of such differences can never be exhaustively determined."4
Cases selectivity preference
Never be exhaustively determined
Copyright © 2020 Dr. Lance Eliot. All rights reserved.
83

Figure 83

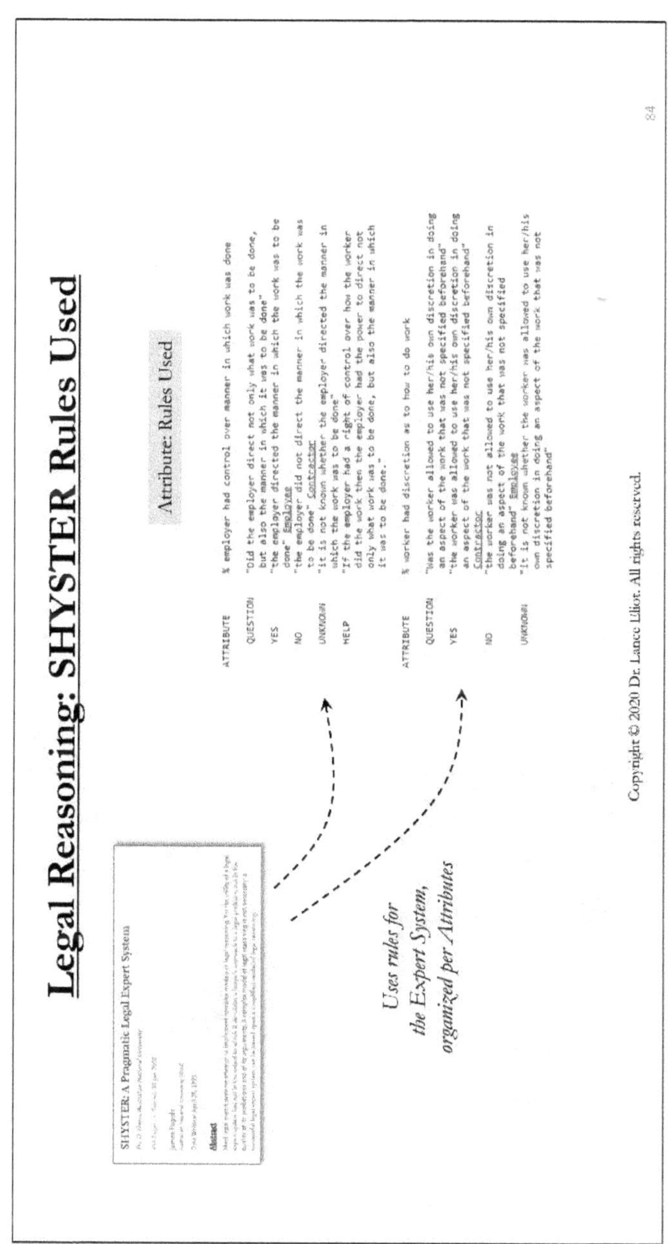
Legal Reasoning: SHYSTER Rules Used
SHYSTER: A Pragmatic Legal Expert System
Abstract
Attribute: Rules Used
ATTRIBUTE % employer had control over manner in which work was done
QUESTION "Did the employer direct not only what work was to be done, but also the manner in which it was to be done"
YES "the employer directed the manner in which the work was to be done" Employee
NO "the employer did not direct the manner in which the work was to be done" Contractor
UNKNOWN "it is not known whether the employer directed the manner in which the work was to be done"
HELP "If the employer had a right of control over how the worker did the work then the employer had the power to direct not only what work was to be done, but also the manner in which it was to be done."
ATTRIBUTE % worker had discretion as to how to do work
QUESTION "Was the worker allowed to use her/his own discretion in doing an aspect of the work that was not specified beforehand"
YES "the worker was allowed to use her/his own discretion in doing an aspect of the work that was not specified beforehand" Contractor
NO "the worker was not allowed to use her/his own discretion in doing an aspect of the work that was not specified beforehand" Employee
UNKNOWN "it is not known whether the worker was allowed to use her/his own discretion in doing an aspect of the work that was not specified beforehand"
Uses rules for the Expert System, organized per Attributes
Copyright © 2020 Dr. Lance Eliot. All rights reserved.
84

Figure 84

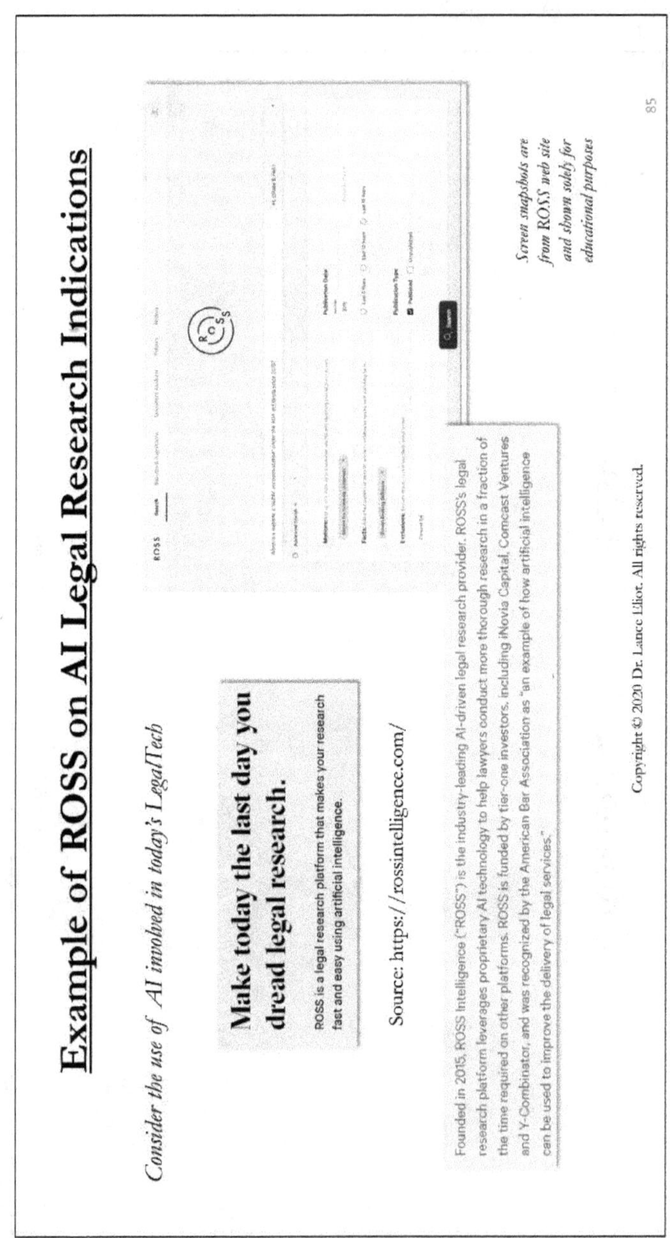

Example of ROSS on AI Legal Research Indications
Consider the use of AI involved in today's LegalTech
Make today the last day you dread legal research.
ROSS is a legal research platform that makes your research fast and easy using artificial intelligence.
Source: https://rossintelligence.com/
Founded in 2015, ROSS Intelligence ("ROSS") is the industry-leading AI-driven legal research provider. ROSS's legal research platform leverages proprietary AI technology to help lawyers conduct more thorough research in a fraction of the time required on other platforms. ROSS is funded by tier-one investors, including iNovia Capital, Comcast Ventures and Y-Combinator, and was recognized by the American Bar Association as "an example of how artificial intelligence can be used to improve the delivery of legal services."
Screen snapshots are from ROSS web site and shown solely for educational purposes
85
Copyright © 2020 Dr. Lance Eliot. All rights reserved.

Figure 85

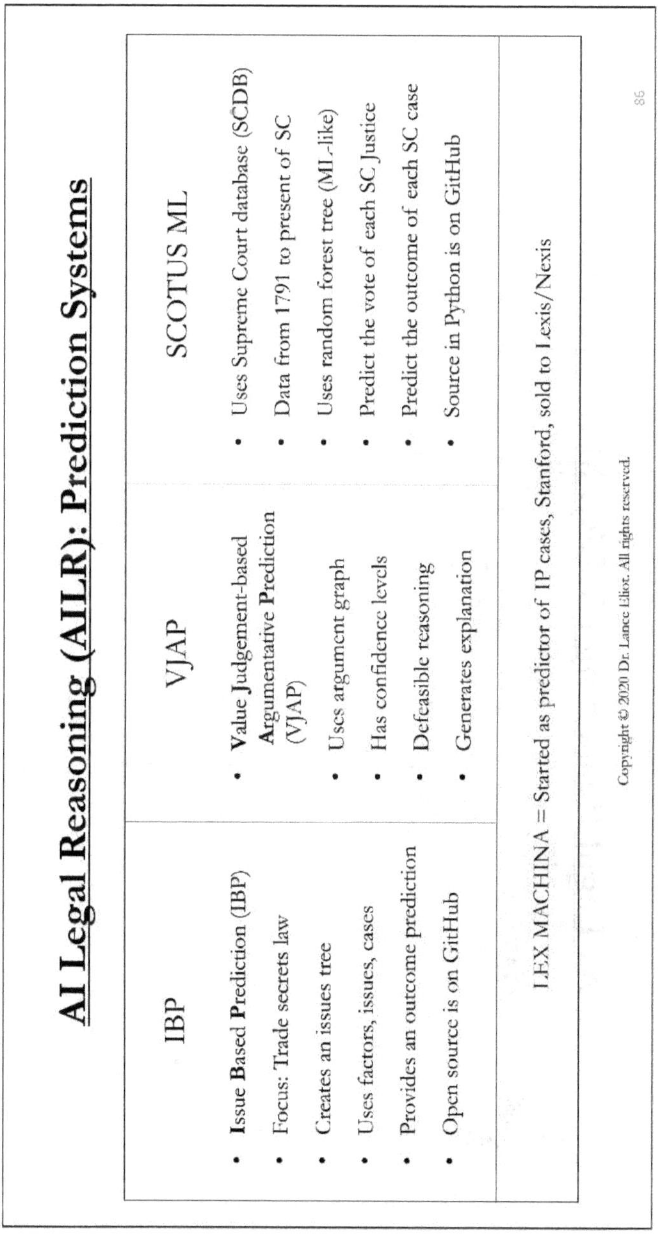

AI Legal Reasoning (AILR): Prediction Systems

IBP	VJAP	SCOTUS ML
• **I**ssue **B**ased **P**rediction (IBP)	• **V**alue **J**udgement-based **A**rgumentative **P**rediction (VJAP)	• Uses Supreme Court database (SCDB)
• Focus: Trade secrets law	• Uses argument graph	• Data from 1791 to present of SC
• Creates an issues tree	• Has confidence levels	• Uses random forest tree (ML-like)
• Uses factors, issues, cases	• Defeasible reasoning	• Predict the vote of each SC Justice
• Provides an outcome prediction	• Generates explanation	• Predict the outcome of each SC case
• Open source is on GitHub		• Source in Python is on GitHub

LEX MACHINA = Started as predictor of IP cases, Stanford, sold to Lexis/Nexis

86

Figure 86

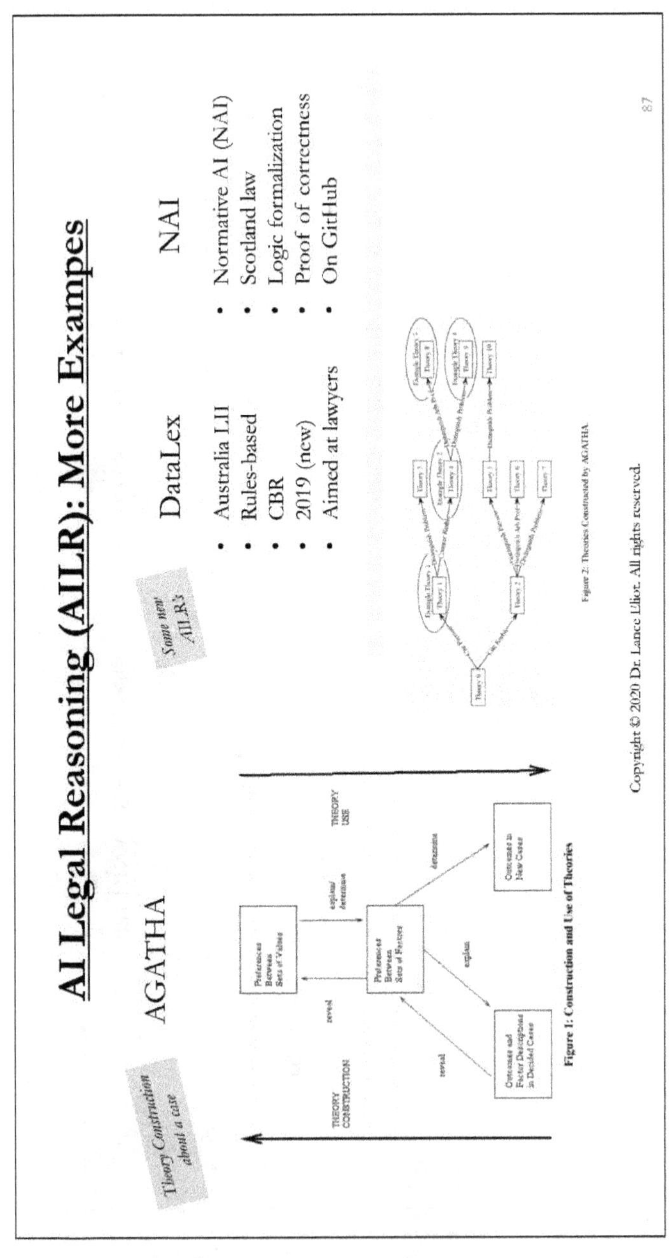
AI Legal Reasoning (AILR): More Exampes
Theory Construction about a case
Some new AILR's
AGATHA
DataLex
• Australia LII
• Rules-based
• CBR
• 2019 (new)
• Aimed at lawyers
NAI
• Normative AI (NAI)
• Scotland law
• Logic formalization
• Proof of correctness
• On GitHub
THEORY CONSTRUCTION
THEORY USE
Figure 1: Construction and Use of Theories
Copyright © 2020 Dr. Lance Eliot. All rights reserved.
87

Figure 87

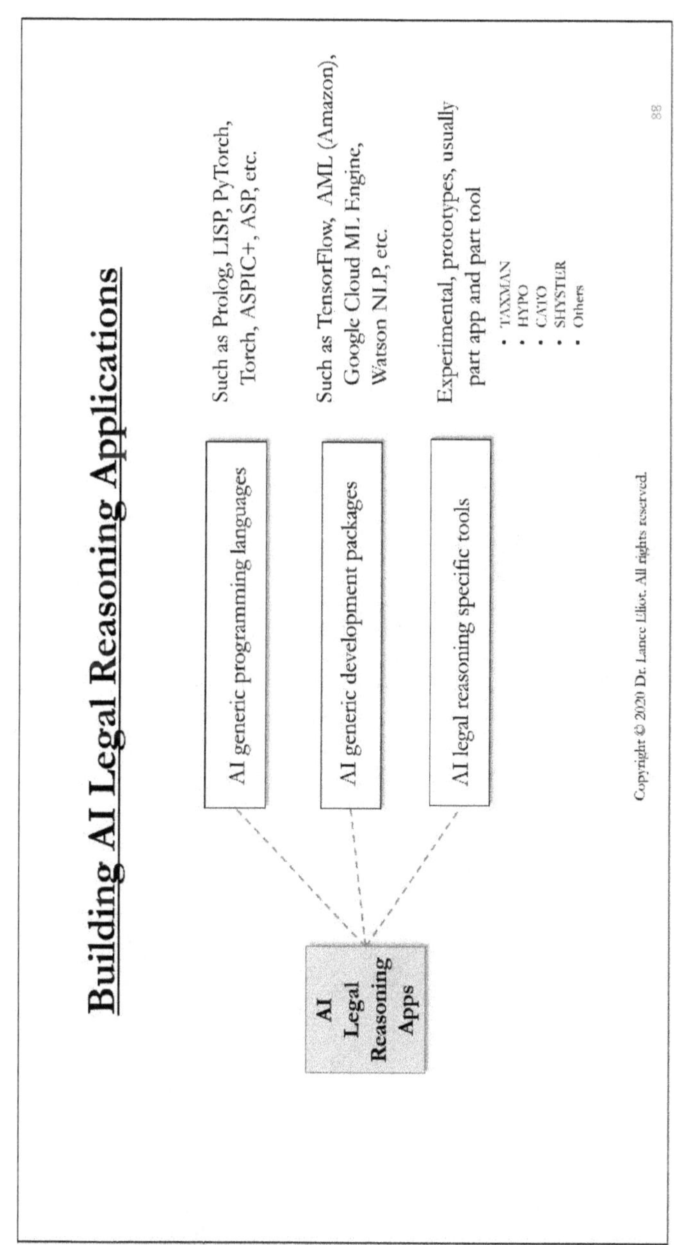
Building AI Legal Reasoning Applications
AI Legal Reasoning Apps
AI generic programming languages
AI generic development packages
AI legal reasoning specific tools
Such as Prolog, LISP, PyTorch, Torch, ASPIC+, ASP, etc.
Such as TensorFlow, AML (Amazon), Google Cloud ML Engine, Watson NLP, etc.
Experimental, prototypes, usually part app and part tool
• TAXMAN
• HYPO
• CATO
• SHYSTER
• Others
Copyright © 2020 Dr. Lance Eliot. All rights reserved.
88

Figure 88

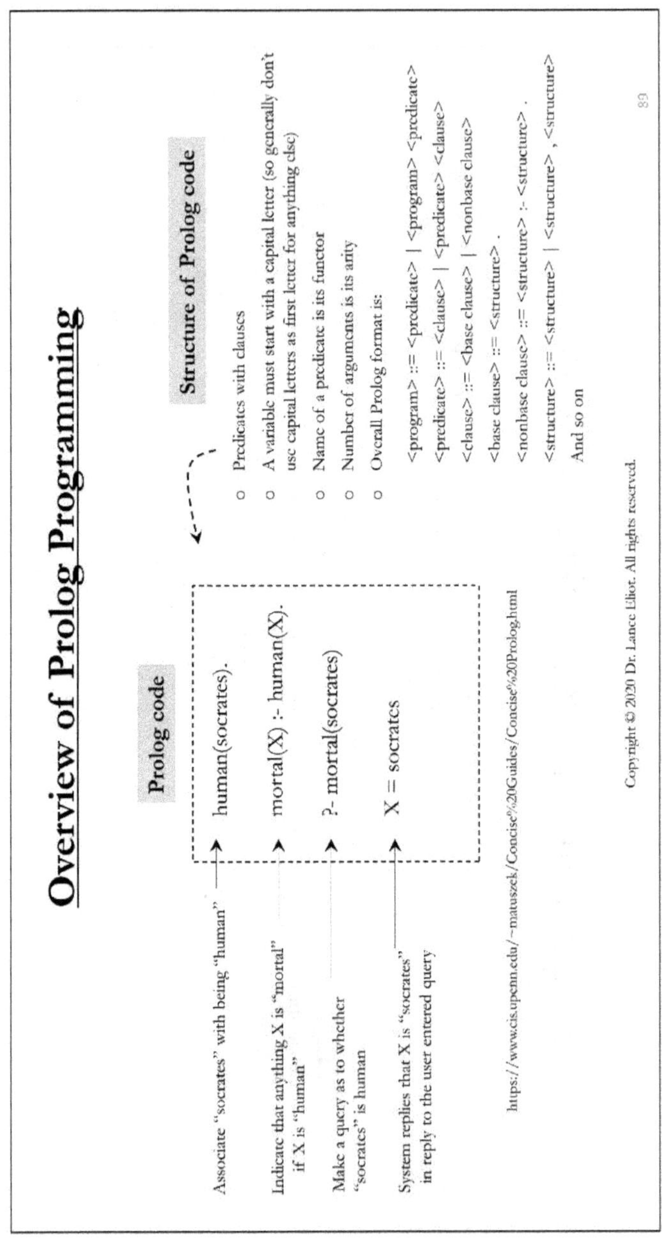
Overview of Prolog Programming
Prolog code
Associate "socrates" with being "human"
human(socrates).
Indicate that anything X is "mortal" if X is "human"
mortal(X) :- human(X).
Make a query as to whether "socrates" is human
?- mortal(socrates)
System replies that X is "socrates" in reply to the user entered query
X = socrates
https://www.cis.upenn.edu/~matuszek/Concise%20Guides/Concise%20Prolog.html
Structure of Prolog code
Predicates with clauses
A variable must start with a capital letter (so generally don't use capital letters as first letter for anything else)
Name of a predicate is its functor
Number of arguments is its arity
Overall Prolog format is:
<program> ::= <predicate> | <program> <predicate>
<predicate> ::= <clause> | <predicate> <clause>
<clause> ::= <base clause> | <nonbase clause>
<base clause> ::= <structure> .
<nonbase clause> ::= <structure> :- <structure> .
<structure> ::= <structure> | <structure> , <structure>
And so on
Copyright © 2020 Dr. Lance Eliot. All rights reserved.
89

Figure 89

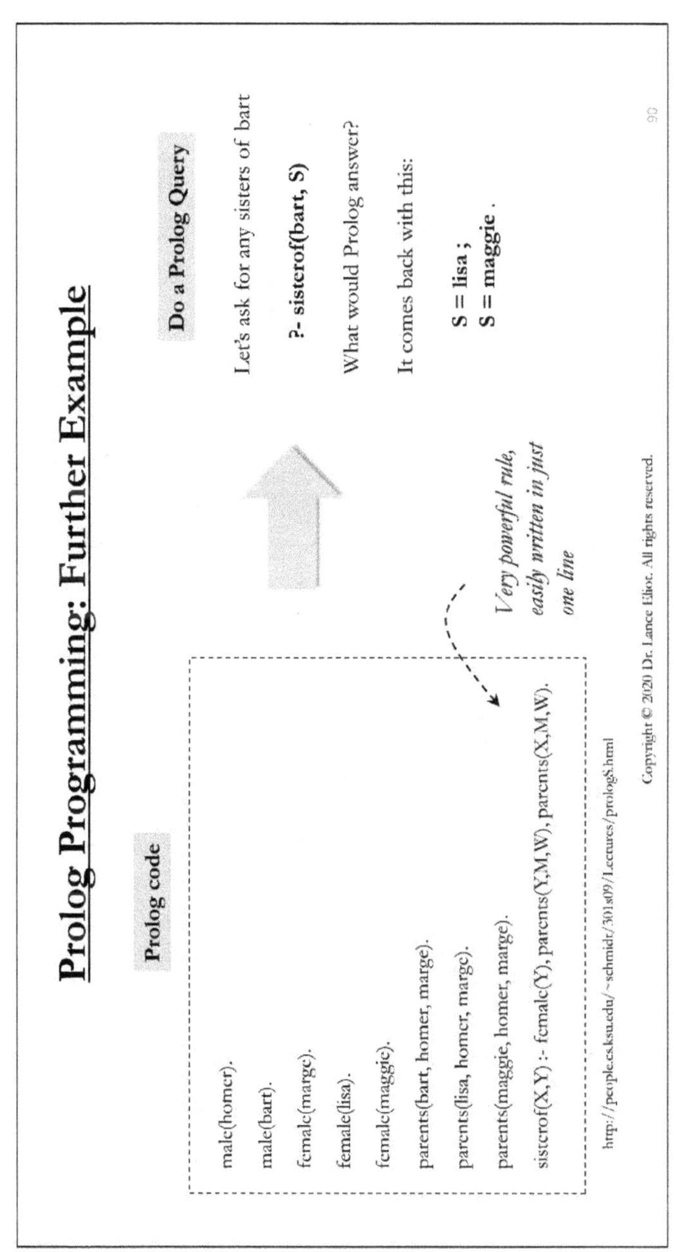
Prolog Programming: Further Example
Prolog code
male(homer).
male(bart).
female(marge).
female(lisa).
female(maggie).
parents(bart, homer, marge).
parents(lisa, homer, marge).
parents(maggie, homer, marge).
sisterof(X,Y) :- female(Y), parents(Y,M,W), parents(X,M,W).
http://people.cs.ksu.edu/~schmidt/301s09/Lectures/prologS.html
Very powerful rule, easily written in just one line
Do a Prolog Query
Let's ask for any sisters of bart
?- sisterof(bart, S)
What would Prolog answer?
It comes back with this:
S = lisa ;
S = maggie .
Copyright © 2020 Dr. Lance Eliot. All rights reserved.
90

Figure 90

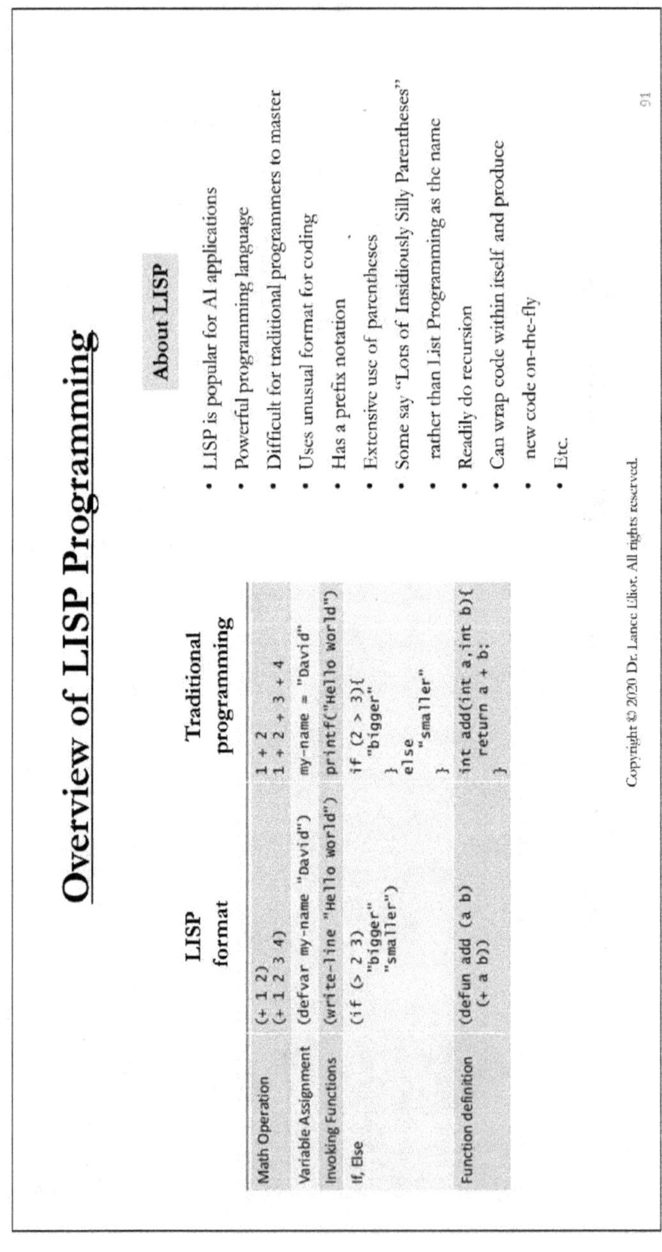
Overview of LISP Programming
LISP format
Traditional programming
Math Operation
(+ 1 2)
(+ 1 2 3 4)
1 + 2
1 + 2 + 3 + 4
Variable Assignment
(defvar my-name "David")
my-name = "David"
Invoking Functions
(write-line "Hello world")
printf("Hello world")
If, Else
(if (> 2 3)
"bigger"
"smaller")
if (2 > 3){
"bigger"
}
else
"smaller"
}
Function definition
(defun add (a b)
(+ a b))
int add(int a,int b){
return a + b;
}
About LISP
LISP is popular for AI applications
Powerful programming language
Difficult for traditional programmers to master
Uses unusual format for coding
Has a prefix notation
Extensive use of parentheses
Some say "Lots of Insidiously Silly Parentheses"
rather than List Programming as the name
Readily do recursion
Can wrap code within itself and produce
new code on-the-fly
Etc.
Copyright © 2020 Dr. Lance Eliot. All rights reserved.
91

Figure 91

Famous LISP Program: ELIZA

About ELIZA Program

- ELIZA is a famous early "AI" program (1960s)
- Pretends to be an interactive psychotherapist
- Used simplistic NLP (Natural Language Processing)
- Just obvious pattern match and text substitution
- Was kind of a poke at psyche-babble and parroting
- Developed by Joseph Weizenbaum (MIT)
- Named after Eliza Doolittle in Bernard Shaw's *Pygmalion*
- Revealed how people can be easily fooled
- Some people convinced of its "intelligence"
- Important insight for Turing Test ramifications

Example of ELIZA "dialogue"

```
Please tell me what's been bothering you.
Well, it's my boss.
Your boss?
Yes.  He's not very friendly.
I see.
He is always upset.
When?
Always.  Especially when things are hectic.
Can you think of a specific example?
Well, yesterday he said he was unhappy with all of us.
That is interesting. Please continue.
He says I am too lazy.
Is it because you are too lazy that you came to me?
I'm not lazy.
Do you believe it is normal to be not lazy?
```


92

Figure 92

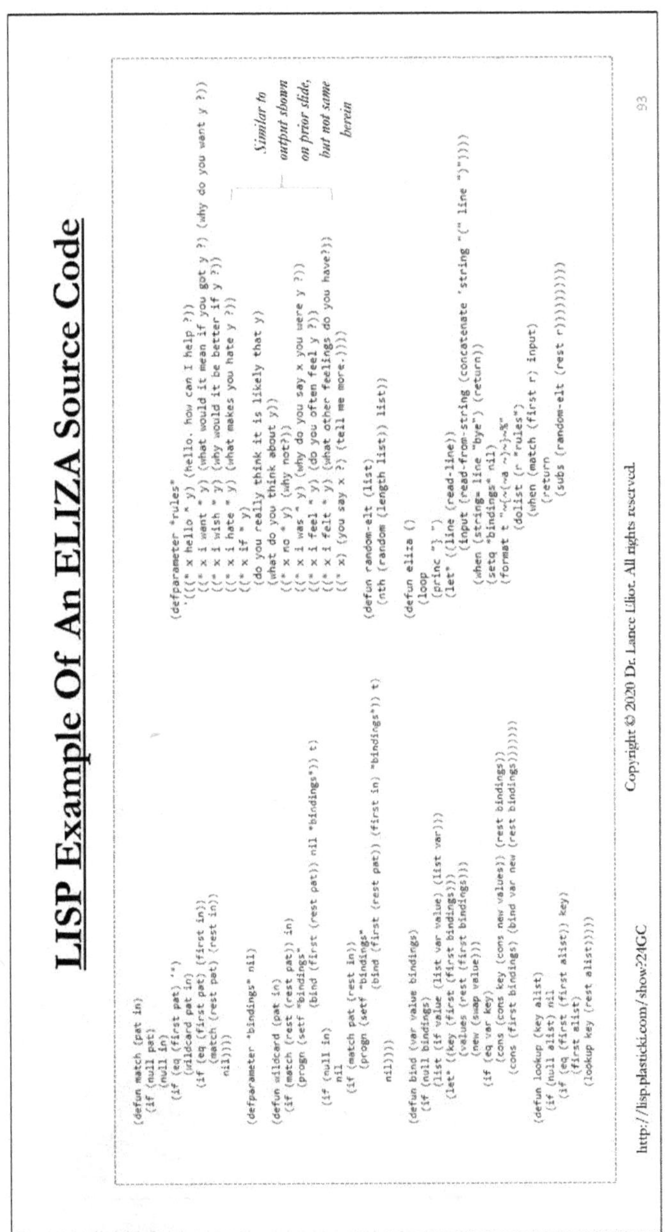
LISP Example Of An ELIZA Source Code
(defun match (pat in)
(if (null pat)
(null in)
(if (eq (first pat) '*)
(wildcard pat in)
(if (eq (first pat) (first in))
(match (rest pat) (rest in))
nil))))
(defparameter *bindings* nil)
(defun wildcard (pat in)
(if (match (rest (rest pat)) in)
(progn (setf *bindings*
(bind (first (rest pat)) nil *bindings*)) t)
(if (null in)
nil
(if (match pat (rest in))
(progn (setf *bindings*
(bind (first (rest pat)) (first in) *bindings*)) t)
nil))))
(defun bind (var value bindings)
(if (null bindings)
(list (if value (list var value) (list var)))
(let* ((key (first (first bindings)))
(values (rest (first bindings)))
(new (swap value)))
(if (eq var key)
(cons (cons key (cons new values)) (rest bindings))
(cons (first bindings) (bind var new (rest bindings)))))))
(defun lookup (key alist)
(if (null alist) nil
(if (eq (first (first alist)) key)
(first alist)
(lookup key (rest alist)))))
(defparameter *rules*
'(((* x hello * y) (hello. how can I help ?))
((* x i want * y) (what would it mean if you got y ?) (why do you want y ?))
((* x i wish * y) (why would it be better if y ?))
((* x i hate * y) (what makes you hate y ?))
((* x if * y)
(do you really think it is likely that y)
(what do you think about y))
((* x no * y) (why not?))
((* x i was * y) (why do you say x you were y ?))
((* x i feel * y) (do you often feel y ?))
((* x i felt * y) (what other feelings do you have?))
((* x) (you say x ?) (tell me more.))))
Similar to output shown on prior slide, but not same herein
(defun random-elt (list)
(nth (random (length list)) list))
(defun eliza ()
(loop
(princ "} ")
(let* ((line (read-line))
(input (read-from-string (concatenate 'string "(" line ")"))))
(when (string= line "bye") (return))
(setq *bindings* nil)
(format t "~{~(~a ~)~}~%"
(dolist (r *rules*)
(when (match (first r) input)
(return
(subs (random-elt (rest r))))))))))
http://lisp.plasticki.com/show?24GC
Copyright © 2020 Dr. Lance Eliot. All rights reserved.
93

Figure 93

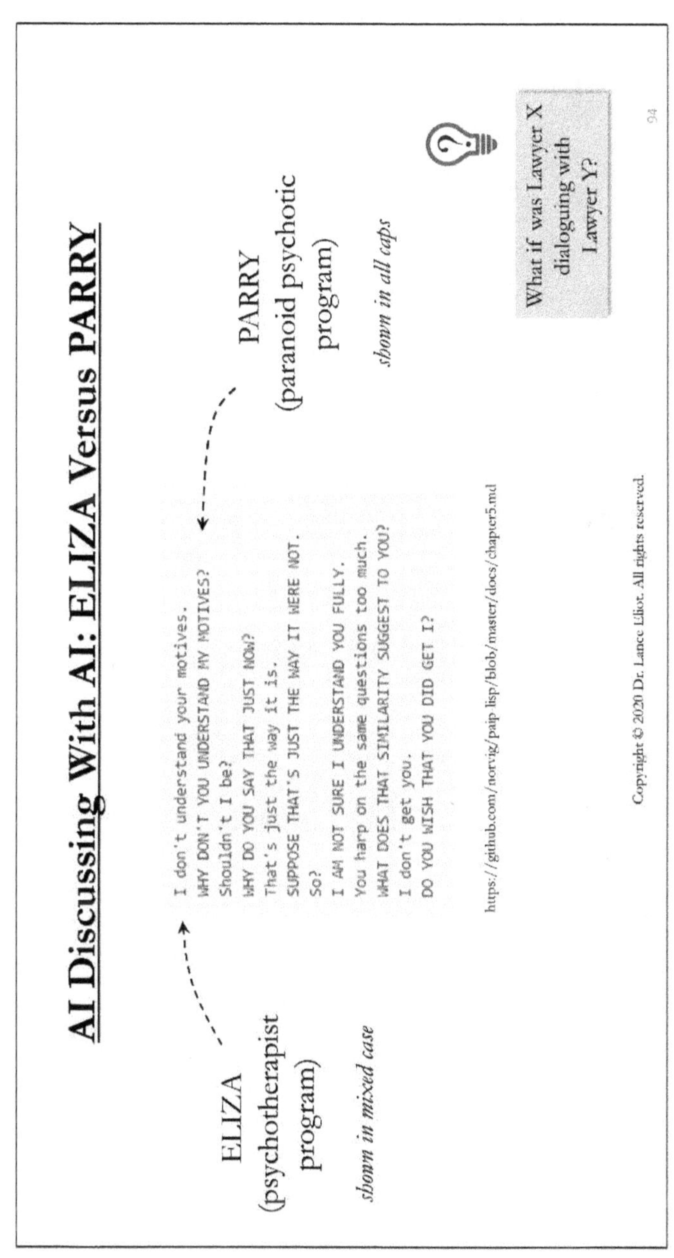
AI Discussing With AI: ELIZA Versus PARRY
ELIZA
(psychotherapist
program)
shown in mixed case
PARRY
(paranoid psychotic
program)
shown in all caps
I don't understand your motives.
WHY DON'T YOU UNDERSTAND MY MOTIVES?
Shouldn't I be?
WHY DO YOU SAY THAT JUST NOW?
That's just the way it is.
SUPPOSE THAT'S JUST THE WAY IT WERE NOT.
So?
I AM NOT SURE I UNDERSTAND YOU FULLY.
You harp on the same questions too much.
WHAT DOES THAT SIMILARITY SUGGEST TO YOU?
I don't get you.
DO YOU WISH THAT YOU DID GET I?
https://github.com/norvig/paip-lisp/blob/master/docs/chapter5.md
What if was Lawyer X dialoguing with Lawyer Y?
94
Copyright © 2020 Dr. Lance Eliot. All rights reserved.

Figure 94

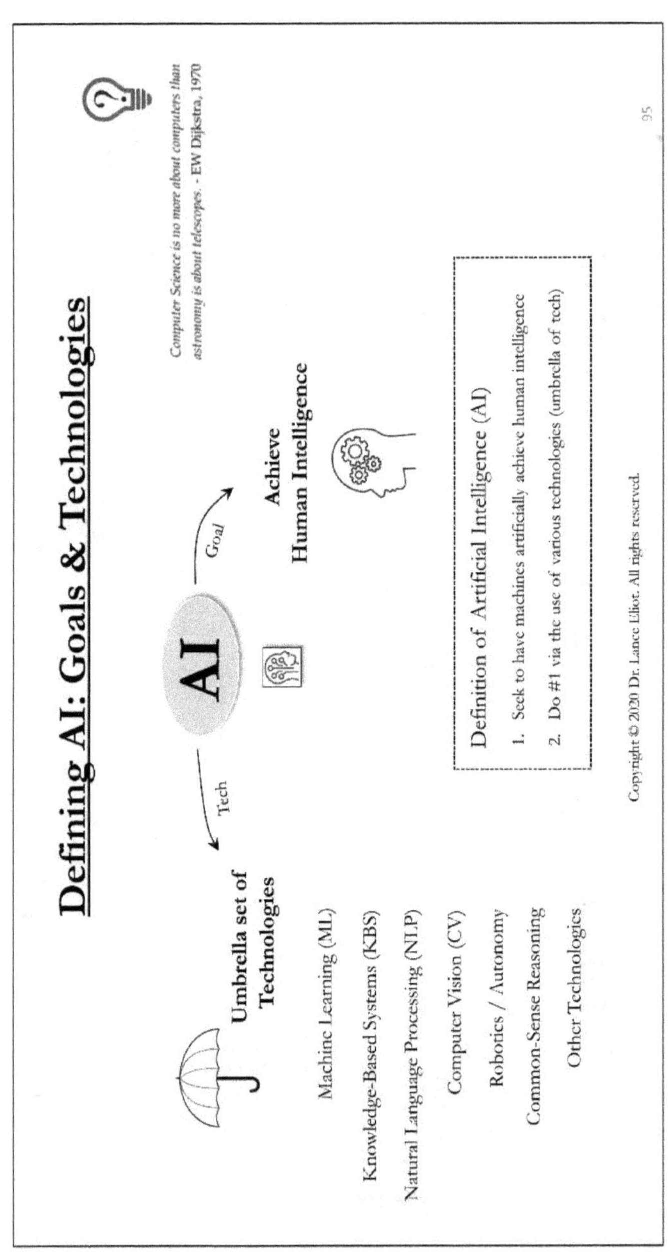
Defining AI: Goals & Technologies
Computer Science is no more about computers than astronomy is about telescopes. - EW Dijkstra, 1970
AI
Tech
Goal
Umbrella set of Technologies
Achieve Human Intelligence
Machine Learning (ML)
Knowledge-Based Systems (KBS)
Natural Language Processing (NLP)
Computer Vision (CV)
Robotics / Autonomy
Common-Sense Reasoning
Other Technologies
Definition of Artificial Intelligence (AI)
1. Seek to have machines artificially achieve human intelligence
2. Do #1 via the use of various technologies (umbrella of tech)
Copyright © 2020 Dr. Lance Eliot. All rights reserved.
95

Figure 95

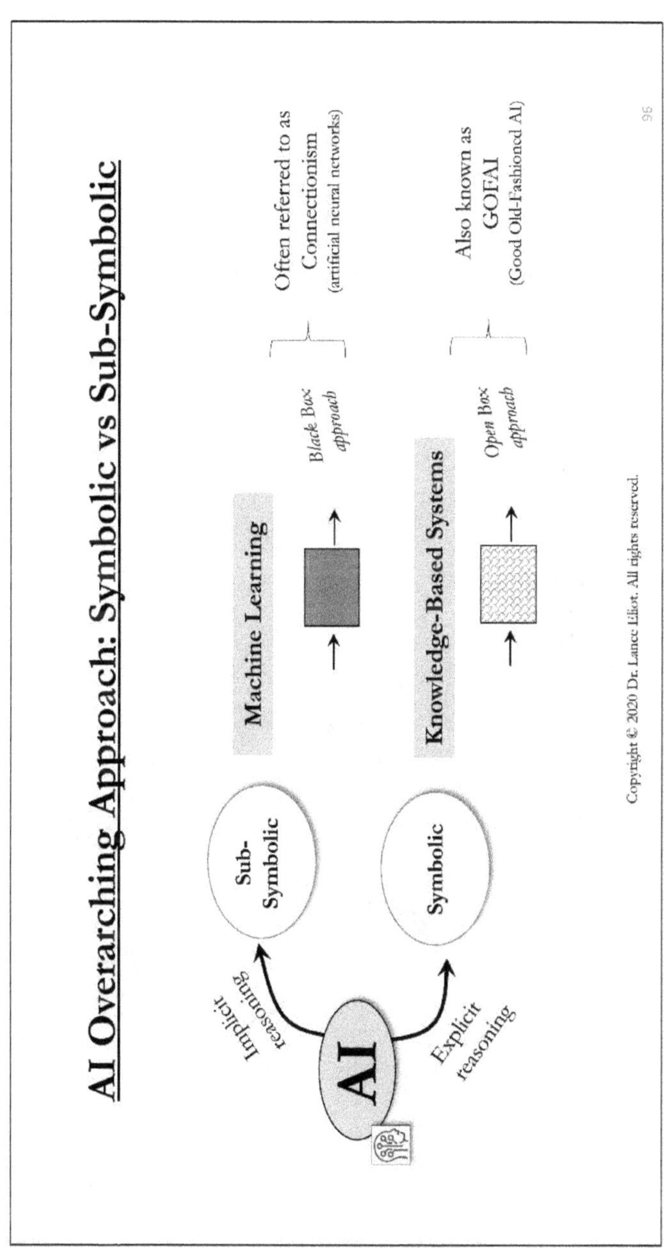
AI Overarching Approach: Symbolic vs Sub-Symbolic
AI
Implicit reasoning
Explicit reasoning
Sub-Symbolic
Symbolic
Machine Learning
Black Box approach
Often referred to as Connectionism
(artificial neural networks)
Knowledge-Based Systems
Open Box approach
Also known as GOFAI
(Good Old-Fashioned AI)
Copyright © 2020 Dr. Lance Eliot. All rights reserved.
96

Figure 96

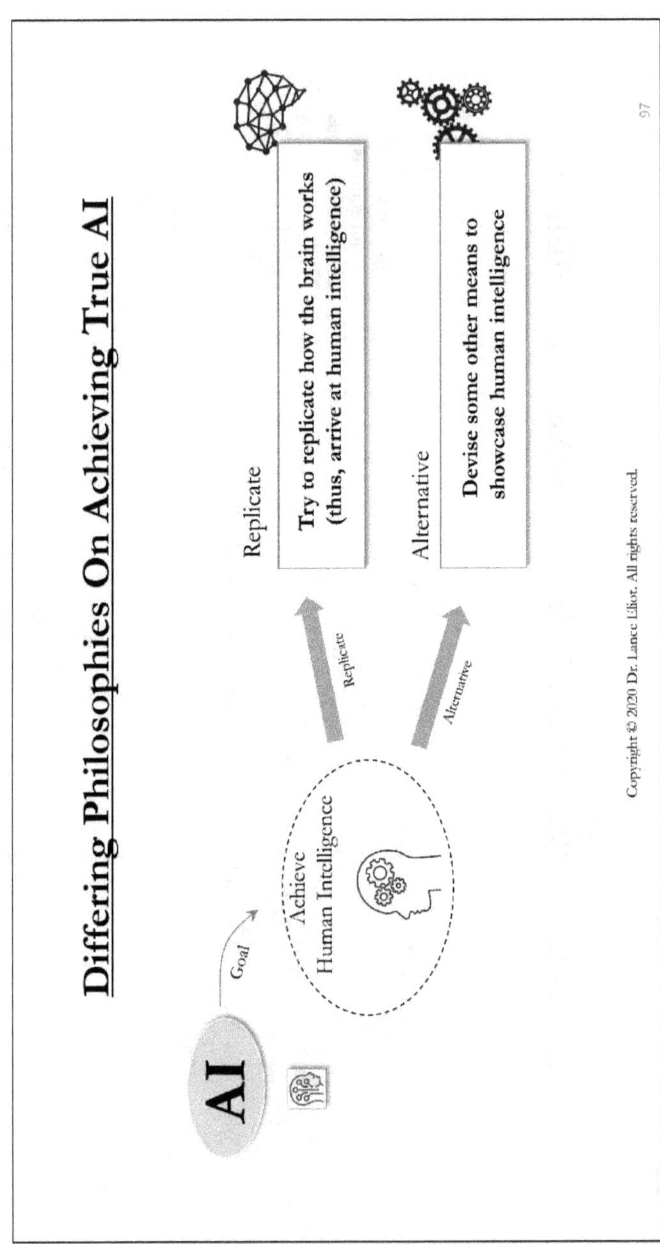
Differing Philosophies On Achieving True AI
AI
Goal
Achieve
Human Intelligence
Replicate
Alternative
Replicate
Try to replicate how the brain works
(thus, arrive at human intelligence)
Alternative
Devise some other means to
showcase human intelligence
Copyright © 2020 Dr. Lance Eliot. All rights reserved.
97

Figure 97

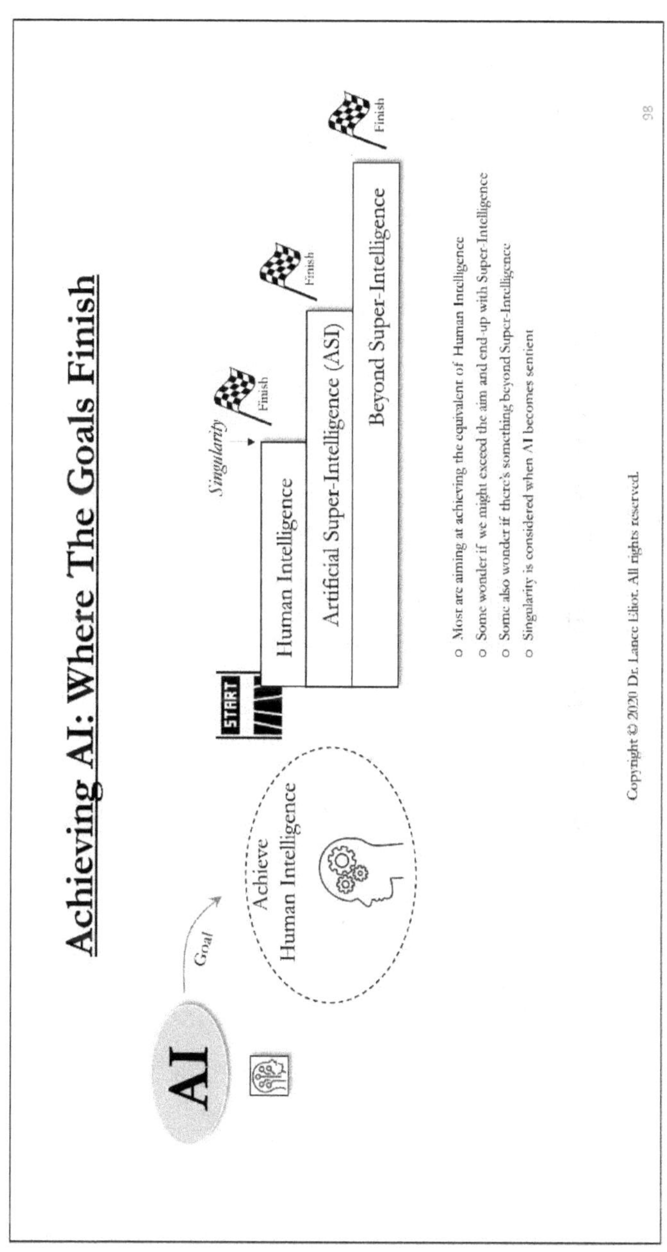
Achieving AI: Where The Goals Finish
AI
Goal
Achieve
Human Intelligence
START
Human Intelligence
Artificial Super-Intelligence (ASI)
Beyond Super-Intelligence
Singularity
Finish
Finish
Finish
o Most are aiming at achieving the equivalent of Human Intelligence
o Some wonder if we might exceed the aim and end-up with Super-Intelligence
o Some also wonder if there's something beyond Super-Intelligence
o Singularity is considered when AI becomes sentient
Copyright © 2020 Dr. Lance Eliot. All rights reserved.
98

Figure 98

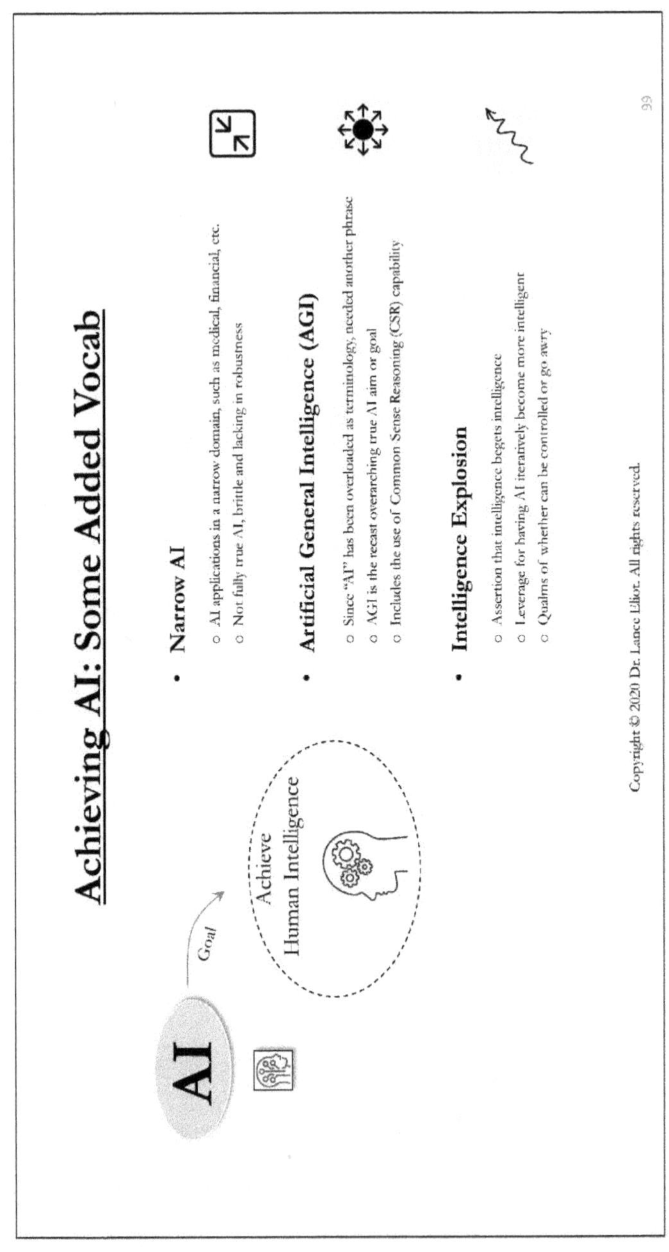
Achieving AI: Some Added Vocab
AI
Goal
Achieve
Human Intelligence
Narrow AI
AI applications in a narrow domain, such as medical, financial, etc.
Not fully true AI, brittle and lacking in robustness
Artificial General Intelligence (AGI)
Since "AI" has been overloaded as terminology, needed another phrase
AGI is the recast overarching true AI aim or goal
Includes the use of Common Sense Reasoning (CSR) capability
Intelligence Explosion
Assertion that intelligence begets intelligence
Leverage for having AI iteratively become more intelligent
Qualms of whether can be controlled or go awry
Copyright © 2020 Dr. Lance Eliot. All rights reserved.
99

Figure 99

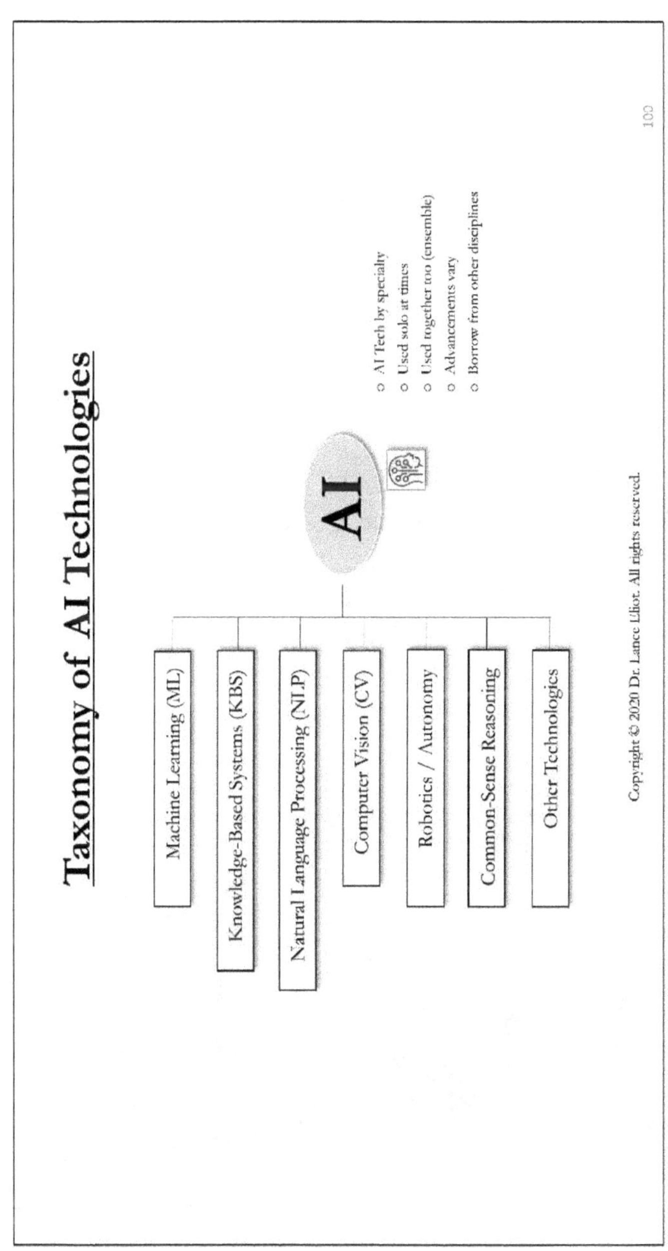
Taxonomy of AI Technologies
Machine Learning (ML)
Knowledge-Based Systems (KBS)
Natural Language Processing (NLP)
Computer Vision (CV)
Robotics / Autonomy
Common-Sense Reasoning
Other Technologies
AI
o AI Tech by specialty
o Used solo at times
o Used together too (ensemble)
o Advancements vary
o Borrow from other disciplines
Copyright © 2020 Dr. Lance Eliot. All rights reserved.
100

Figure 100

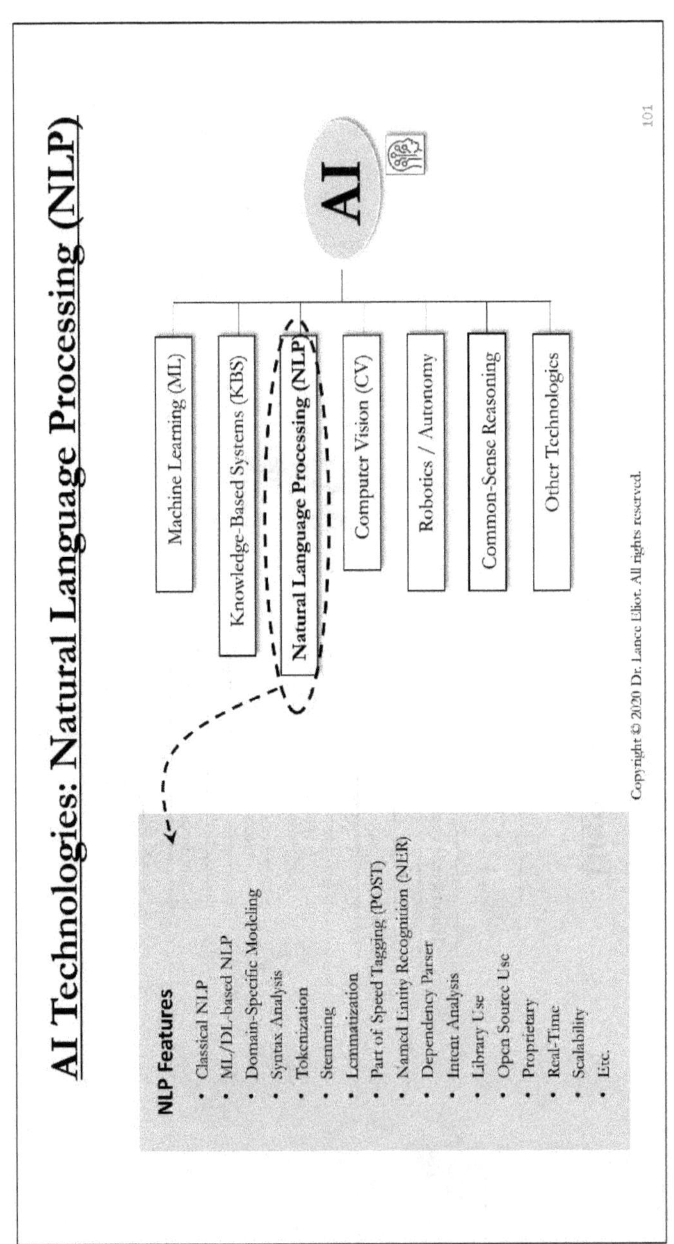
AI Technologies: Natural Language Processing (NLP)
AI
Machine Learning (ML)
Knowledge-Based Systems (KBS)
Natural Language Processing (NLP)
Computer Vision (CV)
Robotics / Autonomy
Common-Sense Reasoning
Other Technologies
NLP Features
• Classical NLP
• ML/DL-based NLP
• Domain-Specific Modeling
• Syntax Analysis
• Tokenization
• Stemming
• Lemmatization
• Part of Speed Tagging (POST)
• Named Entity Recognition (NER)
• Dependency Parser
• Intent Analysis
• Library Use
• Open Source Use
• Proprietary
• Real-Time
• Scalability
• Etc.
Copyright © 2020 Dr. Lance Eliot. All rights reserved.
101

Figure 101

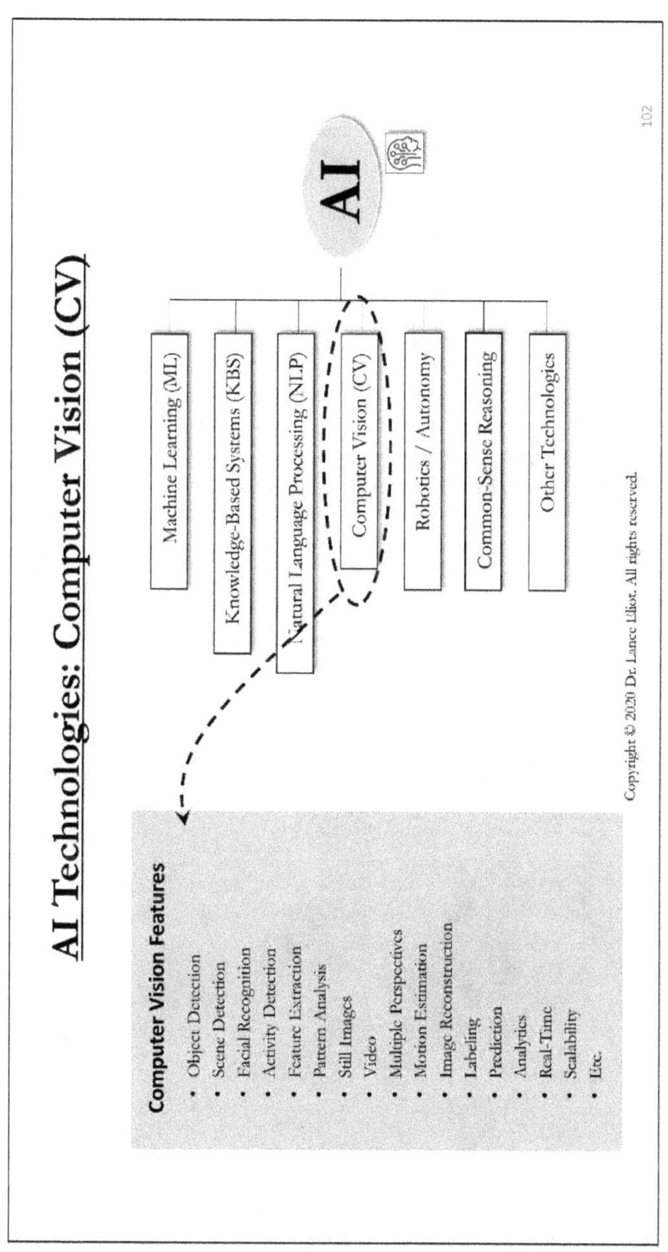
AI Technologies: Computer Vision (CV)
AI
Machine Learning (ML)
Knowledge-Based Systems (KBS)
Natural Language Processing (NLP)
Computer Vision (CV)
Robotics / Autonomy
Common-Sense Reasoning
Other Technologies
Computer Vision Features
• Object Detection
• Scene Detection
• Facial Recognition
• Activity Detection
• Feature Extraction
• Pattern Analysis
• Still Images
• Video
• Multiple Perspectives
• Motion Estimation
• Image Reconstruction
• Labeling
• Prediction
• Analytics
• Real-Time
• Scalability
• Etc.
Copyright © 2020 Dr. Lance Eliot. All rights reserved.
102

Figure 102

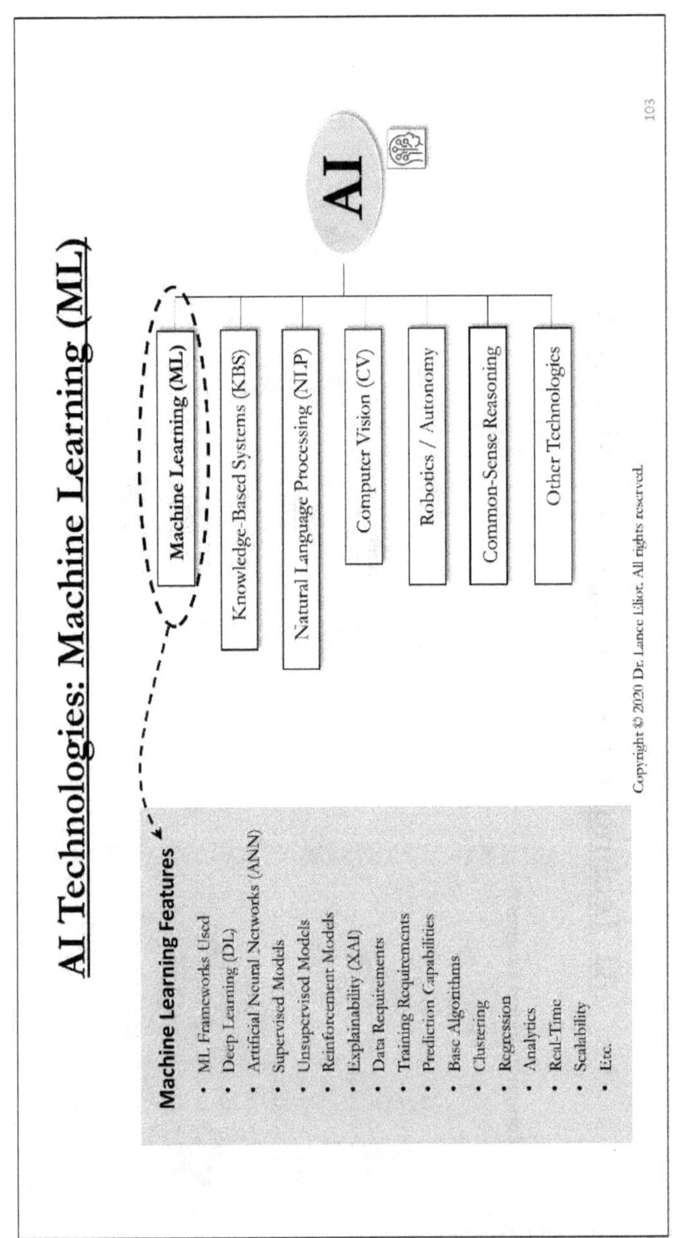
AI Technologies: Machine Learning (ML)
Machine Learning Features
• ML Frameworks Used
• Deep Learning (DL)
• Artificial Neural Networks (ANN)
• Supervised Models
• Unsupervised Models
• Reinforcement Models
• Explainability (XAI)
• Data Requirements
• Training Requirements
• Prediction Capabilities
• Base Algorithms
• Clustering
• Regression
• Analytics
• Real-Time
• Scalability
• Etc.
Machine Learning (ML)
Knowledge-Based Systems (KBS)
Natural Language Processing (NLP)
Computer Vision (CV)
Robotics / Autonomy
Common-Sense Reasoning
Other Technologies
AI
Copyright © 2020 Dr. Lance Eliot. All rights reserved.
103

Figure 103

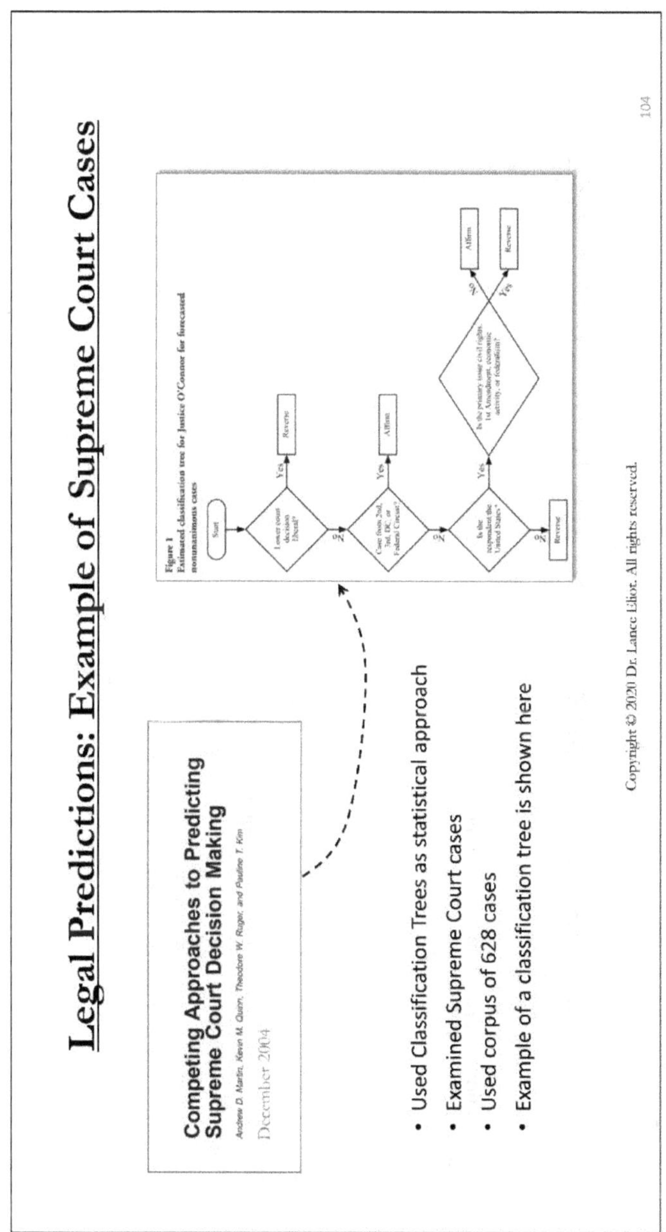
Legal Predictions: Example of Supreme Court Cases
Competing Approaches to Predicting Supreme Court Decision Making
Andrew D. Martin, Kevin M. Quinn, Theodore W. Ruger, and Pauline T. Kim
December 2004
Figure 1
Estimated classification tree for Justice O'Connor for forecasted nonunanimous cases
Start
Lower court decision liberal?
Yes
Reverse
No
Case from 2nd, 3rd, DC, or Federal Circuit?
Yes
Affirm
No
Is the respondent the United States?
Yes
Is the primary issue civil rights, 1st Amendment, economic activity, or federalism?
No
Affirm
Yes
Reverse
No
Reverse
• Used Classification Trees as statistical approach
• Examined Supreme Court cases
• Used corpus of 628 cases
• Example of a classification tree is shown here
Copyright © 2020 Dr. Lance Eliot. All rights reserved.
104

Figure 104

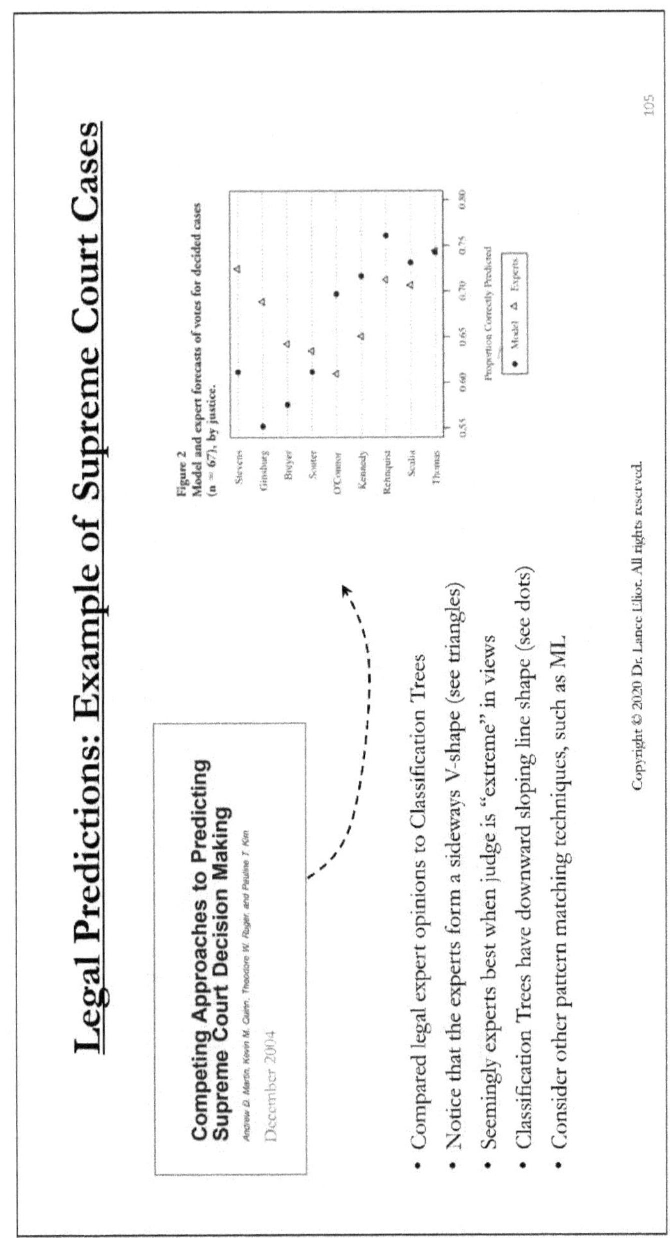
Legal Predictions: Example of Supreme Court Cases
Competing Approaches to Predicting Supreme Court Decision Making
Andrew D. Martin, Kevin M. Quinn, Theodore W. Ruger, and Pauline T. Kim
December 2004
Figure 2
Model and expert forecasts of votes for decided cases (n = 67), by justice.
Stevens
Ginsburg
Breyer
Souter
O'Connor
Kennedy
Rehnquist
Scalia
Thomas
0.55
0.60
0.65
0.70
0.75
0.80
Proportion Correctly Predicted
Model
Experts
• Compared legal expert opinions to Classification Trees
• Notice that the experts form a sideways V-shape (see triangles)
• Seemingly experts best when judge is "extreme" in views
• Classification Trees have downward sloping line shape (see dots)
• Consider other pattern matching techniques, such as ML
Copyright © 2020 Dr. Lance Eliot. All rights reserved.
105

Figure 105

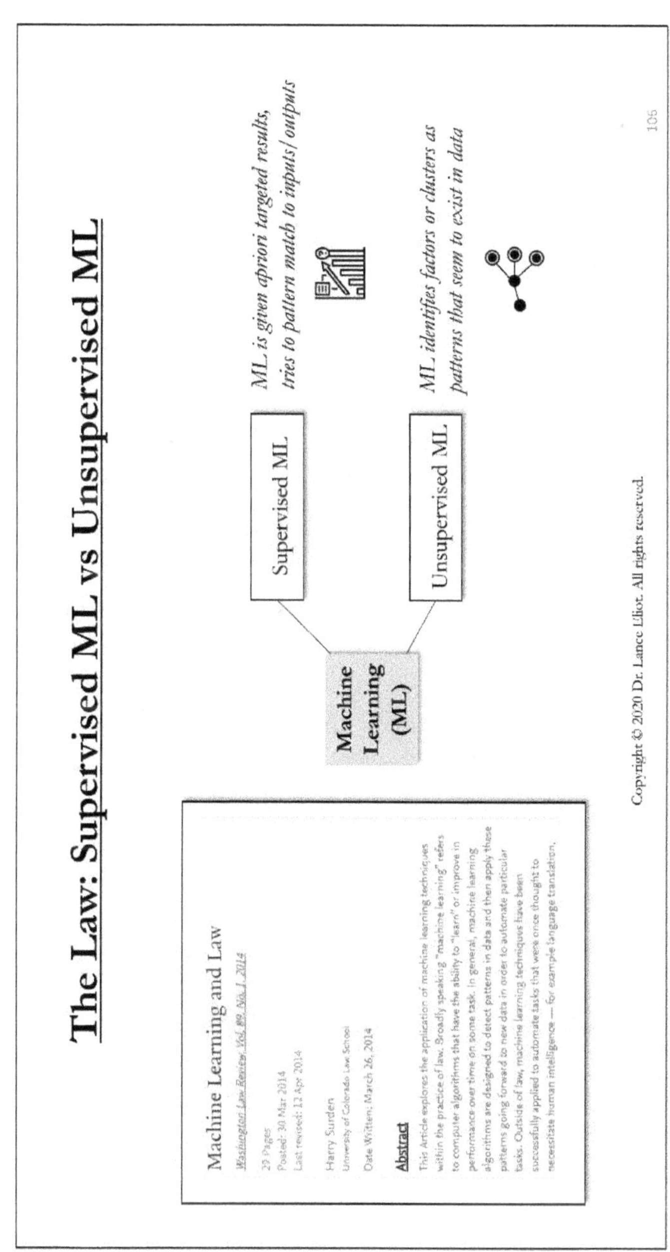
The Law: Supervised ML vs Unsupervised ML
Machine Learning and Law
Washington Law Review, Vol. 89, No. 1, 2014
29 Pages
Posted: 30 Mar 2014
Last revised: 13 Apr 2014
Harry Surden
University of Colorado Law School
Date Written: March 26, 2014
Abstract
This Article explores the application of machine learning techniques within the practice of law. Broadly speaking "machine learning" refers to computer algorithms that have the ability to "learn" or improve in performance over time on some task. In general, machine learning algorithms are designed to detect patterns in data and then apply these patterns going forward to new data in order to automate particular tasks. Outside of law, machine learning techniques have been successfully applied to automate tasks that were once thought to necessitate human intelligence — for example language translation,
Machine Learning (ML)
Supervised ML
ML is given apriori targeted results, tries to pattern match to inputs/outputs
Unsupervised ML
ML identifies factors or clusters as patterns that seem to exist in data
Copyright © 2020 Dr. Lance Eliot. All rights reserved.
106

Figure 106

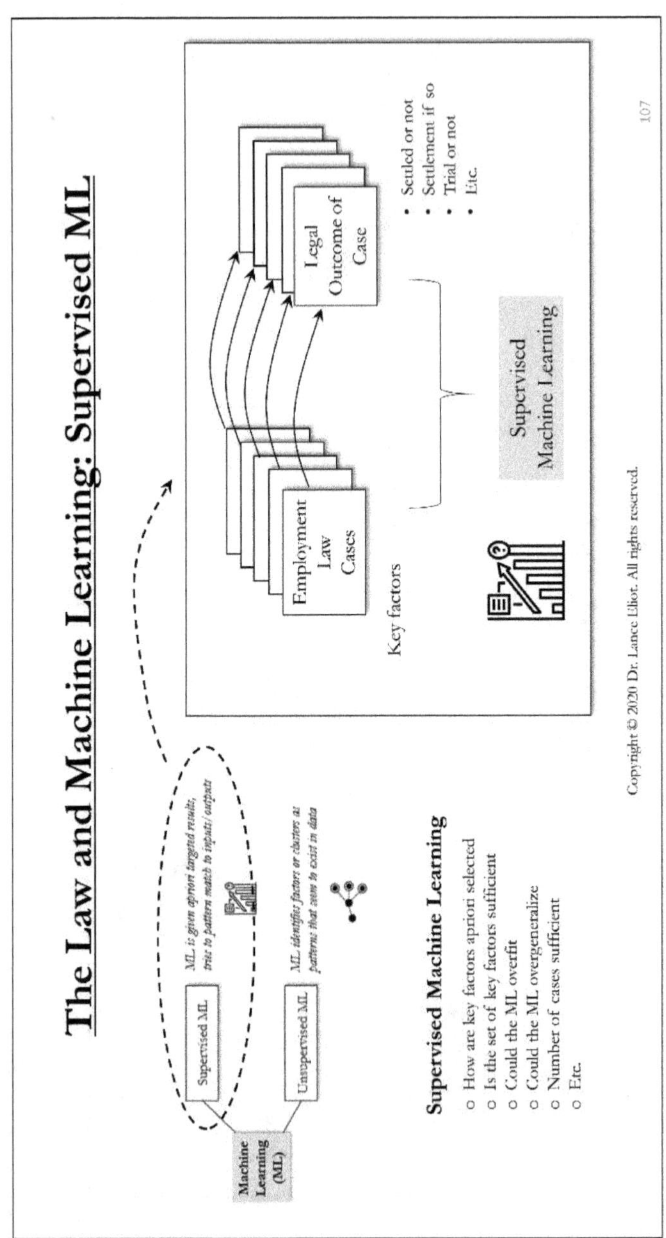
The Law and Machine Learning: Supervised ML
Machine Learning (ML)
Supervised ML
ML is given apriori targeted results; tries to pattern match to inputs/outputs
Unsupervised ML
ML identifies factors or clusters as patterns that seem to exist in data
Supervised Machine Learning
o How are key factors apriori selected
o Is the set of key factors sufficient
o Could the ML overfit
o Could the ML overgeneralize
o Number of cases sufficient
o Etc.
Employment Law Cases
Legal Outcome of Case
Key factors
Supervised Machine Learning
• Settled or not
• Settlement if so
• Trial or not
• Etc.
107
Copyright © 2020 Dr. Lance Eliot. All rights reserved.

Figure 107

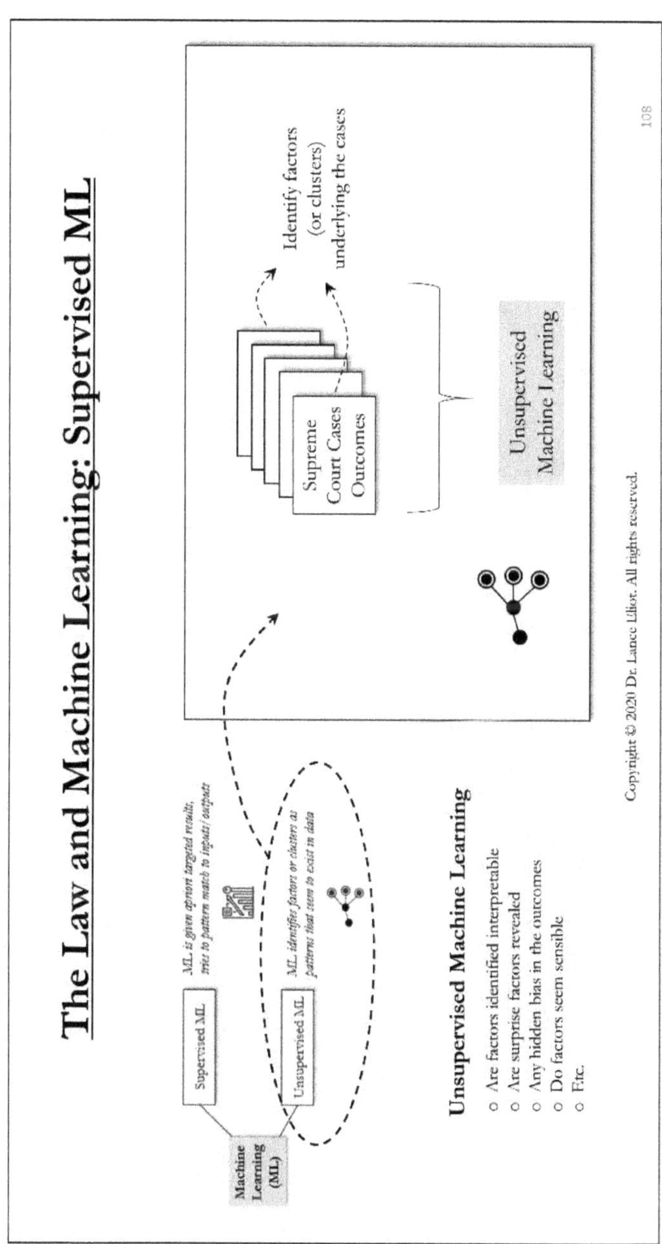

The Law and Machine Learning: Supervised ML
Machine Learning (ML)
Supervised ML
ML is given apriori targeted results; tries to pattern match to inputs/outputs
Unsupervised ML
ML identifies factors or clusters as patterns that seem to exist in data
Supreme Court Cases Outcomes
Identify factors (or clusters) underlying the cases
Unsupervised Machine Learning
Unsupervised Machine Learning
o Are factors identified interpretable
o Are surprise factors revealed
o Any hidden bias in the outcomes
o Do factors seem sensible
o Etc.
Copyright © 2020 Dr. Lance Eliot. All rights reserved.
108

Figure 108

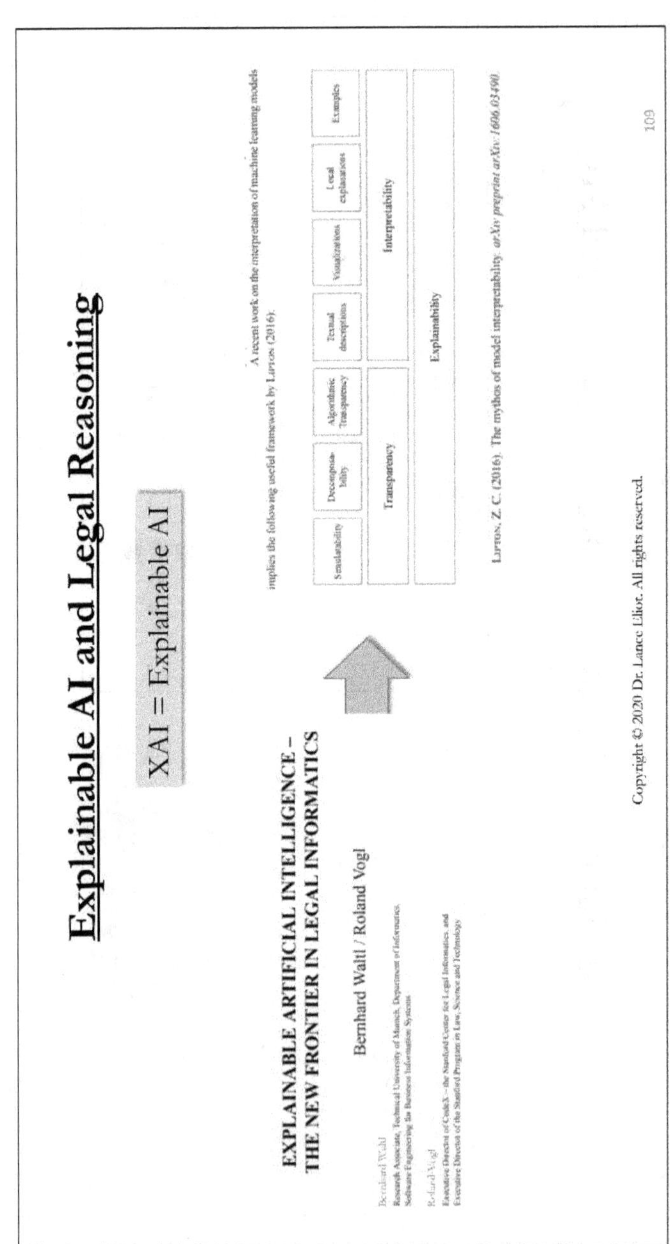
Explainable AI and Legal Reasoning
XAI = Explainable AI
EXPLAINABLE ARTIFICIAL INTELLIGENCE – THE NEW FRONTIER IN LEGAL INFORMATICS
Bernhard Waltl / Roland Vogl
A recent work on the interpretation of machine learning models implies the following useful framework by Lipton (2016).
Simulatability
Decomposability
Algorithmic Transparency
Textual descriptions
Visualizations
Local explanations
Examples
Transparency
Interpretability
Explainability
Lipton, Z. C. (2016). The mythos of model interpretability. arXiv preprint arXiv:1606.03490.
Copyright © 2020 Dr. Lance Eliot. All rights reserved.
109

Figure 109

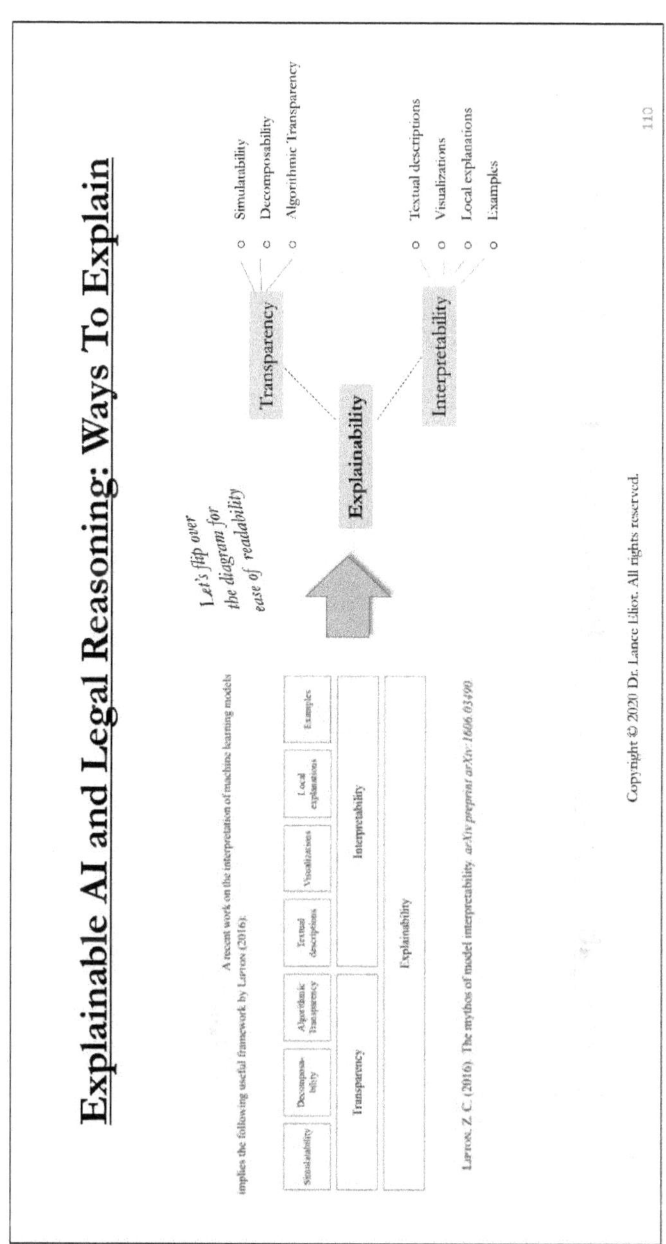
Explainable AI and Legal Reasoning: Ways To Explain
A recent work on the interpretation of machine learning models implies the following useful framework by Lipton (2016):
Simulatability
Decomposability
Algorithmic Transparency
Textual descriptions
Visualizations
Local explanations
Examples
Transparency
Interpretability
Explainability
Lipton, Z. C. (2016). The mythos of model interpretability. arXiv preprint arXiv:1606.03490
Let's flip over the diagram for ease of readability
Explainability
Transparency
Simulatability
Decomposability
Algorithmic Transparency
Interpretability
Textual descriptions
Visualizations
Local explanations
Examples
Copyright © 2020 Dr. Lance Eliot. All rights reserved.
110

Figure 110

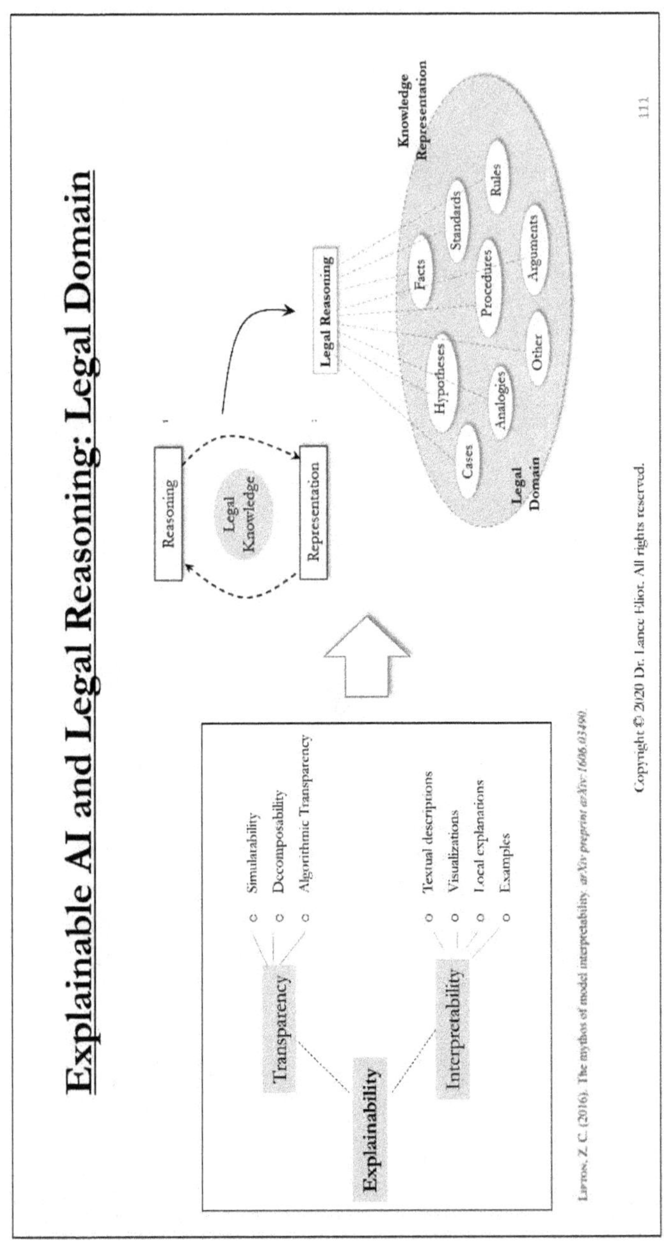
Explainable AI and Legal Reasoning: Legal Domain
Explainability
Transparency
Interpretability
Simularability
Decomposability
Algorithmic Transparency
Textual descriptions
Visualizations
Local explanations
Examples
Lipton, Z. C. (2016). The mythos of model interpretability. arXiv preprint arXiv:1606.03490.
Reasoning
Legal Knowledge
Representation
Legal Reasoning
Facts
Standards
Rules
Hypotheses
Procedures
Arguments
Cases
Analogies
Other
Legal Domain
Knowledge Representation
Copyright © 2020 Dr. Lance Eliot. All rights reserved.
111

Figure 111

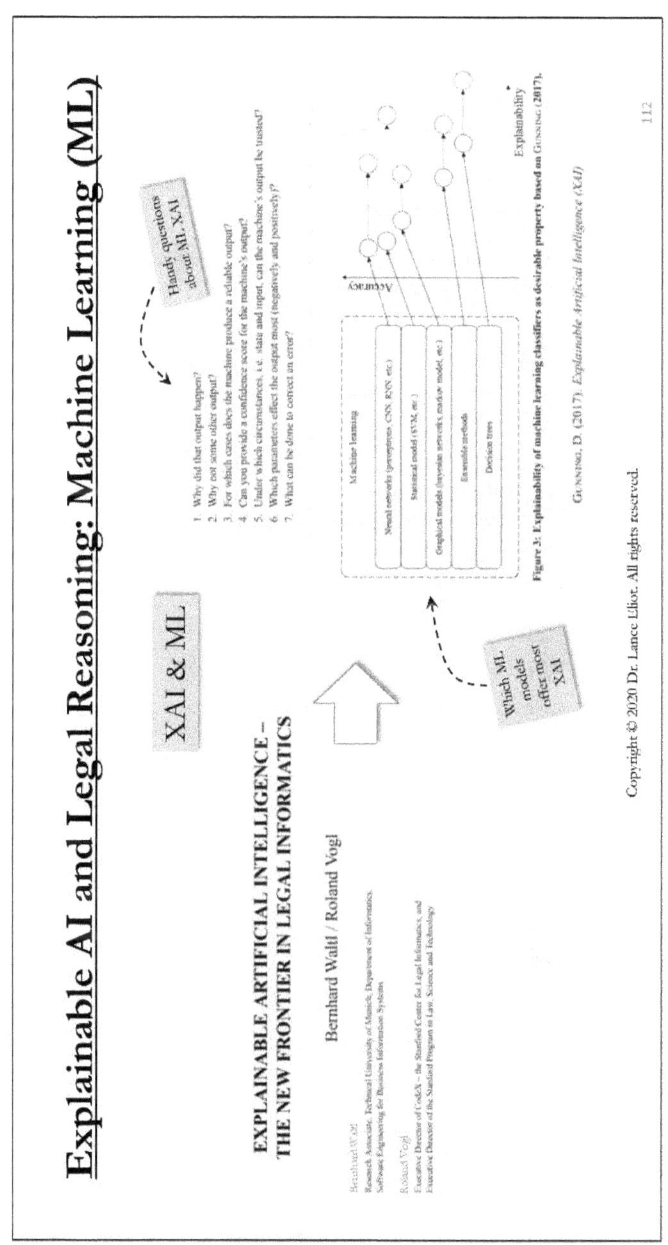

Explainable AI and Legal Reasoning: Machine Learning (ML)
XAI & ML
EXPLAINABLE ARTIFICIAL INTELLIGENCE – THE NEW FRONTIER IN LEGAL INFORMATICS
Bernhard Waltl / Roland Vogl
Handy questions about ML XAI
1. Why did that output happen?
2. Why not some other output?
3. For which cases does the machine produce a reliable output?
4. Can you provide a confidence score for the machine's output?
5. Under which circumstances, i.e. state and input, can the machine's output be trusted?
6. Which parameters effect the output most (negatively and positively)?
7. What can be done to correct an error?
Machine learning
Neural networks (perceptrons, CNN, RNN, etc.)
Statistical model (SVM, etc.)
Graphical models (bayesian networks, markov model, etc.)
Ensemble methods
Decision trees
Accuracy
Explainability
Figure 3: Explainability of machine learning classifiers as desirable property based on GUNNING (2017).
GUNNING, D. (2017). Explainable Artificial Intelligence (XAI)
Which ML models offer most XAI
Copyright © 2020 Dr. Lance Eliot. All rights reserved.
112

Figure 112

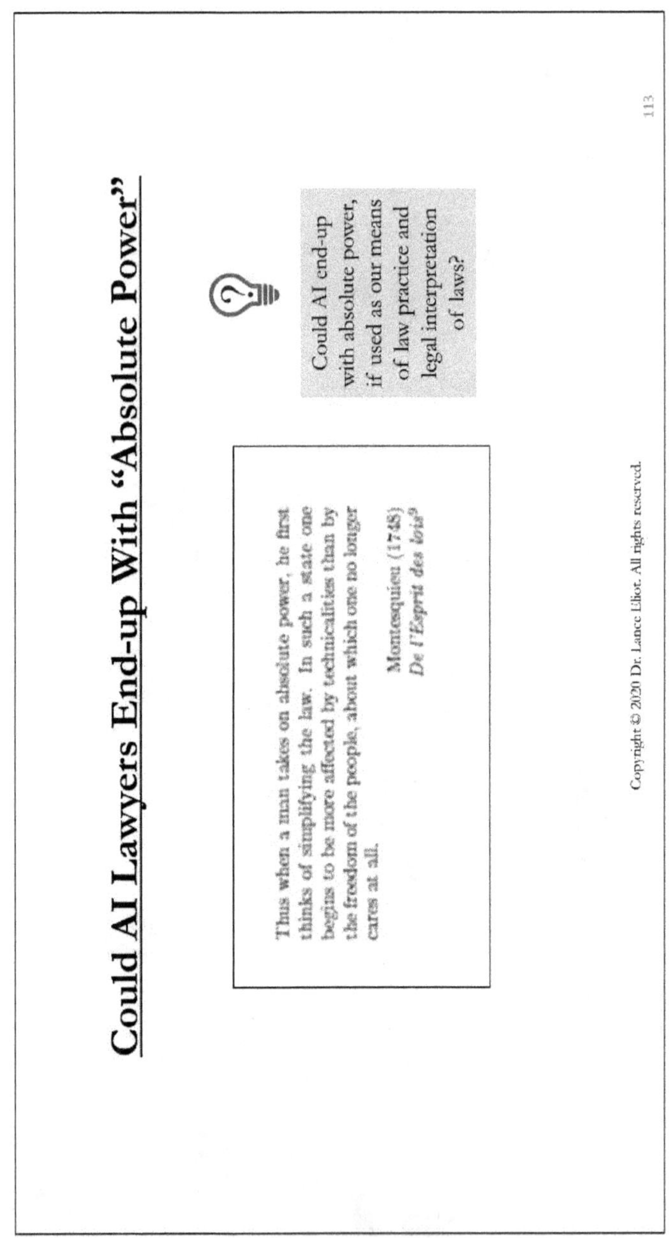
Could AI Lawyers End-up With "Absolute Power"
Thus when a man takes on absolute power, he first thinks of simplifying the law. In such a state one begins to be more affected by technicalities than by the freedom of the people, about which one no longer cares at all.
Montesquieu (1748)
De l'Esprit des lois[9]
Could AI end-up with absolute power, if used as our means of law practice and legal interpretation of laws?
Copyright © 2020 Dr. Lance Eliot. All rights reserved.
113

Figure 113

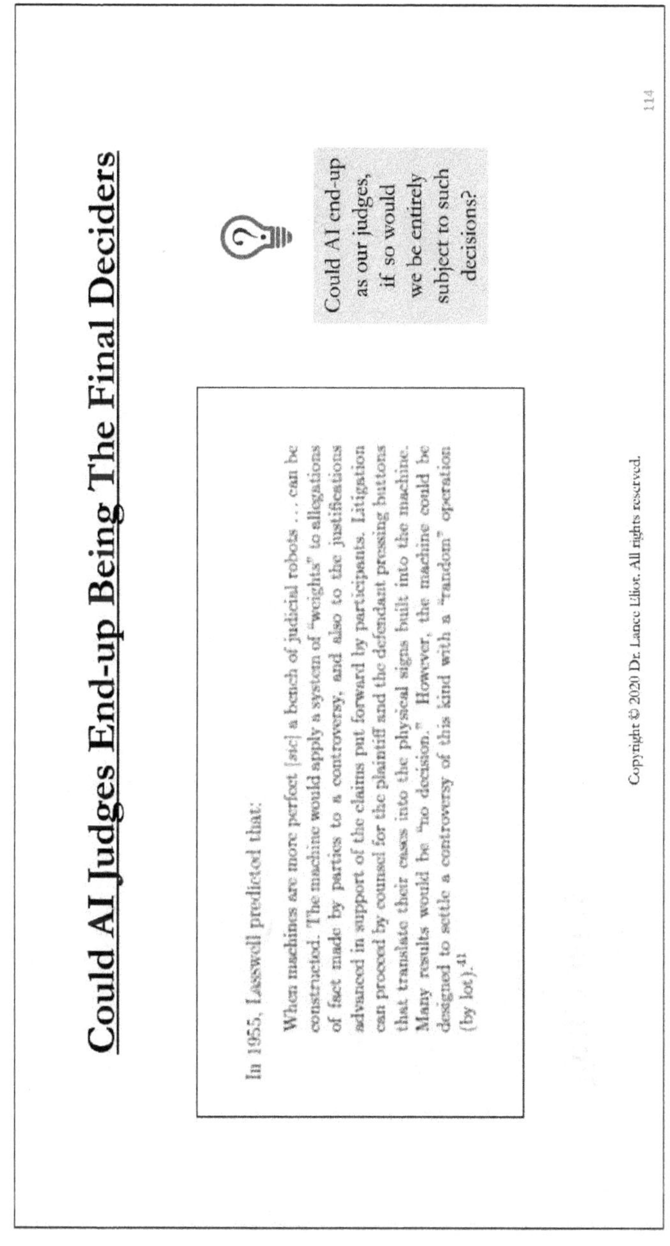
Could AI Judges End-up Being The Final Deciders
In 1955, Lasswell predicted that:
When machines are more perfect [sic] a bench of judicial robots . . . can be constructed. The machine would apply a system of "weights" to allegations of fact made by parties to a controversy, and also to the justifications advanced in support of the claims put forward by participants. Litigation can proceed by counsel for the plaintiff and the defendant pressing buttons that translate their cases into the physical signs built into the machine. Many results would be "no decision." However, the machine could be designed to settle a controversy of this kind with a "random" operation (by lot).[41]
Could AI end-up as our judges, if so would we be entirely subject to such decisions?
Copyright © 2020 Dr. Lance Eliot. All rights reserved.
114

Figure 114

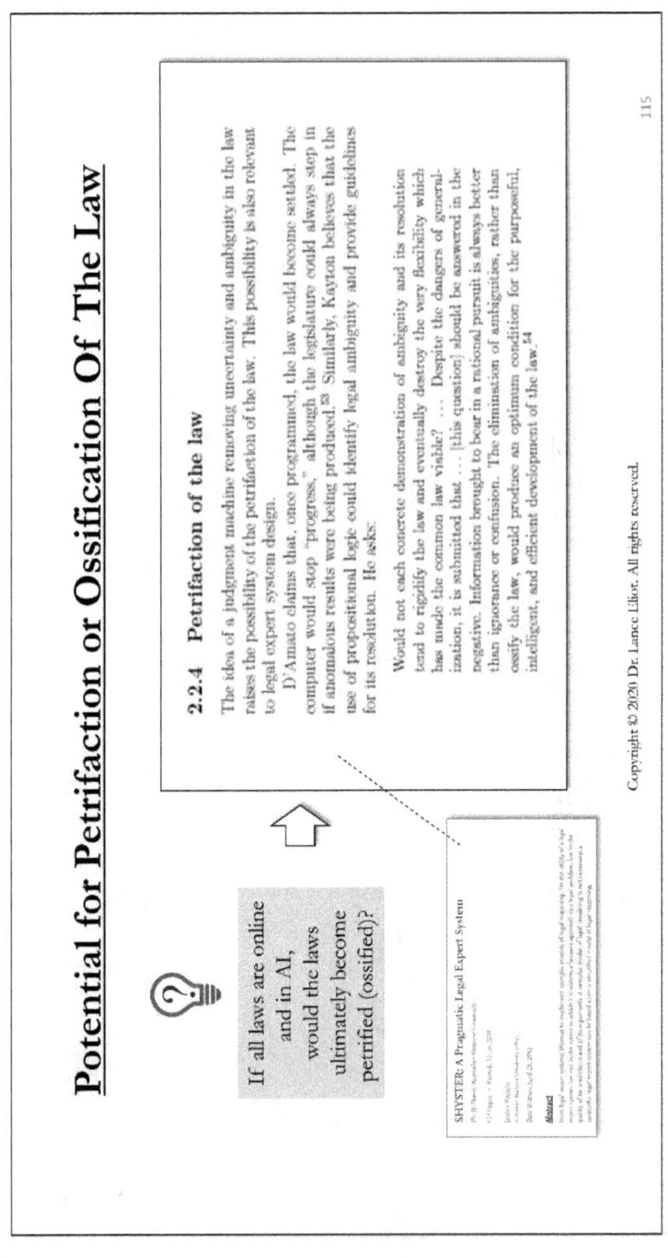
Potential for Petrifaction or Ossification Of The Law
If all laws are online and in AI, would the laws ultimately become petrified (ossified)?
SHYSTER: A Pragmatic Legal Expert System
Abstract
2.2.4 Petrifaction of the law
The idea of a judgment machine removing uncertainty and ambiguity in the law raises the possibility of the petrifaction of the law. This possibility is also relevant to legal expert system design.
D'Amato claims that, once programmed, the law would become settled. The computer would stop "progress," although the legislature could always step in if anomalous results were being produced.53 Similarly, Kayton believes that the use of propositional logic could identify legal ambiguity and provide guidelines for its resolution. He asks:
Would not each concrete demonstration of ambiguity and its resolution tend to rigidify the law and eventually destroy the very flexibility which has made the common law viable? ... Despite the dangers of generalization, it is submitted that ... [this question] should be answered in the negative. Information brought to bear in a rational pursuit is always better than ignorance or confusion. The elimination of ambiguities, rather than ossify the law, would produce an optimum condition for the purposeful, intelligent, and efficient development of the law.54
Copyright © 2020 Dr. Lance Eliot. All rights reserved.
115

Figure 115

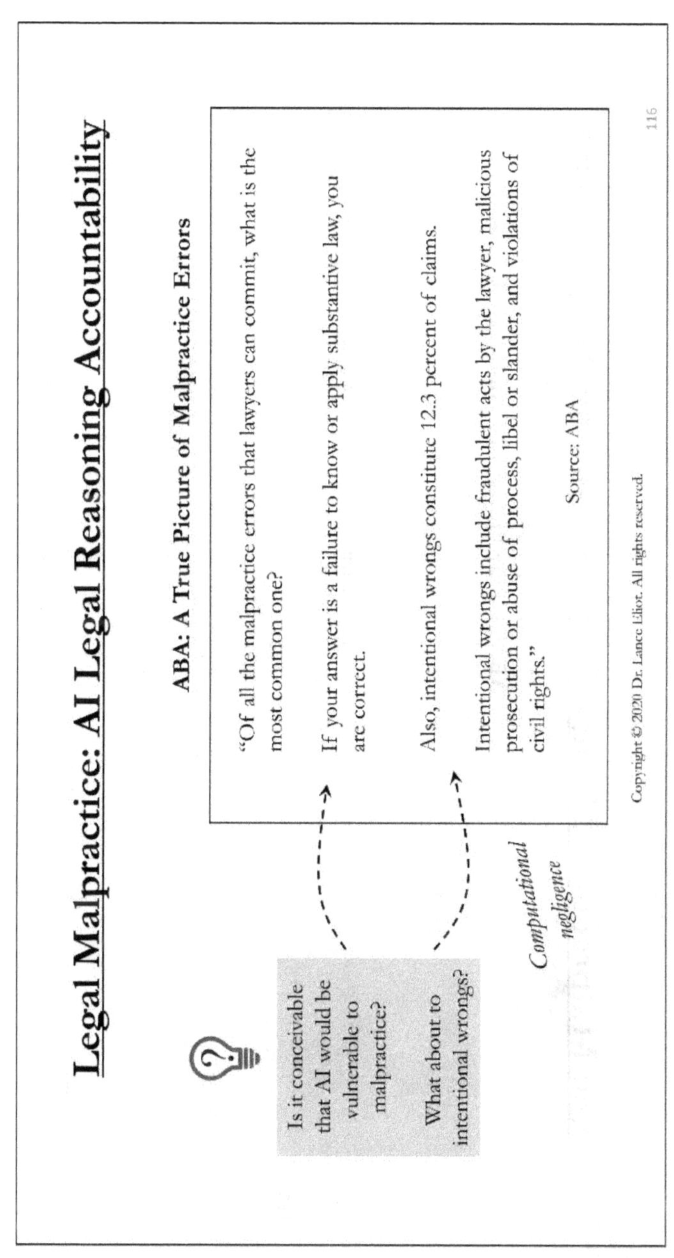
Legal Malpractice: AI Legal Reasoning Accountability
ABA: A True Picture of Malpractice Errors
"Of all the malpractice errors that lawyers can commit, what is the most common one?
If your answer is a failure to know or apply substantive law, you are correct.
Also, intentional wrongs constitute 12.3 percent of claims.
Intentional wrongs include fraudulent acts by the lawyer, malicious prosecution or abuse of process, libel or slander, and violations of civil rights."
Source: ABA
Is it conceivable that AI would be vulnerable to malpractice?
What about to intentional wrongs?
Computational negligence
Copyright © 2020 Dr. Lance Eliot. All rights reserved.
116

Figure 116

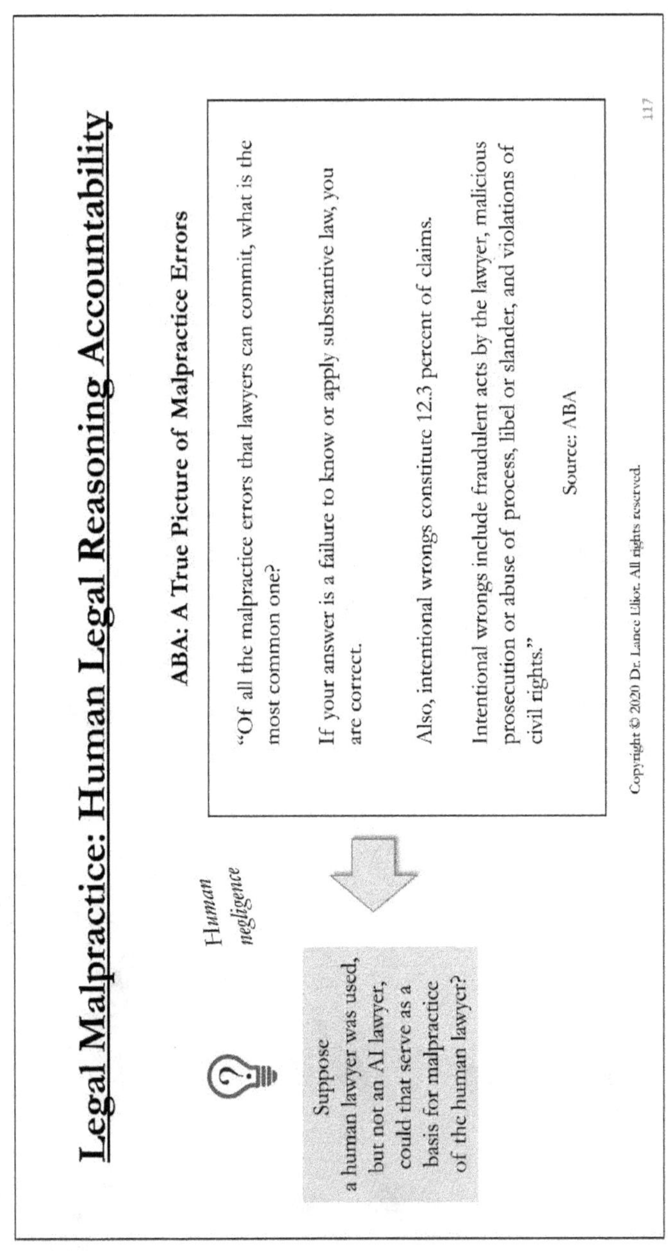
Legal Malpractice: Human Legal Reasoning Accountability
ABA: A True Picture of Malpractice Errors
"Of all the malpractice errors that lawyers can commit, what is the most common one?
If your answer is a failure to know or apply substantive law, you are correct.
Also, intentional wrongs constitute 12.3 percent of claims.
Intentional wrongs include fraudulent acts by the lawyer, malicious prosecution or abuse of process, libel or slander, and violations of civil rights."
Source: ABA
Human negligence
Suppose a human lawyer was used, but not an AI lawyer, could that serve as a basis for malpractice of the human lawyer?
Copyright © 2020 Dr. Lance Eliot. All rights reserved.
117

Figure 117

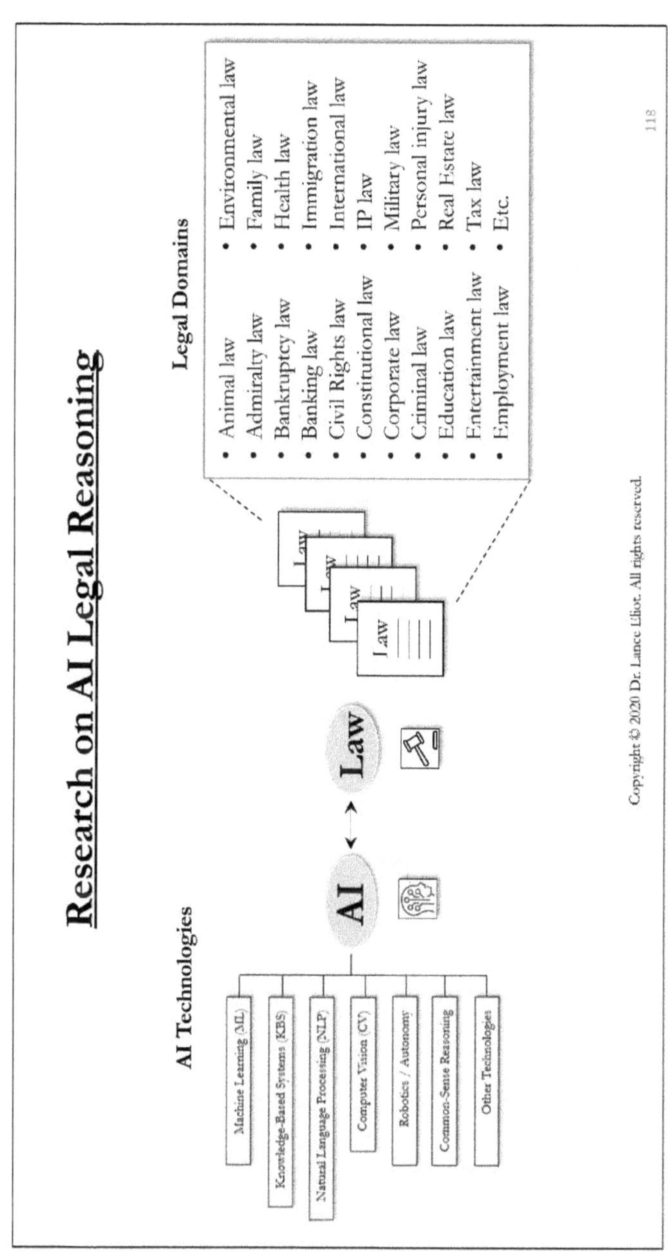
Research on AI Legal Reasoning
AI Technologies
Machine Learning (ML)
Knowledge-Based Systems (KBS)
Natural Language Processing (NLP)
Computer Vision (CV)
Robotics / Autonomy
Common-Sense Reasoning
Other Technologies
AI
Law
Law
Law
Law
Law
Legal Domains
• Animal law
• Admiralty law
• Bankruptcy law
• Banking law
• Civil Rights law
• Constitutional law
• Corporate law
• Criminal law
• Education law
• Entertainment law
• Employment law
• Environmental law
• Family law
• Health law
• Immigration law
• International law
• IP law
• Military law
• Personal injury law
• Real Estate law
• Tax law
• Etc.
Copyright © 2020 Dr. Lance Eliot. All rights reserved.
118

Figure 118

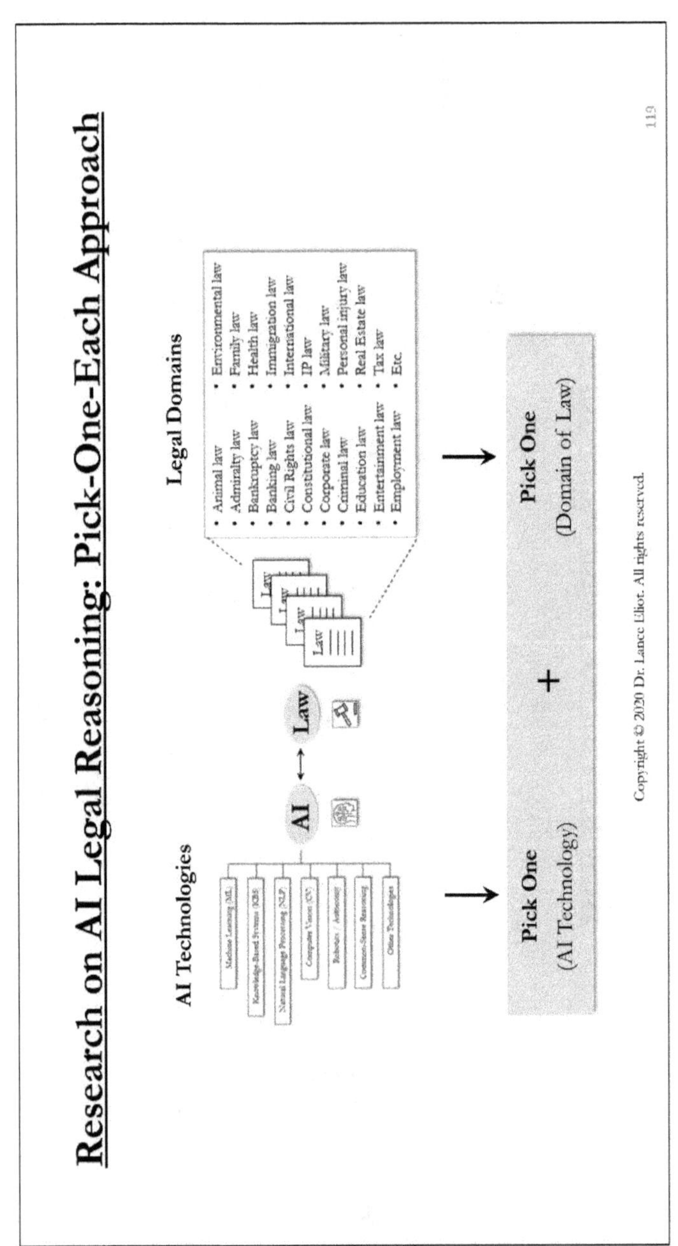
Research on AI Legal Reasoning: Pick-One-Each Approach
AI Technologies
Machine Learning (ML)
Knowledge-Based Systems (KBS)
Natural Language Processing (NLP)
Computer Vision (CV)
Robotics / Autonomous
Common-Sense Reasoning
Other Technologies
AI
Law
Law
Legal Domains
• Animal law
• Admiralty law
• Bankruptcy law
• Banking law
• Civil Rights law
• Constitutional law
• Corporate law
• Criminal law
• Education law
• Entertainment law
• Employment law
• Environmental law
• Family law
• Health law
• Immigration law
• International law
• IP law
• Military law
• Personal injury law
• Real Estate law
• Tax law
• Etc.
Pick One
(AI Technology)
+
Pick One
(Domain of Law)
Copyright © 2020 Dr. Lance Eliot. All rights reserved.
119

Figure 119

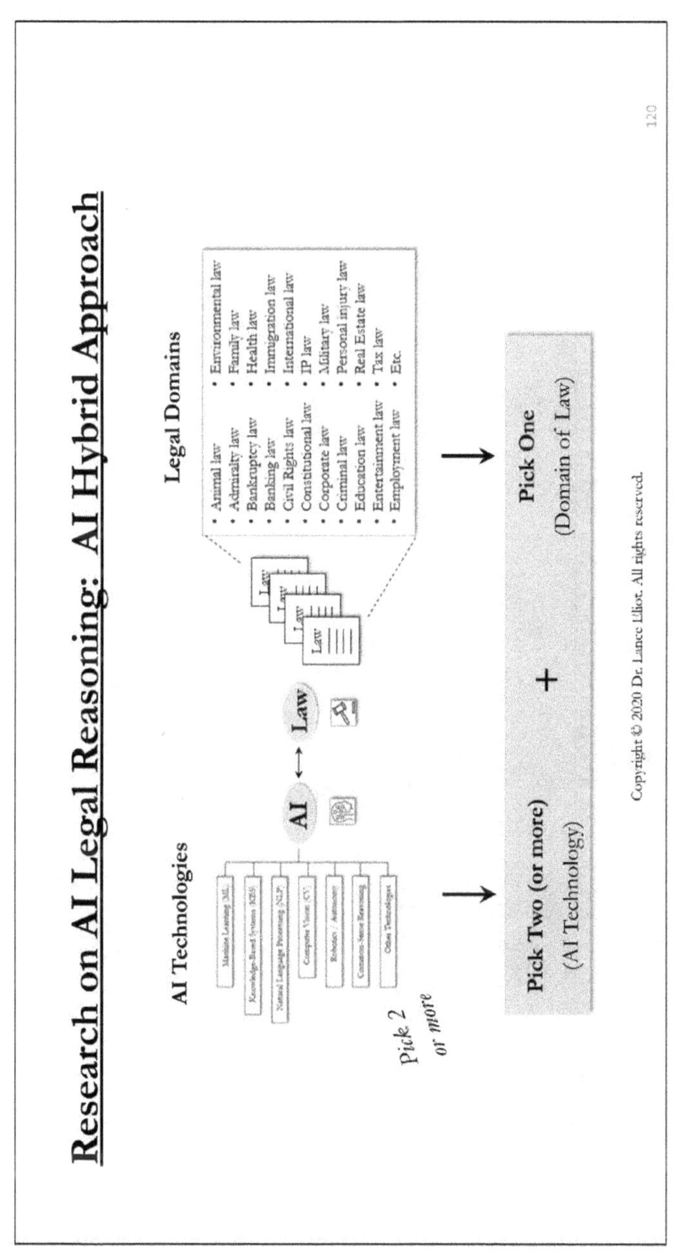
Research on AI Legal Reasoning: AI Hybrid Approach
AI Technologies
Machine Learning (ML)
Knowledge-Based Systems (KBS)
Natural Language Processing (NLP)
Computer Vision (CV)
Robotics / Autonomous
Common-Sense Reasoning
Other Technologies
AI
Law
Law
Legal Domains
• Animal law
• Admiralty law
• Bankruptcy law
• Banking law
• Civil Rights law
• Constitutional law
• Corporate law
• Criminal law
• Education law
• Entertainment law
• Employment law
• Environmental law
• Family law
• Health law
• Immigration law
• International law
• IP law
• Military law
• Personal injury law
• Real Estate law
• Tax law
• Etc.
Pick 2 or more
Pick Two (or more)
(AI Technology)
+
Pick One
(Domain of Law)
Copyright © 2020 Dr. Lance Eliot. All rights reserved.
120

Figure 120

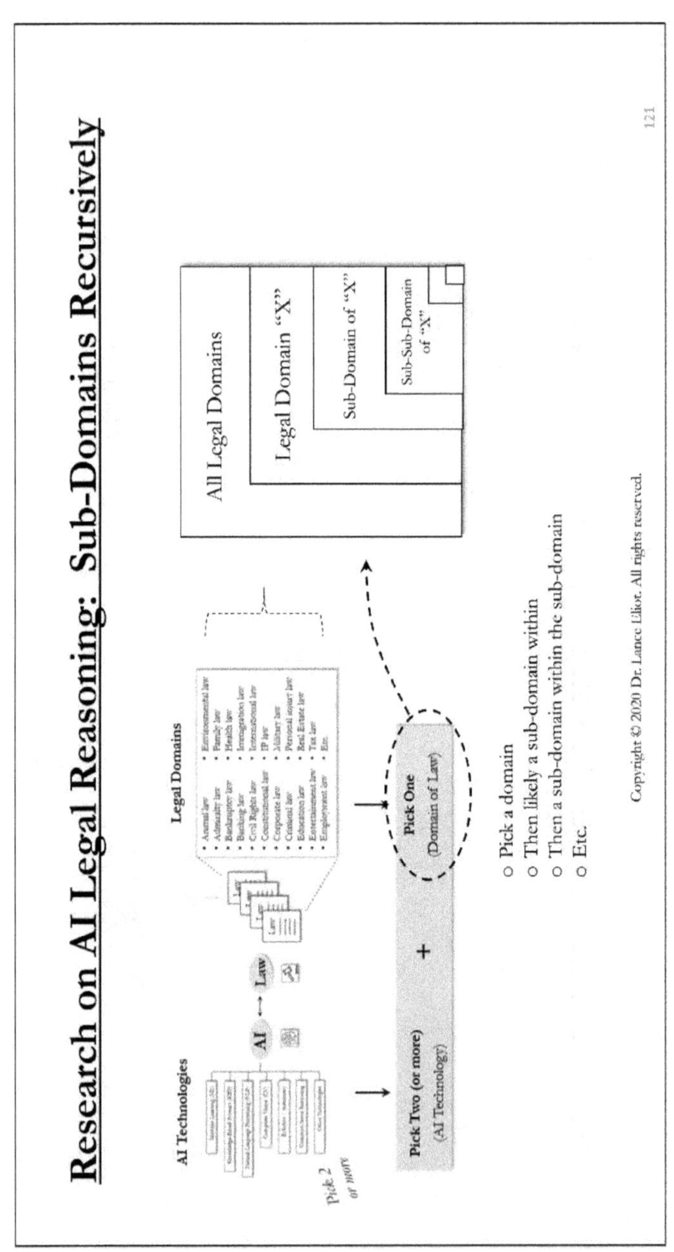

Research on AI Legal Reasoning: Sub-Domains Recursively
AI Technologies
AI
Law
Legal Domains
Animal law
Admiralty law
Bankruptcy law
Banking law
Civil Rights law
Constitutional law
Corporate law
Criminal law
Education law
Entertainment law
Employment law
Environmental law
Family law
Health law
Immigration law
International law
IP law
Military law
Personal injury law
Real Estate law
Tax law
Etc.
Pick 2 or more
Pick Two (or more)
(AI Technology)
+
Pick One
(Domain of Law)
All Legal Domains
Legal Domain "X"
Sub-Domain of "X"
Sub-Sub-Domain of "X"
o Pick a domain
o Then likely a sub-domain within
o Then a sub-domain within the sub-domain
o Etc.
Copyright © 2020 Dr. Lance Eliot. All rights reserved.
121

Figure 121

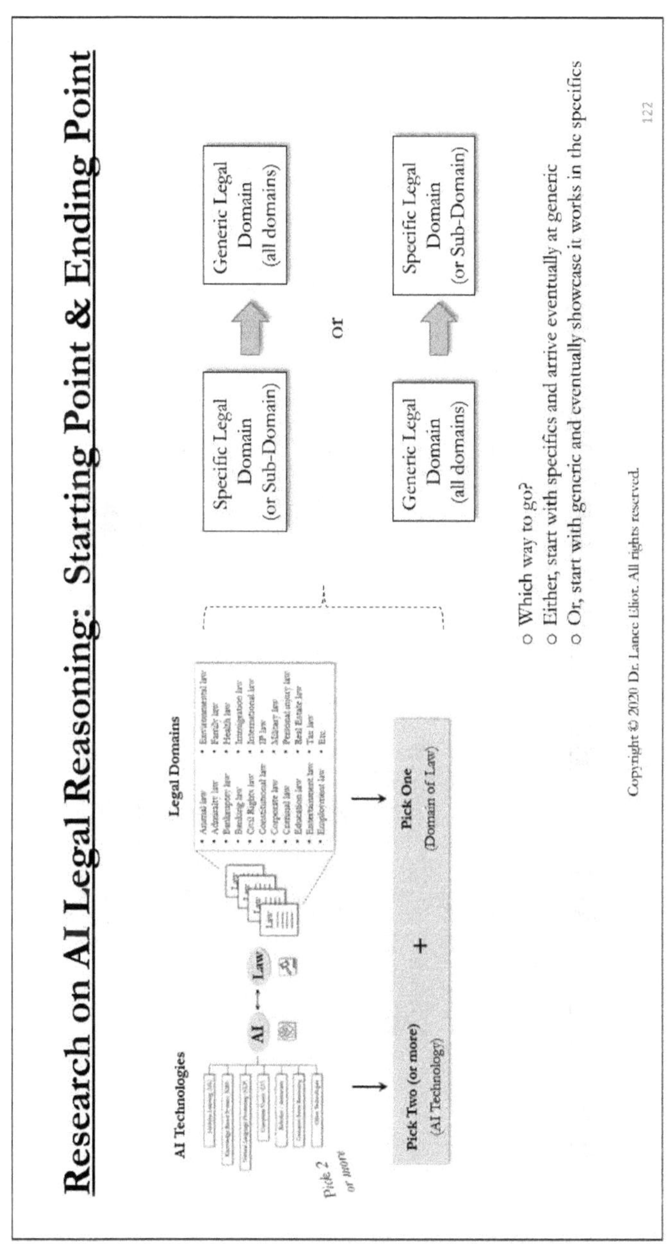
Research on AI Legal Reasoning: Starting Point & Ending Point
AI Technologies
AI
Law
Legal Domains
Pick 2 or more
Pick Two (or more)
(AI Technology)
+
Pick One
(Domain of Law)
Specific Legal Domain (or Sub-Domain)
Generic Legal Domain (all domains)
or
Generic Legal Domain (all domains)
Specific Legal Domain (or Sub-Domain)
Which way to go?
Either, start with specifics and arrive eventually at generic
Or, start with generic and eventually showcase it works in the specifics
Copyright © 2020 Dr. Lance Eliot. All rights reserved.
122

Figure 122

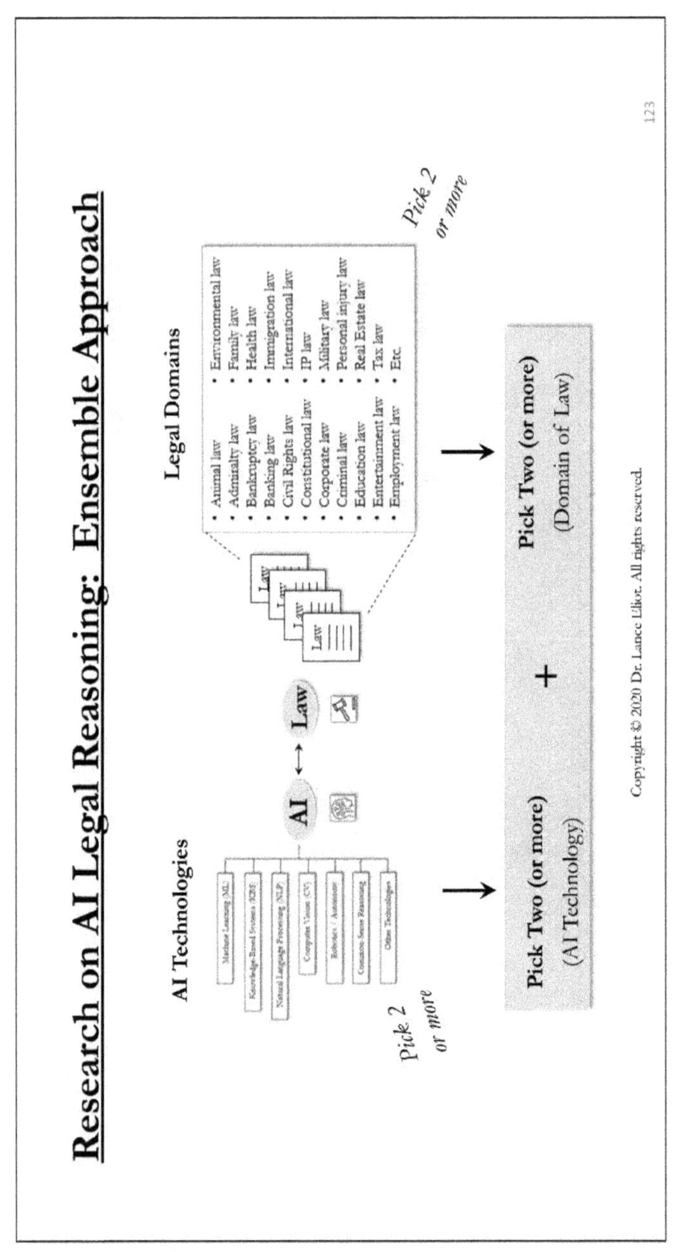
Research on AI Legal Reasoning: Ensemble Approach
AI Technologies
Machine Learning (ML)
Knowledge-Based Systems (KBS)
Natural Language Processing (NLP)
Computer Vision (CV)
Robotics / Autonomous
Common-Sense Reasoning
Other Technologies
AI
Law
Legal Domains
Animal law
Admiralty law
Bankruptcy law
Banking law
Civil Rights law
Constitutional law
Corporate law
Criminal law
Education law
Entertainment law
Employment law
Environmental law
Family law
Health law
Immigration law
International law
IP law
Military law
Personal injury law
Real Estate law
Tax law
Etc.
Pick 2 or more
Pick 2 or more
Pick Two (or more) (AI Technology)
+
Pick Two (or more) (Domain of Law)
Copyright © 2020 Dr. Lance Eliot. All rights reserved.
123

Figure 123

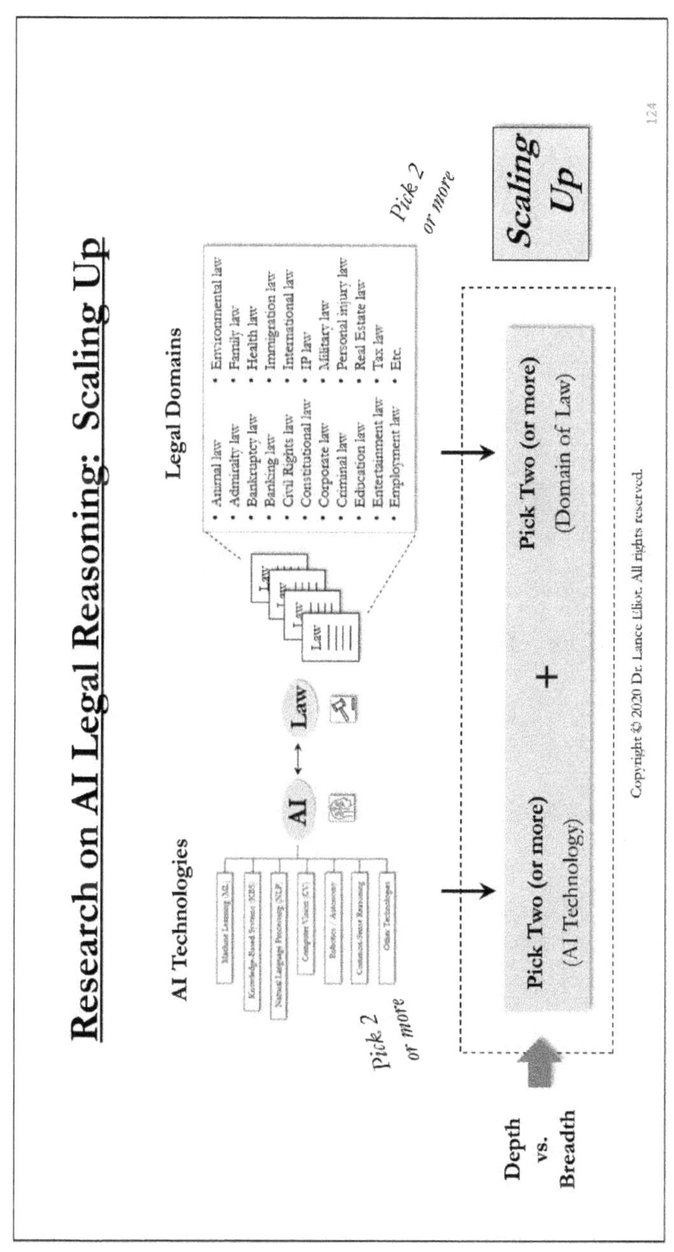

Research on AI Legal Reasoning: Scaling Up
AI Technologies
AI
Law
Legal Domains
Animal law
Admiralty law
Bankruptcy law
Banking law
Civil Rights law
Constitutional law
Corporate law
Criminal law
Education law
Entertainment law
Employment law
Environmental law
Family law
Health law
Immigration law
International law
IP law
Military law
Personal injury law
Real Estate law
Tax law
Etc.
Pick 2 or more
Pick 2 or more
Depth vs. Breadth
Pick Two (or more) (AI Technology)
+
Pick Two (or more) (Domain of Law)
Scaling Up
Copyright © 2020 Dr. Lance Eliot. All rights reserved.
124

Figure 124

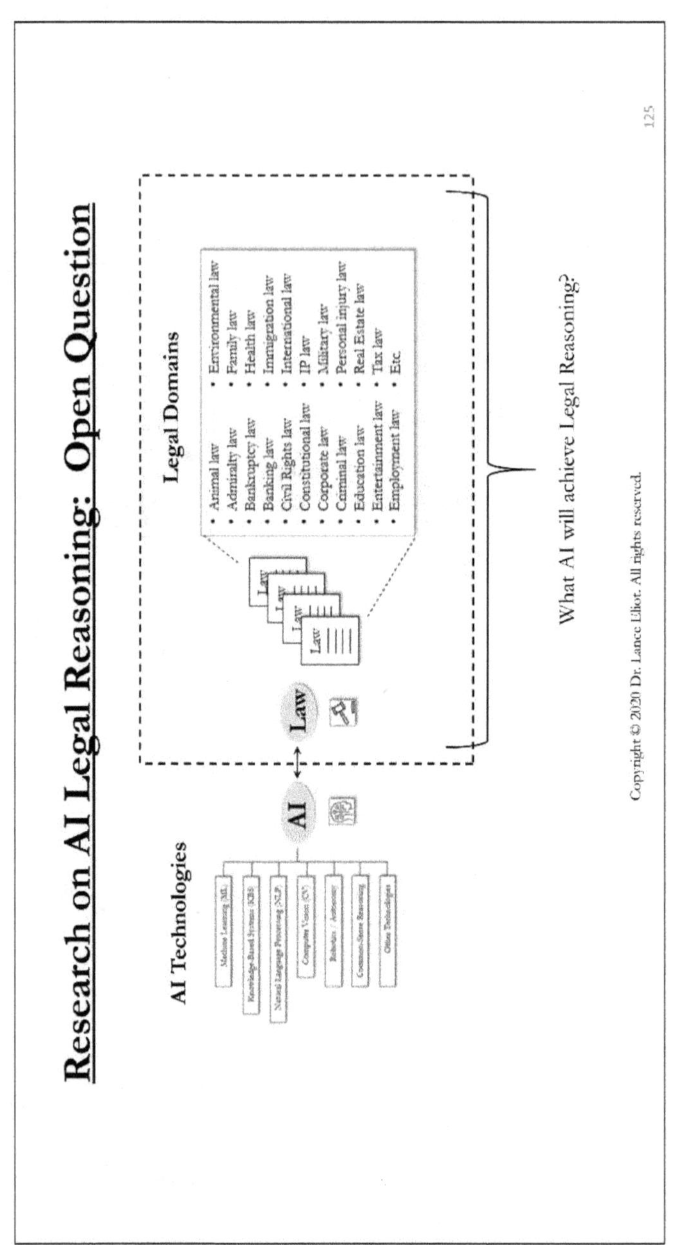
Research on AI Legal Reasoning: Open Question
AI Technologies
AI
Law
Legal Domains
Law
• Animal law
• Admiralty law
• Bankruptcy law
• Banking law
• Civil Rights law
• Constitutional law
• Corporate law
• Criminal law
• Education law
• Entertainment law
• Employment law
• Environmental law
• Family law
• Health law
• Immigration law
• International law
• IP law
• Military law
• Personal injury law
• Real Estate law
• Tax law
• Etc.
What AI will achieve Legal Reasoning?
Copyright © 2020 Dr. Lance Eliot. All rights reserved.
125

Figure 125

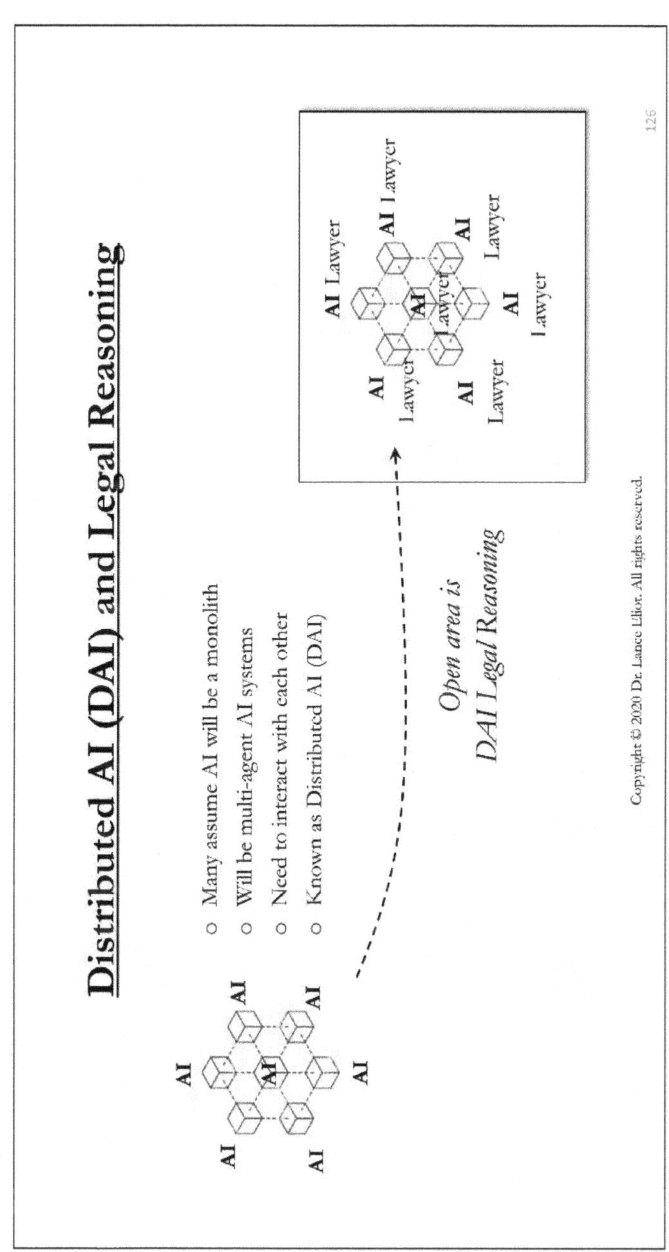
Distributed AI (DAI) and Legal Reasoning
Many assume AI will be a monolith
Will be multi-agent AI systems
Need to interact with each other
Known as Distributed AI (DAI)
AI
AI
AI
AI
AI
AI
AI
Open area is
DAI Legal Reasoning
AI Lawyer
AI Lawyer
AI Lawyer
AI Lawyer
AI Lawyer
AI Lawyer
AI Lawyer
Copyright © 2020 Dr. Lance Eliot. All rights reserved.
126

Figure 126

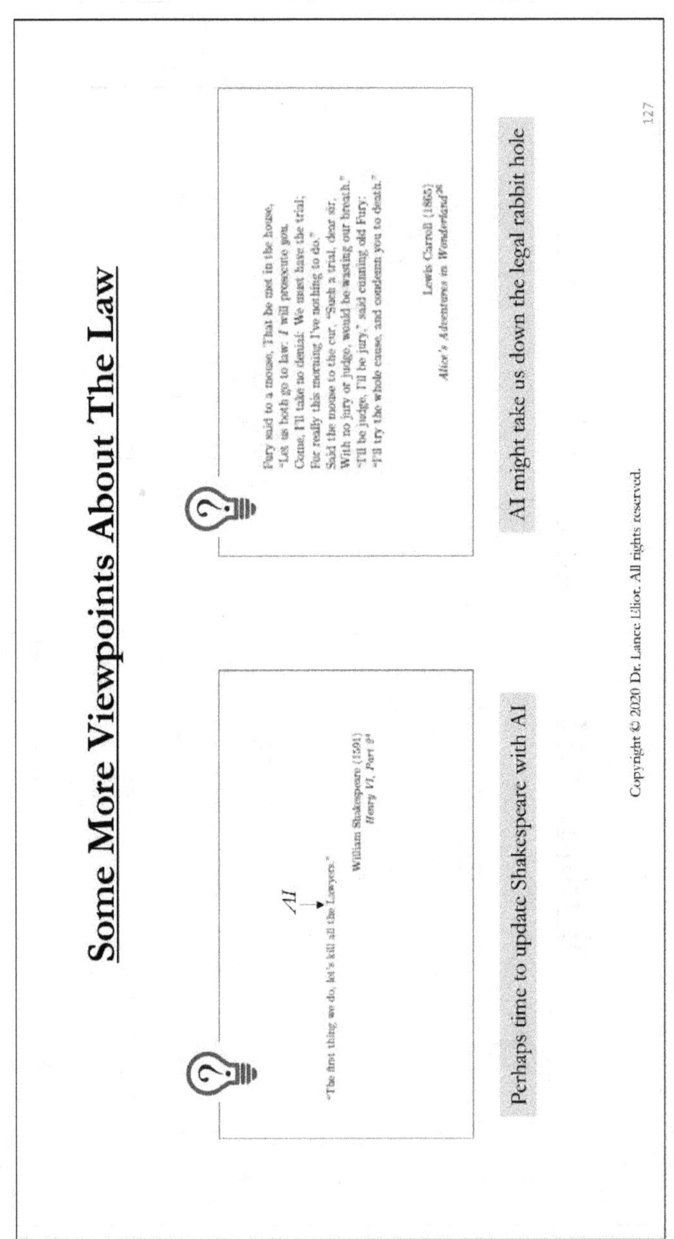
Some More Viewpoints About The Law
AI
"The first thing we do, let's kill all the Lawyers."
William Shakespeare (1591)
Henry VI, Part 2[4]
Perhaps time to update Shakespeare with AI
Fury said to a mouse, That he met in the house,
"Let us both go to law: I will prosecute you.
Come, I'll take no denial: We must have the trial;
For really this morning I've nothing to do."
Said the mouse to the cur, "Such a trial, dear sir,
With no jury or judge, would be wasting our breath."
"I'll be judge, I'll be jury," said cunning old Fury:
"I'll try the whole cause, and condemn you to death."
Lewis Carroll (1865)
Alice's Adventures in Wonderland[26]
AI might take us down the legal rabbit hole
Copyright © 2020 Dr. Lance Eliot. All rights reserved.
127

Figure 127

ABOUT THE AUTHOR

Dr. Lance B. Eliot, Ph.D., MBA is a globally recognized AI expert and thought leader, an experienced top executive and corporate leader, a successful entrepreneur, and a noted scholar on AI, including that his Forbes and AI Trends columns have amassed over 2.8+ million views, his books on AI are ranked in the Top 10 of all-time AI books, his journal articles are widely cited, and he has developed and implemented numerous AI systems.

He currently serves as the CEO of Techbruim, Inc. and has over twenty years of industry experience including serving as a corporate officer in billion-dollar sized firms and was a partner in a major consulting firm. He is also a successful entrepreneur having founded, ran, and sold several high-tech related businesses.

Dr. Eliot previously hosted the popular radio show *Technotrends* that was also available on American Airlines flights via their in-flight audio program, he has made appearances on CNN, has been a frequent speaker at industry conferences, and his podcasts have been downloaded over 100,000 times.

A former professor at the University of Southern California (USC), he founded and led an innovative research lab on Artificial Intelligence. He also previously served on the faculty of the University of California Los Angeles (UCLA) and was a visiting professor at other major universities. He was elected to the International Board of the Society for Information Management (SIM), a prestigious association of over 3,000 high-tech executives worldwide.

He has performed extensive community service, including serving as Senior Science Adviser to the Congressional Vice-Chair of the Congressional Committee on Science & Technology. He has served on the Board of the OC Science & Engineering Fair (OCSEF), where he is also has been a Grand Sweepstakes judge, and likewise served as a judge for the Intel International SEF (ISEF). He served as the Vice-Chair of the Association for Computing Machinery (ACM) Chapter, a prestigious association of computer scientists. Dr. Eliot has been a shark tank judge for the USC Mark Stevens Center for Innovation on start-up pitch competitions and served as a mentor for several incubators and accelerators in Silicon Valley and in Silicon Beach.

Dr. Eliot holds a Ph.D. from USC, MBA, and Bachelor's in Computer Science, and earned the CDP, CCP, CSP, CDE, and CISA certifications.

ADDENDUM

AI And Legal Reasoning Essentials

Advanced Series On

Artificial Intelligence (AI) and Law

By

Dr. Lance B. Eliot, MBA, PhD

For special orders of this book, contact:

LBE Press Publishing

Email: LBE.Press.Publishing@gmail.com

www.ingramcontent.com/pod-product-compliance
Lightning Source LLC
Chambersburg PA
CBHW071101050326
40690CB00008B/1076

9781734601657